T0271198

INDIGENOUS PEOPLES, POVERTY, AND DEVELOPMENT

This is the first book that documents poverty systematically across the world's three major developing regions: Asia, Africa, and Latin America. In so doing, the volume compiles poverty estimates and social indicators for roughly 80 percent of the world's indigenous peoples. It draws on nationally representative data to compare trends in countries' poverty rates and other social indicators with those for indigenous subpopulations and provides comparable data for a wide range of countries all over the world. It estimates global poverty numbers and analyzes other important development indicators, such as schooling, health, and social protection. Provocatively, the results show a marked difference in results across regions, with rapid poverty reduction among indigenous (and nonindigenous) populations in Asia contrasting with relative stagnation – and in some cases falling back – in Latin America and Africa.

Two main factors motivate the book. First, there is a growing concern among poverty analysts worldwide that countries with significant vulnerable populations – such as indigenous peoples – may not meet the Millennium Development Goals, and thus there exists a consequent need for better data-tracking conditions among these groups. Second, there is a growing call by indigenous organizations, including the United Nations Permanent Forum on Indigenous Peoples, for solid, disaggregated data analyzing the size and causes of the "development gap."

Gillette H. Hall is Visiting Associate Professor at the Georgetown University Public Policy Institute in Washington, DC. A development economist on leave from the World Bank, she has published journal articles and papers on poverty and development in Latin America and is a coeditor, with Harry Anthony Patrinos, of the book, *Indigenous Peoples, Poverty and Human Development in Latin America* (2006). At Georgetown, Dr. Hall teaches a range of applied graduate courses and received the Leslie Whittington Outstanding Faculty Award in 2010. At the World Bank, in addition to research, she has worked widely with governments across Latin America on poverty analysis and social protection policy reform. She holds a PhD in Economics from the University of Cambridge. She has also taught at the Johns Hopkins School of Advanced International Studies (SAIS) and the University of Oregon.

Harry Anthony Patrinos is Lead Education Economist at the World Bank. He specializes in all areas of education, including labor market outcomes, quality of education, school-based management, demand-side financing, and public-private partnerships. He has published more than forty journal articles and coauthored or coedited several books, including: *Making Schools Work* (2011); *The Role and Impact of Public-Private Partnerships in Education* (2009); *Indigenous Peoples, Poverty and Human Development in Latin America* (with Gillette H. Hall, 2006); *Policy Analysis of Child Labor: A Comparative Study* (1999); *Decentralization of Education: Demand Side Financing* (1997); and *Indigenous People and Poverty in Latin America: An Empirical Analysis* (1994). Dr. Patrinos previously worked as an economist at the Economic Council of Canada. He holds a PhD from the University of Sussex.

Indigenous Peoples, Poverty, and Development

Edited by

GILLETTE H. HALL
Georgetown University

HARRY ANTHONY PATRINOS
World Bank, Washington, DC

CAMBRIDGE
UNIVERSITY PRESS

CAMBRIDGE UNIVERSITY PRESS
Cambridge, New York, Melbourne, Madrid, Cape Town,
Singapore, São Paulo, Delhi, Mexico City

Cambridge University Press
32 Avenue of the Americas, New York, NY 10013-2473, USA

www.cambridge.org
Information on this title: www.cambridge.org/9781107020573

First published 2012
Reprinted 2013

A catalog record for this publication is available from the British Library.

Library of Congress Cataloging in Publication Data
Indigenous peoples, poverty, and development / edited by Gillette H. Hall, Harry Anthony
Patrinos.
  p. cm.
Includes bibliographical references and index.
ISBN 978-1-107-02057-3 (hardback)
1. Indigenous peoples – Social conditions.   2. Indigenous peoples – Economic conditions.
3. Indigenous peoples – Government relations.   4. Poverty – Cross-cultural studies.
I. Hall, Gillette H., 1962–   II. Patrinos, Harry Anthony.
GN380.I357   2012
305.8–dc23   2011038741

ISBN 978-1-107-02057-3 Hardback

Contents

Contents

Figures

Maps

Tables

Contributors

Prospere Backiny-Yetna
Economist
World Bank
Washington, DC, USA

Arbi Ben-Achour
Lead Social Development Specialist
World Bank
Washington, DC, USA

Hai-Anh Dang
Consultant
World Bank
Washington, DC, USA

Maitreyi Bordia Das
Lead Social Development Specialist
World Bank
Washington, DC, USA

Gillette H. Hall
Visiting Associate Professor
Georgetown Public Policy Institute (GPPI)
Georgetown University
Washington, DC, USA

Emily Hannum
Associate Professor of Sociology and Education
University of Pennsylvania
Philadelphia, PA, USA

Soumya Kapoor
Consultant
World Bank
Delhi, India

Elizabeth M. King
Director, Education
World Bank
Washington, DC, USA

Jerome M. Levi
Professor of Anthropology
Carleton College
Northfield, MN, USA

Kevin Alan David Macdonald
Economist
World Bank
Washington, DC, USA

Biorn Maybury-Lewis
Senior Research Associate
Institute for International Urban Development
Cambridge, MA, USA

Denis Nikitin
Consultant
World Bank
Washington, DC, USA

Harry Anthony Patrinos
Lead Education Economist
World Bank
Washington, DC, USA

Dominique van de Walle
Lead Economist
World Bank
Washington, DC, USA

Meiyan Wang
Associate Professor
Institute of Population and Labor Economics
Chinese Academy of Social Sciences
Beijing, China

Quentin Wodon
Adviser
World Bank
Washington, DC, USA

Introduction

Gillette H. Hall and Harry Anthony Patrinos

INTRODUCTION

This book provides a cross-country assessment of poverty and socio-economic indicators for indigenous peoples. It is motivated by a recent study of indigenous peoples in Latin America (Hall and Patrinos 2006), which finds high poverty rates among these groups, little to no improvement in poverty rates over time, and a continued interest in indigenous peoples socioeconomic status worldwide. Information on indigenous peoples' status by country, as well as analysis of the core drivers of poverty and movements out of poverty, remains lacking and is a significant constraint in implementing policies for the advancement of indigenous peoples across the developing world.

Building on this earlier work, the objective of this book is to assess the extent to which findings from Latin America apply to indigenous peoples in other regions. As such, it explores the extent to which evidence from across the developing world – including Asia and Africa – supports the hypothesis that poverty and deprivation is more severe among indigenous peoples, but more importantly, whether poverty and other trends over time indicate a similar disconnect between indigenous peoples and the overall economy in the countries where they live. The report provides, first, an overview of results for a set of international development indicators, based on the Millennium Development Goals (MDGs), for indigenous peoples, compiled for all countries for which data are readily available, and, second, detailed case studies for seven countries: four in Asia (China, India, Laos, and Vietnam) and three in Africa (Central African Republic, Democratic Republic of Congo, and Gabon). Together with earlier case studies for five Latin American countries (Hall and Patrinos 2006), the case study results cover over 85 percent of the world's indigenous population.

By providing disaggregated data on indigenous peoples, this work is designed to facilitate improved monitoring of national poverty reduction strategies and progress toward international goals (such as the MDGs), allowing indicators to be assessed not only for national averages, but also disaggregated for indigenous peoples. There is significant demand for this data both among international organizations and indigenous civil society organizations themselves. The 2007 passage of the United Nations Declaration of Indigenous Peoples' Rights provides a new global platform for international collaboration toward the advancement of indigenous peoples, in which major development organizations are expected to play a key role. Implementation of the World Bank's revised indigenous peoples policy has been underway for about two years, and includes efforts to shift from a "do no harm" to a "do good" approach in the Bank's operations that include or impact indigenous peoples. Yet an International Labor Organization (ILO) audit of the *Poverty Reduction Strategy Paper* process in Asia, Africa, and Latin America notes the dearth of indigenous-specific indicators as a constraint on adequate incorporation of indigenous development concerns. While indigenous peoples organizations rightly identify a number of limitations to the MDGs in terms of their capacity to capture the structural causes of indigenous poverty, one of their major criticisms is that "indigenous peoples are invisible in country-wide assessments because of the focus of these reports on general averages, which do not reflect the realities of [indigenous peoples]" (Tauli-Corpuz 2005). In fact, the Indigenous Peoples International Centre for Policy Research and Education has produced a list of proposed indicators of material well-being for disaggregation, including all of those compiled in this report (Tebtebba Foundation 2008).

BACKGROUND

It is widely believed and in some cases amply documented that indigenous peoples are the poorest of the poor in terms of income. This is particularly the case in the Americas, New Zealand, and Australia, where disadvantage among indigenous peoples is well documented. Indigenous groups in these countries are severely disadvantaged according to a range of socioeconomic indicators (Gwartney and Long 1978; Snipp and Sandefur 1988; Patrinos and Sakellariou 1992; Borland and Hunter 2000; Kuhn and Sweetman 2002; Maani 2004; Gundersen 2008). During the 1980s, the economic circumstances of indigenous peoples in the United States deteriorated relative to nonindigenous ones, chiefly because of the declining valuation given to indigenous peoples' human capital, particularly for men (Gregory, Abello, and Johnson 1997). Indigenous peoples on reservations are four times more likely to live in poverty than an average U.S. citizen; more recently, however, indigenous people's incomes are growing at about three times the rate of the U.S. economy as a whole (Kalt 2007).

At the same time, there are diverse experiences among indigenous groups, and particularly among "groups within groups" or specific communities within the same country. Some autonomous indigenous communities in Canada thrive and are even trying to obtain their own taxation authority. The Seminole nation of Florida nearly disappeared in the nineteenth century, but in the 1970s, they were the first U.S. indigenous group to enter the gambling industry, and by 2006 had amassed enough wealth to purchase the Hard Rock Café chain (Ward 2006). Yet, more than a quarter of the indigenous population in the United States is estimated to be living below the official poverty line (Kalt 2007). Progress is also slow for other groups around the world, despite increased political visibility.

In the developing world, most work focuses on Latin America, where similar results hold. The first work to systematically establish that indigenous peoples are poorer than the nonindigenous population, for the case of Latin America, was *Indigenous People and Poverty in Latin America* (Psacharopoulos and Patrinos 1994), coinciding with the opening of the United Nations Decade of Indigenous Peoples (1994–2005). That study provided a comprehensive analysis of the socioeconomic conditions of indigenous peoples in the four Latin American countries with the largest indigenous populations. In so doing, that study also set a baseline allowing future progress to be tracked. That study was followed by an update, *Indigenous Peoples, Poverty and Human Development in Latin America* (Hall and Patrinos 2006), which found that even though programs have been launched to improve access to health care and education, indigenous peoples still consistently account for the highest and "stickiest" poverty rates in the region. Thus, despite the fact that indigenous peoples have formed governments in Bolivia and Ecuador in an attempt to claim political rights and social benefits, they remain exceedingly poor with respect to national averages. "Indigenous Peoples in Latin America: Economic Opportunities and Social Networks" (Patrinos, Skoufias, and Lunde 2007) looked at the distribution of, and returns on, income-generating assets – physical and human capital, public assets, and social capital – and the affect these have on income generation strategies. Although providing compelling evidence of the indigenous poverty gap and beginning to explore its determinants, both studies leave open the question as to whether similar findings hold

globally. This slow progress signals a major hurdle for many countries trying to reach the MDG of halving the 1990 poverty rate by 2015; even still,
for other developing regions of the world with large indigenous populations, much less is known about the status of indigenous peoples.

In the developing world, the focus of research has been Latin America,
yet the indigenous population in this region numbers between 28 million
and 43 million, representing no more than 11 percent of the world's total.
With the notable exception of India, very little is known about indigenous or ethnic groups in other countries (see, for example, Van de Walle
and Gunewardena 2001; Hannum 2002; Gustafsson and Shi 2003; Borooah
2005; Eversole, McNeish, and Cimadamore 2006; Gang, Sen, and Yun 2008).
A multitude of ethnographic and anthropologic studies exist for individual indigenous groups, and although useful, these studies are not generally comparable to other studies or written in a form that could be easily
used as input to poverty-reduction monitoring and policy formulation. A
few national poverty assessments now include breakdowns by indigenous
group, with results that are extremely useful at the individual country level,
but the number of countries for which this analysis has been done remains
small, and for those countries covered, results are not often comparable.

On the determinants of the indigenous poverty gap, further scattered evidence by country (on Ecuador, see World Bank 2000; on Peru, see Torero et
al. 2004) continues to highlight the importance of human capital as a determinant of indigenous peoples' progress. Previous studies show that being
indigenous is associated with being poor and that over time that relation has
stayed constant. Furthermore, indigenous peoples suffer from many other
disadvantages, and even when they are able to accumulate human capital,
this does not translate into significantly greater earnings or a closing of the
poverty gap with the nonindigenous population. This holds for countries
where indigenous peoples are a fraction of the overall population, such as
Mexico (Ramirez 2006); countries where a large portion of the population
is indigenous such as in Bolivia (Feiring 2003); in developed countries such
as Australia (Altman et al. 2005); and developing countries such as Vietnam
(Plant 2002). In India, tribal and caste discrimination in the labor market
has been empirically examined (Banerjee and Knight 1985; Bhattacherjee
1985; Dhesi and Singh 1989; Borooah 2005; Das 2006; Deshpande 2007).
Generally, they find that discrimination exists, and that it operates through
job assignment with the scheduled castes entering poorly paid, "dead-end"
jobs. In the case of scheduled tribes, at least one-third of the average income
difference between them and Hindu households is due to the unequal treatment of the former.

The demographic and socioeconomic composition of China's indigenous population (defined here as the ethnic minority population) is described in Poston and Shu (1987). China's minorities comprise about 8 percent of the total population. Even though most groups are integrated into mainstream Han-dominated society, there is still a lack of socioeconomic advancement in a few cases. Gustafsson and Shi (2003) analyze the income gap between minority and majority groups in China and find that the gap grew in the 1990s. Both groups' income grew, but that of minorities grew slower. A statistical breakdown of the gap suggests that the concentration of minorities in regions different from those where majorities are concentrated is the driving force behind growing income gaps. Hannum and Xie (1998) and Hannum (2002) document the educational disadvantages faced by minorities.

Vietnam's ethnic minorities, who tend to live mostly in remote rural areas, typically have lower living standards than the majority does. Differences in levels of living are due in part to the fact that the minorities live in less productive areas characterized by difficult terrain, poor infrastructure, less access to off-farm work and the market economy, and inferior access to education (van de Walle and Gunewardena 2001). Geographic disparities tend to persist because of immobility and regional differences in living standards. There are also large differences within geographical areas even after controlling for household characteristics. Differences in returns to productive characteristics are the most important explanation for inequality. However, minorities do not obtain lower returns to all characteristics. Pure returns to location – even in remote, inhospitable areas – tend to be higher for minorities, albeit not high enough to overcome the large consumption difference with the majority.

There is evidence pointing to significant health and education disadvantage among indigenous groups. Even in the wealthy nations, most studies show an alarming health disadvantage for indigenous peoples – in health indicators as varied as infant mortality, diabetes, various cancers, and mental illness (Sandefur and Scott 1983; Stephens et al. 2005; Bradley et al. 2007; Dixon and Mare 2007; Gunderson 2008). For the rest of the world, less is known about the indigenous peoples' health status or access to health services. The few studies of particular communities indicate that the health of indigenous peoples is substantially poorer than that of the general population, with disease and mortality rates much higher than for the general population (see Hsu 1990 on China). The health of indigenous people is particularly poor for communities whose original ways of life, environment, and livelihoods have been destroyed and often replaced with the worst of Western lifestyle – that is, unemployment, poor housing, alcoholism, and drug use. At the extreme, indigenous peoples suffer systematic repression and deprivation, to the extent that their demographic survival is threatened (Basu 1994). More recently, Lewis and Lockheed (2006) show that it is the rural minority population that is most likely to be excluded from school, and that girls in rural areas are doubly disadvantaged in terms of education access. That is the case for Laos, India, Pakistan, Benin, Ghana, and Malawi.

Indigenous peoples' poverty has been increasingly recognized in the development literature (see, for example, Klitgaard 1991; Chiswick et al. 2000; Alesina and LaFerrara 2005). The relationship between being indigenous and experiencing economic inequality in developing countries has come to the fore in recent years (see, for example, van de Walle and Gunewardena 2001; Nopo, Saavedra, and Torero 2007; Telles 2007). Still, very little investigation has been made into the different economic experiences of the indigenous population within a society, and much less is comparative across countries and over time. For the few countries where the situation of the indigenous population has been investigated, a substantial cost in terms of earnings, poverty, and social development has been estimated, with spillover effects on national economic prospects and social stability. Thus, it is important to consider indigenous peoples in discussions about economic development – which is not often done.

Eversole, McNeish, and Cimadamore (2006) study indigenous poverty from an international perspective. They include chapters on, among other countries, Mexico, Taiwan, Russia, New Zealand, Colombia, Australia, Canada, and the United States. Yet they present case studies with different approaches in each chapter, so the results are not comparable across countries. Thus, despite the fact that they are estimated to be significant in number and are thought to represent a disproportionately large share of the world's poor, research that systematically assesses indigenous peoples' poverty and socioeconomic status in a comparable way across regions and countries remains elusive.

ANALYTICAL APPROACH

The majority of the work to date on the determinants of poverty among indigenous peoples has focused primarily on human capital outcomes. Most studies document that indigenous peoples are disadvantaged in terms of physical and human capital endowments. These low endowments, in turn, lead to significant differences in earnings and, therefore, poverty status – differences that have endured several decades of progress in reducing human capital gaps. In recent years, the social capital and cultural assets of indigenous peoples have been discussed. Social capital, defined as traditional community values and socioeconomic structures, are often referred to as the only productive capital minorities have in abundance (Woolcock and Narayan 2000). These traditional values and structures include collective control and sustainable management of natural resources; reciprocal and mutually supportive work systems; strong social organization and high levels of communal responsibility; a deep respect for the knowledge of their elders; and a close spiritual attachment to their ancestors and the earth. Such cultural assets can play a key role in economic entrepreneurship and in strategies to diversify or intensify livelihoods. Strong network ties, a strong sense of solidarity, and kinship-based exchange relationships also play an important role in providing economic security (Collins 1983).

However, group differences in socioeconomic outcomes can also be explained by looking at the distribution, composition, and returns to income-generating assets. Low asset endowments, for instance in terms of size of land or years of schooling, negatively affect the ability to generate income, whereas low rates of usage and returns stifle economic opportunity (Birdsall and Londoño 1997; Attanasio and Székely 2001). The composition of assets also matters, as the rate of return to one asset is often affected by the ownership or access to other, complementary assets. Empirical studies on Latin America's indigenous population show that social capital does not help promote indigenous socioeconomic advancement. However, low asset endowments can help explain the low overall returns to all assets (see, for example, Escobal and Torero 2005; Patrinos, Skoufias, and Lunde 2007). In addition, discrimination and other exclusionary mechanisms, as well as the internalization of prejudices (stigma), may also affect returns to the assets of excluded minorities (Becker 1971; Darity 1982; Hoff and Pandey 2006).

In sum, six principal (and interrelated) theories emerge from the literature to explain why higher rates of poverty may result among indigenous peoples (Lunde 2008):

1. Spatial Disadvantage: geographic characteristics such as climate, vegetation, access to basic infrastructure, and "remoteness" explain poverty differentials (see, for example, Kanbur and Venables 2007; Shorrocks and Wan 2005).
2. Human Capital: focuses on the lack of education and poor health, and consequent limited productivity in the labor market, as the major determinants of low income and poverty (see, for example, Hannum 2002; Ferreira and Veloso 2004; Hall and Patrinos 2006; Ohenjo et al. 2006).
3. Asset-Based Explanations and Poverty Traps: beyond human capital assets, it is the lack of a minimum asset threshold or combination

of assets, and the inability to cope with shocks ("vulnerability"), that constrain movements out of poverty (see, for example, Dasgupta and Ray 1986).

4. Social Exclusion and Discrimination: even with a sufficient asset base, the chronically poor lack social capital and access to key "networks"; discrimination further causes market segmentation – low returns on assets and/or limited access to services and credit (see, for example, Becker 1971; Wilson 2009).

5. Cultural and Behavioral Characteristics: lack of ability to speak the dominant language, or follow the dominant cultural norms; the poor may be further constrained by own (mal)adaptive behaviors such as adopting a "culture of poverty"; stigma and self-reinforcing stereotype threat; and group-level influences and peer effects (see, for example, Steele and Aronson 1995, 1997; Hoff and Pandey 2004; Fryer 2010).

6. Institutional Path Dependence: beyond characteristics and behaviors of the poor themselves, inequality is structurally reproduced via historically determined social and political relationships, exploitation, and "opportunity hoarding" among elites (see, for example, Aguirre Beltran 1967).

Although the purpose of this report is primarily descriptive, its results provide empirical evidence that can be discussed in light of the theories presented in the preceding list, particularly the first two (spatial disadvantage and human capital theory). To round out these results, it augments the evidence with findings from related microstudies to provide a summary picture of what is known – and not known – about the causes of indigenous disadvantage.

This study provides an assessment of poverty and socioeconomic indicators for seven countries in Africa and Asia for which there are identifiable populations and data. It generates findings that are comparable across countries, so as to begin painting a "global picture" of the conditions and development challenges of indigenous peoples/ethnic minorities. To the extent possible, we will attempt to categorize indigenous disadvantage – across space and time – according to the main hypotheses put forward thus far. However, whereas these and other hypotheses may be useful, especially the more recent and evolving poverty trap literature (see, for example, Bowles, Durlauf, and Hoff 2006; Carter and Barret 2006), our focus here is more on describing the situation and analyzing trends in the countries covered. In doing so, we will focus primarily on indigenous/nonindigenous differences in poverty, human capital (education and health) and labor market outcomes, and access to core social services and programs. Although the purpose of the work is primarily descriptive, where possible, case studies also offer policy suggestions that can contribute to the alleviation of poverty while taking into account the indigenous/ethnic dimension.

FRAMEWORK OF THE BOOK

The book is organized as follows. Chapter 2 addresses the complexities surrounding the issue of indigenous identity. Chapter 3 provides a "global snapshot" of a set of five MDG-like indicators (infant mortality, water deprivation, malnutrition, literacy, and primary school enrollment) for indigenous peoples vis-à-vis national averages for as many countries and groups as the available data allow. The remaining Chapters 4 through 8 offer case studies for seven countries: four in Asia (China, India, Laos, and Vietnam) and three in Africa (Central African Republic, Democratic Republic of Congo, and Gabon). These country studies follow the analytical framework of Hall and Patrinos (2006) to see whether findings from earlier research in Latin America (and the update in Chapter 9) apply also to indigenous peoples in other regions. In conclusion, Chapter 10 draws together the body of results in the context of existing poverty theory in order to move toward an understanding of the causes and drivers of indigenous disadvantage.

The case studies use comparable methodologies to assess:

Poverty Levels and Trends for Indigenous Peoples vis-à-vis National Averages.
Is poverty among indigenous peoples higher and more severe than poverty among the general population in the countries in which they live? Do poverty trends differ between the indigenous and nonindigenous populations? More specifically, do indigenous poverty rates remain stagnant when national poverty rates change? Does being indigenous increase an individual's probability of being poor, even when controlling for other common predictors of poverty (education, employment status, age, region, etc.)?

Differences in Human Capital Assets (Education and Health) and Occupational Attainment
Do indigenous peoples in Asia and Africa lag the general population in terms of schooling? Are they catching up and are educational gaps closing? If so, is this reflected in earnings and household consumption? Are returns to education lower for indigenous peoples? Similarly, how do the indigenous peoples measure up to national averages in terms of access to health services and health indicators?

Labor market outcomes
How large are the earnings and/or consumption gaps between indigenous and nonindigenous peoples, and how much of this gap remains unexplained when controlling for observable factors?

Differences in access to key public social assistance
programs and services
What is the indigenous population's access to basic infrastructure services
(water, sanitation) and major social programs?

HOW MANY INDIGENOUS PEOPLES?

Rough estimates suggest that there are that there are more than 5,000 different groups living in more than 70 countries (IFAD). It has been further
estimated that there are approximately 250–350 million indigenous peoples
worldwide, representing 5 percent of the world's population (IWGIA 2008).
The United Nations Permanent Forum on Indigenous Issues (2006) estimates the indigenous population to be more than 350 million. It is also
estimated that up to 15 percent of the world's poor, and up to one-third
of the rural poor, are indigenous (UNPFII). In one of the first attempts
to show the distribution of the world's indigenous peoples across regions,
Stephens et al. (2005), based on work by Maybury-Lewis (2002), show that
more than half of the world's indigenous peoples are in China and South
Asia (Table 1.1). Given a global population of slightly less than 6 billion in
early 2000, the indigenous population would make up about 4 percent of
the total population.

IWGIA provide a slightly higher estimate of up to 350 million indigenous peoples worldwide, representing 5 percent of the world's population.
These figures are widely cited. Analysis of the annual IWGIA (2008) report,
The Indigenous World 2008, where they have estimates for fifty-three countries, provides a good snapshot. In Table 1.2, we collect these estimates and
put together a regional breakdown. Although not published as a statistical
guide, and a few countries are missing, this estimate is higher than Stephens
et al.'s (2005) and very close to the figure widely cited by the United Nations
and others. The IWGIA gives a global percentage of 5 percent, also higher
than Stephens et al. (2005).

For the seven case studies included in this report, our research also provides estimates of the indigenous population. To cross-check the previously
mentioned estimates, Table 1.3 draws on the data provided in our cases
studies, the estimates for Latin America compiled in Hall and Patrinos
(2006), and extrapolates from Stephens et al. (2005) or IWGIA (2008) for

Table 1.1. *Indigenous population by region*

	(Millions)
China	91.00
South Asia	60.00
Former Soviet Union	28.00
Southeast Asia	26.50
South America	16.00
Africa	14.20
Central America/Mexico	12.70
Arabia	5.00
USA/Canada	2.70
Japan/Pacific Islands	0.80
Australia/New Zealand	0.60
Greenland/Scandinavia	0.12
Total	257.62

Source: Stephens et al. 2005.

Table 1.2. *Indigenous population by region*

	(Millions)
China	105.23
South Asia	94.90
Former Soviet Union	0.40
Southeast Asia	29.84
South America	19.53
Africa	21.98
Central America/Mexico	19.07
Arabia	15.41
USA/Canada	3.29
Japan/Pacific Islands	0.00
Australia/New Zealand	0.46
Greenland/Scandinavia	0.10
Total	310.21

Source: Compiled from IWGIA 2008 by authors.

all other countries. This method yields an estimate of the total global indigenous population of 302 million, which is higher than in Stephens et al. and very close to the IWGIA's, and therefore the figures cited by the UNPFII and IFAD among others. We also get a global population percentage of 5 percent for indigenous peoples.

Table 1.3. *Indigenous population by region*

	(Millions)
China	106.40
South Asia	94.90
Former Soviet Union	0.40
Southeast Asia	29.84
South America	16.00
Africa	21.98
Central America/Mexico	12.70
Arabia	15.41
USA/Canada	3.29
Japan/Pacific Islands	0.80
Australia/New Zealand	0.60
Greenland/Scandinavia	0.12
Total	302.45

Sources: Author estimates (mainly China, India, and Latin America), supplemented by Stephens et al. 2005 and IWGIA 2008.

THE QUESTION OF INDIGENOUS IDENTITY

What do we mean by "indigenous"? There is no widely accepted definition of indigenous peoples. In fact, the United Nations system has not adopted a definition of indigenous peoples, but rather has developed a modern understanding of this term based on: self-identification as indigenous peoples at the individual level and accepted by the community as their member; historical continuity with precolonial and/or pre-settler societies; strong link to territories and surrounding natural resources; distinct social, economic or political systems; distinct language, culture, and beliefs; and the fact that they form nondominant groups of society, and resolve to maintain and reproduce their ancestral environments and systems as distinctive peoples and communities (UNFPII).

Other multilateral organizations have followed suit. At the World Bank, for example, the official position is that "because of the varied and changing contexts in which Indigenous Peoples live and because there is no universally accepted definition of 'Indigenous Peoples,' this policy does not define the term. Indigenous Peoples may be referred to in different countries by such terms as 'indigenous ethnic minorities,' 'aboriginals,' 'hill tribes,' 'minority nationalities,' 'scheduled tribes,' or 'tribal groups'" (Operational Directive 4.10). The UN system further states that the most fruitful approach is to identify, rather than define, indigenous peoples (UNFPII). Even though the term "indigenous" has prevailed as a generic term for many years, in some countries there may be a preference for other terms, including tribes, first peoples/nations, aboriginals, ethnic groups, adivasi, janajati. Terms indicative of occupation and habitat, such as hunter-gatherers, nomads, peasants, pastoralists, and hill people, also exist and can be used interchangeably with indigenous peoples. However, because, as seen in Chapter 2, issues of indigenous identity also become entwined with demands for political recognition and special rights such as those of territory and resources, disagreement over who is and is not indigenous can become heated.

This work makes no attempt to resolve these questions and takes no position on – nor is designed to inform – ongoing or future disagreements over identity. Following the UN and the World Bank (2005), it does not put forth a rule of what does or does not constitute "indigenous." Such an approach would contribute little and would by definition invite controversy over perceived errors of inclusion or omission. The approach taken is instead a pragmatic one. Where data allow, Chapter 3 provides a minimum set of MDG-like indicators for any peoples whom any government or organization – including self-identified indigenous organization (such as International Working Group for Indigenous Affairs, Indigenous People of Africa Coordinating Committee, Africa Commission on Human and Peoples' Rights, and Asia Indigenous Peoples Pact) – describes as satisfying any definition of being indigenous. Country studies were chosen for inclusion in the book based on size of indigenous population and data availability, as well as use terminology and population breakdowns typical in that country. Thus, in China, Vietnam, and Laos, the term "ethnic minority" is used and, where possible, groups are broken down into further subcategories; in India, the constitutionally recognized "Scheduled Tribes" category forms the basis of our analysis. In Africa, where the data available are far more limited, the case studies focus on the pygmy populations for whom data can be disaggregated from household survey data in three countries: Central African Republic, Gabon, and the Democratic Republic of Congo.

References

Aguirre Beltran, G. 1967. *Regiones de Refugio*. Mexico: Instituto Indigenista Interamericano.

Alesina, A. and E. LaFerrara. 2005. "Ethnic Diversity and Economic Performance." *Journal of Economic Literature* 63: 762–800.

Altman, J. C., N. Biddle, and B. H. Hunter. 2005. "A Historical Perspective on Indigenous Socioeconomic Outcomes in Australia, 1971–2001." *Australian Economic History Review* 45(3): 273–295.

Attanasio, O. and M. Székely (eds.). 2001. *Portrait of the Poor: An Asset-Based Approach.* Baltimore: Johns Hopkins University Press.

Banerjee, B. and J. B. Knight. 1985. "Caste Discrimination in the Indian Labour Market." *Journal of Development Economics* 17(3): 277–307.

Basu, S. K. 1994. "A Health Profile of Tribal India." *Health Millions* 2: 12–14.

Becker, G. S. 1971. *The Economics of Discrimination.* Chicago: University of Chicago Press.

Bhattacherjee, D. 1985. "A Note on Caste Discrimination in a Bombay Automobile Firm." *Industrial Relations* 24(1): 155–159.

Birdsall, N. and J.L. Londono. 1997. "Asset Inequality Matters: An Assessment of the World Bank's Approach to Poverty Reduction." *American Economic Review* 87: 32–37.

Borland, J. and B. Hunter. 2000. "Does Crime Affect Employment Status? The Case of Indigenous Australians." *Economica* 67(265): 123–44.

Borooah, V. K. 2005. "Caste, Inequality, and Poverty in India." *Review of Development Economics* 9(3): 399–414.

Bowles, S., S. Durlauf, and K. Hoff. 2006. *Poverty Traps.* Princeton, NJ: Princeton University Press.

Bradley, S., M. Draca, C. Green, and G. Leeves. 2007. "The Magnitude of Educational Disadvantage of Indigenous Minority Groups in Australia." *Journal of Population Economics* 20:547–569.

Carter, M. and C. B. Barret. 2006. "The Economics of Poverty Traps and Persistent Poverty: An Asset-based Approach." *Journal of Development Studies* 42(2): 178–199.

Chiswick, B. R., H. A. Patrinos, and M. E. Hurst. 2000. "Indigenous Language Skills and the Labor Market in a Developing Economy: Bolivia." *Economic Development and Cultural Change* 48(2): 347–367.

Collins, J. L. 1983. "Fertility Determinants in a High Andes Community." *Population and Development Review* 9(1): 61–75.

Darity, Jr., W. A. 1982. "The Human Capital Approach to Black-White Earnings Inequality: Some Unsettled Questions." *Journal of Human Resources* 17: 72–93.

Das, M. 2006. "Do Traditional Axes of Exclusion Affect Labor Market Outcomes in India?" Social Development Papers, South Asia Series Paper no. 97.

Dasgupta, P. and D. Ray. 1986. "Inequality as a Determinant of Malnutrition and Unemployment, 1: Theory." *Economic Journal* 96(4): 10111034.

Deshpande, A. 2007. "Overlapping Identities under Liberalization: Gender and Caste in India." *Economic Development and Cultural Change:* 735–760.

Dhesi, A. S. and H. Singh. 1989. "Education, Labour Market Distortions and Relative Earnings of Different Religion-Caste Categories in India (A Case Study of Delhi)." *Canadian Journal of Development Studies* 10(1): 75–89.

Dixon, S. and D. C. Maré. 2007. "Understanding Changes in Māori Incomes and Income Inequality 1997–2003." *Journal of Population Economics* 20: 571–598.

Eversole, R., J.-A. McNeish, and A. D. Cimadamore. 2006. *Indigenous Peoples and Poverty: An International Perspective.* London: Zed Books.

Feiring, B. 2003. *Indigenous Peoples and Poverty: The Cases of Bolivia, Guatemala, Honduras and Nicaragua.* London: Minority Rights Group International.

Introduction 15

Ferreira, S. and F. Veloso. 2006. "Intergenerational Mobility of Wages in Brazil." *Brazilian Review of Econometrics* 26(2): 181–211.

Gang, I. S. Kunal and M. Yun. 2008. "Poverty in Rural India: Caste and Tribe." *Review of Income and Wealth* 54(1): 50–70.

Gregory, R. G., A. C. Abello and J. Johnson. 1997. "The individual economic well-being of native American men and women during the 1980s: A decade of moving backwards." *Population Research and Policy Review* 16(1–2): 115–145.

Gundersen, C. 2008. "Measuring the Extent, Depth, and Severity of Food Insecurity: An Application to American Indians in the USA." *Journal of Population Economics* 21(1): 191–215.

Gustafsson, B. and L. Shi. 2003. "The Ethnic Minority-Majority Income Gap in Rural China during Transition." *Economic Development and Cultural Change*: 805–822.

Gwarney, J. D. and J. E. Long. 1978. "The Relative Earnings of Blacks and Other Minorities." *Industrial and Labor Relations Review* 31(3): 336–346.

Hall, G. and H. A. Patrinos. 2006. *Indigenous Peoples, Poverty and Human Development in Latin America*. London: Palgrave.

Hannum, E. 2002. "Educational Stratification by Ethnicity in China: Enrollment and Attainment in the Early Reform Years." *Demography* 39(1): 95–117.

Hannum, E. and Y. Xie. 1998. "Ethnic Stratification in Northwest China: Occupational Differences between Han Chinese and National Minorities in Xinjiang, 1982–1990." *Demography* 35(3): 323–333.

Hoff, K. and P. Pandey. 2006. "Discrimination, Social Identity, and Durable Inequalities." *American Economic Review* 96(2): 206–211.

Hsu, H. J. 1990. "Incidence of Tuberculosis in the Hunting Tribe E-Lun-Chun in Northeast China." *Pneumologie* 44(1): 453–454.

International Work Group for Indigenous Affairs (IWGIA). 2008. *The Indigenous World 2008*. Edison, NJ: Transaction Publishers.

Kalt, J. P. 2007. "The State of America's Native Nations." United States, House of Representatives, Committee on Appropriations: Subcommittee on Interior, Environment, and Related Agencies.

Kanbur, R. and A. J. Venables. 2007. "Spatial Inequality and Development: Overview of UNU-WIDER Project." In D. Held and A. Kaya, eds., *Global Inequality*. Cambridge: Polity Press.

Klitgaard, R. 1991. *Adjusting to Reality: Beyond "State versus Market" in Economic Development*. San Francisco: ICS Press.

Kuhn, P. and A. Sweetman. 2002. "Aboriginals as unwilling immigrants: Contact, assimilation and labour market outcomes." *Journal of Population Economics* 15(2): 331–355.

Lewis, M. A. and M. E. Lockheed. 2006. *Inexcusable Absence: Why 60 Million Girls Still Aren't in School and What to Do about It*. Washington, DC: Center for Global Development.

Maani, S. A. 2004, "Why Have Maori Relative Income Levels Deteriorated Over Time?" *Economic Record* 80: 101–124.

Maybury-Lewis, D. 2002. *Indigenous Peoples, Ethnic Groups and the State*. Needham, MA: Allyn & Baker.

Nopo, H., J. Saavedra, and M. Torero. 2007. "Ethnicity and Earning in a Mixed-Race Labor Market." *Economic Development and Cultural Change*: 709–734.

Patrinos, H. A., E. Skoufias, and T. Lunde. 2007. "Indigenous Peoples in Latin America: Economic Opportunities and Social Networks." World Bank Policy Research Working Paper No. 4227.

Plant, R. 2002. *Indigenous Peoples/Ethnic Minorities and Poverty Reduction: Regional Report*. Manila: Asian Development Bank.

Poston, D. L. and J. Shu. 1987. "The Demographic and Socioeconomic Composition of China's Ethnic Minorities." *Population and Development Review* 13(4): 703–722.

Psacharopoulos, G. and H. A. Patrinos. 1994. *Indigenous People and Poverty in Latin America: An Empirical Analysis*. Washington, DC: World Bank.

Ramirez, A. 2006. "Mexico," in G. Hall and H. A. Patrinos, eds., *Indigenous Peoples, Poverty and Human Development in Latin America*. London: Palgrave McMillan.

Sandefur, G. D. and W. J. Scott. 1983. "Minority Group Status and the Wages of Indian and Black Males." *Social Science Research* 12: 44–68.

Snipp, M. and G. D. Sandefur. 1988. "Earnings of American Indians and Alaskan Natives: The Effects of Residence and Migration." *Social Forces* 66(4): 994–1008.

Stephens, C., C. Nettleton, J. Porter, R. Willis, and S. Clark. 2005. "Indigenous Peoples' Health – Why Are They Behind Everyone, Everywhere?" *The Lancet* 366(9479): 10–13.

Tauli-Corpuz, V. 2005. "Indigenous Peoples and the Millennium Development Goals." Paper submitted to 4th Session of UN Permanent Forum on Indigenous Issues, New York, May 16–27, 2005. http://www.choike.org/documentos/mdgs_cso_viky.pdf

Tebtebba Foundation. 2008. *Indicators Relevant for Indigenous Peoples: A Resource Book*. Philippines: Indigenous Peoples International Centre for Policy Research and Education.

Telles, E. E. 2007. "Race and Ethnicity and Latin America's United Nations Millennium Development Goals." *Latin American and Caribbean Ethnic Studies* 2(2): 185–200.

Torero, M., J. Escobal, J. Saavedra, and M. Torero, 2004. "The Economics of Social Exclusion in Peru: An invisible Wall," in M. Buvinic, J. Mazza, and R. Deutsch, eds., *Social Inclusion and Economic Development in Latin America*. Washington, DC: Inter-American Development Bank.

UNPFII. 2006. UN Economic and Social Council, Permanent Forum on Indigenous Issues, Fifth Session. "Action Programme for Second Indigenous Decade Launched." May 15, 2006.

van de Walle, D. and D. Gunewardena. 2001. "Sources of Ethnic Inequality in Viet Nam." *Journal of Development Economics* 65(1): 177–207.

Ward, A. 2006. "Seminole High Rollers Obscure Tribal Hardship." *Financial Times*, December 9.

Wilson, W. J. 2009. *More than Just Race: Being Black and Poor in the Inner City (Issues of Our Time)*. New York: W.W. Norton & Company.

Woolcock, M. and D. Narayan. 2000. "Social Capital: Implications for Development Theory, Research, and Policy." *World Bank Research Observer* 15(2): 225–249.

World Bank. 2000. *Ecuador: Crisis, Poverty and Social Services*. Washington, DC: The World Bank.

World Bank. 2005. *Revised Operational Policy on Indigenous Peoples*. Washington, DC: The World Bank.

2

Indigenous Peoples and Development Goals

A Global Snapshot

Kevin Alan David Macdonald

Both the United Nations Permanent Forum on Indigenous Issues (UNPFII) and the International Labour Organisation (ILO) cite the lack of data on development indicators for indigenous peoples as a major hindrance to both their empowerment and poverty reduction (Tomei 2005: 61; UNPFII 2006). This chapter helps address this knowledge gap by estimating several key development indicators related to progress under the Millennium Development Goals (MDGs) for indigenous peoples around the world. However, this assessment reflects only one concept of development: How peoples define their own development often differs from the notion underlying the MDGs, and for many indigenous peoples, such development has coincided with the loss of the land, economic mode, and language crucial to their identity and own sense of well-being.

METHODOLOGY

Finding a global perspective of indigenous peoples' development can be characterized as a problem first of defining who is indigenous, second of data availability and third of data representativity. This chapter's method is an approach to solving these three problems. First, to approach the problem of defining who is indigenous, this chapter does not use one particular definition, but rather accepts any definition used both in the scholarly literature and by major organizations such as the International Working Group on Indigenous Affairs (IWGIA), the Indigenous Peoples of Africa Coordinating Committee (IPACC), and others. Second, to approach the problem of data availability, development indicators are calculated using major household surveys such as the Demographic and Health Surveys (DHS) and Multiple Indicator Cluster Surveys (MICS) in which ethnic or linguistic groups that are considered indigenous can be identified. Third, to approach the problem of data representativity, this chapter draws on ethnographic and other qualitative sources to help understand how the well-being of these peoples correlates with their likelihood of being sampled in the surveys; a positive or negative correlation results in the well-being of those sampled in the surveys to over or underestimate the well-being of their peoples as a whole.

Ronald Niezen (2003: 19), in *The Origins of Indigenism*, describes the varying definitions of indigeneity and notes the difficulty posed to scholarly analysis by the lack of any single definition. Forming an empirical assessment of indigenous peoples' development, for example, requires an analytic definition of indigenous to determine which peoples' development is to be assessed. However, recent literature on indigeneity has established the inadequacy of the existing analytic definitions, and this is summarized in Chapter 3 by Levi and Maybury-Lewis where some groups whom many consider indigenous reject that moniker, whereas others claim to be indigenous and are not recognized as such; they describe indigeneity as a polythetic class whose members share varying characteristics but not any single defining set of characteristics. Consequently, adopting any of the existing analytic or legal definitions of indigeneity to conduct the present study would not only represent a significant departure from the current discussion on indigeneity but also, as Niezen (2003: 19) notes, would have "the inherent effect of pitting analysis against identity." An alternative approach, the one adopted here, is to provide for a perspective on indigenous peoples' development that is independent of any particular definition: Instead of adopting any particular definition of indigenous, this approach provides the requisite information to assess the development of indigenous peoples based on any existing definition. Accordingly, this chapter identifies and presents development indicators for any people whom major institutions, government or other organization, including self-identified indigenous organizations, describe as satisfying any definition of indigenous. This avoids the need to judge the suitability of any particular definition and increases the relevance of this study.

Because the socioeconomic status of indigenous peoples residing in many high-income countries has been relatively well documented (see, for example, census data provided by U.S. Census Bureau 2004 and Statistics Canada 2008, on Australia's indigenous peoples by Pink and Allbon 2008, or on the Maori peoples by New Zealand Ministry of Social Development 2008), this chapter emphasizes differences in indicator levels between indigenous groups and their encompassing countries for low- and middle-income countries; data on high-income countries from censuses and previous studies are also provided for comparison. Which peoples and indicators can actually be included in this study is constrained heavily by the availability of data. The study draws principally on Demographic and Health Surveys (DHS) and Multiple Indicator Cluster Surveys (MICS) because they allow calculation of indicators that most closely measure progress under the MDGs while being computable or available for as many peoples as possible. These data sets record basic information on sampled household members as well as detailed health information on women typically aged between fifteen and fifty-to-sixty years old depending on the data set; similar information may be collected from males also depending on the data set. With these data, five indicators are presented in this study, which reflect the MDGs on eradicating poverty and hunger, universal education, gender equality, and child health: (1) the under-five mortality rate over the past ten years; (2) the prevalence of safe-water deprivation calculated as the proportion of individuals with a water source being either more than thirty minutes away or being surface water or unimproved springs; (3) the prevalence of stunting calculated as the proportion of children under three years old whose height-for-age ratio is less than -3 standard deviations for the international reference population; (4) the male and female literacy rate; and (5) the male and female country-specific net primary enrollment rate. For several of these countries, per capita household consumption relative to the national average is also presented from a variety of budget and expenditure surveys.[1] The appendix contains details and sources of the indicators. In addition to the information required to calculate these indicators, the household survey data sets typically contain information on the respondent's self-identified ethnicity or the respondent's language either spoken at home or with the enumerator. With this information, this study calculates and presents the indicators among the surveyed subsamples that identify either ethnically or linguistically with the peoples satisfying any definition of indigenous.

However, of interest to this study is not just the indicator levels among the members of a particular people who were sampled in these surveys, but also the indicator levels among those members who were not sampled. Because the surveys used in this study are not designed to be representative of ethnic or linguistic groups, the development indicators of their samples

---

[1] The author is grateful to Claudio Montenegro for providing all calculations of per-capita consumption.

may differ from that of their peoples as a whole, primarily for two reasons: (1) an individual's well-being may be correlated with his or her tendency to identify ethnically with or speak the language of a particular people; and (2) an individual's well-being may be correlated with his or her likelihood to be included in the sample. First, if well-being positively correlates with the tendency of an individual to identify with a people, then the well-being of the sample will overstate the development of the people because those of lower well-being would be underrepresented. Alternatively, if well-being negatively correlates with the tendency to identify, then the sample understates the people's well-being. Evidence of these types of correlations exists, for example, when language is used to identify indigenous peoples in Latin America; the process of language shift, or loss of an indigenous language in favor of Spanish, is more prevalent among less-remote settlements with better MDG outcomes. Also, in India and Nepal, the processes of "sanskritization," when tribal people identify with nontribal people, or "de-sanskritization," when nontribal people identify as tribal, are often closely linked to well-being. Second, if a people's well-being and the likelihood of their inclusion in the sample are positively correlated, then the sample overrepresents the well-being of the people; in cases of a negative correlation, the sample underrepresents their well-being. An individual's inclusion in the sample hinges both on being in a household included in the sampling frame and being present at the time of the interview if his or her household is drawn for interview. The link between remoteness, mobility, and well-being of many of the peoples studied in this chapter – including, for example, the forest peoples of the Congo Basin, Hill Tribes of Southeast Asia, or the pastoralists of the Sahel – presents likely sources of correlation between well-being and sample inclusion; for example, the Thai census of 2000 excludes "hill tribes having no permanent place of residence" (Boonperm 2004: 3). To help establish how the development indicators of samples correspond to that of their respective peoples' populations, this study presents characteristics of peoples drawn from ethnographic and other qualitative studies related to how well-being correlates with (1) the tendency of an individual to identify ethnically or linguistically with the people, (2) the likelihood of being included in the census and therefore the sampling frame, and (3) the likelihood of being present at the time of the interview.

Each section begins with a discussion of which peoples are considered to be or satisfy at least one of the various definitions of indigenous in a region; results for these core MDG-like indicators are then compared across groups and against national averages, followed by a discussion of their representativity. The chapter begins with Africa, followed by Asia and the Pacific, Latin America, and concludes with North America.[2]

AFRICA

Saugestad (2008) attributes the introduction of the concept of "indigenous" in Africa to the first UN International Decade of the World's Indigenous People (Minde 2008: 10), which witnessed the recognition and trans-national organization of Africa's indigenous peoples, including the creation of the Indigenous People of Africa Coordinating Committee (IPACC) in 1997 and the adoption of the report of the Working Group of Experts on Indigenous Populations by the Africa Commission on Human and Peoples' Rights (ACHPR) in 2003. Recognition of a "communality" among African groups identifying as indigenous also emerged during this period and forms the concept of indigeneity currently underlying the IPACC, the ACHPR, and other organizations; this communality includes the occupation or use of territory prior to others, political or economic marginalization, and the display of cultural characteristics, mode of production, and identity "that link hunting and herding peoples with their home environments in deserts and forests," among others (Saugestad 2008: 165). This concept of indigeneity is typically associated with peoples traditionally engaged in "transhumant pastoralism, hunting and gathering, and drylands horticulture including oasis cultures" (IPACC 2007; Saugestad 2008: 165).

The ACHPR, IWGIA, and IPACC provide examples of peoples who identify as indigenous and satisfy this broad definition: These include the forest peoples of central and southern Africa, pastoralist groups in West Africa, including the Fulani and Tuareg peoples, forest peoples in eastern Africa such as the Ogiek, as well as pastoralists groups in eastern Africa, including the Somali, Afars, and Maasai, among others (ACHPR 2006: 15–16; Wessendorf 2008). However, the existing data provides only a small sample for forest peoples such as the Pygmies and San Bushmen, and groups such as the Ogiek are not recorded in the samples at all. Additionally, there is no widespread agreement on many peoples' classification as indigenous;

---

[2] The Saami, known previously as "Laplanders," are generally defined as indigenous in Europe and live in northern Scandinavia; however, they have been the subject of relatively few studies, and empirical development data on them as a whole are generally not available (Dixon and Scheurell 1995: 176). Lund (2008) cites the assimilation policies of their encompassing nation-states as removing the focus on ethnicity as well as the collection of ethnicity information.

for example, some governments and organizations reject many pastoralist groups' claims to being indigenous.

Central and Southern Africa

The equatorial forests of the Congo Basin are home to an estimated 300,000 to 500,000 "Pygmy" hunter-gatherer forest peoples, whereas the Kalahari Depression is the traditional home for the estimated 85,000 to 90,000 hunter-gatherer "San" bushmen (Ohenjo et al. 2006) in southern Africa. Table 2.1 presents human development indicators for sampled households identifying either ethnically or linguistically with these groups.

Previous research on the health of the Congo Basin forest peoples is limited, but Ohenjo et al. (2006) have compiled some health statistics from various field studies from the 1980s and 1990s and found under-five mortality rates ranging from 27 percent among the Mbendjele in northern Republic of Congo to 40 percent among the Twa in Uganda. Forest peoples inhabit ten central African countries (Köhler and Lewis 2002), but many of the DHS and MICS for these countries either do not contain information with which to identify forest people or contain only a few households in the sample; their human development and relative consumption estimates are presented in Table 2.1. Among the few sampled households, under-five mortality rates ranged from 16 percent in Gabon to 29 percent in the Republic of Congo, representing significant departures from the corresponding national averages. Among the thirty-nine households included in the Republic of Congo DHS, only 4.5 percent of females are literate and slightly less than 30 percent of males are literate, compared to national averages of 79 percent and 90 percent, respectively. Net primary enrollment among boys from these households are less than a third of the national average, at 25 percent, and among girls, it is less than half the national average, at 33 percent.

How representative these sample-based indicators are of the actual population of forest peoples depends on how the indicator levels of the households that were excluded from the sample differ from those that were included. The mobility and isolation of forest peoples reduces the likelihood of inclusion in censuses (Turnbull 1965: 26; Knight 2003: 90) and subsequently the household survey-sampling frames. Forest people generally "lead a semi-sedentary life, and cultivate crops to some extent, although they still maintain forest life, depending largely on the wild animals and plants, at least for a part of the year" (Ichikawa and Kimura 2003: 4), but the extent to which a particular band is sedentary varies. For example, in Sato's (1992) study of Baka forest people in the Sangha River

Table 2.1. *Central and Southern Africa: Basic well-being indicators*

	Under 5 mortality (per 1,000 exposed)	Water deprivation (% of h.h. members)	Stunting (% of children)	Literacy rate		Net primary enrollment		Households in sample (total)	Per capita H.H. consumption (% of nat'l avg)
				(% of males)	(% of females)	(% of boys)	(% of girls)		
Cameroon 1998	146	42.3	10.7	m.	m.	m.	m.	662	m.
peulh	191	4.5	14.2	m.	m.	m.	m.	15	m.
pygmee	201	93.1	21.9	m.	m.	m.	m.	3	m.
fulfulde[1]	221	21.4	14.9	m.	m.	m.	m.	43	m.
Cameroon 2004	148	28.5	13.0	80.0	65.0	81.9	78.9	10,462	m.
peulh	170	21.5	11.1	43.0	18.7	61.6	55.0	387	m.
pygmee	160	53.6	53.6	17.1	10.3	71.5	100.0	18	m.
fulfulde[1]	192	25.9	17.9	27.3	13.4	60.7	51.9	1,632	m.
Congo 2005	123	20.0	10.3	90.5	78.5	88.9	88.0	5,879	m.
pygmee	287	11.7	28.9	29.6	4.5	24.8	33.4	39	m.
Congo Democratic Republic 2007	155	58.1	18.7	85.3	59.0	71.0	67.6	8,886	
pygmy	0	57.3	25.0	22.6	0.0	50.0	100.0	7	62.8
Gabon 2000	91	19.0	6.7	m.	m.	m.	m.	6,203	m.
pygmee	162	51.0	51.0	m.	m.	m.	m.	8	m.
Namibia 2000	60	11.6	7.2	84.9	87.5	86.3	86.9	6,392	m.
san	24	27.3	11.7	25.9	21.1	20.6	17.7	80	46.1
Namibia 2006	69	15.9	7.3	88.9	91.4	87.5	87.9	9,200	m.
san[1]	104	10.7	25.6	37.1	22.2	48.2	72.2	81	m.

Notes: [1] Language; [2] Religion.

Sources: Cameroon DHS 1998, Cameroon DHS 2004, Congo 2005, DRC DHS 2007, DRC Enquete Aupres des Menages 2005, Gabon 2000, Namibia DHS 2000, Namibia Household Income and Expenditure Survey 1993, Namibia DHS 2006.

area in northwestern Republic of Congo, all forest people were primarily sedentary and settled next to roads or rivers, although some still participated in short hunting and gathering excursions into the forest. In Knight's (2003) study of the Bongo and other forest peoples of Gabon, almost all bands had settlements next to roads or rivers, but many occupied them only during the rainy seasons; during the dry season, they lived deeper in the forest, engaging in hunting and gathering (Knight 2003: 93). This seasonal occupancy of base settlements during the rainy seasons is also described in a number of studies of the "Mbuti" and "Efe" forest peoples in DRC (Bahuchet 1991: 213) and is problematic for inclusion in the DHS samples because these surveys are generally conducted during the dry seasons. Although more sedentary settlements imply a greater likelihood of access to public facilities, as exemplified by the most sedentary settlements in Knight's (2003: 92) study having access to a school and electricity, health conditions among households living in more sedentary bands can be poorer than those living in less sedentary bands, as documented by Dounais and Froment (2006). In their study, poor living conditions and poor sanitation among sedentary Mbuti in DRC, Aka, Kola and Medjan in Cameroon cause higher instances of transmissible and parasitic diseases than would have occurred in less sedentary life in the forest. Additionally, they find the hunting and gathering lifestyle supplies better diets to forest peoples; an excess intake of "energy-dense foods that are rich in fat and free sugars but low in complex carbohydrates" were consumed among sedentarized Baka and Kola forest peoples (Dounais and Froment 2006: 31). More sedentary forest people may also be less well off than the less sedentary ones if they were forced to sedentarize due to poor hunting and gathering conditions; Knight (2003) reports how the Bagama groups in southwestern Gabon near the coast have been forced to sedentarize because "forest resources in the area have been seriously depleted through prolonged logging" (Knight 2003: 95).

Table 2.1 also presents estimates for "San" bushmen peoples in Namibia. Among the 81 households identifying linguistically with the San language in the 2006 Namibia DHS, the under-five mortality rate for the preceding 10 years was 104 per 1,000 – much higher than 69 per 1,000 of the national sample. The literacy rate of males, at 37.1 percent, is less than half that of the national sample, whereas for females, it is less than one-third of the national sample, at 22 percent. The net primary enrollment rate for males is slightly more than half that of the national sample, at 48.2 percent, and for girls, it stands at 72 percent. However, these indicators may overestimate the well-being of their population as a whole, because many Bushman people in

Namibia have been displaced and forced into resettlement camps with poor living and health conditions (Ohenjo et al. 2006).

West Africa

The two major pastoralist peoples in West Africa are the Fulani and Tuareg, who, among others, are included as examples of peoples identifying as indigenous by the ACHPR and IWGIA (ACHPR 2006: 15–16; Wessendorf 2008). Table 2.2 presents human development indicators for households sampled in either the DHS or MICS, which identify ethnically with either of these groups or speak one of their languages. Relative per-capita household consumption levels for these households are also presented, where available.

The Fulani (or Fulbe, Peul, and Peuhl, among other names) inhabit much of the Sahel and consequently emerge in all west African DHS and MICS surveys that record a respondent's self-reported ethnicity or language. As Table 2.2 reveals, the well-being of the sampled Fulani households varies by country. The under-five mortality rate among sampled households over the preceding 10 years ranges from 133 per 1,000 live births in the Benin 2006 sample to 268 per 1,000 in the 2003 sample and 288 per 1,000 in the 1998 sample of *foulfouldé*-speakers for Burkina Faso. The prevalence of safe-water deprivation exhibits a similar wide range for the sampled Fulani households. In the 2005 Guinea sample, 60.6 percent of members of sampled Fulani households had either access only to surface water or only to water that was more than thirty minutes away; in the 2006 Mali sample, 3.7 percent of the members of households identifying ethnically as Fulani were subject to safe-water deprivation. The prevalence of stunting among children, measured as the proportion of children under the age of three whose height-for-age ratios are less than -3 standard deviations of the international reference population, varies from 35.5 percent of children among *foulfouldé*-speakers in the 2003 Burkina Faso sample down to 8.3 percent among the Fulani in the 2005 Senegal sample. The largest disparity between male and female literacy rates among sampled Fulani occurs in the 2006 Mali sample, where 21.8 percent of sampled males are literate compared to only 5.9 percent of females. The lowest net primary enrollment rates for sampled Fulani children are in the 2003 Burkina Faso sample, at approximately 14 percent. Departures in the well-being of sampled Fulani from the average levels of their encompassing countries vary. In Benin, the under-five mortality rate in the preceding 10 years for the Fulani sample falls slightly below the national sample average, whereas in the Burkina Faso sample, the

Table 2.2. *West Africa: Basic well-being indicators*

	Under 5 mortality (per 1,000 exposed)	Water deprivation (% of h.h. members)	Stunting (% of children)	Literacy rate		Net primary enrollment		Households in sample (total)	Per capita H.H. consumption (% of nat'l avg)
				(% of males)	(% of females)	(% of boys)	(% of girls)		
Benin 2001	163	18.6	10.7	47.9	25.0	63.5	48.0	5,769	m.
peulh	182	46.8	19.7	15.6	4.7	26.9	6.2	188	
Benin 2006	136	18.3	18.2	54.7	28.0	66.9	58.8	17,511	
peulh and related	133	39.1	31.6	10.7	4.1	16.2	15.6	533	93.0
Burkina Faso 1998	224	23.0	16.6	m.	m.	m.	m.	4,812	m.
fulfulde/peul	269	21.6	15.5	m.	m.	m.	m.	272	m.
touareg/bella	28	29.7	0.0	m.	m.	m.	m.	18	m.
fulfulde[1]	288	12.2	14.2	m.	m.	m.	m.	149	m.
Burkina Faso 2003	193	24.4	19.4	31.5	16.0	35.7	28.8	9,097	
fulfulde/peul	250	47.4	31.3	12.8	8.1	15.3	14.5	502	103.4
touareg/bella	274	59.7	22.1	25.0	7.9	39.5	38.2	117	m.
foulfouldé/peul[1]	268	55.3	35.5	4.0	2.4	19.4	18.7	352	m.
Chad 2004	203	27.1	23.2	35.2	12.1	m.	m.	5,369	
peul	272	27.2	22.5	16.8	8.1	m.	m.	83	100.2
Gambia 2005	m.	12.3	8.3	m.	5.9	70.7	71.9	6,071	
Pulaar	m.	12.9	8.7	m.	5.4	79.1	82.2	1,412	m.
Pulaar[1]	m.	13.3	8.8	m.	5.0	79.1	81.9	1,377	m.
Guinea 1999	195	32.3	10.1	m.	m.	m.	m.	5,090	
peulh	172	40.6	9.3	m.	m.	m.	m.	1,509	m.

Guinea 2005	188	58.9	15.1	44.2	16.1	57.2	48.9	6,282	
peulh	171	60.6	11.8	40.0	13.8	55.5	45.6	2,228	m.
Mali 2001	238	10.8	19.1	30.8	14.8	44.9	33.3	2,320	
peulh	228	11.0	20.2	27.8	13.4	42.4	36.7	310	m.
tamacheck	257	17.4	19.5	27.5	10.9	48.9	37.3	72	m.
peuhh/foulfould¹	282	31.3	23.3	m.	1.5	20.2	12.8	105	m.
tamacheck/bella¹	238	m.	m.	m.	m.	m.	m.	m.	m.
Mali 2006	215	5.7	16.3	37.4	17.1	47.9	40.4	12,998	
peulh	229	3.7	16.2	30.7	16.1	38.4	35.4	1,400	m.
tanachek	194	19.8	17.2	27.7	11.4	41.0	27.0	815	m.
peulh¹	214	6.4	19.8	21.8	5.9	26.6	23.1	748	m.
tanachek¹	145	22.9	20.7	25.8	7.1	38.5	25.0	711	m.
Niger 1998	303	18.5	19.5	m.	m.	m.	m.	5,875	m.
peul	240	20.8	15.6	m.	m.	m.	m.	247	m.
touareg	330	17.1	21.3	m.	m.	m.	m.	392	m.
tamasheq¹	312	12.3	11.0	m.	m.	m.	m.	15	m.
fulfude¹	187	21.5	26.7	m.	m.	m.	m.	45	m.
Niger 2006	218	27.9	29.4	27.9	11.6	44.5	30.1	7,660	
peul	200	34.5	31.7	12.1	9.0	23.9	24.3	432	m.
touareg	215	43.2	34.6	19.7	6.4	27.7	23.4	882	m.
peul¹	204	38.5	32.8	4.9	5.2	17.3	20.1	350	m.
touareg¹	204	51.8	30.4	16.6	5.2	30.1	32.2	635	m.
Senegal 2005	135	10.5	5.3	53.8	34.7	58.2	58.7	7,407	
poular	137	13.0	8.3	44.3	29.2	57.0	56.5	1,990	m.

Notes: ¹ Language; ² Religion.

Sources: Benin DHS 2001, Benin DHS 2006, Benin QUIBB 2003, Burkina Faso DHS 1998, Burkina Faso DHS 2003, Burkina Faso DHS 2003, Burkina Faso Enquete Prioritaire 1994, Gambia MICS3 2005, Guinea DHS 1999, Guinea 2005, Mali DHS 2001, Mali DHS 2006, Niger DHS 1998, Niger DHS 2006, Senegal DHS 2006.

rate for the Fulani of 250 per 1,000 differs starkly from the national average of 193 per 1,000.

There exists extensive ethnographic and other research on the Fulani with which to understand how these indicator levels for the households included in these samples correspond to those excluded. One important determinant of this correspondence stems from a combination of the Fulani's traditional mobility and the low capacity of low-income countries to sufficiently include highly mobile or isolated subpopulations in their census or DHS and MICS sampling frames. For example, the Sahelian ecology, in conjunction with the loss of herding lands to sedentary farming and game reserves, systematically force portions of the Fulani population to abandon nomadism and become sedentary because of what Burnham (1999: 279) describes as "impoverishment through cattle disease, drought and other foreseeable, but unpredictable, natural risks." This settlement of impoverished Fulani potentially causes the sampled households' indicator levels to understate the population's human development because the mobility of those better-off, nomadic Fulani decreases the likelihood of their inclusion in the survey sample. This understatement, however, may be offset if detrimental ecological factors do not cause households to sedentarize but instead cause them to increase their mobility or to permanently migrate to a different area, excluding them from surveys. Basset and Zwéli (1999) document such migration patterns in response to deteriorating grazing conditions among the Fulani in the Katiali area of northern Côte d'Ivoire; whereas some households responded to these conditions by leaving the area permanently, others adopted a seasonal, 100–150 kilometer southern transhumance during the dry season, returning with the rainfall in late May and June. A similar response to deteriorating herding conditions is reported by van Driel (1999) for Fulani pastoralists along the Niger River valley in the Karimama area of northern Benin. This increase in household mobility or permanent migration in response to declining herding conditions reduces the likelihood that the affected households would be included in the survey samples relative to the unaffected households, especially given that surveying generally occurs during the dry seasons. The correspondence of the sampled indicators is also affected by the correlation between the tendency of an individual to identify with Fulani and his or her well-being. Both positive and negative correlations are evident: Whereas impoverished and non-nomadic Fulani often maintain their identity (Burnham 1999: 279), "others leave society and survive on newly-established networks" (de Bruijn 1999: 302). In a study of street youth in Dakar by Understanding Children's Work (2007), 66 percent of children were of Fulani origin.

Accompanying the Fulani in parts of the Sahel, but more predominantly in the deserts surrounding the west Saharan massifs of Ahaggar, Tassili-n-Ajjer, Aïr, and Adrar-n-Iforas, are the seminomadic Tuareg peoples (Keenan 2004: 68). As Table 2.2 reveals, their households emerge in data from Burkina Faso, Niger, and Mali where they are also identified as speakers of their Berber language, Tamachek (Seligman 2006: 22). Similar variations in indicator levels exist for the sampled Tuareg. For example, the under-five mortality rate ranges from 145 per 1,000 among the sampled speakers of Tamachek in the 2006 Mali sample up to 274 per 1,000 among Fulani in the 2003 Burkina Faso sample. Differences between the national average and various indicators for the Tuareg also vary. The water deprivation rate among sampled Tuareg household members in the 2003 Burkina Faso sample is more than twice the national average of 24.4 percent, while stunting rates are similar to the national averages. Like the Fulani, the Tuareg are subject to the same ecological phenomena that link settlement and mobility patterns to poverty, consequently affecting how their survey-sampled indicators correspond to that of their population. This is exemplified by Rasmussen's (2001 study of Tuareg settlement patterns in an area near the Aïr massif of central Niger. Although Tuareg peoples have generally maintained their traditional economic mode of pastoralism, trans-desert caravan trade, and sedentary oasis gardening (Rasmussen 2002: 237), more households in this area were becoming less mobile by adopting oasis gardening or becoming more mobile by participating in migrant labor in response to deteriorating herding conditions (Rasmussen 2001: 7).

East Africa

The Horn of Africa's diverse climates support a number of different pastoralist and agro-pastoralist groups (Smith 1992: 169), and several included among the examples of peoples identifying as indigenous by the ACHPR and IWGIA (ACHPR 2006: 15–16; Wessendorf 2008) emerge in the Demographic and Health Surveys for Ethiopia and Kenya. Those with samples of around 100 or more households include the Somali generally located in the Ogaden, Somalia, and northeastern Kenya; the Affar of central Ethiopia; the semi-pastoral Maasai located through the Rift Valley and highlands of central and southern Kenya as well as northern Tanzania (Spear 1993: 2, 3); and the Nuer between the Sobat and White Nile rivers in Sudan and Ethiopia.

Table 2.3 presents indicator levels for the sampled households identifying either ethnically or linguistically with these groups. In the latest surveys, the

Table 2.3. *East Africa: Basic well-being indicators*

	Under 5 mortality (per 1,000 exposed)	Water deprivation (% of h.h. members)	Stunting (% of children)	Literacy rate (% of males)	Literacy rate (% of females)	Net primary enrollment (% of boys)	Net primary enrollment (% of girls)	Households in sample (total)	Per capita H.H. consumption (% of nat'l avg)
Ethiopia 2000	188	53.2	25.9	52.7	24.4	37.5	30.1	14,072	
affar	217	91.7	28.0	19.3	6.7	15.5	8.2	467	m.
somalie	177	85.3	27.9	26.3	7.5	21.3	17.6	626	m.
afarigna¹	224	92.3	28.7	9.2	4.7	14.7	7.6	465	m.
somaligna¹	179	86.3	26.6	27.0	7.1	22.3	17.9	598	m.
Ethiopia 2005	132	45.3	23.8	59.0	29.2	42.9	42.8	13,721	
affar/adal, danakil, denkel	118	91.0	21.8	13.9	2.9	16.1	9.8	510	m.
dasenech/geleb, gelaba, marle	m.	m.	m.	m.	100.0	m.	m.	m.	m.
hamer/bashada, bana, karo	144	31.6	18.8	0.0	12.0	17.7	6.9	17	m.
somalie	93	73.9	31.0	21.5	6.2	16.0	11.8	599	m.
nuwer/abigar	101	85.5	19.3	42.4	4.2	22.3	32.2	99	m.
nyangatom/turkana, bume, men, bum, rogegeno, tobola	m.	m.	0.0	m.	100.0	m.	m.	m.	m.
Kenya 1998	105	52.1	11.4	m.	m.	m.	m.	8,380	
masai	67	27.8	15.8	m.	m.	m.	m.	53	m.
Somali	315	0.0	0.0	m.	m.	m.	m.	8	m.
masai¹	64	25.9	18.8	m.	m.	m.	m.	51	m.
Kenya 2003	113	51.7	10.8	88.2	78.7	76.7	77.9	8,561	
masai	50	72.7	11.2	55.3	31.8	51.8	45.0	145	m.
Somali	162	51.7	13.9	38.1	14.3	49.0	33.6	507	m.
masai¹	60	68.1	10.3	47.6	28.1	49.6	49.1	114	m.
somali¹	172	55.2	14.5	34.1	11.9	45.9	32.3	439	m.

Notes: ¹ Language; ² Religion.
Sources: Ethiopia DHS 2000, Ethiopia DHS 2005, Kenya DHS 1998.

sampled Somali in Ethiopia have lower rates of under-five mortality at 93 per 1,000 relative to the national sample, but a much higher prevalence of safe-water deprivation at 73.9 percent and stunting among children at 31 percent; in the Kenya 2003 sample, their under-five mortality rate exceeds the national average at 172 per 1,000 among Somali-speakers but have close to the same prevalence of water and slightly higher child-stunting rate at 55.2 percent and 14.5 percent. Somali households also exhibit large disparity in literacy rates between males and females at, for example, 34.1 and 11.9 percent in Kenya and moderate disparities among net primary enrollment rates for males and females. Among Afar households in the latest Ethiopian survey, the infant mortality rate lies slightly below that of the national sample at 118 per 1,000, but the safe-water deprivation rate is 91.2 percent. The literacy rate among males is 13.9 percent, which is nearly five times that of the female literacy rate of 2.9 percent. A smaller but still large gender disparity exists in net primary enrollment rates as well. The sampled Maasai households experienced lower under-five mortality rates than the national sample at 50 per 1,000, a higher prevalence of safe-water deprivation at 72.7 percent, and a similar child-stunting rate at 11.2 percent. Literacy and net primary enrollment rates for the sampled Maasai are much lower than the national samples. The Nuer households also exhibit low literacy and net primary enrollment rates, better child nutrition and under-five mortality rates, and a worse water deprivation rate than the Ethiopian sample as a whole.

The factors that determine how accurate these peoples' sampled household indicators are for those households not included in the survey are largely similar to that of the west African pastoralists: The ecology links well-being both positively and negatively to inclusion in the sample by affecting mobility and sedentarization. Additional links are also evident. For example, Getachew (2001) surveys Afar pastoralist households in and around the town of Malka Warar in the Afar Region of Ethiopia and finds those with residences within towns have much higher incomes than those with residences only outside of town (Getachew 2001: 161, table 14). This suggests those living in remote areas who are more likely to be excluded from the household survey samples also have lower well-being. However, the opposite is found in a study of Maasai household surveys in the Longido area in northern Tanzania by Homewood et al. (2006). Here, it is the poorer households that locate closer to towns to diversify their economic mode with wage labor as a response to pastoral land scarcity resulting from commercial cultivation, conservation, and other reasons (Homewood et al. 2006: 21). Survey enumeration during the dry season in conjunction with unique seasonal migration patterns exemplify an additional reason for the

sampled household indicators to over- or understate that of their populations. Farah et al. (2004) study the stock-splitting strategy of Somali drom-
edary camel herders in the Moyale district in northern Kenya's rangelands
where younger males accompany non-lactating animals to distant pastures
for grazing during the dry season months of December through March,
whereas other household members remain with their lactating stock closer
to their settlements (Farah et al. 2004: 51). Because this will often occur
during dry seasons, these males who are accompanying the non-lactating
stock farther away from their more permanent settlements would be underrepresented in household samples. If human-development-related factors
such as school attendance determine whether a male remains with the
settlement instead of accompanying the lactating stock, then males exhibiting these factors would be overrepresented. However, this source of selection bias is unique to the type of stock and does not apply uniformly to all
Somali because those in different ecological areas herd different types of
stock, such as cattle in Ethiopia's Ogaden (Farah 1993: 62). The dry season
is also the most resource-scarce time of year for Somali pastoralists (FSAU
2001: 3); surveying during or just after this period may understate the average of some indicators such as nutrition measures or access to water for the
household's full consumption cycle.[3] Fieldwork for the Kenya 2003 DHS
survey began just after the end of the dry season, fieldwork for the Ethiopia
2000 DHS occurred during the dry season, and fieldwork for the other surveys occurred in both seasons.

Summary

The lack of consensus on who is considered indigenous and the lack of data
for many groups such as the Ogiek limit the characterization of development among indigenous peoples in Africa. For example, the Pygmy forest peoples and San bushmen have very few households included in the
national surveys examined here. Among these few households, however,
indicators are generally worse than those for their respective national samples. The other peoples included in this study have larger sample sizes, and
are primarily nomadic or seminomadic pastoralists; however, there is less
consensus about their status as indigenous. For these peoples, under-five
mortality and child malnutrition rates are high, and both may exceed or
fall below that of their national levels; water deprivation rates generally are

---

[3] In addition, the previous civil conflict in Somalia and the ongoing insecurity has left
    approximately 500,000 Somalis living in refugee camps in Kenya and Ethiopia (Luling
    2002: 227).

higher than the national levels. Education indicators for these peoples are lower than the national averages and this gap as a proportion of the national levels is much higher than that of the other indicators.

Because the peoples included in this section are traditionally mobile, either pursuing a nomadic pastoralist or hunting and gathering economic mode, their mobility and settlement patterns are important determinants for how the indicators for their sampled households correspond to that for their people's respective populations; generally, there is evidence of both positive and negative correlations between well-being and survey inclusion. Further qualitative research on the well-being of these peoples needs to understand the possible links between settlement, mobility, and well-being and sample these peoples accordingly to eliminate selection biases.

ASIA AND PACIFIC

While few national governments in Asia officially define subpopulations as indigenous – exceptions include the Philippines and Nepal – in most countries, the term is not commonplace, and some governments reject the concept entirely. Nevertheless, there exist numerous self-defined indigenous organizations in the region. For example, the Asia Indigenous Peoples Pact (AIPP), which began in 1992 and is funded by numerous international and national government agencies, includes as members twenty-eight organizations representing peoples from South, South East, and East Asia and is in communication with eighty more (AIPP 2009). In addition, the IWGIA (Wessendorf 2008) discusses several peoples who identify as indigenous.

Many peoples are either represented by the AIPP or its affiliates or are included among the peoples discussed by the IWGIA. In South Asia, these include the Adivasi or Scheduled Tribes of India, the Adavasi Janajati of Nepal, the Jumma peoples of the Chittagong Hill Tracts and others of Bangladesh, and the Vadda of Sri Lanka. The Ainu of northern Japan and the Okinawans of the Ryukyu Islands, the indigenous peoples of Taiwan, and several minority groups concentrated mainly in southwest China but also in the east and north of it comprise the peoples generally considered indigenous in East Asia. Those in Southeast Asia primarily include the hill tribe peoples in the highlands of Vietnam, Laos, Thailand, and Myanmar, such as the Hmong, Kammu, Karen, and others, as well as the Orang Asli of Peninsular Malaysia, the Orang Ulu of Sarawak, the Igorot of the Luzon Cordillera, the Lumad of Mindanao in the Philippines, the Masyarakat Adap including the Komunitas Terpencil of Indonesia and over half the inhabitants of West Papua. The government of Australia defines the Aboriginal and

Torres Straight Islanders as indigenous, while the Maori of New Zealand are those generally defined as indigenous. Using these definitions of indigenous, the Asia and Pacific region has the highest absolute number of indigenous peoples in the world, at approximately 230 million (see Chapter 1).

Census data and health studies are available for the indigenous peoples of Australia and for the Maori of New Zealand, but for the other countries, data are limited owing either to their not participating in a DHS or MICS, or to the absence of an ethnicity or language variable or a suitable ethnic or language category. For example, data on under-five mortality, nutrition, and water access are unavailable either disaggregated by ethnic minority or for the minorities as a whole. This section presents census-derived indicators of human development for Australia and New Zealand as well as DHS- and MICS-computed indicators for India, Nepal, and Bangladesh in South Asia, and for Laos, Vietnam, Thailand, and the Philippines in South East Asia.

South Asia

The government of India recognizes more than 500 scheduled tribes, but approximately half of India's scheduled tribe population is classified as part of the six major tribes of the Gond, Bhil, Mina, Kunda, Oroaon, and Santhal (Nag 1990: 115). The India DHS for 1998 and 2005 only reports whether the household head or individual self-identifies as a member of a scheduled tribe; which tribe, although recorded by the enumerator, is not reported in the data sets. Sinha (1990) categorizes the geographic locations of scheduled tribes into seven geographic regions, which is largely reflected in Table 2.4's presentation of the DHS samples' human development indicators. This categorization generally, although not perfectly, reflects the habitats of the major tribes. The Bhil peoples, for example, inhabit the western Indian Satpura and Vindhya mountains, primarily in Rajasthan with the Mina, although many have also migrated to and are employed in the tea gardens of the northeastern state of Tripura. The Chota Nagpur plateau area of eastern India contains the largest concentration of Oraon peoples and is the origin of Santhal peoples who are now concentrated to the north in Bihar state and east into Tripura state. The habitats of the Gond peoples span several of these regional categories stretching from the Satpura mountains in western India to eastern India's Chota Nagpur Plateau area and south to the Godavari River (Singh 1994; Whitehead 2007).

Human development indicator levels for the India sample are presented in Table 2.4, including each state's sample as a whole and for those sampled households identifying as scheduled tribes for both the 1998 and 2005 India National Family Health Surveys. For both samples as a whole, households

Table 2.4. *India: Basic well-being indicators*

	Under 5 Mortality (per 1,000 exposed)	Water Deprivation (% of h.h. members)	Stunting (% of children)	Literacy Rate		Net Primary Enrollment		Households in Sample (total)	Per Capita H.H. Consumption (% of nat'l avg)
				(% of males)	(% of females)	(% of boys)	(% of girls)		
India 1998	101	8.0	22.6	m.	m.	m.	m.	48,660	76.0
scheduled tribe	126	12.6	27.5	m.	m.	m.	m.	4,822	
Northeast									
assam	80	13.5	33.9	m.	m.	m.	m.	1,342	m.
scheduled tribe	74	18.1	27.4	m.	m.	m.	m.	234	m.
manipur	61	27.0	11.2	m.	m.	m.	m.	528	m.
scheduled tribe	67	28.6	16.7	m.	m.	m.	m.	181	m.
meghalaya	128	17.7	24.6	m.	m.	m.	m.	324	m.
scheduled tribe	126	17.9	27.0	m.	m.	m.	m.	287	m.
mizoram	59	17.6	14.0	m.	m.	m.	m.	385	m.
scheduled tribe	59	17.7	14.0	m.	m.	m.	m.	378	m.
nagaland	68	20.7	11.6	m.	m.	m.	m.	298	m.
scheduled tribe	68	21.6	8.7	m.	m.	m.	m.	244	m.
arunachalpradesh	86	15.0	11.9	m.	m.	m.	m.	400	m.
scheduled tribe	89	14.8	10.9	m.	m.	m.	m.	257	m.
tripura	68	12.7	22.2	m.	m.	m.	m.	456	m.
scheduled tribe	16	20.5	33.0	m.	m.	m.	m.	82	m.
East									
bihar	110	5.7	33.5	m.	m.	m.	m.	3,944	m.
scheduled tribe	117	7.9	36.5	m.	m.	m.	m.	423	m.
orissa	116	12.5	17.6	m.	m.	m.	m.	1,954	m.
scheduled tribe	138	16.6	19.9	m.	m.	m.	m.	336	m.
sikkim	84	14.0	9.8	m.	m.	m.	m.	507	m.
scheduled tribe	97	11.0	7.6	m.	m.	m.	m.	142	m.

(continued)

Table 2.4 (continued)

	Under 5 mortality (per 1,000 exposed)	Water deprivation (% of h.h. members)	Stunting (% of children)	Literacy rate		Net primary enrollment		Households in sample (total)	Per capita H.H. consumption (% of nat'l avg)
				(% of males)	(% of females)	(% of boys)	(% of girls)		
west bengal	71	6.8	19.4	m.	m.	m.	m.	2,170	m.
scheduled tribe	100	9.9	22.5	m.	m.	m.	m.	93	m.
Central									
madhya pradesh	145	11.0	28.3	m.	m.	m.	m.	3,492	m.
scheduled tribe	180	14.3	33.8	m.	m.	m.	m.	642	m.
West									
goa	50	12.1	4.8	m.	m.	m.	m.	500	m.
scheduled tribe	m.	14.0	m.	m.	m.	m.	m.	2	m.
gujarat	91	8.0	23.3	m.	m.	m.	m.	1,819	m.
scheduled tribe	95	9.7	29.3	m.	m.	m.	m.	362	m.
maharashtra	70	7.9	14.2	m.	m.	m.	m.	2,791	m.
scheduled tribe	92	9.1	19.0	m.	m.	m.	m.	195	m.
rajasthan	125	10.7	29.1	m.	m.	m.	m.	3,458	m.
scheduled tribe	155	14.1	38.6	m.	m.	m.	m.	507	m.
South									
andhra pradesh	91	10.0	14.2	m.	m.	m.	m.	2,103	m.
scheduled tribe	116	12.2	12.8	m.	m.	m.	m.	130	m.
karnataka	83	8.7	15.8	m.	m.	m.	m.	2,060	m.
scheduled tribe	121	8.2	22.1	m.	m.	m.	m.	133	m.
kerala	26	7.2	7.4	m.	m.	m.	m.	1,153	m.
scheduled tribe	38	18.5	0.0	m.	m.	m.	m.	11	m.
tamil nadu	65	8.1	12.1	m.	m.	m.	m.	2,348	m.
scheduled tribe	137	10.5	53.5	m.	m.	m.	m.	17	m.

North

haryana	79	8.9	24.3	m.	m.	m.	m.	1,319	m.
scheduled tribe	m.	15.3	0.0	m.	m.	m.	m.	2	m.
himachal pradesh	48	11.9	18.2	m.	m.	m.	m.	1,081	m.
scheduled tribe	0	17.4	0.0	m.	m.	m.	m.	6	m.
jammu	79	17.4	17.3	m.	m.	m.	m.	1,107	m.
scheduled tribe	81	23.9	13.8	m.	m.	m.	m.	27	m.
punjab	70	7.1	17.2	m.	m.	m.	m.	1,240	m.
scheduled tribe	0	12.7	0.0	m.	m.	m.	m.	2	m.
uttar pradesh	132	3.5	31.0	m.	m.	m.	m.	5,609	m.
scheduled tribe	125	9.5	41.8	m.	m.	m.	m.	126	m.
new delhi	58	7.6	17.9	m.	m.	m.	m.	1,010	m.
scheduled tribe	56	9.9	0.0	m.	m.	m.	m.	3	m.
India 2005	85	6.3	19.5	77.6	55.1	72.5	70.0	109,041	70.2
Scheduled Tribe	112	16.7	25.3	58.8	33.6	68.6	63.0	11,892	

Northeast

assam	95	5.1	16.3	76.5	63.9	80.5	77.5	2,828	m.
scheduled tribe	83	12.3	12.0	75.6	59.2	74.0	69.7	250	m.
manipur	50	42.7	10.1	91.6	74.8	66.5	66.4	3,009	m.
scheduled tribe	71	38.5	15.6	87.2	70.5	65.3	57.2	653	m.
meghalaya	74	18.8	25.6	74.2	70.5	51.9	50.5	1,500	m.
scheduled tribe	74	20.7	26.4	73.4	71.0	52.6	49.2	1,213	m.
mizoram	48	14.1	13.3	94.3	94.5	80.1	78.9	1,272	m.
scheduled tribe	49	14.3	13.4	95.3	94.7	79.8	79.4	1,241	m.
nagaland	70	22.3	16.1	85.1	76.9	52.8	55.0	2,850	m.
scheduled tribe	66	22.9	15.4	87.7	80.1	56.5	56.9	1,961	m.
tripura	73	8.1	12.1	76.2	68.9	77.5	80.9	1,368	m.
scheduled tribe	110	19.5	18.6	60.0	45.8	72.4	70.8	227	m.

(continued)

Table 2.4 (continued)

	Under 5 mortality (per 1,000 exposed)	Water deprivation (% of h.h. members)	Stunting (% of children)	Literacy rate		Net primary enrollment		Households in sample (total)	Per capita H.H. consumption (% of nat'l avg)
				(% of males)	(% of females)	(% of boys)	(% of girls)		
East									
arunachal pradesh	98	13.2	18.8	77.5	52.7	61.4	56.0	1,195	m.
scheduled tribe	101	17.7	18.3	77.4	53.1	63.1	58.6	752	m.
bihar	95	1.3	23.7	69.7	37.0	52.2	45.7	2,514	m.
scheduled tribe	62	0.0	10.0	51.1	59.4	40.0	0.0	10	m.
chhattisgarh	106	7.9	19.8	73.1	44.9	81.5	77.2	2,519	m.
scheduled tribe	129	15.8	21.6	61.8	30.4	79.5	71.7	684	m.
jharkhand	112	14.7	22.0	68.6	37.6	62.3	57.2	2,077	m.
scheduled tribe	138	24.1	25.1	51.4	24.2	61.0	52.1	501	m.
orissa	95	9.0	15.6	74.1	52.2	71.4	72.0	3,221	m.
scheduled tribe	136	18.8	24.5	49.4	22.3	64.9	61.3	674	m.
sikkim	42	21.7	13.5	82.4	72.6	65.5	65.5	1,489	m.
scheduled tribe	36	23.8	18.9	83.0	70.3	65.1	61.9	503	m.
west bengal	65	2.8	13.1	73.6	59.1	77.3	77.9	4,829	m.
scheduled tribe	82	5.8	21.3	57.8	28.2	72.1	67.2	171	m.
West									
goa	32	4.6	6.9	90.7	84.1	78.6	81.0	2,445	m.
scheduled tribe	73	6.5	6.2	86.8	76.2	69.0	75.8	104	m.
gujarat	77	4.5	20.9	82.9	64.0	74.3	73.4	2,635	m.
scheduled tribe	116	8.3	30.5	57.3	43.2	70.0	77.1	274	m.
haryana	59	9.9	14.8	83.0	60.5	75.8	73.2	1,930	m.
scheduled tribe	62	12.9	0.0	50.0	37.0	66.7	80.7	13	m.
madhya pradesh	108	16.8	23.3	72.5	44.5	68.7	71.2	4,460	m.
scheduled tribe	141	20.6	31.1	50.4	23.5	59.9	60.6	713	m.

maharashtra	53	3.4	16.6	88.3	70.7	79.5	78.4	6,428	m.
scheduled tribe	70	11.1	28.0	66.2	43.5	76.2	73.7	555	m.
rajasthan	93	14.5	19.0	72.3	36.2	75.8	64.9	2,649	m.
scheduled tribe	114	19.2	23.9	60.6	18.2	76.5	53.0	337	m.
South									
andhra pradesh	79	5.1	15.3	70.8	49.7	71.5	63.8	5,207	m.
scheduled tribe	112	11.4	25.4	46.3	22.6	76.5	65.0	269	m.
karnataka	66	12.8	16.6	75.3	60.0	77.1	77.8	4,266	m.
scheduled tribe	78	11.7	23.8	63.7	40.3	61.2	69.2	287	m.
kerala	20	1.9	5.2	95.4	93.6	88.7	90.4	2,451	m.
scheduled tribe	52	18.2	15.7	89.5	66.6	90.9	100.0	41	m.
tamil nadu	45	5.5	8.2	83.8	69.4	89.9	90.7	4,582	m.
scheduled tribe	34	23.4	11.1	55.8	49.0	64.3	78.5	39	m.
North									
himachal pradesh	43	9.0	12.2	93.7	79.6	81.1	85.2	2,185	m.
scheduled tribe	42	14.0	11.1	94.8	66.0	73.1	86.2	89	m.
jammu and kashmir	54	18.9	10.8	78.3	54.1	75.3	73.7	2,056	m.
scheduled tribe	38	52.9	14.8	69.0	26.5	73.3	74.8	162	m.
punjab	55	0.9	13.2	82.3	68.8	80.8	75.8	2,430	m.
scheduled tribe	m.	0.0	m.	60.0	60.5	100.0	m.	3	m.
uttar pradesh	112	1.5	27.2	76.0	44.9	72.7	70.2	8,170	m.
scheduled tribe	139	27.8	39.2	50.0	17.4	69.6	56.5	61	m.
uttaranchal	70	14.0	18.8	86.4	65.0	82.1	83.8	2,059	m.
scheduled tribe	94	3.5	21.1	53.7	38.3	88.6	87.2	68	m.
delhi	46	8.0	16.0	90.2	77.4	75.8	75.2	2,392	m.
scheduled tribe	88	17.6	26.6	76.5	54.4	89.3	65.7	37	m.

Notes: [1] Language; [2] Religion; *For exposures over the past five years.

Sources: India NFHS 1998 and 2005, India NSSO Socio-Economic Survey 1999, India DHS 2005, India NSSO Socio-Economic Survey 2004.

identifying as members of a scheduled tribe have lower indicator levels than the national sample as a whole. The under-five mortality rate for the scheduled tribe household samples is 112 per 1,000 as compared to 85 per 1,000 for the national sample in 2005; the prevalence of water deprivation rate of 16.7 percent for sampled scheduled tribe households is 2.7 times that of the national sample, and the prevalence of stunting among children is 25.3 percent compared to the national sample level of 19.5 percent. Literacy among the 2005 sampled female scheduled tribe members is 33.6 percent, which is almost half the 58.8 percent among males. The male net primary enrollment exceeds female net primary enrollment slightly, 68.6 percent to 63.0 percent. Within each state, the indicator levels for the scheduled tribe sample relative to the state sample as a whole varies. The northeastern state scheduled tribe samples generally have indicators closer to that of their state samples, but several states such as Mizoram and Meghalaya have very high proportions of their samples identifying as members of scheduled tribes. The states of Jharkhand, Chhattisgarh, Orissa, Madhya Pradesh, Rajasthan, and Uttar Pradesh have poor indicator levels for the sampled scheduled tribes, but the state samples also have poor indicators. In contrast, indicator levels for households identifying as scheduled tribes in Gujarat and Andhra Pradesh are just as poor, but indicators for the state sample as a whole are generally higher than the national levels.

Establishing how the indicator levels among the scheduled tribe households included in the surveys' samples correspond to the indicator levels among those households not included in the samples lies more in understanding the correlation between well-being and the tendency to identify with a scheduled tribe than in understanding the correlation between well-being and the likelihood of inclusion in the sample. The scheduled tribes are generally characterized traditionally as practitioners of swidden (shifting) agriculture as well as hunting and gathering, but land scarcity and land dispossession has transformed their economic mode into one characterized by horticulture, terrace cultivation, animal husbandry, agricultural labor, and migrant labor (Fuchs 1992:133–38; Singh 1994: 2). This more sedentary way of life, in conjunction with little debate about the accuracy of scheduled tribe population estimates, suggests that the census-based sampling frame of the DHS survey includes almost all scheduled tribe households, precluding a correlation between sampling frame inclusion and well-being. There is evidence, however, of both a positive and negative correlation between well-being and the tendency to self-identify with a scheduled tribe. For example, a tendency of tribes to emulate and identify with nontribal peoples has been widely documented in a process entitled "sanskritization." Unnithan-Kumar (1997) describes the claim by the Girasia people of Rajasthan to be members of the Rajput caste; some researchers describe these people as "tribal" but "emulating Rajput customs to gain higher status," whereas other describe them as "tribalized," who had lost their Rajput status long ago after being forced into reclusion (Unnithan-Kumar 1997: 17–18). This process raises the possibility of a positive correlation between well-being and tendency of a household to self-identify as a scheduled tribe if those who are worse off or belong to worse-off tribal groups are more likely to identify as something other than a scheduled tribe. In other cases, however, a positive correlation may exist. Dudley-Jenkins (2003) discusses the process of "re-tribalization" or "de-sanskritization" in response to government programs and benefits directed toward scheduled tribes, and illustrates this with the dramatic increase in the census-estimated population of the Halba tribe in Maharashtra, from 7,205 members in 1971 to 242,819 members in 1981. A large portion of this increase owes to members of a particular subcaste now self-identifying as tribal; "that a group is trying to become a Scheduled Tribe shows the government's indirect influence on identity claims through the construction of a particular menu of categories and a related opportunity structure" (Dudley-Jenkins 2003: 104–06). The incentive for such a group to identify as a scheduled tribe only exists when the opportunities associated with being scheduled exceed the group's current opportunities. If these opportunities associate with actual well-being, then well-being would negatively correlate with the tendency to self-identify as a member of a scheduled tribe; the measured well-being of the households self-identifying as part of a scheduled tribe would underestimate that of the households whom the government or some researchers define as scheduled.

In Nepal, the National Committee on Nationalities recognizes fifty-nine different Janajati groups comprising 31 percent of Nepal's total population, forty-one of which are classified as Hill Janajati who traditionally inhabit the Himalayan mountains, and eighteen of which are classified as Tarai Janajati who traditionally inhabit the portion of the Indo-Gangetic plains immediately below. Also included among the Janajati are the Newar people comprised of forty distinct cultural groups and sharing Newari as a common mother tongue (Dahal 2005: 90; Bennett 2008). The Hill Janajati include such groups as the agro-pastoralist Magar of central Nepal along with the Gurung in the Annapurna and Dhaulagiri ranges, and the Sherpa in the Solu and Khumbu Tracts, whereas the Tarai Janajati include the numerous rice-cultivating Tharu peoples (Macfarlane 1976; Fuchs 1992; Guneratne 2002). Table 2.5 presents human development indicators for the DHS-sampled households belonging to these groups and others, as well as for the Tarai, Hill, and Newar Janajati peoples as wholes. Overall, the Janajati sample has indicators that are generally comparable to that of the national sample, such

Table 2.5. *Nepal: Basic well-being indicators*

	Under 5 mortality (per 1,000 exposed)	Water deprivation (% of h.h. members)	Stunting (% of children)	Literacy rate (% of males)	Literacy rate (% of females)	Net primary enrollment (% of boys)	Net primary enrollment (% of girls)	Households in sample (total)	Per capita H.H. consumption (% of nat'l avg)
Nepal 2001	108	22.0	21.3	69.6	35.3	80.0	67.2	8,602	m.
Janajati	102	20.1	19.9	72.4	41.3	84.2	78.9	2,424	m.
Tarai Janajati	99	0.1	15.5	65.5	30.0	81.7	73.8	551	m.
dhanuk	88	0.0	29.0	63.1	14.5	74.6	63.3	72	57.4
dhimal	0	0.0	0.0	100.0	20.0	100.0	80.0	4	80.3
rajbanshi	93	0.0	11.1	66.7	43.9	100.0	91.7	33	98.2
tharu	102	0.1	12.4	65.4	32.6	81.3	73.6	442	67.2
Hill Janajati	112	28.9	23.0	72.8	41.7	84.3	79.5	1,510	m.
chepang	228	7.0	56.3	64.3	12.6	51.9	46.2	40	43.6
danuwar	134	0.0	19.0	100.0	41.5	66.7	100.0	14	62.5
darai	0	0.0	0.0	100.0	66.7	100.0	m.	2	67.2
gurung	90	33.6	11.4	95.6	55.6	87.2	84.0	94	151.7
kumhal	135	55.5	32.3	0.0	48.3	100.0	0.0	4	48.4
limbu	123	24.2	18.2	72.5	44.9	84.6	79.6	188	77.4
magar	85	25.8	18.4	79.0	52.8	88.3	85.8	415	87.0
majhi	172	32.6	21.4	24.2	29.3	78.6	82.5	17	53.6
mugrali/humli/kar bhote	380	79.2	66.7	14.3	0.0	50.0	m.	11	144.7
rai	126	45.8	18.8	70.0	44.5	94.4	83.1	209	74.2
sherpa	102	48.5	17.3	77.7	34.8	91.9	73.0	67	129.0
tamang	96	27.4	25.5	68.3	28.6	82.7	76.1	431	56.8
thami	196	0.0	40.0	66.7	20.0	66.7	12.5	15	82.6
Newar	46	17.5	12.6	83.8	59.7	89.5	85.2	363	250.8

Nepal 2006	79	16.0	15.2	78.7	54.5	87.7	83.3	8,707	m.
Janajati	77	15.7	14.1	78.3	58.9	90.0	86.6	2,625	m.
Tarai Janajati	87	1.0	5.6	73.4	51.5	91.8	88.4	645	m.
dhanuk	81	0.0	7.0	62.5	25.7	93.5	93.0	26	m.
rajbanshi	7	7.1	0.0	100.0	56.8	100.0	98.6	12	m.
santhal/satar	136	0.0	12.3	50.0	19.0	26.3	m.	7	m.
tharu	89	0.9	5.2	72.9	52.5	89.3	85.2	597	m.
Hill Janajati	77	25.0	19.5	79.1	60.2	88.2	85.4	1,632	m.
bhote	130	0.0	100.0	0.0	36.4	100.0	100.0	2	m.
chepang/praja	128	29.8	43.2	39.1	21.6	36.8	58.8	31	m.
darai	0	0.0	0.0	50.0	26.3	100.0	100.0	6	m.
dunuwar	213	0.0	13.6	57.3	44.5	100.0	100.0	12	m.
gharti/bhujel	87	18.6	5.4	71.9	77.3	100.0	75.6	25	m.
gurung	42	7.2	8.9	90.3	68.4	95.6	92.7	185	m.
jirel	0	18.5	10.0	93.8	57.9	87.5	83.3	22	m.
kumal	77	11.0	14.4	78.5	34.2	73.9	100.0	17	m.
lepcha	0	28.6	0.0	100.0	75.0	100.0	66.7	4	m.
limbu	84	18.0	12.0	87.2	80.9	90.0	83.7	194	m.
magar	92	26.3	25.9	83.8	58.3	89.7	92.8	484	m.
majhi	48	45.2	24.5	67.1	42.7	74.6	88.7	28	m.
rai	56	26.4	22.2	83.7	69.7	90.9	89.2	184	m.
sherpa	14	34.1	21.5	79.6	61.2	91.9	100.0	61	m.
sunuwar	0	54.8	38.0	100.0	82.5	100.0	29.5	9	m.
tamang	72	32.5	15.9	69.4	48.3	86.1	74.5	369	m.
Newar	43	12.3	4.7	89.8	74.6	94.1	87.9	348	m.

Notes: [1] Language; [2] Religion.
Sources: Nepal DHS 2001, Nepal Nepal Living Standards Survey II 2003, Nepal DHS 2003.

as an under-five mortality rate of 102 per 1,000 compared to the national 108 per 1000 in 2001 and 77 per 1,000 compared to the national 79 per 1,000 in 2006. Compared to the Hill Janajati, the Tarai Janajati have better water deprivation and stunting rates but lower literacy rates in both surveys and lower net primary enrollment rates in the 2001 survey; the under five mortality rate was lower than the Hill Janajati sample in 2001 but higher in 2006. The sampled Newar households in both surveys have better indicators across the board. The sample size for many of the individual Janajati groups is small, although some figures stand out. For example, among the forty Chepang households sampled in 2001, the under-five mortality rate from the preceding ten years is 22.8 percent, and 12.8 percent among the thirty-one households sampled in 2006; the Chepang are among twelve Janajati groups that the Nepal Federation of Indigenous Nationalities categorizes as "highly marginalized" (UNDP 2004).

How well the indicator levels of each group's sampled households represent those of their households excluded from the samples depends on the correlations between well-being and both seasonal migration patterns and the tendency to identify as a member of certain people. In addition to the migratory patterns of any traditionally nomadic peoples such as the traditionally forest-dwelling Chepang near the Seti and Trisuli rivers (Fuchs 1992: 99), who may still pursue this economic mode, seasonal labor migration has been increasingly documented. For example, in Fricke's (1994) study of the isolated Tamang village of Timling above the Ankhu Khola River in central Nepal, "more and more of Timling's households send members from the village to participate in the wage labor economy of Nepal" during the months of late December to February "when the labor requirements in the village are reduced and when porter work is most available" (Fricke 1994: 30). If the seasonal migration period causes a member of any particular Janajati to be absent during the DHS enumeration periods, which begin at the end of January and early February, and if the decision to send household members to participate in the wage economy is related to lower household well-being or poverty, then a negative correlation exists between well-being and sample inclusion. The same correlation may occur if lower socioeconomic status also increases the likelihood of more permanent labor migration, as exemplified by the large number of Tamang members engaged in emigrant wage labor in the Darjeeling tea gardens, noted by Fuchs (1992 97). Another source of this correlation arises from a group's self-identification as a different group similar to the process of "sanskritization" discussed among the Bhils and others previously. This is exemplified by Fisher's (2001) observation of Panchagaon groups of Thak Khola in western Nepal's Himalayan

Dhaulagiri zone claiming to be Thakali. However, their claim stems not from a desire "to be of the same endogamous group as the Thakali," but rather to be of equal status with their neighbors. If the tendency for one group to identify as another group is more likely when the group has a lower socioeconomic status than the other, then this is a potential source of correlation between well-being and self-identification.

Development indicators for the Bangladesh Chittagong Hill Tracts and other peoples are presented in Table 2.6. Water deprivation rates among the sampled household members for all groups are higher than that of the national sample of 64.1 percent except for the Saontal. Female literacy rates are generally comparable to that of the national sample at 61.9 percent, with the exception of the sample that identifies as Chakma and Marma. Male and female net primary enrollment rates are also comparable to the national sample rates of 86.8 and 88.7 percent, respectively. Most of these groups, including those of the Chittagong Hill Tracts, also live in the adjacent parts of India and traditionally practice the same economic mode of swidden or *jum* cultivation (Adnan 2004: 97); the links between well-being and sample inclusion likely reflect that of the scheduled tribes, but unique links also emerge due to the large movement of refugees out of the Chittagong Hill Tracts during the conflict that ended in 1997 (Mohsin 2003: 13) and displacement caused by high in-migration of Bengali settlers to the region, as well as the flooding of farmlands resulting from the Kaptai hydroelectric project in the 1960s (Adnan 2004).

South East Asia

Development indicators for hill tribe peoples identifiable in the available MICS household surveys for Laos, Thailand, and Vietnam are presented in Table 2.7. The rate of water deprivation ranges from 9.8 percent among the Muong sample in the 2006 Vietnam MICS to 72.6 percent among the Kammy sampled in the 2000 Lao MICS. Female literacy rates among the hill tribe sample in the Thailand 2005 MICS is approximately two-thirds of the national level while the net primary enrollment rate for sampled hill tribe girls and boys is comparable to the national average at 95 percent.

Many of the factors affecting how these sample-based indicator levels for each people relate to that of the households not included in the samples stem from correlations between well-being and sample inclusion through the remoteness or mobility of households. Censuses generally underestimate hill tribe populations because of their mobility and isolation stemming from their traditional swidden or shifting slash-and-burn economic

Table 2.6. *Bangladesh: Basic well-being indicators*

	Under 5 mortality (per 1,000 exposed)	Water deprivation (% of h.h. members)	Stunting (% of children)	Literacy rate		Net primary enrollment		Households in sample (total)	Per capita H.H. consumption (% of nat'l avg)
				(% of males)	(% of females)	(% of boys)	(% of girls)		
Bangladesh 2006	m.	2.6	m.	m.	61.9	86.8	88.7	62,463	
Chakma	m.	22.7	m.	m.	51.8	90.6	88.0	872	m.
Garo	m.	8.0	m.	m.	59.5	92.6	91.1	754	m.
Marma	m.	16.7	m.	m.	54.3	92.1	92.0	592	m.
Saontal	m.	0.0	m.	m.	63.7	84.1	71.9	286	m.
Tripura	m.	17.2	m.	m.	62.7	89.1	77.1	217	m.

Notes: [1] Language, [2] Religion.
Sources: Bangladesh MICS3 2006

Table 2.7. *South East Asia: Basic well-being indicators*

	Under 5 mortality (per 1,000 exposed)	Water deprivation (% of h.h. members)	Stunting (% of children)	Literacy rate		Net primary enrollment		Households in sample (total)	Per capita H.H. consumption (% of nat'l avg)
				(% of males)	(% of females)	(% of boys)	(% of girls)		
Lao PDR 2000	m.	42.0	20.8	m.	28.6	72.1	67.6	1,001	m.
Hmong	m.	48.9	32.4	m.	9.6	66.8	48.6	39	75.8
Leu	m.	35.5	16.3	m.	26.3	82.4	77.8	37	m.
Kammu	m.	72.6	20.8	m.	14.3	57.2	46.7	62	m.
Philippines 2003	42	5.9	m.	95.0	96.4	86.9	87.6	12,586	m.
ibaloi	18	9.7	m.	100.0	98.3	93.7	93.5	45	m.
ifugao	0	0.0	m.	77.8	93.6	88.5	91.0	37	m.
igorot	18	3.7	m.	88.5	91.9	79.0	86.7	38	m.
kankanaey	21	1.6	m.	100.0	100.0	91.6	100.0	43	m.
manabo	96	26.8	m.	61.3	65.8	55.5	62.9	36	m.
Thailand 2005	m.	1.3	1.9	m.	91.5	94.7	94.7	40,511	m.
Hill Tribe	m.	62.6	5.3	m.	57.0	94.6	95.7	190	24.5
Vietnam 2006	m.	6.9	m.	m.	67.1	92.4	91.1	8,337	m.
BaNa	m.	53.6	m.	m.	28.6	76.7	77.8	72	m.
H Mong	m.	28.6	m.	m.	8.4	96.1	97.2	187	36.7
Hre	m.	13.8	m.	m.	15.4	85.7	81.8	34	m.
Muong	m.	9.8	m.	m.	69.4	91.9	91.7	399	48.4

Notes: [1] Language; [2] Religion.
Sources: Lao PDR MICS2 2000, Lao PDR Expenditure and Consumption Survey 2002, Philippines DHS 2003, Thailand MICS3 DHS 2005, Thailand Socio-Economic Survey 2006, Vietnam MICS3 2006, Vietnam Household Budget Survey 2005.

mode; for example, the 2000 census in the wealthiest country of those included, Thailand, excluded all "hill tribes having no permanent place of residence" (Boonperm 2004: 3). This exclusion from censuses generally implies exclusion from the MICS sampling frames, and, as a result, a correlation between sample inclusion and well-being ensues if well-being correlates with isolation and mobility. Cases of a positive such correlation do exist. A household's isolation and mobility is in part determined by the availability of new land, which is crucial to the success of swidden agriculture and in part by the type of swidden practiced. Sutthi (1989) categorizes the Hmong, Mien, Lisu, and Lahu as "pioneer" swidden cultivators who continually farm a plot of land and, once its soil is depleted, then clear a new plot; the Karen, Lua, and Kammu peoples practice "cyclical" swidden that allows plots to fallow. Early studies from the 1960s and 1970s of Hmong households in northern Thailand and Laos suggest high mobility with average household residence in a particular location to range between 5 and 8.6 years; more recent studies suggest much less mobility, with average residence periods ranging from 5 to 30 years (Ireson 1995: 208). One reason for this reduction in household mobility is a reduction in land availability caused by both increased population growth and immigration, as well as government programs to restrict pioneer clearing. This reduction in land availability has a negative impact on hill tribe well-being. For example, Cooper (1984) studies a collection of Hmong villages in the Tanen mountains around Chang Mai, Thailand, and finds 90 percent of respondents have reported not having enough food but being unable to relocate because of the unavailability of land, whereas more remote areas were not affected as much (Cooper 1984: 214). However, this positive correlation between well-being and isolation and mobility is being offset by households in less isolated areas adapting to the scarcity of land by changing the composition of their mode of production. For example, in the Green Hmong village of Ban Suay in Chang Mai province, Michaud (1997) finds an increase in sedentarized commercial agricultural and income from other sources including from stock breeding, tourism, and opium production comprising 14 percent, 7.5 percent, and 23 percent of the village's net income, respectively (Michaud 1997: 227). Labor migration to increase wage income has also been documented among Kammu men in Laos migrating to Thailand (Ireson 1996: 92), among refugee Pa-O men from northern Thailand migrating to Chang Mai and Bangkok (Christensen and Kyaw 2006: 51), and among Lua and Karen men migrating to towns during the dry season. Hayami and Darlington (2000: 143) characterize many Karen villages as being populated mostly by women and children.

Table 2.7 also presents indicators for Philippine groups in the Cordillera, including the Ifugao who traditionally inhabit the slopes of Mount Data and its proximity, the Ibalois and Kankanaey in the southern Cordillera[4] (ADB 2002: 7), and the Manabo who inhabit southeastern areas of the island of Manabao. For all these groups, the number of households is quite small – less than fifty. Among these households, human development indicator levels vary. The 36 households identifying as Manabo have had a much higher rate of under-five mortality, at 96 per 1,000 live births, relative to the whole sample at 42 per 1,000 over the preceding 10 years. The safe-water deprivation rate among these households is also much higher than the national sample average, and literacy and net primary enrollment for both genders is much lower than the national sample. Among the households identifying as Ibaloi, Igorot, or Kankanaey, the under-five mortality rate over the past 10 years has been lower than that of the national sample at 18 per 1,000 for the Ibaloi and Igorot and 21 per 1,000 for the Kankanaey. Literacy and net primary enrollment rates for the sampled Ibaloi and Kankanaey are slightly higher than the national sample, while it is lower among those households identifying as Manabo. Given that there has been no thorough enumeration of Philippine's indigenous peoples since 1916 (Wessendorf 2008: 278), their isolation likely relates sample inclusion to well-being similarly to that of the highlanders of Indochina. All these groups traditionally practice swidden agriculture and, for those groups in the Cordillera of Luzon, terraced rice cultivation (ADB 2002: 7), but similar changes in economic mode are documented. The extent of out-migration is exemplified by McKay (2005) in a study of the Ifugao barangay of Haliap on the eastern slopes of the Antipolo Valley in the central Cordillera; she adopts the term "translocality" to describe how out-migrants who identify as members of the community live in metropolitan areas within the Philippines and many other places in the world (McKay 2005: 465).

Pacific

The indigenous peoples of Australia and the Maori of New Zealand have been the subject of previous health and well-being research both academically and by government agencies and programs. This section presents some basic indicators available from government and academic sources to highlight their well-being. Table 2.8 presents the infant mortality rate from 2001 to 2005 for three states and one territory combined, the maternal mortality

[4] The Igorot includes these groups and is a more general term.

Table 2.8. *Australia: Infant and maternal mortality, education, and income*

	Infant mortality rate		Maternal mortality rate	School Ret. to Yr 12		Med. Indiv. income
	Male	Female		1998	2007	2006
Non-Indigenous	4.6	3.9	8.7	72.7	75.6	473
Indigenous	14.3	9.5	45.9	32.1	42.9	278

Source: Pink and Allbon 2008. Infant mortality rates are per 1,000 live births from 2001 to 2005 for QLD, WA, SA, and NT only; maternal mortality rates are per 100,000 births from 2000 to 2002; median weekly individual income is for individuals aged fifteen and older.

rate from 2000 to 2002, the rate of school retention to year 12, and the median individual weekly income for indigenous and nonindigenous peoples in Australia. Indigenous peoples experience large, negative departures in their well-being from that of the nonindigenous population. The infant mortality rate among indigenous males of 14.3 per 1,000 live births is more than three times that of the nonindigenous population, whereas the rate for females of 9.5 per 1,000 is more than twice that of nonindigenous females. The maternal mortality rate among indigenous peoples of 45.9 per 100,000 births is more than five times that of nonindigenous peoples. The rate of school retention to year 12 among indigenous peoples was 42.9 percent in 2007, up from 32.1 percent in 1998 compared to 75.6 percent among the nonindigenous in 2007. Median weekly income for individuals over the age of 15 is AUS$473 whereas for the indigenous population it is AUS$278.

For the Maori in New Zealand, Table 2.9 provides estimates for two time periods of the under-five male and female mortality rates, upper secondary completion rates, and median hourly earnings relative to the national median. From the period of 1995 to 1997 to the period of 2000 to 2002, the under-five mortality rate for Maori declined from 13.3 to 10.6 deaths per 1,000 for males and 11.9 to 9.0 per 1,000 for females; for both genders, the gap between Maori and the national average declined as well. The upper secondary completion rates for Maori is estimated at 43.9 percent for 2007, well below the 65.5 percent of the national average; however, it represents a significant increase from the 28.8 percent of 2003 and a major decrease in the gap between Maori and the national average. However, even though the gap between the Maori and national levels for these indicators has declined over the various time periods, in the ten years between 1997 and 2007, the median hourly earnings of Maori has remained basically unchanged at around 86 percent of the national median.

Table 2.9. *New Zealand: Child mortality, education, and income*

	Under 5 mortality, male		Under 5 mortality, female		Upp. Sec. completed		Relative Med. earnings	
	2000–2002	1995–1997	2000–2002	1995–1997	2007	2003	2007	1997
Total	7.7	9.0	6.5	7.7	65.5	52.6		
Mäori	10.6	13.3	9.0	11.9	43.9	28.8	85.2	86.7

Sources: Under five mortality, Statistics New Zealand (2005), New Zealand Ministry of Social Development (2008). Under five mortality rates are per 1,000 live birthds, upper secondary school are percent of all school leavers, and relative median hourly earnings is percent of national averages.

Summary

Whereas the peoples studied in this section generally have worse indicator levels than their national averages, the disaggregation by group reveals various outliers lying above their national levels. Under-five mortality rates are only available for Nepal and India; the Nepalese Janajati samples' levels are distributed around their national level but as a whole are below the national level, whereas in India, they are above the national level. Water deprivation rates both exceed or fall short of their national levels. Among the Hill Tribe sampled households in Thailand, the Kammu and Leu samples in Laos, and the Hmong, Muong, and BaNa peoples in Vietnam, these rates are the worst. Stunting among children is worse among the Hmong sample in Laos and the Magar sample in Nepal, representing a large departure from their national levels, whereas Thailand's hill tribe sample exhibits the lowest deprivation rates. Male literacy rates are only available for the Scheduled Tribe sample of India and the Nepalese Janajati sample; the Scheduled Tribe sample exhibits the worst among these, whereas the Gurung sample from Nepal exhibits the best. Lao Kammu, Leu, and Hmong samples have the highest levels of primary enrollment and are closest to their national levels.

The representativity of the available data depends primarily on how well-being is correlated with, for India and Nepal, a household's tendency to self-identify with a particular people, and, for Southeast Asia, a household's mobility and isolation. Additionally, data does not exist for many groups either because they are too small to be included in DHS and MICS datasets or the country does not participate in these surveys. This includes, for example, China; but school enrollment and attainment data for seven- to sixteen-year-olds for Chinese minorities is reported in Tables 5.14, 5.15, 5.19, and 5.21 in Hannum and Wang (Chapter 5 in this volume). Future research and data collection on peoples in South Asia needs to account for the tendency of groups to self-identify with other groups in order to produce a more representative, quantitative study, and in Southeast Asia, the issues of mobility and isolation need to be addressed due to their correlation with well-being.

LATIN AMERICA

The problem of defining indigenous in Latin America is less whether groups such as the Maya, Quechua, Aymara, Mapuche, and others satisfy a definition of indigenous, but more of whether an individual or household belongs to such a group. For example, and as pointed out by Layton and Patrinos (2006: 27), under the definition employed by the Ecuadorian government, 6 percent of the population of Ecuador are indigenous, whereas according to the definition used by the National Confederation of Indigenous Nationalities of Ecuador, 32 percent are indigenous. Researchers typically use three criteria when counting or analyzing indigenous peoples in Latin America: self-identification, language, and geographic concentration (Layton and Patrinos 2006: 25). For the DHS and MICS surveys utilized in this analysis, language is the only identifier for indigenous groups in Peru for both survey years, for Bolivia in 1998, and for the various Mayan subgroups in Guatemala,[5] whereas for the others, self-identified ethnicity exists as well. The primary problem with using language to classify an individual as a member of a particular people is that individuals, their descendents, as well as whole communities lose their language and adopt Spanish. Consequently, the extent to which sampled household indicators of development for a particular linguistic group represents that of their population depends on how this "language shift" correlates with well-being. If such a correlation is positive, as is seemingly evident, then the sampled household indicators understate that for their population; if those people from a particular group who no longer speak its language were included as part of the linguistic group in the survey sample, then the resultant levels of development would be higher.

South America

Table 2.10 presents estimates of development and relative per capita consumption for South American DHS or MICS sampled households for

[5] Those who self-identify as "Indian" can be determined.

Table 2.10. *South America: Basic well-being indicators*

	Under 5 mortality (per 1,000 exposed)	Water deprivation (% of h.h. members)	Stunting (% of children)	Literacy rate (% of males)	Literacy rate (% of females)	Net primary enrollment (% of boys)	Net primary enrollment (% of girls)	Households in sample (total)	Per capita H.H. consumption (% of nat'l avg)
Bolivia 1998	99	10.8	9.4	m.	m.	m.	m.	12,109	
aymara[1]	163	15.8	12.3	m.	m.	m.	m.	483	m.
quechua[1]	165	38.2	19.1	m.	m.	m.	m.	1,273	m.
guarani[1]	56	25.0	24.0	m.	m.	m.	m.	20	m.
Bolivia 2003	93	9.7	7.8	97.0	91.1	82.7	82.3	19,207	
quechua	111	16.1	11.1	95.0	83.1	83.9	82.2	4,602	73.8
aymara	99	7.4	8.1	98.6	93.1	75.0	75.9	2,376	72.7
guarani;	78	1.6	4.6	98.0	92.3	90.9	88.8	266	157.7
Guyana 2005	49	1.2	m.	m.	m.	89.5	88.6	2,608	
amerindian	8	9.0	m.	m.	m.	91.8	91.2	171	41.6
Peru 2000	60	15.5	7.7	m.	91.3	m.	m.	28,900	
quechua[1]	114	37.9	17.2	m.	59.8	m.	m.	2,610	m.
aymara[1]	66	13.4	11.3	m.	78.9	m.	m.	253	m.
Peru 2004	41	16.5	5.8	m.	93.0	91.1	92.0	13,211	
quechua[1]	71	31.4	15.4	m.	62.5	93.0	93.4	1,155	m.
aymara[1]	40	10.1	3.9	m.	81.9	93.2	94.2	123	m.
Ecuador 1998–2003	76.7	m.	3.0	m.	m.	m.	m.	m.	
indigenous	138	m.	3.0	m.	m.	m.	m.	m.	54.5

Notes: [1] Language, [2] Religion.

Sources: Bolivia DHS 2003, Bolivia MECOVI 2002, Guyana 2005 DHS, Guyana LSMS 1992. Larrea and Torres 2005. Under five mortality for 2001 (indigenous includes official definition, language and self-identification), nutrition deprivation for 1998, and per capita income for 2003.

which various groups could be identified. In Guyana, the question used to identify the "Amerindians" is self-reported ethnicity as is the question used to identify Quechua and Aymara peoples in the Bolivia 2003 DHS. In Peru, only language is asked.

Quechua comprises several varieties, although its two traditionally recognized groups are Quechua I, whose varieties' speakers are concentrated in central Peru and Quechua II, whose varieties' speakers are concentrated in Ecuador and northern Peru as well as in southern Peru, Bolivia, Chile, and Argentina (Hornberger and King 2001). In the DHS for Peru and Bolivia, no subvarieties of Quechua were distinguished. As Table 2.10 reveals, sampled Quechua speakers in both countries and for both years of collection in Peru had much lower levels for all indicators except for net primary enrollment rates than the national averages. In the 1998 Bolivia DHS, sampled households experienced an under-five mortality rate of 165 per 1,000 live births compared to 99 per 1,000 for the national sample of households; in 2003 sample, these figures became 111 per 1,000 and 93 per 1,000, respectively. Disparity between stunting rates among the Quechua sample and national sample is most apparent in the 2004 Peru DHS sample, with a stunting rate of 15.4 percent among sampled Quechua speakers compared to 5.8 among the national sample as a whole.

These indicator levels for the sample of households identifying linguistically as Quechua are likely lower-bound estimates for the broader Quechua peoples, because there is evidence that language shift from Quechua to Spanish is a consequence of absorption into the encompassing Spanish-speaking, national economy and positively correlates with well-being. For example, in the Loja province of Ecuador's Andean sierra, King (2001) documents the advanced state of language shift from Quechua to Spanish among the Saraguro who are one of Ecuador's two most economically successful indigenous groups (King 2001: 33). In the Quechua town of Lagunas, she attributes this transition to "the economic and scholastic advantages pulling them towards Spanish, and the concomitant prejudice, harassment, and discrimination pushing them away from Quichua," which began with exposure to the Spanish-speaking national culture from the close proximity of the Pan-American highway completed in the 1940s (King 2001: 74). In contrast, Stark (1985a) describes the isolated and almost entirely monolingual Quichua-speaking "Platillos" who inhabit the northern slopes of Mount Chimborazo in central Ecuador; they primarily engage in herding and the subsistence agriculture of root crops, with few nearby "public facilities such as schools, health centers, and churches" (Stark 1985a: 465).

That language shift is highly correlated with urbanization and development is further evinced in Myers's (1973) study of language shift among indigenous migrants living inside Lima, Peru, in the then-squatter settlements of Villa María del Perpetuo Socorro and El Planeta. In her survey, "98 per cent of those with a mother tongue of Quechua have gained some knowledge of Spanish" (Myers 1973: 57), and that the extent of language shift measured by the location and frequency of migrants' Spanish use is positively associated with years of schooling, especially those between ages fifteen and thirty-four (Myers 1973: 103, table 23), as well as other variables related to development. Those who remain in less-developed rural areas can retain their language, as shown by Mannheim's (1985) finding that "the linguistic domination of the southern highlands of Peru by Quechua speakers (save for a large concentration of Aymara speakers in Puno) continues to be pervasive" as a result of not economic factors but that "Quechua speakers treat the boundary between Quechua- and Spanish-speakers as of primordial importance in their social universe" (Mannheim 1985: 487). This rural, linguistic pervasion is likely echoed in Bolivia as well: Stark (1985b) observes that in the isolated mountain towns of the province of Franz Tamayo in the La Paz department, campesino parents see little need for their children to be educated in Spanish, unlike other areas of Latin America (Stark 1985b: 525). However, the extent of language shift in Bolivia is much less than compared to the rest of South America; "the dominant minority speaks only Spanish, while the majority that they dominate speak only Quechua, with a few bilingual mediators in between" (Stark 1985b). The levels of development for Quechua speakers in Bolivia in 1998, consequently, are likely to be closer to that of the broader Quechua people than in Peru where the language shift of Quechua peoples more integrated into the national economy is more advanced.

The second major indigenous group in the Andes are the Aymara who, numbering around 2 million, are primarily concentrated on the high Andean plains surrounding Lake Titicaca in Peru and Bolivia as well as northern Argentina and Chile (Hardman 1981: 3; Briggs 1985a: 546). Table 2.10 reveals development estimates for sampled households identifying linguistically in both Peru DHS and in the 1998 Bolivia DHS, as well as those identifying ethnically in the Bolivia 2003 DHS. In Bolivia, Aymara indicators tend to be higher than that for the Quechua, especially in the later survey, and in Peru, Aymara estimates also indicate much higher levels of well-being than for the Quechua; in the later survey, they are often similar to the national averages except for literacy rates. Analogous to the Quechua case, the development indicators for the Aymara households identified linguistically are likely lower-bound estimates for their broader populations. Evidence of this can be found of the rural pervasion of Aymara where in Bolivia approximately one-third of the population speaks Aymara, whereas in Peru it is around 3 percent. Myers's (1973) study of the squatter communities in Lima, while primarily focused on Quechua, also collected some data on Aymara speakers. She found that 1.3 percent of her survey had Aymara as a mother tongue, but only 0.2 percent could actually speak it. Consequently, language shift is likely correlated with isolation and development as is the case for Quechua.

Table 2.10 also presents some indicators for Ecuador's indigenous peoples derived from Larrea and Torres (2006). However, specific groups cannot be identified. Indicators are calculated from samples from different years and also use different definitions of indigenous. The under-five mortality figure of 138 per 1,000 is from the 2001 national census and defines indigenous "based on an extended version of the definition of 'indigenous' in the 2001 census and adding self-identification and the language spoken at the household level" (Larrea and Torres 2006: 69). The prevalence of stunting, which is equal to the national sample, is drawn from the 1998 Living Conditions Survey in which indigenous is identified by language. The per-capita household income for indigenous people as proportion of the national sample level is 54.5 percent; this figure stems from the Ecuador Employment, Unemployment, and Underemployment Survey of 2003.

Central America and Mexico

The second group of countries for which DHS or MICS data exist on indigenous households are Belize and Guatemala, where indigenous peoples are primarily Mayan peoples. For both countries, the questions on both ethnicity and language were included in the surveys, although in Belize, it was not recorded exactly which of the Mayan peoples participated, whereas in Guatemala, the main subgroups, including Kaqchikel, Q'eqchi', K'iche', Mam, are only identifiable by language. Table 2.11 presents the estimates for each of the ethnic and linguistic groups. In Belize, except for enrollment, the estimates for both ethnically Mayan and speakers of Mayan are worse than that of the national average.

Those sampled households who identify as ethnically Mayan have similar estimates for those who speak Mayan, although those who speak Mayan have slightly worse estimates for most indicators; this is consistent with language shift correlating with well-being as shown for Quechua and

Table 2.11. *Central America: Basic well-being indicators*

	Under 5 mortality (per 1,000 exposed)	Water deprivation (% of h.h. members)	Stunting (% of children)	Literacy rate (% of males)	Literacy rate (% of females)	Net primary enrollment (% of boys)	Net primary enrollment (% of girls)	Households in sample (total)	Per capita H.H. consumption (% of nat'l avg)
Belize 2006	m.	1.2	4.9	m.	86.9	92.1	92.0	1,832	m.
Garifuna	m.	0.4	3.9	m.	93.7	97.9	100.0	151	85.3
Maya	m.	6.0	10.0	m.	80.1	97.9	94.3	217	58.6
Mestizo	m.	0.4	4.6	m.	88.3	89.7	87.6	775	96.1
Garifuna[1]	m.	0.5	2.9	m.	94.2	100.0	100.0	112	m.
Maya[1]	m.	7.5	11.1	m.	77.4	98.8	94.7	163	m.
Guatemala 1998	65	8.1	21.2	m.	m.	m.	m.	5,587	m.
indian	79	15.4	35.3	m.	m.	m.	m.	1,656	m.
kaqchiquel[1]	81	8.0	41.8	m.	m.	m.	m.	261	70.7
qeqchi[1]	68	54.5	19.7	m.	m.	m.	m.	382	47.2
k'iche'[1]	89	5.5	42.2	m.	m.	m.	m.	355	72.1
mam[1]	106	6.0	53.7	m.	m.	m.	m.	133	47.7
poqomchi'[1]	33	8.8	30.4	m.	m.	m.	m.	42	17.9
tzu'utuhil[1]	56	7.7	28.2	m.	m.	m.	m.	41	80.6
kanjobal[1]	63	12.2	39.9	m.	m.	m.	m.	70	31.2
chorti[1]	m.	m.	m.	m.	m.	m.	m.	1	87.2
pocomam[1]	0	100.0	900.0	m.	m.	m.	m.	1	41.6
mayan[2]	37	22.3	49.5	m.	m.	m.	m.	26	m.
Mexico 2000–2003	m.	m.	m.	93.6	90.1	m.	m.	m.	m.
non-indigenous*	27	m.	14.5	m.	m.	m.	m.	m.	100.0
indigenous*	52	m.	44.3	82.9	68.4	m.	m.	m.	26.2

Notes: [1] Language; [2] Religion; *Defined by language except for under five mortality and per capita income, which are defined according to cut-off proportion of community inhabitants speaking an indigenous language.

Sources: Belize MICS3 2006, Belize Poverty Assessment Study 1995, Guatemala DHS 1998, Guatemala MECOVI 2002, Ramirez 2005. Literacy figures for 2000, under five mortality and nutrition deprivation for 2003, per capita consumption for 2003, per capita monthly income and is from 2002. Nutrition deprivation is proportion below −2 standard deviations (see appendix for definition of indicator).

Aymara in the Andes. In Guatemala, those sampled households who identify themselves as "Indian" had worse levels than the national averages for
all indicators. Among the speakers of the different Mayan languages, Mam-
speakers included in the sample exhibited the worse under-five mortality
rate at slightly more than 106 per 1,000 live births and the worst estimate
for the prevalence of stunting among children at 53.7 percent. The K'iche'
and Kaqchikel also have notably higher levels of under-five mortality than
the national average, at around 9 percent and 8.1 percent of all live births,
respectively; these higher figures are echoed in the estimates of the rate of
stunting among children as well. The Q'eqchi' speakers have under-five mortality and stunting estimates closer to that of the national population. For
the other reported linguistic groups, the number of households included
in the sample are very small, and their levels are more consistent with the
national figures.

The close association between isolation from the encompassing national
economy and retention of language, which exists among Quechua and
Aymara speakers, also persists among the various Mayan groups; consequently, the development levels for the Mayan subgroups are likely lower-
bound estimates for their respective populations. Case studies of Kaqchikel
and Spanish language shift in two Mayan towns in Guatemala compiled by
Garzon et al. (1998a) illustrates this link. Richards (1998), for example,
reports no Spanish use among the inhabitants of 12-square-kilometer San
Marcos La Laguna on the northeastern shore of Lake Atitlán; it is isolated
from surrounding communities by "high promontories" and accessible
almost exclusively by boat (Richards 1998: 62, 90). This is contrasted by
McKenna Brown's (1998) discussion of the inhabitants of San Antonio
Aguas Callientes in the Quinizilapa Valley of whom many sell textiles,
produce, and low-cost manufactured goods and receive a large number
of tourists from nearby Antigua and Guatemala City. Here, parents are
bilingual but many "speak only Spanish to their children"; she cites a
1987 language survey of the community in which none of the children
between one and four years old were learning Kaqchikel as a first language
(McKenna Brown 1998: 117). In Belize, the proportion of Mayan inhabitants of Belize district that contains Belize City more than doubled in the
1980s, from 0.8 percent to 1.8 percent of the district's population (Woods
1996: table 3), but evidence of the Mayan language persisting as a first
language in isolated rural areas is documented among Mopan-speaking
Mayans by Danziger (2001) in Belize. In all three of these studies of language use in Mayan towns, language shift among individuals is highly correlated to educational attainment and integration with the encompassing

economy, but it is not necessarily correlated with loss of Mayan or Indian as documented, for example, by Garzon (1998b) in San Juan Comalapa near Guatemala's capital.

Table 2.11 also presents indicators for Mexico derived from a variety of sources and presented by Ramirez (2006); however, the information is not disaggregated by people. Most indicators are calculated either for indigenous or nonindigenous peoples, and the definition of these varies by indicator. The under-five mortality rate for indigenous peoples of 52 per 1,000 is nearly double that of the national sample and stems from a 2003 study. "Indigenous" people are defined as those inhabiting communities that contain 75 percent or more indigenous people defined by language, whereas those who are "nonindigenous" dwell in communities with less than 5 percent indigenous people. Stunting rates are drawn also from a 2003 study and show a rate three times higher than that of the national population. Data from the national census of 2000 provides literacy rates. Whereas the male literacy rate at the national level of 93.6 percent only exceeds the female rate by 3.5 percent, the indigenous male rate of 82.6 percent exceeds that of indigenous females by 14.5 percent. The average per-capita monthly income is 26.2 percent and is from the National Income and Consumption Survey of 2002. For this figure, indigenous is defined as being located in a community inhabited by at least 10 percent indigenous people defined by language.

Summary

The latest indicator levels by country for the Latin American samples tend to be worse than that of their national samples. Under-five mortality levels are mostly higher than the national averages, with the worst among speakers of the Mam language in Guatemala in 1998 and those who identified as Quechua in Bolivia in 2003. The lowest under-five mortality is among the Amerindian sample from the Guyana 2005 DHS. Water deprivation rates are generally evenly dispersed around the national levels, the worst being sampled speakers of the Q'eqchi, with nearly seven times that national level. Child stunting rates are generally higher than national levels for these peoples, with the Mam-speaking sample from Guatemala and the Quechua-speaking sample in the Peru 2004 DHS having nearly double the level of their national samples; the Guatemalan peoples have the highest rates, however. Male literacy rates are only available for one country's survey, and female literacy rates are only available for a few. The lowest female rates are among the Quechua-speaking sample in Peru. Both male and female net primary enrollment rates are similarly distributed around their national levels and do not exhibit any drastic departures from the national levels. The lowest levels are among the self-identified Aymara samples in Peru. Generally, the indicators presented for groups identified by language likely understate that of their broader populations because of language shift correlating positively with the development indicators presented here.

NORTH AMERICA

The indigenous peoples of North America include the various North American Indian tribal groups, but also Native Hawaiians in the United States and the Inuit and Métis in Canada. North American peoples have been the subject of previous research, and this section presents some basic census-based indicators to highlight their well-being in relation to that of their respective countries.

United States

Table 2.12 presents census 2000 figures for the 2.5 million American Indian and the 400,000 Native Hawaiian and other Pacific Islanders, as well as for the 39 tribal groups. Disparity between American Indians and the United States as a whole is immediately apparent. High school attainment among American Indians older than twenty-five of 70.9 percent is 10 percent lower than that of the country. Median household income is 72.9 percent of the national median of $41,994. More than a quarter of American Indian individuals are below the poverty level whereas 28.1 percent of members of families with children younger than five years are below the poverty level. For Native Hawaiians and other Pacific Islanders, the indicators are higher than Native Americans but still lower than the national average, except for median household income. Among the tribal groups, the Tohono O'Odham of southwest United States have the lowest median household income at 55 percent of the national level, the highest proportion of individuals below the poverty level at 39.6 percent, and the highest proportion of members of families with children under five below the poverty level at 44.8 percent. The Delaware people have the highest median household income at 96 percent of the national median and lowest poverty level indicators, with both below 10 percent. Table 2.13 presents infant mortality rates of white and American Indian people in the United States for the time periods of 1989 to 1991 and 1998 to 2000. Between these two periods, infant mortality

Table 2.12. *United States: Education, income, and poverty*

	Population (total)	H. School Grad. (percent)	Med. H.H. Income (% of nat'l)	Percent below (individuals)	Poverty level (families w/ young child)
United States	281,421,906	80.4	$41,994	12.4	17.0
Amer. Ind. / Alaska Nat.	2,475,956	70.9	72.9	25.7	28.1
Nat. Hawaiian and other Pac.	398,835	78.3	101.7	14.6	19.2
Arctic					
Alaskan Athabascan	14,520	75.4	66.2	22.9	33.5
Aleut	11,941	77.5	87.9	15.0	14.5
Eskimo	45,919	70.3	77.4	21.3	26.2
Great Basin					
Comanche	10,120	82.6	75.6	36.8	27.8
Paiute	9,705	77.2	70.8	24.6	33.7
Ute	7,309	74.2	56.4	33.9	44.7
Great Plains					
Blackfeet	27,104	76.6	71.6	25.4	33.7
Cheyenne	11,191	74.3	61.1	36.0	40.1
Chippewa	105,907	77.9	76.7	23.7	32.3
Cree	2,488	75.0	85.9	22.0	30.2
Crow	9,117	79.4	71.2	32.7	42.6
Kiowa	8,559	81.1	67.7	26.6	33.7
Osage	7,658	91.8	84.9	12.2	27.0
Potawatomi	15,817	83.5	92.2	13.2	11.6
Shoshone	7,739	75.1	64.8	29.0	30.8
Sioux	108,272	76.2	59.8	38.9	47.7
North East					
Delaware	8,304	83.4	96.0	9.6	9.3
Iroquois	45,212	79.6	85.0	19.0	26.5
Menominee	7,883	79.4	68.8	26.2	32.0
Ottawa	6,432	80.7	90.5	11.8	17.6

(continued)

Table 2.12 (*continued*)

	Population (total)	H. School Grad. (percent)	Med. H.H. Income (% of nat'l)	Percent below (individuals)	Poverty level (families w/ young child)
Pacific Northwest					
Puget Sound Salish	11,034	73.4	76.2	25.4	32.0
Tlingit-Haida	14,825	82.4	87.8	15.2	19.1
Plateau Region					
Colville	7,833	80.7	71.0	23.7	31.3
Yakama	8,481	73.0	73.1	32.0	36.2
South East					
Cherokee	281,069	76.6	77.7	18.1	24.2
Chickasaw	20,887	82.3	80.1	17.3	23.0
Choctaw	87,349	79.6	77.7	18.5	25.1
Creek	40,223	81.9	79.7	18.0	25.0
Houma	6,798	51.5	83.1	21.6	19.4
Lumbee	51,913	64.7	78.5	18.2	28.9
Seminole	12,431	75.5	70.1	25.6	27.8
South West					
Apache	57,060	69.0	67.8	59.3	38.8
Navajo	269,202	62.7	56.7	37.0	40.4
Pima	8,519	65.7	75.5	31.2	34.8
Pueblo	59,533	76.3	67.0	29.1	35.4
Tohono O'Odham	17,466	64.5	55.0	39.6	44.8
Yaqui	15,224	58.6	76.3	28.3	35.2
Yuman	7,295	66.1	64.5	32.1	44.9
Other					
Latin American Indian	104,354	48.0	81.0	23.1	27.3

Source: U.S. Census Bureau (2004). Families with young child are those with relative less than five years old. Poverty level used by the U.S. Census Bureau is based on a set of "money income thresholds that vary by family size to detect who is poor." Poverty and household income figures are for 1999; educational attainment of secondary or above is for individuals aged twenty-five years or older.

Table 2.13. *United States: Infant mortality*

	1989–1991	1998–2000
White	6.3	4.8
Amer. Ind. / Alaska Nat.	11.8	8.0

Source: Tomashek et al. 2006, table 2. Figures per 1,000 live births at and above 20 weeks gestation. Race defined by mother's reported race on birth certificate.

Table 2.14. *Canada: Infant mortality, education, and income*

	Population (total)	Med. income (dollars)	Low income (percent)	Less than Sec. Edu. (percent)	1980	1991	2000
Canada	31,241,030	25,615	8.6	23.8	10.4	6.4	5.3
American Indian	1,253,620	17,781	16.5	39.2	23.7	12.3	6.4
Métis	409,065	22,269	10.9	31.4	m.	m.	m.
Inuit	65,885	17,764	11.5	53.4	m.	m.	m.

Sources: Statistics Canada (2008), Human Resources and Skills Development Canada (2009), Treasury Board of Canada Secretariat (2005). Excludes census data for one or more incompletely enumerated Indian reserves or Indian settlements. Ethnicity is based on respondent's self-reported ethnic origin of their ancestors and includes single and multiplie ethnic origin responses. Median income are for individuals aged fifteen years and older, low income are for members of economic families, less than secondary education are for individuals aged fifteen years or older, and infant mortality figures are per 1,000 live births.

dropped from 11.8 per 1,000 live births to 8.0 per 1,000 live births, as well as the departure from white levels of infant mortality, which in the second period stood at 4.8 percent.

Canada

Table 2.14 presents several indicators for the census-defined North American Indian, Métis, and Inuit peoples residing in Canada. The proportion of members of economic families experiencing "low income" are much higher for the North American Indian, Métis, and Inuit peoples, at 16.5 percent, 10.9 percent, and 11.5 percent, respectively, compared to 8.6 percent nationally. Higher proportions of these peoples over the age of fifteen have education attainment less than secondary, with the highest being the Inuit at 53.4 percent. Infant mortality rates have dropped dramatically for North American Indian peoples, from 23.7 per 1,000 live births in 1980 to 6.4 per 1,000 live births in 2000, which is only slightly higher than the national level of 5.3 per 1,000 live births.

CONCLUSIONS

This study reveals that indigenous peoples' development, from a global perspective, exhibits at least two broad characteristics. First, although the well-being of indigenous peoples lags considerably that of nonindigenous people in many countries, this is not true for all countries. For example, in several African countries, India, several Southeast Asian countries, Australia, New Zealand, and the Americas, the development indicators of those peoples considered to be indigenous lag considerably behind that of their countries as wholes, but in other African countries, Nepal, Bangladesh, and other Southeast Asian countries, this lag either does not exist or is reversed. It is notable that in some of the poorest countries included in this study, such as Nepal, Bangladesh, Mali, and Niger, there exists no clear difference in the well-being of those considered as indigenous and those not, whereas in some of the richest countries included in this study, such as the United States, Canada, Australia, and New Zealand, the difference is clear and substantial. This observation suggests that the gap in well-being between indigenous and nonindigenous emerges through the process of development; however, the proceeding chapters on East Asian countries show this exclusion of indigenous peoples from development is not a necessity. The second characterization revealed by this study is that within countries, the experiences of different indigenous peoples are heterogeneous. For example, in Nepal, the well-being of the Gurung people generally exceeds that of the national average, whereas that of the Magar lags. In many northeastern states of India, such as Mizoram and Nagaland, many indicators for the scheduled tribes, including under-five mortality and stunting, are better than the national averages. This is also true for the Aymara of Bolivia and Peru. Heterogeneity in well-being is apparent among the various Mayan peoples in Guatemala and American Indian tribal groups in the United States. Consequently, this study suggests that the development of indigenous peoples from a global perspective is one characterized by heterogeneity both across countries and within.

Future empirical research to explore these characterizations of indigenous peoples' development requires additional data collection both within the countries where data exist and in countries where data do not exist. Data collection must be conducted in a way to ensure representativity. This includes taking into account the seasonal mobility patterns related to well-being such as those documented among Fulani pastoralists in the Sahel, Tuareg pastoralists in the Sahara, and other pastoralists in the Horn of Africa. Sampling in remote areas needs to occur as well, because the remoteness of settlements relates to well-being as documented among the forest peoples in the Congo Basin and the various hill tribe peoples in Indochina. Furthermore, until a single definition of indigenous emerges in the literature, the identification of peoples in the data must cater to different definitions of these peoples. For example, data on which ethnic or linguistic group a survey respondent self-identifies with are relevant only to self-identity definitions of either indigenous or ethnicity. Such phenomena as sanskritization and de-sanskritization documented among various scheduled tribes in India and Janajati in Nepal, as well as language shift among the Quechua, Aymara, and Maya peoples in Latin America, renders data on self-identity insufficient if other definitions of indigeneity or ethnicity are of interest to a researcher, such as descent or official census categories. Data collection exhibiting these considerations would produce inclusive and representative samples. This would then allow for the rigorous statistical testing of differences between groups within countries and changes across time that are needed to eliminate the quantitative information deficiency on indigenous peoples' human development that currently persists.

APPENDIX

This appendix describes the methodologies used to develop the indicators presented in this study.

Under-Five Mortality: The under-five mortality rate is the probability of dying before reaching age five and is estimated using a synthetic cohort life table approach identical to that used by ORC Macro, the provider of the DHS data sets. This method estimates and combines the survival probabilities of eight age segments of increasing length between zero and five years old from exposure and death over the ten years preceding the survey. The method adjusts for the partial exposure of those born fifteen years prior to the survey and five years prior to the survey. For more information, see Rutstein and Rojas (2006: 69–75).

Safe-Water Deprivation Prevalence: This is the proportion of household members whose household's primary source of water is either more than thirty minutes (round trip) away from the place of residence, or only from surface water such as ponds and streams or unimproved springs. This indicator is adopted from Gordon et al. (2003).

Child Stunting Rate: The stunting rate is the proportion of children younger than three years whose height-to-age ratio is below -3 standard deviations for that of the NCHS/CDC/WHO international reference population. Those below -3 standard deviations are described as experiencing severe stunting, which is a general reflection of inadequate nutritional intake (Rutstein and Rojas 2006: 122). This method is generally robust to race as racial differences in average height do not begin to emerge at least until age five (de Onis and Yip 1996).

Literacy Rate: This is the proportion of either females or males who are either able to read all or part of a sentence provided by the survey enumerator, or have completed secondary school. Those for whom the enumerator did not have a sentence with the language spoken by the respondent were excluded from the calculation.

Net Primary Enrollment Rate: The net primary enrollment rate is the proportion of country-specific primary-age students attending primary school. If the survey occurs more than six months after the start of the school year, the child's age is assumed to be one year less at the time the school year began; this adjustment provides a more accurate measure of the net enrollment rate because it excludes children who were too young to start school that year.[6] See Porta et al. (2011) for more information.

Per-Capita Mean Household Consumption: This is the mean level of per-capita household consumption measured either in currency or by an index depending on the data set and expressed as a percentage of the national mean.

Ethnicity and Language: Ethnicity is either that self-reported by the respondent or that of the household head, depending on the data set. Language is either the "mother tongue" of the respondent, the language spoken at home, the language spoken by the household head, the language spoken by the interviewer, or the language of the questionnaire. Household ethnicity and language, when household members reported differently from each other, is the one reported most by the household members. For this reason, indicators are calculated for "usual residents" of the household only.

---

[6] This methodology is adapted from the World Bank's ADePT Education software; the author is grateful to Emilio Porta for his advice calculating education indicators based on household survey data

References

Adnan, Shapan (2004). *Migration, land alienation, and ethnic conflict: causes of poverty in the Chittagong Hill Tracts of Bangladesh.* Dhaka: Research and Advisory Services.

Africa Commission on Human and People's Rights (2006). *Indigenous peoples in Africa: The forgotten peoples?* Banjul: ACHPR.

Asia Indigenous Peoples Pact (2009). Membership. Chiang Mai, Thailand: AIPP. Accessed April 22, 2009 at http://www.aippnet.org///content/blogcategory/23/40/

Asian Development Bank (2002). *Indigenous peoples: ethnic minorities and poverty reduction, Philippines.* Manila, Philippines: Environment and Social Safeguard Division, Regional and Sustainable Development Dept., Asian Development Bank.

Bahuchet, S. (1991). Spatial mobility and access to resources among the African Pygmies. In: Casimir, M. J. and A. Rao (Eds.), *Mobility and territoriality: social and spatial boundaries among foragers, fishers, pastoralists and peripatetics.* New York: Berg Publishers, pp. 205–257.

Basset, T. J. and K. B. Zwéli (1999). Fulbe livestock raising and environmental change in Northern Côte d'Ivoire. In: V. Azarya et al. (Ed.), *Pastoralists under pressure?* Boston: Brill, pp. 139–160.

Bennett, L. et al. (2008). *Caste, ethnicity and regional identity in Nepal: Further analysis of the 2006 Nepal demographic and health survey.* Washington, DC: United States Agency for International Development.

Boonperm, Jirawan (2004). *Census 2000 and its implementation in Thailand: Lessons learnt for 2010 Census.* UN Department of Economic and Social Affairs. Accessed March 7, 2009 at http://www.unescap.org/stat/meet/census2004/census2004_thailand.pdf

Briggs, L. T. (1985a). A critical survey of the literature on the Aymara language. In: H. E. Manelis Klein and L. R. Stark (Eds.), *South American Indian languages: retrospect and prospect.* Austin: University of Texas Press, pp. 546–594.

(1985b). Dialectical variation in Aymara. In: H. E. Manelis Klein and L. R. Stark (Eds.), *South American Indian languages: retrospect and prospect.* Austin: University of Texas Press, pp. 595–616.

Burnham, P. (1999). Social change in Fulbe society. In: V. Azarya et al. (Ed.), *Pastoralists under pressure?* Boston: Brill, pp. 269–283.

Christensen, Russ and Sann Kyaw (2006). *The Pa-O: rebels and refugees.* Chiang Mai: Silkworm Books.

Cooper, Robert (1984). *Resource scarcity and the Hmong response: patterns of settlement and economy in transition.* Kent Ridge: Singapore University Press.

Dahal, Dilli Ram (2005). Social composition of the population: caste/ethnicity and religion in Nepal. In: Central Bureau of Statistics, *Population monograph of Nepal, volume 1.* Kathmandu, Nepal: Central Bureau of Statistics. Acccessed February 27, 2009 at http://www.cbs.gov.np/Population/Monograph/default_volume1.htm

Danziger, E. (2001). *Relatively speaking: language, thought, and kinship among the Mopan Maya.* New York : Oxford University Press.

de Bruijn, M. (1999). The pastoral poor. In: V. Azarya et al. (Ed.), *Pastoralists under pressure?* Boston: Brill, pp. 285–312.

68 *Macdonald*

de Onis M. and R. Yip (1996). The WHO growth chart: historical considerations and current scientific issues. *Bibliotheca Nutrito et Dieta*, 53:74–89.

Dixon, John E. and Robert P. Scheurell (1995). *Social welfare with indigenous peoples.* New York: Routledge.

Dounias, E. and A. Froment (2006). When forest-based hunter-gatherers become sedentary: consequences for diet and health. *Unsaylva 224*, 57:26–33.

Dudley-Jenkins, Laura (2003). *Identity and identification in India: defining the disadvantaged.* New York : RoutledgeCurzon.

Farah, K. O. (2004). The Somali and the camel: ecology, management and economics. *Anthropologist*, 6 (1): 45–55.

Farah, M. I. (1993). *From ethnic response to clan identity: a study of state penetration among the Somali nomadic pastoral society of northeastern Kenya.* Uppsala: Academiae Ubsaliensis.

Fisher, William F. (2001). *Fluid boundaries: forming and transforming identity in Nepal.* New York: Columbia University Press.

Food Security Analysis Unit (2001). Pastoralists under pressure. *Focus.* October 2001. FSAU, Food and Agricultural Organization.

Fricke, Thomas E. (1994). *Himalayan households: Tamang demography and domestic processes.* New York : Columbia University Press.

Fuchs, Stephen (1992). *The aboriginal tribes of India*, 3rd Ed. New Delhi: Inter-India.

Garzon, S. (1998a). Indigenous groups and language their contact relations. In: Garzon, S. et al. (Eds.), *The life of our language: Kaqchikel Maya maintenance, shift, and revitalization.* Austin: University of Texas Press, pp. 9–43.

(1998b). Case study three: San Juan Comalapa. In: Garzon, S. et al. (Eds.), *The life of our language: Kaqchikel Maya maintenance, shift, and revitalization.* Austin: University of Texas Press, pp. 129–154.

Getachew, K. N. (2001). *Among the pastoralist Afars in Ethiopia.* Utrecht: International Books.

Gordon, David et al. (2003). *Child poverty in the developing world.* Bristol: The Policy Press

Guneratne, Arjun (2002). *Many tongues, one people: the making of Tharu identity in Nepal.* Ithaca: Cornell University Press, pp. 91–106.

(2007). The Tharu of Chitwan, Nepal. In: Brower, Barbara A. and Barbara Rose Johnston (Eds.), *Disappearing peoples?: indigenous groups and ethnic minorities in South and Central Asia.* Walnut Creek, CA: Left Coast Press.

Hardman, M. J. (1981). Introductory essay. In: Hardman, M. J. (Ed.), *The Aymara language in its social and cultural context.* Gainesville: University Presses of Florida, pp. 3–31.

Hayami, Y. and S. M. Darlington (2000). The Karen of Burma and Thailand. In: Sponsel, L. E. (Ed.), *Endangered peoples of Southeast and East Asia: struggles to survive and thrive.* Westport, CT: Greenwood Press, pp. 137–156.

Homewood, K. et al. (2006). Maasai pastoralists: diversification and poverty. In: *Pastoralism and poverty reduction in East Africa: a policy research conference*, June 27–28, 2006, International Livestock Research Institute (unpublished).

Hornberger, N. H. and K. A. King (2001). Reversing the Quechua language shift in South America. In: Fishman, J. A. (Ed.), *Can threatened languages be saved?* Buffalo, NY: Multilingual Matters, pp. 67–105.

Human Resources and Skills Development Canada (2009). Infant mortality/health/ indicators of well-being in Canada. Accessed March 4, 2009 at http://www4.hrsdc. gc.ca/indicator.jsp?indicatorid=2&lang=en

Ichikawa, M. and D. Kimura (2003). Recent advances in Central African hunter-gatherer research. *African Study Monographs*, Suppl. 28: 1–6.

Indigenous Peoples of Africa Co-ordinating Committee (2007). Who is indigenous in Africa? *IPACC*, Accessed March 8, 2009 at http://www.ipacc.org.za/eng/ who.asp

Ireson, Carol J. (1996). *Field, forest, and family: women's work and power in rural Laos.* Boulder, CO: Westview Press.

Ireson, W. Randall (1995). Hmong demographic changes in Laos: causes and ecological consequences. *SOJOURN*, 10 (2): 198–232.

Keenan, J. (2004). *The lesser gods of the Sahara.* London: Frank Cass.

King, Kendall A. (2001). *Language revitalization processes and prospects: Quichua in the Ecuadorian Andes.* Buffalo, NY: Multilingual Matters.

Knight, J. (2003). Relocated to the roadside. *African Study Monographs*, Suppl. 28: 81–121.

Köhler, A. and J. Lewis (2002). Putting hunter-gatherer and farmer relations in perspective: a commentary from Central Africa. In: Hunt, S. (Ed.), *Ethnicity, hunter-gatherers, and the "other": association or assimilation in Africa.* Washington, DC: Smithsonian Institute, pp. 276–305.

Larrea, Carlos and Fernando Montenegro Torres (2006). Ecuador. In: Hall, G. and H. A. Patrinos (Eds.), *Indigenous peoples, poverty and human development in Latin America.* New York: Palgrave Macmillan.

Layton, Heather M. and Harry A. Patrinos (2006). Estimating the number of indigenous peoples in Latin America. In: Hall, G. and H. A. Patrinos (Eds.), *Indigenous peoples, poverty and human development in Latin America.* New York: Palgrave Macmillan, pp. 25–39.

Luling, V. (2002). Somali of the Horn of Africa. In: Hitchcock, R. K. and A. J. Osorn (Eds.), *Endangered peoples of Africa and the Middle East.* Westport, CT: Greenwood Press, pp. 219–234.

Lund, E. et al. (2008). The Sami – living conditions and health. *International Journal of Circumpolar Health*, 67 (1):6–8.

Macfarlane, Alan (1976). *Resources and population: a study of the Gurungs of Nepal.* New York : Cambridge University Press.

Mannheim, B. (1985). Southern Peruvian Quechua. In: Manelis Klein, H. E. and L. R. Stark (Eds.), *South American Indian languages: retrospect and prospect.* Austin: University of Texas Press, pp. 481–515.

McKenna Brown, R. (1998). Case study two: San Antonio Aguas Calientes and the Quinizilapa Valley. In: Garzon, S. et al. (Eds.), *The life of our language: Kaqchikel Maya maintenance, shift, and revitalization.* Austin: University of Texas Press, pp. 101–128.

McKay, Deirdre (2005). Rethinking locality in Ifugao: Tribes, domains, and colonial histories. *Philippine Studies*, 53 (4):459–490.

Michaud, Jean (1997). Economic transformation in a Hmong village of Thailand. *Human Organization*, 56 (2): 222.

Minde, H. (2008). Introduction. In: Minde H. (Ed.), *Indigenous peoples: self-determination, knowledge, and indigeneity*. Delft: Eburon Publishers, pp. 1–28.

Mohsin, Amena (2003). *The Chittagong hill tracts, Bangladesh: on the difficult road to peace*. Boulder, CO: Lynne Rienner Publishers.

Myers, S. K. (1973). *Language shift among migrants to Lima, Peru*. Chicago: University of Chicago Press.

Nag, N. G. (1990). Some demographic characteristics of scheduled tribes with special reference to Gujarat, Madhya Pradesh, Rajasthan and Maharashtra. In: Bose, A. et al. (Eds.), *Demography of tribal development*. Delhi: B. R. Publishing Corporation.

New Zealand Ministry of Social Development (2008). *The social report 2008*. Wellington: Ministry of Social Development.

Niezen, R. (2003). *The origins of indigenism: human rights and the politics of identity*. Berkeley: University of California Press.

Ohenjo, N., R. Willis, D. Jackson, C. Nettleton, K. Good and B. Mugarura (2006). Health of indigenous people in Africa. *The Lancet*, 367: 1937–1945.

Pink, Brian and Penny Allbon (2008). *Health and welfare of Australia's Aboriginal and Torres Strait Islander people 2008*. Canberra: Australian Bureau of Statistics, Australian Institute of Health and Welfare.

Porta, E., G. Arcia, K. Macdonald, S. Radyakin, M. Loshkin (2011). *Assessing Sector Performance and Inequality in Education*. Washington, DC: The World Bank.

Ramirez, Alejandro (2006). Mexico. In: Hall, G. and H. A. Patrinos (Eds.), *Indigenous peoples, poverty and human development in Latin America*. New York: Palgrave Macmillan, pp. 150–198.

Rasmussen, S. J. (2001). *Healing in community: medicine, contested terrains, and cultural encounters among the Tuareg*. Westport, CT: Bergin and Garvey.

  (2002). The Tuareg. In: Hitchcock, R. K. and A. J. Osorn (Ed.), *Endangered peoples of Africa and the Middle East*. Westport, CT: Greenwood Press

Richards, J. B. (1998). Case study one: San Marcos La Laguna. In: Garzon, S. et al. (Eds.), *The life of our language: Kaqchikel Maya maintenance, shift, and revitalization*. Austin: University of Texas Press, pp. 62–100.

Rutstein, S. O. and G. Rojas (2006). *Guide to DHS statistics*. Calverton, MD: ORC Macro.

Sato, H. (1992). Notes on the distribution and settlement pattern of hunter-gatherers in North Western Congo. *African Study Monographs*. 13(4): 203–216.

Saugestad, S. (2008). Beyond the "Columbus Context": new challenges as the indigenous discourse is applied to Africa. In Minde, H. (Ed.), *Indigenous Peoples: Self-determination, knowledge, and indigeneity*. Delft: Eburon Publishers, pp. 157–176.

Seligman, T. K. (2006). An introduction to the Tuareg. In: Seligman, T. K. and K. Loughran (Eds.), *The art of being Tuareg*. Los Angeles: UCLA Fowler Museum of Cultural History, pp. 19–27.

Sharma, Anima (2003). *Socio-economic development of Indian tribes*. New Delhi: Mohit Publications.

Singh, Kumar Suresh (1994). *The scheduled tribes*. Delhi: Anthropological Survey of India.

Sinha, U. P. (1990). Demographic profile of tribal population in India. In: Bose, A. et al. (Eds.), *Demography of tribal development*. Delhi: B. R. Publishing Corporation

Smith, A. B. (1992). *Pastoralism in Africa*. Athens: Ohio University Press.

Sutthi, C. (1989). Highland agriculture: From better to worse. In: McKinnon, J. and B. Vienne (Eds.), *Hill tribes today: problems in change*. Bangkok: White Lotus, pp. 107–142.

Spear, T. (1993). Introduction. In: Spear, T. and R. Waller (Eds.), *Being Maasai: ethnicity and identity in East Africa*. Athens: Ohio University Press, pp. 1–18.

Stark, L. R. (1985a). Ecuadorian Highland Quechua: History and Current Status. In: H. E. Manelis Klein and L. R. Stark (Eds.), *South American Indian languages: retrospect and prospect*. Austin: University of Texas Press, pp. 443–480.

(1985b). The Quechua language in Bolivia. In: H. E. Manelis Klein and L. R. Stark (Eds.), *South American Indian languages: retrospect and prospect*. Austin: University of Texas Press, pp. 516–545.

Statistics Canada (2008). 2006 Census: topic based tabulations. Accessed March 3, 2009 at http://www12.statcan.ca/english/census06/data/topics/Index.cfm

(2008b). More information on ethnic origin. Accessed March 4, 2009 at http://www12.statcan.ca/english/census06/reference/dictionary/pop030a.cfm

Statistics New Zealand (2005). Appendix 3: five-year age group mortality and survivorship rates, 1995 – 2002. Accessed March 2, 2009 at http://www.stats.govt.nz/analytical-reports/nz-life-tables-2000-2002/appendix3.htm

Tomashek, Kay M. et al. (2006). Infant mortality trends and differences between American Indian / Alaska Native infants and white infants. *American Journal of Public Health*, 96 (12):2222–2227.

Tomei, Manuela (2005). *Indigenous and tribal peoples: an ethnic audit of selected poverty reduction strategy papers*. Geneva: International Labour Organization.

Treasury Board of Canada Secretariat (2005). *Canada's performance 2005: The government of Canada's contribution*. Ottawa: Treasury Board of Canada Secretariat.

Turnbull, Colin M. (1965) *Wayward servants: the two worlds of the African pygmies*. Garden City, NY: Natural History Press.

Understanding Children's Work (2007). *Enfants mendiants dans la region de Dakar*. Rome: Understanding Children's Work.

United Nations Development Programme (2004). *Nepal human development report*. Kathmandu: UNDP.

United Nations Permanent Forum on Indigenous Issues (2006). Data collection and disaggregated data. Accessed March 5, 2009 at http://www.un.org/esa/socdev/unpfii/en/data.html

United States Census Bureau (2004). Census 2000 data for 249 population groups, including 39 tribal groups. Accessed March 3, 2009 at http://factfinder.census.gov/home/aian/sf2_sf4.html

Unnithan-Kumar, Maya (1997). *Identity, gender, and poverty: new perspectives on caste and tribe in Rajasthan*. Providence, RI: Berghahn Books.

van Driel, A. (1999). The end of the herding contract: decreasing complimentary linkages between Fulbe pastoralists and Dendi agriculturalists in Northern Benin. In: V. Azarya et al. (Eds.), *Pastoralists under pressure?* Boston: Brill, pp. 191–210.

Wessendorf, K. (2008). *The indigenous world 2008*. Copenhagen: The International
    Working Group for Indigenous Affairs.
Whitehead, Judith (2007). The Bhils. In: Brower, Barbara A. and Barbara Rose Johnston
    (Eds.), *Disappearing peoples?: indigenous groups and ethnic minorities in South and
    Central Asia*. Walnut Creek, CA: Left Coast Press, pp. 73–90.
Woods, L.A. et al. (1996). International Migration and the Ruralization of Belize, 1970–
    1991. In: Phillips, M. D. (Ed.), *Belize: selected proceedings from the second interdis-
    ciplinary conference*. Lanham, MD: University Press of America, pp. 173–190.

3

Becoming Indigenous

Identity and Heterogeneity in a Global Movement

Jerome M. Levi and Biorn Maybury-Lewis

INTRODUCTION

The Declaration on the Rights of Indigenous Peoples was signed into international law by the United Nations General Assembly on September 13, 2007. Although the difficult work of implementation still lies ahead, the ratification of this treaty signals a sea change in attitude toward the globe's indigenous peoples, a population that numbers 300 million worldwide. The Declaration heralds, at the dawn of this millennium, that the genocide, exploitation, and forced assimilation of indigenous peoples, not to mention the calculated dispossession of their resources and involuntary removal from their lands, as well as the elimination of their languages, religions, and cultures, will no longer be tolerated in the international community.

This chapter traces, in broad brushstrokes, how we got to this point in history and suggests possible trajectories that might be taken in the future. It seeks answers to fundamental questions about the indigenous movement and how it got on the world's agenda: Why is indigenous identity, based on numerous local, "aboriginal" societies, not only a new phenomenon, but also a global one? Who are indigenous peoples and what accounts for the creation of indigeneity? How is the struggle for indigenous rights in Africa and Asia different from that found in the Americas, Australia, and New Zealand? Why are most indigenous peoples among the poorest populations in almost every country where there exist data, yet in other cases, indigenous peoples have been quite successful? How does the global mobilization of indigenous peoples relate to the issues of representation, recognition, resources, and rights?

Although the aforementioned UN accord is now a formal covenant, indigenous peoples still stand precipitously on the brink of an uncertain future. The goal of this chapter is to give an overview of both the promises and challenges at this historic moment as well as outline the sheer heterogeneity beneath the common struggle of today's global indigenous movement. The current situation is aptly summarized in the poignant words of Anna Tsing (2007: 33): "The global indigenous movement is alive with promising contradictions. Inverting national development standards, it promises unity beyond plurality: diversity without assimilation. It endorses authenticity and invention, subsistence and wealth, traditional knowledge and new technologies, territory and diaspora." The creative potential unleashed on the world's stage through the conjunction of these seeming antinomies is the topic this chapter explores.

RETHINKING INDIGENOUS IDENTITY

Our starting point is the question of indigenous identity, which on cursory appraisal seems straightforward enough, but identity actually is a slippery concept. Social scientists debate endlessly about it and the topic fills the stacks of newsstands and libraries alike. Ethnic identity, national identity, gender identity, the identity of religions, cultures, and classes, not to mention the way these overlap or interconnect, are all analyzed in minute detail without much discussion, let alone agreement, about what identity means in the first place. This may, in part, be the source of the problem. Philosophers and mathematicians, by contrast, seem to have comparatively less difficulty with the concept. For them, the meaning of identity is about as tight as a concept can be. Technically speaking, a thing is identical only with itself. As Wittgenstein put it, according to Quine, "to say of anything that it is identical with itself is trivial, and to say that it is identical with anything else is absurd. What then is the use of identity?" (Quine 1987: 90).

"Genuine questions of identity," says Quine, "can arise because we may refer to something in two ways and leave someone wondering whether we referred to the same thing" (1987: 90). Thus when we are introduced to a man in the village of Mishongnovi on Second Mesa in Arizona, in the southwestern portion of the United States, we are told his name and that he is a member of the Coyote Clan. When he goes on business to the nearby town of Window Rock, capital of the Navajo Nation, he specifies that he is a Hopi; at a lecture he delivers in Chicago he claims to be Native American; and at the Palais Wilson in Geneva, as he sits between a Dayak woman from Kalimantan, Indonesia, and an Ogiek man from Kenya while attending an international human rights conference, he identifies himself, and is identified by others, as indigenous. The same man has claimed four different identities, yet none are inconsistent and all are true. How so?

Heraclitus as well as Hume both noted that although identity has to do with the notion of sameness, it becomes salient, paradoxically, only through the recognition of difference. Two points emerge, following their analyses. Genuine questions of identity arise in reference to differences in *nomenclature*; furthermore, the concept of identity is ineluctably *relational*. As the preceding example shows, although in one sense the man's identity persisted throughout, in another sense different facets of that identity were created or inflected instrumentally. That is, whereas at one level his underlying personhood did not change, the contexts did, and this altered the structures of identification.

Like other collective or social identities, such as ethnicity according to Ronald Cohen (1978), indigenous identity arises contextually as part of a series of nested dichotomizations in relation to the social distance between oneself and one's interlocutors. Unlike these other identities, however, indigenous identity is an apical or universal category that subsumes others within it – without, however, diluting or challenging their integrity or existence. Furthermore, it emerges not only in the widest possible field of sociopolitical relations – international contexts of conquest, states, and empires (and thus is a phenomenon that is both new and truly global in its reach), but also designates the preconquest, nondominant, and marginalized sectors within these political arenas as Starn and de la Cadena (2007) and Friedman (2008) observe.

Indigenous Peoples and the Creation of Indigeneity

If authentic questions about identity are both relational and nomenclatural in nature, then as new identities emerge in the context of new social relations, new terminology – or at least new understandings of old words – is likewise required (Levi and Dean 2003: 4–9). Such is the case with the popular neologism "indigeneity." The term designates a fresh conceptualization of indigenous identity under recent conditions of globalization, or what Niezen similarly intends by the word "indigenism," a term he uses "to describe the international movement that aspires to promote and protect the rights of the world's 'first peoples'" (Niezen 2003: 4). Increasingly over the last two decades, disenfranchised peoples from around the world are discovering the useful potential of the term "indigenous" and claiming this identity as a badge of pride wrested from trying conditions, thereby allowing actors from diverse local cultures access to a universal category of collective empowerment predicated on primordial attachments. Put simply, these groups are becoming indigenous. As Hodgson says while comparing indigenous movements in Africa and the Americas: "Increasing numbers of historically marginalized groups are 'becoming' indigenous by joining transnational networks and alliances that promote indigenous mobilization and by demanding recognition of rights from their respective nation-states and the international community" (2002: 1037).

The genealogy of this idea, which essentially has to do with postcolonial political mobilization across boundaries of various sorts, has salient historical antecedents, none more noteworthy than the creation of the category "Indian" in the Americas, although it too shares a colonial kinship with similar words like *native*, *aborigine*, and *tribal*, which in recent decades similarly have undergone emancipatory revaluations in meaning inverting the implications of social hierarchy, backwardness, and savagery that the terminology connoted in earlier practice. In his seminal essay, "Becoming Indian in Lowland South America," David Maybury-Lewis begins with the observation that "[i]t was the European invaders of the Americas who, through a famous confusion, started to refer to the inhabitants of the new world indiscriminately as Indians. The Indians for their part had little sense of possessing common characteristics that distinguished them from the Europeans. Their Indianness was a condition imposed upon them by the invaders" (1991: 207). He goes on to show, however, that this imposed category enabled diverse Native American peoples of Brazil, Argentina, and Chile to have a change in consciousness increasingly throughout the 1970s and 1980s that allowed them to transcend preexisting "tribal" identities in order to form new pan-ethnic organizations at the level of the nation-state, concluding "that becoming Indian in lowland South America is a difficult process of trying to create Indian organizations at a national level that are strong enough and astute enough politically to be able to defend Indian lives and interests locally" (Maybury-Lewis 1991: 233; see also Jackson 1991). In this chapter, we make a cognate argument, but substitute the concept of indigeneity for Indian, and move the playing field from the national to the international level.

THE HETEROGENEITY OF INDIGENEITY

Indigeneity enables groups that from a conventional anthropological perspective would seldom, if ever, be lumped together – peoples as ethnologically dissimilar as Saami reindeer herders, Karen, Lahu, and other shifting cultivators known as "hill tribes" on the Thai-Burmese frontier, diverse groups of forest dwellers, formerly known as "Pygmies" and traditionally hunter-gatherers, scattered throughout the Congo basin, Andean peasants,

Australian Aborigines, and Native Hawaiians, to name but a few – to all find common cause under the universalizing banner of indigenism. Thus, rather than being a specific *type* of society, indigenous peoples instead represent a particular *position* or subjectivity vis-à-vis fields of power.

Yet this transcultural, essentially politico-economic characterization only scratches the surface. Beyond ethnological differences, divergence in modern political orientations and economic philosophy similarly abound.

Consider two contrasting examples. In Alaska, the Kaktovik Inupiat Corporation – an organization made up of Kaktovikmiut and local whaling captains – supports oil development in the Arctic National Wildlife Refuge (ANWR), which some native people feel was created without adequate consultation in the first place. This group has clashed with environmentalists, and wants to work with the Shell Oil Company. By contrast, Bolivian President Evo Morales, the first self-declared indigenous president in modern Andean history,[1] ordered troops to occupy his country's oil and gas fields ceded earlier to multinational corporations. "Capitalism is the worst enemy of humanity," he announced together with his intention to renegotiate all contracts (Starn and de la Cadena 2007).

These contrasts are hardly isolated cases. On the contrary, the global indigenous movement is rife with diverse strategies for indigenous empowerment. Notwithstanding neat depictions of a "general indigenous model," based on romantic notions of culture, supposedly typifying peoples as diverse as the Lakota, Wampanoag, Mapuche, Miskito, Adivasi, Maori, Kurds, and Pashtun as all more or less egalitarian, spiritual, consensus-building, harmonious custodians of nature universally resisting capitalist encroachment (Fenelon and Hall 2008), in fact, the global indigenous movement is far more complex and resists, if anything, a facile politics or an ideology of closure.

One recalls, as do Nash (2001) and Stephen (2003), that Mayan Zapatista rebels signaled their protest to increased neoliberal economic reforms brought about through Mexico's signing of the North American Free Trade Agreement (NAFTA) by launching an armed insurrection in the southeastern state of Chiapas on January 1, 1994 – precisely so as to coincide with the date that NAFTA went into effect, whereas on the other side of the border in the United States, what Stull (1990) terms "reservation economic developments" ranging from mining and forestry to tourism and

[1] Alejandro Toledo, President of Peru, also makes this claim owing to the fact that he was elected president before Morales in Bolivia and that he comes from a family of Quechua *campesinos*.

commercial industry – not to mention the "casino capitalism" of the 367 American Indian–owned gaming establishments (the latter industry alone generating \$19.4 billion in 2004) – have now become legend (Harvard Project on American Indian Economic Development 2008: 148). And in Canada, whereas Coyne (2008) points out that Exxon Mobil showcases the broad support exhibited among Aboriginal and Métis peoples in the Cold Lake region of northeastern Alberta for the economic benefits – in the form of training, employment, and scholarships through the Native Internship Program – created by its affiliate Imperial Oil Resources, a company that operates the largest thermal in situ oil-recovery project in the world; on the other hand, *The Latin American Herald Tribune* (2009) reports that in the Ecuadorian Amazon, considerable concern has been registered over the negative impacts the OCP (Oleoducto de Crudos Pesados) project's 503 kilometer heavy crude oil pipeline is having on the indigenous population of that region. Meanwhile, Tuhiwai Smith (2007) affirms that the varied responses of Maori activists and entrepreneurs who sought to set up Maori language immersion schools in the wake of New Zealand's recent dismantling of its welfare state in favor of privatization reflect the push and pull of competing understandings of the individual and community, as well as the way that multicultural neoliberal regimes engender novel indigenous subjectivities.

The lesson that the literature reveals is that today, indigenous experience cannot be reduced either to capitalism or communism, the principles of free market competition, structural inequality, individual profiteering, and environmental degradation being as likely to be found in indigenous communities (sometimes with their blessings, sometimes without) as are redistributive economies, egalitarian social structures, and eco-friendly, communitarian values.

Scales of Difference, Dimensions of Divergence

To merely observe that there exists heterogeneity in the identities, interests, and tactics deployed by those involved in the global indigenous movement will not suffice. Rather, we need to stipulate the form, range, and valences of these differences. First, social scientists observe that not only between countries or regions, but also within them there is dramatic heterogeneity among indigenous peoples in terms of political mobilization and levels of economic development. For example, the Harvard Project on American Indian Economic Development (2008: 115) reports that even though it is true that, as an aggregate, Native Americans consistently have a significantly higher poverty rate than any other ethnic group in the nation – a statistic that unfortunately characterizes indigenous people in virtually every country where they exist – tremendous discrepancies in wealth, and ipso facto power, exist among different indigenous peoples as much in industrialized countries as in developing ones.

Thus, The Harvard Project (2008: 118–119) continues, in the United States for the year 2000, on the Crow Creek Reservation in South Dakota, per capita income was $4,043. By contrast, in the Shakopee Mdewakanton Sioux Community in Minnesota, the per capita income in 2000 was $113,509 – a difference in excess of nearly $110,000, thanks to the latter being a gaming reservation located in suburban Minneapolis-St. Paul, a major metropolitan area, whereas the former is situated on a desolate patch of land in rural Midwest America.

At the other end of the spectrum of international development is Nepal, one of the poorest countries in Asia, uncomfortably sandwiched between India and China, two burgeoning economic powerhouses. Yet just as in the United States, according to NEFIN (2008), Nepal too exhibits a range of economic development among its diverse indigenous peoples. The Nepal Federation of Indigenous Nationalities classifies each of its sixty-one Adibasi Janajati – that is, indigenous or tribal peoples – into one of five categories representing a continuum of politico-economic development. This ranges from peoples like the Lepcha and Majhi, categorized as "endangered" and "highly marginalized" through merely "marginalized" and "disadvantaged" groups such as the Tharu and Gurung, to "advanced" peoples like the Newar and Thakali, the latter now being successful businessmen in many parts of Nepal.

Another component of these differences is the degree to which different groups are represented in umbrella organizations and transnational alliances (International Work Group on Indigenous Affairs, hereafter IWGIA), Euro-American advocacy organizations (Cultural Survival), and electronic media (Internet), the combination of which has been critical to the articulation of modern indigenous rights movements, discourses, and practices. In Tanzania, for example, the national indigenous movement took shape through an umbrella organization known as PINGOs (Pastoral and Indigenous Non-Governmental Organizations) and, as elsewhere in Africa, focused largely on hunting and herding societies. However, representation in PINGOs was unequal. In its member organizations, Maasai representation dominated over that of other pastoral nomads, like the Barabaig; this despite the fact that today, many Maasai are no longer full-time transhumant pastoralists and instead rely on sedentary agriculture, wage labor, and other forms of income. The sustained participation and political voice in PINGOs of Tanzanian hunter-gatherers such as the Hadzabe, during the 1990s, writes Igoe (2006), was minimal at best.

Salient differences in economic development, organizational pluck, and cultural politics exist not only between indigenous societies, but also *within* them. There is a tendency in much scholarship about indigenous peoples to speak of them in terms of *groups* rather than *individuals*. This has the unfortunate effect of eliding cross-cutting hierarchies of knowledge, gender, age, geography, and class that increasingly stratify indigenous peoples throughout the world. Following Turner (1995), whether it exists informally, as when one person dominates another in a conversation, or formally, for instance when a king dominates his subjects, inequality is a feature of most human interactions, notwithstanding important experiences of *communitas*. However, much of the literature on indigenous peoples still utilizes idealistic and essentialized images, failing to differentiate, on the one hand, between an ethos of normative community equality commonly found in many indigenous communities and, on the other, the very different reality, equally common, of inequalities among individuals in knowledge, power, and resources, a situation that is often a source of tension (Levi 1999). Even among famously egalitarian hunter-gatherers, they are not all equally egalitarian. According to Friedl (1975), there exists a spectrum of inequality, in this case gender inequality, among foraging societies determined by gender relations in subsistence activities, the relative dependence on hunting versus gathering, and the variable opportunity women have to distribute meat (a valued resource) outside the family.

So too, according to the research of Rus (1994), Harvey (1998), and Levi (2002), intra-ethnic inequality has fueled much organizing in the indigenous world. The aforementioned Zapatista rebellion (and ensuing violence that followed in the wake of the creation of indigenous autonomous communities) was not only an armed insurrection against corrupt local non-Indians who had obtained indigenous lands by nefarious means and siphoned off indigenous labor and resources, as well as a revolt against the Mexican state that had forgotten its early-twentieth-century revolutionary compact with indigenous peoples in its zealous pursuit of late-twentieth century capitalism. It was also a decisive battle in a long-festering virtual civil war within the Indian community itself, between impoverished Tzotzil and Tzeltal Mayans in the highlands of Chiapas, on one hand, and a corrupt but equally indigenous oligarchy, on the other. Over decades, the latter had usurped the leadership in their towns, which they ran as personal fiefdoms, maintained Mexico's strong-arm single party system in the countryside in exchange for patronage from state officials, squelched alternative peasant and religious organizations that challenged "traditional" (that is, oligarchic) authority, and freely killed, maimed, or expelled individuals who opposed the status quo – thus creating, on the eve of the rebellion, many thousands of displaced and disgruntled indigenous Chiapanecos ready to support the Zapatista cause.

Less dramatic but equally noteworthy are peacetime differentiations of individuals in indigenous communities. Claudia Briones (2007) discusses various constructions of self and cultural style in terms of diverse idioms, all expressing variations on a common theme of Mapuche identity in Chile. She notes that the diverse cultural politics of belonging at contemporary Mapuche gatherings encompass people who articulate their identity by dressing in *bombacha* garb to inflect their attachment to rural identities and "traditional" Mapuche culture, as well as urban youth in jeans and face piercings who identify as part of the new movement known as *mapunky* (punk Mapuches) and *mapuheavy* (heavy metal Mapuches). All of this is part of the Mapuche experience today (Briones 2007).

What accounts for such radical differences within and between indigenous groups? There are no easy answers, but undoubtedly it has to do with an imprecise calculus of internal cultural variables articulating with exogenous political and economic structures. Variations in economic vitality, political consciousness, and social reawakening among indigenous peoples are surely correlated with some combination of differences in their natural and cultural resources, different demographic factors, different levels of education, differential skills in organizing, networking, and coalition building, differential access to capital, information, and global media, and different histories of interactions with both state agencies and nongovernmental organizations (NGOs). The impressive economic success of the Nepalese Thakali mentioned earlier no doubt is in part attributable to the fact that they were able to parlay their traditional knowledge and skill as salt traders, whose home territory was located along the main caravan route between Tibet and India, into modern business savvy. In the same way, the predominance of Maasai in Tanzanian indigenous rights fora trades on the political marketing of their handsome cultural distinctiveness and warrior aesthetics, traits that have captivated variously the fascination, horror, and admiration of outsiders since British colonial days.

Similarly, the variables that determined the difference between the aforementioned Crow Creek Reservation, which is one of the poorest Indian reservations per capita in the United States, and the Shakopee Mdewakanton reservation, which is one of the wealthiest, stem directly from the political

and military decisions their respective ancestors took during the same critical event: the Minnesota Dakota War of 1862. That uprising, not unlike
the turmoil and violence that split Mayan communities in Chiapas during
the late twentieth century, was both a war against whites and the federal
government that had usurped their land and a tragic civil war within the
Dakota Nation itself, the painful wounds of which have not healed to this
day. The 1862 conflict represented a crisis of conscience and divided loyal-
ties that tore apart the Dakota, a divide between "friendlies" and "cut-hairs"
who were Christianized Indians who had taken up farming and – most
importantly, from the perspective of Abraham Lincoln – had aided white
settlers and government soldiers during the war, on the one hand, and so-
called "hostiles" and "long hairs," on the other The latter were more tren-
chant in maintaining the ways of their forebears, including ultimately rising
up in arms to defend their land and feed their families, now on the brink
of starvation, from the invaders. In the end, according to Anderson and
Woolworth (1988), the small group of farmer Indians or so-called "Peace
Party" was rewarded by being allowed to stay at a few tiny places in the
tribe's home region of Minnesota – hence the Shakopee community –
whereas the rest of the Dakota people (men, women, and children), after
being interred in a virtual concentration camp at Fort Snelling and enduring at Mankato the largest mass execution in United States history, were
ultimately shipped off to desolate reservations, such as Crow Creek, far out
on the windswept plains.

In other situations, it is not tribal history so much as new structural openings and strategic maneuverings made possible through modern regime
changes, democratization, capital flows, decentralization, and economic
liberalization that have to do with contemporary indigenous realities. The
case of indigenous peoples in Siberia during the post-Soviet era is instructive. As Balzer (2003) demonstrates, the Sakha, known to outsiders by the
ethnonym Yakut, had a more or less successful history of negotiations with
Moscow, clearly related to the vast unexploited subsurface energy and
mineral wealth of their lands – and even though today they are one of the
poorest per capita republics in Russia, they did manage to secure regional
autonomy. Thus they exist as the Sakha Republic, or Yakutia, and overall
are a "rich and pivotal" indigenous people of Siberia (Balzer 2003:115).
At the other end of the spectrum of success, but still partially within the
Sakha Republic, according to Balzer (2003: 123–130) are the "poor and
despised" Yukagir, a tiny minority of 1,142 persons (according to the 1989
census) with a vocal intelligentsia but without a land-based "homeland."
Between these two extremes are the 22,500 Khanty who, like the Sakha

are "mired in oil" but, like the Yukagir, are a traditionally hunting, fishing, and reindeer-breeding post-tribal people now deploying their shamanic religion and dramatic rituals of reindeer sacrifice (which were prohibited under Soviet rule) as strategic vehicles for public protest, cultural revival, and political mobilization.

Indigenous Spaces: Tradition, Civilization, and Its Discontents

Nor can sentimental attachments to ethnic essentialism, "unchanging tradition," cultural purity, preindustrial technology, territorial integrity, or rooted intimacy with the land be marshaled anymore as ubiquitous or defining traits of indigenous peoples (if indeed they ever could). True, in May 2008, CNN broadcast images around the world of an "uncontacted tribe" in the western Amazon near the Peru-Brazil border – naked men painted red and black shooting arrows at the low-flying plane that took the photos – but conditions of such pristine aboriginality are not only the rare exception, but are so at variance with most experiences today, indigenous and otherwise, as to make them newsworthy internationally. More typical of many indigenous lives in the twenty-first century are those of Australian Aborigines who, even though they are still stereotypically associated with the "outback," nowadays, according to Merlan (2007) are more likely to be found in Sydney and other urban centers, just as "[i]n the United States the majority of Native Americans live in cities" (Ramirez 2007: 1), although again the popular conception is that Indian issues are largely confined to reservations in the rural west.

In like manner, the Baguio Declaration of the Second Asian Indigenous Women's Conference, ratified by 100 indigenous women from 12 Asian countries, addressed explicitly the emergent problems faced by pastoralists in Mongolia transitioning to cities on account of the loss of their livestock due to climate change, as well as the heightened vulnerability of indigenous women similarly forced to become urban dwellers after being displaced from tribal areas (Baguio Declaration 2004). Whereas most indigenous peoples fall somewhere in between uncontacted Amazonian tribes, on the one hand, and citified Indians in the United States, on the other, in general, following Clifford (2007), "diaspora" as well as "homeland" are equally descriptive of the traditional centers and geographical distensions characterizing indigenous peoples today.

To be sure, in some places, uncanny cultural continuity as well as territorial integrity still does exist: The historical and ethnographic work of Marlowe (2002) informs us that the Hadzabe in Tanzania, for instance, have managed to remain in the same general area and maintain a foraging way of life that has changed little in centuries, perhaps even millennia, despite having long been in contact with both pastoral and agricultural societies and, increasingly after the 1990s, tourists intent on seeing Africa's last nomadic hunter-gatherers. Yet where indigenous communities have been torn asunder by the forces of colonial or neoliberal dismemberment, as is often the case, there are also creative mechanisms of "re-membering," reconstruction, and reconciliation; lost members and even nonmembers connecting in novel ways in addition to new identities being woven from the shreds and patches of old ones. Thus, the studies of Nagel (1996) and Ramirez (2007) help us understand that it was in the wake of the "Indian termination policy" of the 1950s, whereby the United States sought to abrogate its obligations to federally recognized tribes, that there arose, during the 1960s and 1970s, the pan-Indian movement as Native Americans from various tribes and reservations increasingly gathered into urban Indian *hubs*. One does not normally think of Silicon Valley, California, as a particularly "indigenous" place, but with the reinvigoration of the Muwekma Ohlones who were always native to the area, in concert with the in-migration of Native Americans from across the United States, Mexico, and beyond, it has increasingly become so (Ramirez 2007). Imaginative redefinitions of belonging and expansive notions of membership are also exhibited by recent efforts at reconciliation between Aboriginal and non-Aboriginal peoples in northern Australia. There McIntosh's work (2003) tells us that the Yolngu symbolically tied in Australian "white fellas" with their community based on the hydrological metaphor of the mingling of fresh water and salt water in the estuaries of Arnhemland, an ecological phenomenon where two come together as one without either losing its identity. In the face of politico-economic realities, reconstruction and representation can also demand that indigenous peoples remake themselves in the stereotyped cultural image that the world expects of them, rather than allowing them to be seen as they actually are. Consequently, to regain lost homelands, Namibia's Omaheke San, "a landless underclass of farm laborers, domestic servants, and squatters" (Sylvain 2002:1074; 2005), are today compelled to deploy what Gayatri Spivak has aptly termed "strategic essentialism" (see Kilburn 1996), instrumentally manipulating their identity so as to conform to popular (mis)conceptions of "authentic Bushmen" as timeless hunters and gatherers, trackers of wild game still roaming the vast Kalahari, people essentially naked or scantily dressed only in skins, rooted inseparably to the land since time immemorial – never mind that for the Omaheke San today, this image exists only as a dim and fading memory in the minds of a few ancient elders.

The dialectics of indigenous spaces may be defined, but not exhausted, by the thesis and antithesis of homeland and displacement. Instead, the seeming antinomies are partially resolved through their synthesis in an entirely new kind of space: cyberspace. Telecommunications in general and the digital revolution in particular go a long way toward answering the question: Why now? Why at this stage of world history is there a global indigenous movement? In our media-saturated world, where news and images can be flashed around the globe in seconds, bounced off satellites, modulated via airwaves, no country is really isolated, no place so remote that contact cannot somehow be made, sites located, communication achieved. Text-messaging, cell phones, chat rooms, e-mail, blogs, Web sites, and video conferencing via the Internet not only regularly connect transnational migrant K'iché men working in the United States with family members back home in their communities in the highlands of western Guatemala, but create and maintain the linkages that gave rise to the global indigenous movement in the first place, enabling communication between Tuscarora (in New York) and Turkana (in Kenya), Saami (in Finland) and Seminole (in Florida), Ainu (in Japan) and Innu (in Labrador), and all of them with multilateral organizations and international institutions, such as the UN Permanent Forum on Indigenous Issues, Cultural Survival, the Indigenous Peoples of Africa Co-ordinating Committee, and so on. Furthermore, as Niezen argues in "Digital Identity: The Construction of Virtual Selfhood in the Indigenous Peoples' Movement," the emergence, spread, and relative affordability of new information and communication technologies has encouraged local, primordial identities to be reimagined in terms of a global and virtually borderless geography (Niezen 2005).

The veracity of the preceding information notwithstanding, a digital divide still exists, perhaps in the indigenous world more than elsewhere – separating on opposite sides of an ocean of difference an elite cadre of Internet insiders from the vast majority of those who do not even have access to electricity. At the same time, it must be recalled that the modalities of intimate, organic, and embodied communication occurring in the context of face-to-face interaction that takes place in small-scale societies where most of the world's indigenous people still reside contrasts strikingly with the disembodied and segmented communications that typify the talk in cyberspace. Nevertheless, new communication technology offers a radical and phenomenally empowering medium that allows people

to transcend instantaneously both spatial and cultural distances, as indigenous peoples and their supporters forge social and political alliances of
all types in all corners of the globe. There is no turning back of the clock.
Pen pals and snail-mail could never have achieved this kind of connectiv-
ity and immediacy.

POLYTHETIC CLASSIFICATION: A FLEXIBLE
APPROACH TO UNITY AMID DIVERSITY

Given the tremendous historical, political, economic, and cultural variety
of peoples who identify as being indigenous, and are mutually recognized
as such by others, one might well ask: Is there any common core or set
of determinative characteristics that sets them apart from other groups?
Furthermore, how does this diversity square with a more or less "unitary"
global movement? In fact, although there exists "no universally accepted
definition" of indigenous peoples (MacKay 2007: 51), several working
understandings are widely consulted, as well as critiqued, by academics,
advocates, and multilateral organizations working in the field.

Perhaps the definition most commonly used, implicitly and explicitly,
is the one provided by José Martinez Cobo, Special Rapporteur to the
Subcommission on Prevention of Discrimination and Protection of
Minorities, in his detailed 1986 report to the UN, *Study of the Problem
of Discrimination against Indigenous Populations*:

Indigenous communities, peoples and nations, are those which have a historical
continuity with pre-invasion and pre-colonial societies that developed on their territories, consider themselves distinct from other sectors of society now prevailing
in those territories, or parts of them. They form at present non-dominant sectors of
society and are determined to preserve, develop, and transmit to future generations
their ancestral territories, and their ethnic identity, as the basis of their continued
existence as peoples, in accordance with their own cultural patterns, social institutions, and legal systems (Cobo 1986: 379).

Even though the preceding definition is widely used, none of the initiatives of the United Nations concerning indigenous peoples – neither the
Permanent Forum on Indigenous Issues, nor the Regional Initiative on
Indigenous Peoples' Rights and Development, nor even the Declaration
on the Rights of Indigenous Peoples – has a legally binding definition of
indigenous peoples (a situation that has caused consternation among some
member states). At the present time, "the only definition of indigenous
peoples that is legally binding to ratifying states is the one included in
the Indigenous and Tribal Peoples Convention 169 that was adopted in

1989 by the International Labour Organization" (Hodgson 2002:1038). However, this definition, like the one used by the World Bank (MacKay 2007), does not differ substantially from Cobo's paradigmatic conceptualization, although Saugestad points out that Cobo's characterization links indigeneity to the method of colonization, thereby separating the definition of indigenous peoples in Africa and Asia from those in the Americas and Australia, in essence bifurcating what would otherwise be a global indigenous peoples movement (Saugestad 2008). Significantly, she notes that the UN Working Group on Indigenous Populations "brings out four principles to be taken into account in any possible definition of indigenous peoples:

a) priority in time, with respect to the occupation and use of a specific territory;

b) the voluntary perpetuation of cultural distinctiveness, which may include aspects of language, social organisation, religion and spiritual values, modes of production, laws and institutions;

c) self-identification, as well as recognition by other groups, as well as State authorities, as a distinct collectivity; and

d) an experience of subjugation, marginalisation, dispossession, exclusion or discrimination, whether or not these conditions persist." (Saugestad 2008:165)

These four features – historical antecedence, cultural distinctiveness, self-identification, and nondominance – appear repeatedly as fundamental criteria defining indigenous peoples. Still, problems remain if the intent is to deploy all in a universal definition. The first problem is the notion of prior occupancy. The Maasai, for example, are by far the most prominent actors in indigenous rights movements of East Africa, yet they are not, nor claim to be, "first peoples" in the region because, according to Hodgson (2002: 1087), they migrated south into Kenya and northern Tanzania probably only in the last several hundred years. Thus, there exist other peoples in these countries who antedate them historically, yet are not included in the indigenous peoples movement.

Similarly, as Rosaldo (1989) and Kenrick and Lewis (2004: 8) point out, the difficulty with the criterion of cultural distinctiveness is that it may be linked to arbitrary markers of altereity, and thus the problematic logic equating "culture" with "difference." Some groups therefore have had had trouble being recognized as indigenous precisely because they were unable to demonstrate sufficient cultural distinctiveness. We have in mind here the difficulty certain groups of Native Americans, such as the Mashpee in

Massachusetts (Clifford 1988) or the Lumbee in North Carolina (Blu 2001), have had in gaining federal recognition as bona fide "tribes" because they do not conform to stereotypic images of American Indians, and in other respects may be largely indistinguishable from surrounding populations (Lambert 2007). A similar dilemma has faced certain San groups in post-apartheid Southern Africa (Lee 2003, Sylvain 2002, 2005b) as well as some Aboriginal peoples in Australia (Povinelli 1998; Bell 2001) and Canada (Pinkowski and Asch 2004).

So too, if *self-identification* is called forth as a critical criterion of indi-geneity, what is one to make of situations where groups, who by all other indices are unequivocally indigenous, do not aspire to label themselves as such, either because they do not know that the "indigenous" category exists, as in the case of the previously mentioned "uncontacted Amazonian tribe," or because they actively and assertively disavow the label, as is the case described by Quetzil Castañeda in a provocatively titled article, "'We Are Not Indigenous!': An Introduction to the Maya Identity of Yucatan" (2004). Are we to conclude therefore that these peoples are *not* indigenous because they have not self-identified as such?

Finally, indigenous peoples are conventionally defined as *nondominant*, because they are minority populations or are otherwise dominated, subju-gated, or marginalized. Yet in Bolivia, Indians are in the numerical major-ity, the Quechua and Aymara alone number an estimated 62 percent of the country's population, not even counting the smaller populations of Indian peoples in the eastern part of the country. On the other hand, if nondomi-nance is interpreted not in terms of population but rather marginalization or economic standing, then the Newar and Thakali minorities might not qualify as indigenous; these peoples are among the most prosperous in Nepal, and have been for years, the Newars being renowned throughout the Himalayas as merchants and fine artisans, just as the Thakali historically were long-distance traders. Or again, consider the Otavalo: a Quichua-speaking group in highland Ecuador, a people who are simultaneously profoundly traditional yet remarkably successful entrepreneurs marketing Andean tex-tiles and music throughout the world via an ethnically based transnational trade network of producers, distributors, and retailers (Colloredo-Mansfeld 1999; Meisch 2002), a cultural practice that sometimes has garnered them, according to Freeman (1997) the dubious distinction of being called the "Jews of the Andes."

In sum, if even the four basic principles stipulated as necessarily being part of any definition of indigenous people cannot be applied universally, then, as Beteille (1998), Kuper (2003), and Igoe (2006) have argued, given the apparent ambiguity of the concept, is it better to dispense with it altogether, and perhaps call into question the legitimacy of the international rights movement predicated on the concept, on grounds that are at once scholarly, practical, and political?

Our view is that the idea of "indigenous peoples" is neither vacuous nor uncircumscribed, and its conceptual complexity demands not that we disqualify it as a meaningful analytic category on which to base a social movement, but only that it be understood as a heuristic device in the manner of a polythetic rather than a monothetic class. The latter is the kind of category most people have in mind when they think of demarcating the boundaries of a particular class or kind of phenomena: Certain traits are specified and the possession of said traits are both necessary and sufficient criteria for inclusion in the class. This, however, is not the only way to delimit a category. Polythetic classification, a concept that draws on the Wittgensteinian idea of "family resemblances" and is used regularly in fields as diverse as biology, philosophy, linguistics, psychology, anthropology, and sociology (Needham 1975), offers an alternate way to reduce the complexity of phenomena into conceptually meaningful categories. As Bailey (1973: 294) puts it:

Unlike a monothetic type, a polythetic type has no unique set of defining features. It can be formed from many different combinations of values on the component variables, hence the name polythetic. As Sokal and Sneath (1963: 14) say: 'A polythetic arrangement, on the other hand, places together organisms that have the greatest number of shared features, and no single feature is either essential to group membership or is sufficient to make an organism a member of the group.' In a polythetic group each feature is shared by many members, and each member possesses many features. If no single feature is possessed by all members, the group is termed fully polythetic.

It appears to us (see also the concurring discussion in Barume 2000: 35–37) that this is precisely the scenario that obtains in the delimitation of "indigenous peoples." The pronounced heterogeneity of indigenous peoples we have reviewed so far – in terms of political mobilization, economic standing, territoriality, history, discrimination, prior occupancy, organizational savvy, structural dislocation, poverty, international connections, technological access, cultural distinctiveness, rootedness to the land, and self-ascription as indigenous, to name a few of the dimensions of difference that have been discussed – can all be easily accommodated with the notion of a polythetic class.

	A	B	C	D	E
1	x	x	x		
2		x	x	x	
3			x	x	x
4	x	x			x
5	x	x		x	
6	x			x	x
7		x	x		x

Figure 3.1. Polythetic classification, showing the variable interrelationships among components.

Consider a set in which there are seven features (1, 2, 3, etc.) spread among five indigenous societies or peoples (A, B, C, etc.) with each feature being represented among three societies. No society possesses all the features, and there is no single feature possessed by all the societies (Figure 3.1). In like manner, a rope is made because many fibers overlap and interweave in complex ways, not because there exists a single golden thread that runs throughout. So too the integrity that holds together the polythetic class of indigenous peoples is attributable not to their uniformity, but on the contrary, to the combination and diversity of their complex interrelationships.

The *idée fixe* of indigenous peoples, which is the central organizing principle for the global indigenous movement, can be further thought of as akin to what anthropologist Victor Turner famously articulated as a *multivocal* symbol (see Turner 1967), a symbol that has multiple and diverse meanings, condensing a fan of referents into a single metaphor, image, or concept that functions as a powerful mode of communication, often found in political and religious settings. The more public the symbol, the bolder and more ambitious its assertions, the more open it is to ambiguous and even contradictory interpretations. But therein lies its power, for it enables a wide variety of audiences to find meaning in its broad connotative range. Indeed, the polysemous quality of political language and multivocal symbols is at the heart of much social and political organizing, illustrated, for example, by the relationship between national flags and political parties. "While the existence of different political parties shows that not everyone agrees about what their country stands for, everyone does agree that their country's flag stands for their country" (Levi 2007: 251).

The flexible character of the indigenous movement is conceptually analogous to this. It is a banner, a rallying point, a dynamic effort at collective organization and political action seeking justice and social reform. It is a social *movement*, not a social stasis, a process more than a category, a diligent work in progress with delicate negotiations taking place across contested boundaries on multiple fronts. It encompasses, without apology, divergent discourses, practices, ideologies, and philosophies. Indigenous peoples, so it seems, would have it no other way. Why? Because more than any other people they have been denied, literally as well as rhetorically, the very terms of *life*. They are people who frequently have been treated as living fossils, leaving open to them only two routes, equally unsatisfactory, toward their place in the future: either be swept aside in the name of progress or preserved as fragile relics in virtual museums. The global indigenous movement and its allies insist that neither is a viable choice. Instead, for the first time in history, indigenous peoples are increasingly demanding – and getting – their rightful places at the bargaining table.

Most importantly, the legitimacy of the indigenous rights movement derives not from its logical consistency or formal features as a recognizable category, but rather because it exists as a political fact and global social movement in reality, commanding the attention of advocates and academics alike. Thus, contrary to the objections of critics like Béteille (1998), the question is not whether "indigenous peoples" makes sense scientifically as a generalizable category, or whether it is sound ethnologically when applied either globally or to particular cultural areas, such as India. Ultimately, the question is not whether it is *admissible anthropologically*, but rather whether it is *justifiable politically*. On this matter, Kuper's (2003) criticism of indigeneity as a platform for collective empowerment gets closer to the real issue, but in the end also misses a crucial point of the indigenous movement. Kuper argues much too closely to the group and not sufficiently in regard to the group's relationship with outside power holders in his critique of the term "indigenous" and indigenous peoples' movements. This becomes clear when he takes as an example the case of Canada:

[In Canada, one] has rights only if one has a certain number of appropriate grandparents. This might be fairly called the Nuremberg principle. A drift to racism may be inevitable where so called cultural identity becomes the basis for rights, since any cultural test (knowledge of a language for example) will exclude some who might lay claim to an identity on grounds of descent. In the indigenous-peoples movement, descent is tacitly assumed to represent the bedrock of collective identity (Kuper 2003: 392).

In the first place, we argue in the development of the polythetic approach that descent is but one of a number of important factors that *may* define indigeneity; but is neither necessary nor sufficient. True, indigeneity may often involve indigenous descent, but it does not have to, nor does it always in actuality. One has only to recall the case of the Choctaw Freedmen in the United States, former African slaves and their descendants who were incorporated as citizens into the Choctaw Nation of Oklahoma in 1885, or even more strikingly and recently Sub-Comandante Marcos, the eloquent, masked, pipe-smoking spokesmen of the Zapatistas whose words revolutionized the indigenous consciousness of a nation – the son of Spanish immigrants – to realize that membership in the indigenous movement cannot be neatly distilled as race. More than anything, indigeneity is a political identity. And in the second place, to equate those defined as indigenous with dominant peoples with plausible world power aspirations and capabilities, such as pre–World War II Nazis, fails to take into account a salient (although again, neither necessary nor sufficient) characteristic of indigeneity: people who have had an experience of subjugation, marginalization, dispossession, exclusion or discrimination, whether or not these conditions persist (Saugestad 2008: 165). For that reason, indigenous peoples should not be equated with state regimes intent on using racist criteria to impose themselves on others. As Alcida Ramos puts it bluntly in her comment on Kuper, "[T]o put in the same category indigenous claims for legitimate difference, Nazi racism, and South African apartheid is to miss the point of differential power" (Ramos 2003: 392). In sum, indigeneity is a discourse of empowerment and social justice for the most disadvantaged members of society, not a rhetoric of world power and domination. Just which strands in the polythetic class will be activated and chosen to count as "indigenous" is a radically contingent event. *Ultimately, indigeneity is conjunctural.*

Finally, we contend that the multiplex differences among indigenous groups do not weaken their collective struggle for recognition and rights. On the contrary, we argue that it is precisely these *differences* within the movement that are often its source of greatest *strength*. The divergences within and between groups *self-identifying as indigenous*, thereby claiming membership in this self-ascribed polythetic category, fosters creative engagements across boundaries of various sorts insofar as they partake of a relational vocabulary of belonging at different levels. From this perspective, political, economic, and cultural oppositions constitute not the undoing of the movement or the conceptual category on which it is based, but conversely the terms for greater organic complementarity and overall integrity within it.

For example, consider how the differences that have resulted among indigenous peoples whose territories were bisected by the international boundary separating the United States and Mexico – originally constituting crises and sources of considerable pain – in recent years have been reimagined as bases for cultural sharing and collective reorganization. In this international border region, the Kumeyaay of southern California, who retained into the twentieth century comparatively more ceremonial knowledge and fared better economically due to the demarcation of reservations (Shipek 1968) and, more recently, substantial gaming revenues, have used their newfound wealth to host cultural gatherings with the Kumiai of northern Baja California, Mexico who, although poorer monetarily, are richer in the twenty-first century by having retained greater knowledge of the indigenous language, material culture, ethnobotany, and subsistence arts (Levi 1992).

Whereas the preceding example shows how cross-border differences have been utilized creatively *within* a single group of indigenous people, the illustration that follows shows how the self-ascribed category of indigeneity allows peoples *without* historical connections, common cultural ties, or geographical contiguity to still make a virtue of their differences. Ronald Niezen, comparing the involvement of the Tuareg and Cree in the global indigenous movement, writes that several decades ago:

> The Tuaregs of the West African Sahara and the Crees of northern Canada would have had little or nothing in common. One is a nomadic pastoral people of the desert and arid savannah, the other a hunting, fishing, and gathering people of the northern boreal forest. One is a people with rigid class distinctions and with chiefs drawn from a nobility; the other an egalitarian society with a tradition of leadership based on hunting skill. One is a people in conflict with governments that are ready to use deadly force to restrict their mobility and their suprastate exercise of self-determination; the other is in conflict with a liberal democracy subject to embarrassment and public censure for the use of unnecessary force.

> Yet in recent years these two groups have somehow come together in the same meetings under the same rubric: as indigenous peoples. Under these circumstances the basic common features of their histories become more important than the contrasts of environment, subsistence, social structure and politics. When we look for the things that indigenous peoples have in common, for what brings them together and reinforces their common identity, we find patterns that arise from the logic of conquest and colonialism.... They are similarities based largely on the relationship between indigenous peoples and states ... [which] usually fall into one of three categories ... assimilative state education, loss of subsistence, and state abrogation of treaties (Niezen 2003: 86–87).

Facing common problems, indigenous peoples have learned from each other's diverse circumstances, successes, and failures in dealing with their respective nation-states. The identity that indigenous peoples share therefore is born, so to speak, of their common differences. From an organizational perspective, their differences do not weaken the movement, but rather supply the sources of ingenious, and truly "multicultural," transnational, collective global action.

INDIGENOUS IDENTITY IN CONTINENTAL
CONTEXTS: "SETTLER SOCIETIES" VERSUS THE
AFRICAN/ASIAN CONTROVERSY

The first crucial dichotomy of any analysis of the world's indigenous peoples begins with a discussion of the differences in the identification of indigenous peoples in so-called settler societies, as took shape in the Americas, Australia, and New Zealand, on the one hand, and in African and Asia, on the other – a process set in motion by the global consequences of what has come to be known sparely as "The Conquest." The European trans-oceanic expansion of the then-known "Western" world began powerfully in the late fifteenth century, with groups of Spaniards purposely traversing the South Atlantic to the Caribbean, the Antilles, and the Americas to begin the installation of what would eventually become Spanish America. They began doing so in what they thought was an archipelago off the coast of India. In a similar effort to reach India by sea, as opposed to the arduous land journey to "the East" of the previous centuries, Portuguese seafarers, soldiers, priests, adventurers, and traders, in the same period, circumvented the African continent, sailing around the Cape of Good Hope and penetrating the African hinterland and later India. One such Portuguese, Pedro Álvarez Cabral, sailing toward the Cape of Good Hope in 1500, was blown off course by a storm, "discovering" Brazil, thus beginning Portuguese America on the Brazilian Atlantic coast. These dual processes, supplemented in the seventeenth and eighteenth centuries by Dutch, English, French, Danish, and other European incursions into the Americas, had profound impacts on the peoples the Europeans encountered. Europeans entering overseas lands already occupied by indigenous societies normally resulted in an all-too-familiar pattern that is widely documented: uneasy contact, warfare, ethnocide, and genocide (for classic scholarly accounts of European exploration, discovery, and colonization, see Parry 1971 and 1981).

The definitional issue of who are the "indigenous peoples" was and remains much less problematic in regions where peoples of European origins overran indigenous peoples to form "settler" societies in the Americas and, later, in New Zealand and Australia. But the definitional issue remains quite problematic in Asia and Africa. Although Europeans eventually went around the world to all the continents, they did not take over and remake, to the same degree, the entire social order, during centuries of colonization, outside the areas that we designate, here, as "settler societies." In the Americas, Australia, and New Zealand, even after independence, peoples of European origins continued to rule and to dominate the Indians,

Aborigines, and Maoris, respectively. Although European traders, adventurers, and colonists did, of course, enter into the Asian and African hinterlands, their descendants did not maintain long-term power as in the post-independence contexts of the Americas, Australia, and New Zealand.

Thus, of equal or greater significance than the different conditions of conquest, it was the varied circumstances of the postcolonial world that has shaped indigeneity in modern times. That is, in the postcolonial states of Africa and Asia, after independence, the colonials – by and large – went "home." Not so in the Americas, Australia, and New Zealand, where the descendants continued to dominate, politically and economically, and usually numerically as well. In Africa and Asia, however, after departure of the colonial European powers, these newly independent states concluded that the remaining peoples in these places were *all* indigenous. In the vigorous attempt to foster national unity in the new states, the argument that some minority peoples were indigenous whereas others were not was often interpreted as a recrudescence of "tribalism" and invitation to ethnic conflict, although in actuality it often served as just another way to legitimize the right to rule for dominant groups. The articulation of indigenous rights in the postcolonial scenarios of Africa and Asia, thus, has historically encountered particular difficulties.

The first geopolitical dichotomy, then, when analyzing the world's indigenous peoples today, is between the "settler societies" – the places where Europeans established governing colonies and, later, their descendants founded independent states – and those that did not follow this pattern. Indigenous peoples are and remain clearly those who are non-European "First Peoples" in these settler societies (although the phenomena of Mestizo and Métis peoples poses interesting issues from another direction), whereas the problem of defining who is and is not indigenous in the rest of the world is complicated in other ways (D. Maybury-Lewis 2002: 6).

Hodgson offers an insightful summary of this issue and why claims of indigeneity are so problematic, today, beyond the "settler societies" (Hodgson 2002: 1042):

In contrast to their American counterparts, African groups, as well as many Asian groups who identify themselves as indigenous, face a different set of issues. First and foremost, while most groups are recognized as "indigenous" on the international scale, they are still struggling for similar recognition by their national governments. Moreover, they are doing so, at least initially, in terms of an international discourse and definition of *indigenous* that has been shaped by the experiences of indigenous peoples from the Americas, Australia, and elsewhere. The term has been used in Africa and Asia by distinct cultural minorities who have been historically repressed by majority populations in control of the state apparatus. Although few claim to be "first people" as such, these groups argue that they share a similar structural position vis-à-vis their nation-states as indigenous peoples in the Americas and Australia: the maintenance of cultural distinctiveness; a long experience of subjugation, marginalization, and dispossession by colonial and postcolonial powers; and, for some, a historical priority in terms of the occupation of their territories. Perhaps, most importantly, in terms of the ILO and Cobo definitions, these groups now *self-identify* as indigenous, despite the arguments of their national governments to the contrary. They argue for what scholars and advocates have termed a "constructivist," "structural," or "relational" definition of *indigenous* that encompasses and reflects their situation, rather than more "essential," "substantial," or "positivist" definitions.

These self-identified indigenous people and their allies argue that whether a national government is controlled by people from another continent or from the same country makes little difference. Minorities like themselves – they argue – in decolonized areas need to assert their indigenous rights and identities if the new states (wherever they may be), which they are confronting, oppress them by jeopardizing indigenous knowledge, culture, and customary patterns of politico-economic activity, following the patterns of domination found typically in the "settler societies." The momentum for Asian, as well as African, claims of indigeneity therefore remains palpable (Kingsbury 1998: 449; Niezen 2003: 73–75).

According to Saugestad (2008), there are also certain differences in the history and organization of the indigenous movement in Africa and the Americas, both in terms of structure and longevity. In the Americas, the indigenous movement was a grassroots struggle that grew organically among a number of organizations and networks from the bottom up, developing initially from the 1970s political consciousness of organizations like the American Indian Movement (AIM) and "Red Power." By contrast, indigenous mobilization in Africa not only began much more recently, just in the 1990s, but also was built from the top down, by indigenous representatives in Geneva and New York, who then went back to their home countries to build coalitions that became the indigenous movement in Africa.

The particular difficulties faced by indigenous peoples in Africa and Asia, fundamentally having to do with struggles to be recognized as "indigenous" by the governments of the nation-states wherein they reside, can best be understood by examining specific cases. Here we will briefly mention the situations in India and China, because these are both important countries with large indigenous populations, and although neither country recognizes these peoples as "indigenous," they are recognized as such by the international community and also self-identify as indigenous peoples, thereby aligning themselves with the global indigenous movement.

"The government of India has taken a firm position on indigenous peoples, insisting that there are none in India or, more precisely, that there are none who can be singled out as indigenous, since most peoples of the subcontinent have been there for thousands of years" (D. Maybury-Lewis 1991: 40). Instead, today there are 461 ethnic groups that the Indian state recognizes as *Scheduled Tribes*, sometimes also known locally as *adivasi*. They constitute 8.2% of India's population, or 84.3 million people. These marginal peoples of the subcontinent are the so-called hill and forest tribes, minority peoples who nevertheless constitute the majority in the "tribal belt" of seven states in northeastern India between Burma/Myanmar and Bangladesh, literally and psychologically "a frontier" region, poor and far away from India's major centers of commerce and industry. The Indian constitution "established special protections for scheduled tribes and also specified that they should receive certain benefits. In 1993, for instance, 41 seats out of 545 were reserved for their representatives in the national parliament and 527 out of a total of 4,061 in the state legislatures" (D. Maybury-Lewis 1991: 41). Notwithstanding this political representation and theoretical legal protection, local authorities have routinely been willing to cooperate with developers and their state allies to aggressively go after tribal lands and resources, pushing aside many of these safeguards in a pattern recognizable in the experiences of indigenous peoples in Canada, the United States, Latin America, Africa, Australia, and other parts of the indigenous world.

Given the antiquity of settlement for most peoples in the subcontinent and thus the virtual inability of determining who were the "natives" and who were the "invaders," Béteille has argued, on anthropological and historical grounds, that in the Indian context, the designation "tribal peoples" is preferable to "indigenous peoples" because the former term refers to a "type of society or stage of evolution [rather] than to the priority of settlement" (1998: 188). Similarly, Kingsbury details the Indian government's rationale for refusing to recognize domestic indigeneity (Kingsbury 1998: 435):

The Indian government's position contains an implied argument that a forensic inquiry into who appeared first in India would be unhelpful and undesirable, for two reasons. First, some groups meriting special protection would be excluded while others not in need of such protection might be included. Second, recognition of special rights and entitlements for having been the earliest or original occupants might spur and legitimate chauvinist claims by groups all over India, many of which might be very powerful locally while in some sense "nondominant" nationally. Claims to historical priority already feature in some "communal" conflicts and incipient chauvinist movements abound, as with the pro-Marathi, Hindu-nationalist Shiv Sena party in Maharashtra. In effect, if some people are "indigenous" to a place, others are vulnerable to being targeted as nonindigenous, and groups deemed to be migrants or otherwise subject to social stigma may bear the brunt of nativist "indigenist" policy. Once indigenousness or "sons of the soil" becomes the basis of legitimation for a politically or militarily dominant group, restraints on abuses of power can be difficult to maintain.

Although defending a distinct regime type and confronting different historical and cultural circumstances, the leaders in the People's Republic of China (PRC) make an analogous argument. State actors in the PRC assert that the nation succeeded, through its revolutionary struggle, to liberate the Chinese people from colonial oppression, bringing in its stead the Maoist revolution. While China supports the United Nations' efforts to promote the rights of ethnic minorities, maintaining (without explaining why) that there are no minority-based rights organizations in the PRC, it can hardly accept that there could be those who need liberation in the "New China," a nation-state whose founding principal was the Marxist-Leninist vision of man's liberation from oppression.

For this reason, there are 105,226,114 people (8.47% of the PRC's population) in 55 government recognized *minzu* or ethnic minority groups, 20 with less than 100,000 each according to the 2000 census, but no "indigenous peoples." The state does not recognize the term "indigenous peoples." The ethnic minorities living in the PRC are concentrated in the southwest, particularly in Yunnan province where there are 25 of the 55 officially recognized. Others live in the north, the east, and on the island of Hainan. They are mostly subsistence farmers, have illiteracy rates of over 50%, and are among China's poorest people (IWGIA 2008: 257). In February 2007, for the first time since the beginning of the Revolution, the China State Council announced, in its 11th Five-Year Plan (2006–2010), policies and plans for the development of ethnic minorities. The goal was to effect improvements in six areas: income, education (increasing the mandatory time youth must remain in school to nine years), infant survival rates, quantity of ethnic language publications, professionalization for employment, and "urbanization" [sic]. It remains to be seen how these policy intentions will be implemented, given the PRC's weak provincial record, in recent years, of working with the poor, rural, and vulnerable citizenry. That these people are outside of the predominant Han ethnic group adds another dimension, according to the IWGIA 2008 Report, to the potential problems surrounding implementation of these plans (256–257).

Not surprisingly, the highest concentration of ethnic minorities in the PRC is in the province of Yunnan, a frontier area bordering the Tibetan Autonomous Republic, India, Burma/Myanmar, Laos, and Vietnam – countries also containing numerous ethnic minorities, particularly in *their* respective border regions. The government has initiated an effort to revitalize

Yunnan's border areas, focusing, again, on keeping youth in school, income generation projects, infrastructure and housing investment, culture, health, and training in science and engineering. The programs are important for showing the good intentions of the PRC government. However, there is little involvement of the minority population in the design or implementation of these projects. Misappropriation of funds and corruption is commonplace. The results of the upcoming five-year plan remain to be seen. What is already clear is that – with the exception of the PRC's current effort to publish more of the minority languages, while giving access to the region to scholars, of the Han majority, to study cultures and languages in order to preserve them – the overriding ethos of the state's effort is assimilationist. Around the world, innumerable scholars have observed that state-mandated assimilationist policies tend to usher in a cluster of problems for cultural survival, especially when associated with nonparticipatory planning. The tendency is to both disrespect and undermine indigenous cultures.

THE "FOUR R'S" OF INDIGENOUS MOVEMENTS

Several authors state that indigenous movements and the scholarship describing them can be summarized in terms of four key concepts, each of which begins with an "r." Harris and Wasilewski (2004) write that indigeneity, as an alternate worldview, is characterized by "Four R's (relationship, responsibility, reciprocity, redistribution) versus Two P's (power and profit)." However, we view this stark dichotomization between indigenous and nonindigenous worldviews, rigidly differentiated in these terms, as more a function of misplaced romanticism than ethnographic reality. We therefore instead follow Hodgson, who observes that the indigenous movement and the expansive literature that has traced its transformations are largely concerned with four cross-cutting issues: representation, recognition, resources, and rights (Hodgson 2002). These "Four R's," as we call them, characterize not only the global indigenous movement, but also individual indigenous movements in different parts of the world.

Representation

The way indigenous peoples are represented in public fora, both by themselves and others, is at the heart of many anthropological studies, because it connects the politics of identity and cultural authenticity debates, on the one hand, with the ability of peoples to be recognized as indigenous by states, the international community, and the media, on the other

(Warren and Jackson 2002). "In the absence of electoral clout, economic prowess, or military might, the 'symbolic capital' accompanying authentically performed cultural identities represents one of the most influential political resources available to indigenous peoples" (Levi and Dean 2003: 15; see also Conklin 1997).

Put simply, the more that indigenous peoples fail to conform to popular stereotypes and essentialized images of who and what indigenous people are, the more they risk being seen as culturally "inauthentic." That is, "the more they become savvy about the media, politically skilled, linked to the international community ... the more they begin to slip out of the 'savage slot' (Trouillot 1991) – whether noble, natural, primitive, or romantic – in spite of the fact that this is the rhetorical position from which they derive much of their symbolic capital, moral authority, and political clout" (Levi and Dean 2003: 2–3). The world community, so it seems, likes its indigenous people culturally distinct in stereotypically recognizable ways.

In many cases, there seems to be an odd calculus at work whereby the less clothes one wears (or the more clothes one wears that are distinctly ethnic), the more one's indigeneity is unassailable – an exotic aesthetic of primitive authenticity that not only perpetuates Western fictions and reinscribes indigenous peoples as perennially subaltern, but poses an unfortunate identity challenge for increasing numbers of real indigenous people. On the one hand, indigenous people who become displaced from their homelands, or are no longer anchored to their putatively timeless traditions – impoverished individuals forced to subsist as rural farm workers or urban slum dwellers – risk losing the acknowledgment of their indigenous identity because they come to be seen as indistinguishable from other sectors of the nation's poor. At the other end of the spectrum, indigenous people who work as doctors, lawyers, politicians, economists, computer scientists, academics, engineers, or other professionals jeopardize their indigeneity by having become *too* successful. Having achieved a certain status, they are now culturally indistinguishable from other educated and accomplished sectors of the nation's dominant class. In both cases – indigenous elite on the one hand and indigenous poor on the other – the individuals in question tend to be characterized pejoratively as people who have "lost touch" with their culture. As such, they are judged more by the affinities they share with others in their *class*; yet the representation and recognition of indigeneity is usually tied to *culture*, often with unfortunate results, for not infrequently it has forced indigenous people, from Africa to the Amazon, to adopt paint and feathers, loincloths and beads, even when these items of material culture were anachronisms or ethnographically foreign (Conklin

1997; Sylvain 2002; Lee 2003). Given the authenticating power the Western gaze casts on the colonized, the subaltern has been compelled to conform to the fantasies of those from the developed world wielding cameras and video-recorders, if only to be *recognized* as indigenous by political leaders and public alike.

Recognition

The politics of representation are inextricably intertwined with the politics of recognition, as suggested in the previous section. The first step toward securing rights as an indigenous people *qua* "indigenous" is being recognized as such by the nation-state wherein the group resides. However, this is often a considerable challenge for two reasons. First, indigenous peoples have to protect resources and demand rights from the very nation-states that historically disenfranchised them in the first place. Second, in some parts of the world, particularly in Asia and Africa, official policy holds that either all citizens are equally indigenous or that no indigenous people exist as a separate category, which amounts to the same thing. Hodgson (2002: 1041) notes: "Demanding such recognition involves indigenous rights activists learning the relevant legal and bureaucratic categories and processes, lobbying at various levels and sites of government, appealing to the popular media, seeking international support, and molding their images, identities, and agendas accordingly, so that they may be properly recognized, remembered, and acknowledged."

One of the central paradoxes implicit in the politics of acknowledgment is not only that oral cultures increasingly are having to become literate to pursue their struggle for rights and recognition, and similarly fluid practices and flexible social boundaries often become fixed, but frequently indigenous peoples ironically are required to break tradition in order to keep tradition – for example, by divulging beliefs and practices to uninitiated audiences in the context of litigation over protection of sacred sites or culturally restricted knowledge, as has happened in Australia, North America, and Melanesia (Weiner 1997, 1999). Furthermore, at the very time indigenous peoples are required to press their claims in ever more sophisticated manners before agents of the nation-state, bureaucratic organizations, and the international community, they must do so in forms that perpetuate essentialist notions of culture. That is, paradoxically, at the very moment that legal and political exigencies are demanding of them profound cultural change, they are compelled, to be recognized as indigenous, to depict themselves as having remained frozen in time. Because bureaucratic and legalistic frames shape the terms by which indigenous identities are pub-licly recognized, too often indigenous peoples have been encouraged "to reify particular practices in order to define themselves as different from the wider society. Both the reifications and the demands which accompany them are products of legal systems" (Harris 1996: 1).

Because cultural distinctiveness is routinely deployed as a marker of indi-geneity, the global indigenist movement has perpetuated the salience of cul-ture over class in its struggles to have indigenous identities recognized. Yet Sylvain has written perceptively of the dilemma this poses for various San groups in southern Africa: "As criteria for recognition increasingly focus on 'cultural' features of indigeneity, to the exclusion of socioeconomic and pol-itical features, the majority of contemporary San find themselves compelled to choose between being excluded from the debate and asserting themselves in essentialist and primordialist vocabulary" (Sylvain 2002: 1074).

Resources

Beside the issues of representation and recognition discussed earlier, one of the most significant and recurring sources of grievance for which indigen-ous activists and their allies seek redress are the conflicts that arise between the assertion of indigenous rights and claims on natural resources. While there is of course both overlap and contradiction in the diverse manners that capitalist resource exploitation, indigenous subsistence, and nation-state interests interact as stakeholders, the relationship between indigenous peoples and economic resources is of continuing concern to the indigenous movement in at least four ways:

1. *Threats to indigenous lands and resources by extractive industries.* This is a problem so central to indigenous experience today and so ubi-quitous throughout the world that examples of it appear on every continent and almost daily in the media, ranging in everything from conflicts over oil exploitation in Siberia and Ecuador to commercial fishing in New Zealand and California.

2. *Dislocation of indigenous peoples from traditional use areas in the name of environmental conservation*: Whereas early on there seemed to be a natural alliance between the environmental and indigenous move-ments, in more recent years there have also been conflicts between environmental rights and indigenous rights. One area where this is evidenced is when increasing numbers of indigenous people become "conservation refugees," a term referring to people who have been

evicted from their lands in order to create conservation areas, game parks, and wilderness areas – a problem that is worldwide in its spread, with a number that is estimated at more than 14 million in Africa alone (Dowie 2006: 9; see Barume 2000 on the "Pygmy" case in the Democratic Republic of Congo).

3. *Linkages between biodiversity and linguistico-cultural diversity, with indigenous knowledge systems providing important keys to understanding and exploiting nature.* Here the problem related to the use of indigenous resources exemplifies overcoming what has come to be known as "bio-piracy," defined as "the appropriation of the knowledge and genetic resources of farming and indigenous communities by individuals or institutions seeking exclusive monopoly control (usually patents or plant breeders' rights) over these resources and knowledge" (Bhatt 2004: 12). Numerous cases illustrate how traditional ethnobotanical knowledge was relied on as a guide in the prospecting of wild plant resources that subsequently were extracted and developed for world markets, yet without the prior permission or compensation of the relevant indigenous community that supplied the critical knowledge in the first place (e.g., Geingos and Ngakaeaja 2002).

4. *Correlation between indigenous peoples and poverty indicators in most of the world.* As various chapters in this book make clear, indigenous people throughout the world overwhelmingly tend to be among the poorest of the poor, as indicated by standard economic measures of health, education, and welfare. Although the situation may be changing in certain countries, especially in Asia, and despite the media attention that has been given to indigenous struggles in recent years, the correlation between indigenous peoples and poverty still characterizes the situation in virtually every country where there exist data.

Rights

The fourth and final issue that universally is of concern to indigenous movements and activists is the whole matter of rights. It is a topic of such centrality that it has already been mentioned in previous sections, but nonetheless here merits brief discussion on its own. It is of course explicit in rights to land and resources, but also encompasses areas of concern beyond these material domains. As Hodgson notes, "indigenous demands for rights ... extend beyond their territorial resources. These demands hinge on the right to self determination and include the right to determine their own

development and to control and protect their cultural knowledge and performances, material remains, languages, indigenous knowledge, and bio-
genetic material" (Hodgson 2002:1041).

There is, however, a salient difference between the way rights are commonly articulated by contemporary states and the notion of rights that typically are of concern to indigenous groups. The former, based largely on the
Western philosophical tradition of social contract theory as initially formulated by Hobbes, Locke, and Rousseau, imagine rights in terms of civil and
political rights, a universal feature of individuals, based on abstract moral
principles. By contrast, indigenous peoples stress the concept of collective
and cultural rights; individuals have rights by token of their membership
in certain groups. Indeed, it is chiefly through their belonging to, and participation in, the locally anchored moral universes defined by these groups
that individuals achieve their social being and essential personhood. In
a social sense, it is what makes them human in the first place (Levi and
Dean 2003: 9–18).

Reflecting this idea of rights as it obtains in Africa, Parker Shipton
observes: "Individuals do not have rights independently of kin groups or
other enduring entities. One could phrase it this way: rights are relative
and relatives have rights. The enduring social entities may be constituted
according to principles other than kinship, such as age grading, territory
or voluntary association" (Shipton 2003: 66). The concept of individual
rights and group rights are different, but they are not incompatible with
each other. In practice, universal human rights predicated on the autonomy of the individual and exemplified in the UN Universal Declaration
of Human Rights can and do accommodate the rights of individuals who
belong to special groups. From this perspective, indigenous rights are like
women's rights or children's rights – that is, the rights of certain categories
of often vulnerable people who by token of their inclusion in this or that
group merit special consideration, but can still fit comfortably under the
rubric of universal human rights. In fact, difference itself may be thought
of as a universal right. "If there is universal positive human right, perhaps it
contains an irony. The American Anthropological Association's Task Force
on Human Rights has recently agreed on a seemingly paradoxical idea: a
universal human right to *difference*" (Shipton 2003: 63).

This idea of the right to be different is largely what indigenous rights are
all about. The primary collective right indigenous groups are interested in
protecting is their right as *peoples*. Yet it is this very conception of rights that
historically has made modern nation-states nervous. Given that in international law, the first right of any *people* is their right to self-determination,

many states historically have been reticent to formally recognize even the existence of an indigenous people, other than the national majority, living within their borders, for in doing so it could ipso facto lead these people to legally claim rights distinct from those of other citizens, according to international covenants. Most importantly, many states fear that acknowledging the rights of indigenous peoples, chief among these being the right to self-determination, creates a dangerous scenario of "nations within nations," leading to balkanization, if not outright secession. In practice, most indigenous peoples seek self-determination in terms of constitutional or limited autonomy rather than wholesale independence from their countries – they are not, by and large, wanting their own seats as separate states in the General Assembly of the United Nations.

Recognizing the need to protect collective rights, and believing that the UN Universal Declaration of Human Rights irredeemably placed the autonomous individual at the center of its philosophical and political concepts and therefore allegedly smacked of Eurocentric bias, African countries developed their own legal instrument, the African Charter on Human and *Peoples'* Rights (emphasis added). Given the inclusion of the word "peoples" in the title, one might have thought that Africa was leading the way in acknowledging the rights of indigenous peoples. Unfortunately, this is not the case. With rare exception, indigenous peoples throughout the continent have struggled for their recognition and rights. As discussed earlier, in part this has to do with the fact that once the European colonial powers departed, it was felt that all Africans were equally indigenous. The argument that some groups were more indigenous than others, so it was held, would only lead to invidious comparisons and conflict in these newly independent states that were already struggling to forge common national identities of their many ethnic groups. It would, in essence, represent a tacit recrudescence of tribalism. Or so runs the argument. Even though the African nations have all signed the UN Declaration on the Rights of Indigenous Peoples, indigenous rights activists declare that generally it is having few practical consequences in Africa.

SUMMARY AND CONCLUSIONS

The signing of the Declaration on the Rights of Indigenous Peoples was a landmark event on a global scale and critical first step more than twenty years in the making. Of greater significance than ratification, however, is the *enforcement* of these declarations, conventions, and treaties – national as well as international – protecting the rights of indigenous peoples.

Moving, then, from theory to practice, one must first determine *who* is indigenous and *what* defines them as such. A related and not inconsequential consideration, in view of the issues at stake, is the question of motive: *Who is doing the defining* and *for what reasons?* On cursory appraisal, a "cut and dry," straightforward, general definition based on abstract principles would seemingly be desirable, but as soon as one begins to apply a "one size fits all" definition cross-culturally, it becomes apparent that whatever might be gained theoretically in terms of its supposedly universal applicability would, on the other hand, be lost the more one is familiar with the particular history, politics, ethnic relations, economics, and ethnography of individual cases. Indigenous identity is shifting, complex, processual, conjunctural, and ultimately relative to context. Realizing this all too well, given the diversity of indigenous peoples and the multiplicity of definitions, the UN Declaration on the Rights of Indigenous Peoples has purposely *not* defined the term "indigenous" in an unequivocal way. Any serious definition of indigeneity therefore cannot be scientifically generalized or stipulated legalistically in advance, although in practice, definitions of indigenous identity tend to cohere around four central features: (1) *prior occupancy*, (2) *cultural distinctiveness*, (3) *self-identification*, and (4) *nondominance*. Ultimately, however, indigenous identity is radically contingent.

The absence of a universal definition of "indigenous peoples" is not a sign of sloppy thinking or lack of methodological rigor. On the contrary, it shows that "indigenous peoples" instantiate what is formally known as a *polythetic* category. Polythetic classification, deployed in a range of human and natural sciences, defines a group in a way such that no single trait or set of traits possessed by an individual is necessary and sufficient to define it as belonging to the group. That is, no trait is possessed by all of the members of the group, but each trait is shared by many members. Consequently, there is a "family resemblance" among them. While it may seem that one could never operationalize such a seemingly vague definition and use it in a pragmatic fashion, in actuality we do it all the time, and on a routine basis. In contradistinction to "semantic formalism," it is what forms the basis of "ordinary language philosophy" – that is, the philosophy of how it is we actually use and understand language in practice rather than in terms of a formal theory of meaning. For example, consider – as did Ludwig Wittgenstein – what it is that all "games" have in common. There are "card games," "ball games," "board games," and many other types of games; not even "rule-guidedness" or the distinction between "winners and losers" defines all games: Sometimes we "make up the rules as we go along" or "play just for fun." Nevertheless, we understand and use the word "game" all the time, notwithstanding the lack of an analytically precise, universally applicable definition. The definition of "indigenous peoples," as we have argued here, is of the same order.

A major point of this chapter has been that diverse peoples throughout the world are self-consciously claiming an indigenous identity, often for the first time in history. That is, "aboriginal," minority peoples who in other contexts may identify as Kumeyaay, Hopi, Shavante, Dayak, Batwa, Tarahumara, Inuit, Taureg, Dogrib, Khanty, Sami, Yolgnu, and so on, or any other of more than 4,000 so-called tribes scattered across the globe are, individually and together, doing something radically innovative. They are *becoming* indigenous.

Liberating the term "indigenous" from its previous colonial entanglements with words like "primitive" and "savage," they have instead realized the emancipatory potential of a label that allows them to shift the parameters of their heretofore local identities in the direction of translocal arenas of power and attach themselves to a global social movement that, ironically, still makes sense to them "culturally." Even though *heterogeneity* seems to be the most common defining trait of indigeneity today, given the diverse political, economic, social, and religious make-up of the peoples identifying as "indigenous," nevertheless one cannot help but notice, if one attends a gathering of indigenous peoples from around the world, that the indigenous representatives there intuitively recognize the "family resemblance" among those who have gathered, perspicaciously acknowledging the indigeneity of others belonging to this polythetic group (notwithstanding the absence of formal guidelines to consult).

Data showing the heterogeneity of indigeneity indicate the vitality and organic complementarity among diverse segments of the twenty-first century's first truly multicultural, global, social movement of empowerment, justice, and reform for the world's most disadvantaged people. The diversity within the movement should not be taken as a sign of either political weakness or deployed as an analytic tool to be used in divide-and-conquer tactics. Indigenous peoples today are rich and poor, educated and illiterate, rural and urban, socialist and capitalist. Some live in their homelands, others in diasporas; some are "traditional," others are "modern." They number among their ranks Christians, Moslems, and animists. They live in jungles, mountains, and deserts, and are to be found on every continent save Antarctica.

Notwithstanding this palpable diversity, certain structural and cultural configurations recur with noticeable frequency. Many indigenous peoples are marginalized in remote and often desolate corners of their countries; are politically oppressed or unrepresented; have mobile settlement patterns, subsistence technologies, and traditional knowledge systems finely calibrated to local environments; manifest worldviews predicated on sharing, reciprocity, and interconnections between cultural, natural, and supernatural dimensions of reality; regard land – as well as certain plants and animals – as sacred; are situated in regions rich in natural resources inviting expropriation by governments and/or capitalist exploitation; and suffer disproportionately from poor health, lack of education, potable water, alcoholism, disease, and cognate social and natural ills. Almost without exception they are among the poorest and most disenfranchised people in the states where they reside.

A number of distinct indigenous peoples throughout the world have been discussed in this chapter and each case is different. Nevertheless, at the risk overgeneralization, we suggest that certain social features and risk patterns emerge cross-culturally through the cases. Some indigenous peoples historically have been at greater risk and more susceptible to impoverishment, marginalization, exploitation, disenfranchisement, and discrimination than others, both by neighboring peoples and development agendas. Our research suggests that on every continent, indigenous societies with settlement patterns that are *mobile* (nomadic, seminomadic, transhumant, semisedentary, etc.) rather than permanent, and *dispersed* rather than nucleated tend be at greater risk.

These settlement patterns correlate with traditional subsistence methods and modes of production. *Foragers* (hunters, gatherers, and fishers) perhaps tend to be most at risk of unsuccessfully asserting their claims to traditional use areas and, once dislodged from their territories, are most likely to become landless squatters in their own homeland. *Shifting cultivators* (peoples practicing swidden or slash-and-burn agriculture) and *nonsedentary pastoralists* (transhumant as well as fully nomadic or migratory) also experience difficulties asserting rights to their territories, although perhaps less so than foragers. Indigenous peoples and peasants living at higher population densities and practicing intensive agricultural regimes appear less likely to be pushed off their lands without major uprisings and political turmoil.

This scale of difference in terms of settlement and modes of production overlaps somewhat, although by no means completely, with a cognate scale of increasing sociopolitical complexity, division of labor, hierarchy, and competitiveness. In general, the more averse to confrontation, the more egalitarian, the more dependent on relations of reciprocity and sharing, the more inclined to deploy forms of passive resistance, the more likely the group will be unsuccessful in sustaining viable negotiations to secure their rights and resources with development agencies, nation-states, and other dominant actors, including other local peoples, both "indigenous" and otherwise. By contrast, the more indigenous peoples have traditions based on social hierarchy, clear lines of authority or leadership, age grades, confrontational forms of resistance, military preparedness, trade or market skills, and competition, the more likely they will be successful in structuring efforts at self-determination and mounting sustained dialogue and viable strategies to retain control over their economic, political, and cultural resources. While the described configurations suggest themselves to us based on our familiarity with the ethnological record and development literature, it was further corroborated by our field research in South and East Africa in March 2009, with special reference to the San, Hadzabe, Datoga (Barabaig), Maasai, and Iraqw.

Another major pattern that emerges from the research is the dichotomy between the identification and subsequent translocal organization of indigenous peoples in what we have called "settler societies," in the Americas, Australia, and New Zealand, on the one hand, and indigenous peoples in Africa and Asia, on the other. Whereas in the Americas, Australia, and New Zealand, the identification of indigenous peoples – sometimes denominated as "First Peoples" – is relatively clear-cut, the postcolonial contexts of Africa and Asia have made the struggle for rights and recognition of indigenous peoples far more contentious. The history and organization of the indigenous movement in Africa and the Americas also differs. In the Americas, it began in the 1970s as a grassroots movement that was built from the bottom up; in Africa, conversely, it was sparked in the 1990s by indigenous representatives meeting in New York and Geneva, and thus, returning to Africa, was built by indigenous elites from the top down.

The final pattern to emerge from the analysis of the indigenous movement – and here we build directly on the insights of Dorothy Hodgson (2002) – is that scholarship on indigenous activism tends to be concerned with for four key issues and the intersections among them: representation, recognition, resources, and rights. These "Four Rs," as we have called them, get played out in distinctive ways in different parts of the world, although there are also overarching commonalities irrespective of ethnographic particularities. *Representation* is concerned with the strategies and politics of display, the arts of stagecraft, the tactical performance of cultural identities, and the manner these intersect with debates on authenticity. Much is at stake in the representation of indigenous peoples, chiefly whether they will be *recognized* as such, and thereby acknowledged, most importantly by the states where they reside. Put simply, to be recognized as indigenous, many such peoples represent themselves, and are represented by others, in conformity with stereotyped images of the "pristine native," thereby deploying a political tactic known in postcolonial theory as "strategic essentialism" that assists in achieving group goals.

The issue of *resources* becomes part of indigenous concerns in at least four ways: extractive industries that jeopardize indigenous lands; the dislocation of indigenous peoples in the name of wildlife conservation; the biopiracy that taps into the nexus between the environment and traditional knowledge systems; and the correlation between indigenous peoples and poverty. Finally, the topic of indigenous *rights* involves not only control over territorial resources, as mentioned earlier, but extends beyond them to nonmaterial domains as well, such as cultural performances, languages, art, symbols, and esoteric knowledge, in addition to exercising rights over their own biological material, such as DNA and burial remains. However, all of these rights are derivative of self-determination that, according to international law, is the preeminent right of any *people*.

The late anthropologist, David Maybury-Lewis, in the course of his more than fifty years as a scholar and advocate of indigenous societies, said once that our question is not *if* we are going to have development in the indigenous world, but *how*. Although well aware of the downfalls indigenous people have gone through as a result of poorly thought-out development or what he termed "developmentalism," he remained a believer in the promise of improving human welfare through sound thinking and action. With him, we believe that we must understand indigenous societies on their own terms, engage them, and ultimately join with them to plan and make common cause. We too remain convinced that an anthropological approach would help us better understand the particularities that create separate cultural identities and ultimately lead us toward the portal where we might glimpse, however briefly, the more fundamental things that bind all humans together.

ACKNOWLEDGMENTS

We wish to acknowledge the opportunity to conduct nearly a month of field research in South Africa, Kenya, and Tanzania in March 2009 that arose in conjunction with this project. We thank, especially, Harry Patrinos and Gillette Hall for their important feedback and collegial support throughout the project and for initiating this critical investigation. We wish to thank Lauren Blacik, research assistant for this project at Carleton College; Gregory A. Finnegan, Head of Reference at Harvard's Tozzer Library; the Indigenous Peoples of Africa Coordinating Committee (IPACC) Director, Nigel Crawhall; the IPACC office personnel, particularly Mala Marchealase and Natalie Kyriacou; Belinda Kruiper, for her support in helping us visit the ≠Khomani San leaders in the southern Kalahari; Anetta Bok, the women's representative from South Africa to IPACC; Dawid Kruiper, Petrus Vaalbooi, and /Una Rooi – chief ≠Khomani elders; Kanyinke Sena, Regional Representative from East Africa to IPACC; Naftali Kitandu, Hadzabe activist and leader; Hadzabe headmen Thomas Yakobo and Jack Bagosh; Meshuko Ole Mapu, Maasai leader, elder, and holy man; Edward Porokawa, Coordinator of Pastoralists and Indigenous Non-Governmental Organizations, in Arusha, Tanzania; Rafique Keshavjee, the Head of Academic Planning at the Faculty of Arts and Sciences at Aga Khan University East Africa; Achola Okeyo, social anthropologist in Nairobi; Matthew Davies and Justin Willis of the British Institute in East Africa; Joseph and Janice Day, Berra Tawahongva, and Shereen Susungkew, of the Hopi nation; and the many indigenous people in North, Central, and South America who over the years have welcomed the authors into their lands, villages, and homes.

References

Anderson, Gary and Alan Woolworth, eds. (1988). *Through Dakota Eyes: Narrative Accounts of the Minnesota Indian War of 1862.* St. Paul: Minnesota Historical Society Press.

Baguio Declaration (2004). Accessed April 30, 2009 at http://www.ikap-mmsea.org/document%20new/BAGUIO%20DECLARATION.pdf

Bailey, Kenneth D. (1973). "Constructing Monothetic and Polythetic Typologies by the Heuristic Method," *The Sociological Quarterly*, V. 14, No. 3: 291–308.

Balzer, Marjorie Mandelstam (2003). "'Hot and Cold' Interethnic Relations in Siberia." In Dean, Bartholomew and Jerome M. Levi, eds. *At the Risk of Being Heard: Identity, Indigenous Rights, and Postcolonial Societies.* Ann Arbor: The University of Michigan Press.

Barume, Albert Kwokwo (2000). *Heading Towards Extinction? Indigenous Rights in Africa: The Case of the Twa of the Kahuzi-Biega national Park, Democratic Republic of Congo.* Copenhagen: IWGIA Document No. 101.

Bell, D. (2001). "Respecting the Land: Religion, Reconciliation, and Romance-An Australian Story." In John A. Grim, ed. *Indigenous Traditions and Ecology.* Cambridge, MA: Harvard University Press.

Béteille, André (1998). "The Idea of Indigenous Peoples," *Current Anthropology*, V. 39, No. 2: 187–191.

Bhatt, Abhinav (2004). "'Bio-Piracy': Some Important Cases," *Singapore Law Gazette* (August): 12–15. Accesed May 1, 2009 at http://74.125.95.132/search?q= cache:q266dtiXxV8J:www.lawgazette.com.sg/2004–8/feature1.pdf+Bhatt+2004+ bio-piracy&cd=1&hl=en&ct=clnk&gl=us&client=firefox-a

Blu, Karen I. (2001). *The Lumbee Problem: The Making of an American Indian People*, 2nd ed. Lincoln: Nebraska University Press.

Briones, Claudia (2007). "'Our Struggle Has Just Begun': Experiences of Belonging and Mapuche Formations of Self." In Starn, Orin and Marisol de la Cadena, eds. *Indigenous Experience Today*. Oxford and New York: Berg.

Castañeda, Quetzil E. (2004). "'We Are Not Indigenous!' An Introduction to the Maya Identity of Yucatan," *Journal of Latin American Anthropology*, V. 9, No. 1: 36–63.

Central Intelligence Agency (2009). *Central Intelligence Agency Factbook: Bolivia*. Accessed May 1, 2009 at https://www.cia.gov/library/publications/the-world-factbook/geos/bl.html

Chennells, Roger (2007). "San Hoodia Case." A Report for GenBenefit, available at: www.uclan.ac.uk/genbenefit

Clifford, James (1988). *The Predicament of Culture: Twentieth Ethnography, Literature, and Art*. Cambridge, MA: Harvard University Press.

(2007). In Orin Starn and Marisol de la Cadena, eds. *Indigenous Experience Today*. Oxford and New York: Berg.

Cobo, José Martinez (1986). "The Study of the Problem of Discrimination against Indigenous Populations." Vols. 1–5. United Nations Document E/CN.4/Sub.2/1986/7. New York: United Nations.

Cohen, Ronald (1978). "Ethnicity: Problem and Focus in Anthropology," *Annual Review of Anthropology*, V. 7: 379–403.

Colloredo-Mansfeld (1999). *The Native Leisure Class: Consumption and Cultural Creativity in the Andes*. Chicago: University of Chicago Press.

Conklin, Beth (1997). "Body Paint, Feathers, and VCRs: Aesthetics and Authenticity in Amazonian Activism," *American Ethnologist*, V. 24, No. 4: 711–737.

Coyne, Amanda (2008). "Aboriginals Have a Good Neighbor at Cold Lake," *The Lamp: An Exxon- Mobil Publication*, No. 4: 3–8.

Dean, Bartholomew and Jerome M. Levi, eds. (2003). *At the Risk of Being Heard: Identity, Indigenous Rights, and Postcolonial Societies*. Ann Arbor: The University of Michigan Press.

Dowie, Mark (2006). "Conservation Refugees: When Protecting Nature Means Kicking People Out," *Seedling*: 6–12.

Fenelon, James V. and Thomas D. Hall (2008). "Revitalization and Indigenous Resistance to Globalization and Neoliberalism," *American Behavioral Scientist*, V. 51, No. 12: 1867–1901.

Freeman, Mark [writer, director, producer] (1997). "Weavers of the World", 24-minute documentary on the Otavalo of Ecuador. Accessed May 1, 2009 at http://www-rohan.sdsu.edu/~mfreeman/films.php?id=9

Friedl, Ernestine (1975). *Women and Men: An Anthropologist's View*. New York: Holt, Rinhart, and Winston.

Friedman, Jonathan (2008). "Indigeneity: Anthropological Notes on a [sic] Historical Variable." In Henry Minde, ed. *Indigenous Peoples: Self-determination, Knowledge, Indigeneity*. Delft: Eburon Academic Publishers.

Geingos, Victoria and Mnathambo Ngakaeaja (2002). "Traditional Knowledge of the San of Southern Africa: Hoodia Gordonii," mimeo 17 pages, presented at Second South-South Biopiracy Summit: "Biopiracy – Ten Years Post Rio," August 22–23, Johannesburg, South Africa,

Harris, La Donna and Jacqueline Wasilewski (2004). "Indigeneity, an Alternative Worldveiw: Four R's (Relationship, Responsibility, Reciprocity, Redistribution) vs. Two P's (Power and Profit). Sharing the Journey Towards conscious Evolution," *Systems Research and Behavioral Science*, V. 21: 1–15.

Harris, Olivia (1996). "Introduction: Inside and Outside the Law." In O. Harris, ed. *Inside and Outside the Law: Anthropological Studies of Authority and Ambiguity.* London: Routledge.

Harvard Project on American Indian Economic Development et al. (2008). *The State of the Native Nations: Conditions Under U.S. Policies of Self-Determination.* New York and Oxford: Oxford University Press.

Harvey, Neil (1998). *The Chiapas Rebellion: The Struggle for Land and Democracy.* Durham, NC: Duke University Press.

Hodgson, Dorothy L. (2002). "Introduction: Comparative Perspectives on the Indigenous Rights Movement in Africa and the Americas," *American Anthropologist*, V. 104, No. 4: 1037–1049.

Igoe, Jim (2006). "Becoming Indigenous Peoples: Difference, Inequality, and the Globalization of East African Identity Politics," *African Affairs*, V. 105, No. 420: 399–420.

Indigenous Peoples of Africa Co-Ordinating Committee (IPACC) (2007). "Briefing Note on the Threat to the Hadzabe People of the Yaida Valley, Karatu District, United Republic of Tanzania," mimeo, Capetown, South Africa, IPACC.

Jackson, Jean (1991). "Being and Becoming an Indian in Vaupés." In Greg Urban and Joel Sherzer, eds. *Nation-States and Indians in Latin America.* Austin: University of Texas Press.

Kenrick, Justin and Jerome Lewis (2004). "Indigenous Peoples' Rights and the Politics of the Term 'Indigenous,'" *Anthropology Today*, V. 20, No. 2 (April): 4–9.

Kilburn, Michael (1996). "Glossary of Key Terms in the Work of Gayatri Chakravorty Spivak." Accessed April 30, 2009 at http://www.english.emory.edu/Bahri/Glossary. html

Kingsbury, Benedict (1998). "'Indigenous Peoples' in International Law: A Constructivist Approach to the Asian Controversy," *The American Journal of International Law*, V. 92, No. 3 (July): 414–457.

Klima, George J. (1985). *The Barabaig: East African Cattle Herders*, 2nd ed. Long Grove, Illinois: Waveland Press.

Kuper, Adam (2003). "The Return of the Native," *Current Anthropology*, V. 44 (June), No 3: 389–395.

Lambert, Valerie (2007). "Choctaw Tribal Sovereignty at the Turn of the 21st Century." In Orin Starn and Marisol de la Cadena, eds. *Indigenous Experience Today.* Oxford and New York: Berg.

Latin American Herald Tribune (2009). "Ecuador Indians Want Oil-Spill Emergency Declared," April 29. Accessed April 29, 2009 at http://www.laht.com/article.asp? CategoryId=14089&ArticleId=328935

Le Roux, Willemien and Alison White, eds. (2004). *Voices of the San.* Cape Town, South Africa: Kwela Books.

Lee, Richard B. (2003). "Indigenous Rights and the Politics of Identity in Post-Apartheid Southern Africa." In Bartholomew Dean and Jerome M. Levi, eds. *At the Risk of Being Heard: Identity, Indigenous Rights, and Postcolonial States*. Ann Arbor: The University of Michigan Press.

Levi, Jerome M. (1992). "Review – Delfina Cuero: Her Autobiography, an Account of Her Last Years, and Her Ethnobotanic Contribution, by Florence Connolly Shipek," *American Indian Culture and Research Journal*, V. 16, No. 4.

  (1999). "Hidden Transcripts Among the Rarámuri: Culture, Resistance, and Interethnic Relations in Northern Mexico," *American Ethnologist*, V. 26, No. 1: 90–113.

  (2002). "A New Dawn or a Cycle Restored? Regional Dynamics and Cultural Politics in Indigenous Mexico, 1978–2001." In David Maybury-Lewis, ed. *The Politics of Ethnicity: Indigenous Peoples in Latin American States*. Cambridge, MA and London: Harvard University Press.

  (2007). "Symbols." In William Darity, ed. *International Encyclopedia of the Social Sciences*. V. 8: 249–253. New York: MacMillan.

Levi, Jerome M. and Bartholomew Dean. (2003). "Introduction." In Bartholomew Dean and Jerome M. Levi, eds. *At the Risk of Being Heard: Identity, Indigenous Rights, and Postcolonial States*. Ann Arbor: University of Michigan Press.

Mackay, Fergus (2007). "World Bank, International Finance Corporation and Indigenous Peoples in Asia." In *Indigenous Peoples and the Human Rights-Based Approach to Development: Engaging in Dialogue*. Bangkok: UNDP Regional Center in Bangkok.

Madsen, Andrew (2000). "The Hadzabe of Tanzania: Land and Human Rights for a Hunter-Gatherer Community." Copenhagen: IWIGIA Document No. 98.

Marlowe, Frank (2002). "Why the Hadza Are Still Hunter-Gatherers." In S. Kent, ed. *Ethnicity, Hunter-Gatherers, and the "Other."* Washington, DC: Smithsonian Institution Press.

Maybury-Lewis, Biorn (1994). *The Politics of the Possible: The Growth and Political Development of the Brazilian Rural Workers' Trade Union Movement, 1964–1985*. Philadelphia: Temple University Press.

Maybury-Lewis, David (1991). "Becoming Indian in Lowland South America." In Greg Urban and Joel Sherzer, eds. *Nation-States and Indians in Latin America*. Austin: University of Texas Press.

  (2002). *Indigenous Peoples, Ethnic Groups, and the State*, 2nd ed. Boston and London: Allyn and Bacon.

McIntosh, Ian S. (2003). "Reconciling Personal and Impersonal Worlds: Aboriginal Struggles for Self-Determination." In Bartholomew Dean and Jerome M. Levi, eds. *At the Risk of Being Heard: Identity, Indigenous Rights, and Postcolonial Societies*. Ann Arbor: The University of Michigan Press.

Meisch, Lynn A. (2002). *Andean Entrepreneurs: Otavalo Merchants and Musicians in the Global Arena*. Austin: University of Texas Press.

Merlan, Francesca (2007). "Indigeneity as Relational Identity: The Construction of Australian Land Rights." In Orin Starn and Marisol de la Cadena, eds. *Indigenous Experience Today*. Oxford and New York: Berg.

  (2009). "Indigeneity: Global and Local." *Current Anthropology*, V. 50, No. 3: 303–333.

Nagel, Joane (1996). *American Indian Ethnic Renewal: Red Power and the Resurgence of Indian identity and Culture*. New York: Oxford University Press.

Nash, June C. (2001). *Mayan Visions: The Quest for Autonomy in an Age of Globalization*. London and New York: Routledge.

Needham, Rodney (1975). "Polythetic Classification: Convergence and Consequences." *Man*, V. 10: 349–369.

Nepal Federation of Indigenous Nationalities (NEFIN) (2008). "Categorization." Accessed April 2009 at http://www.nefin.org.np/indigenous-nationalities/categorization

Niezen, Ronald (2003). *The Origins of Indigenism: Human Rights and the Politics of Identity*. Berkeley: University of California Press.

(2005). "Digital Identity: The Construction of Virtual Selfhood in the Indigenous Peoples' Movement." *Comparative Studies in Society and History*, V. 45, No. 2: 532–551.

Nyamnjoh (2007). "'Ever Diminishing Circles': The Paradoxes of Belonging in Botswana." In Starn, Orin and Marisol de la Cadena, eds. *Indigenous Experience Today*. Oxford and New York: Berg.

Parry, John H. (1971). *Trade and Dominion: The European Overseas Empires in the 18th Century*. London: Wiedenfeld and Nicholson.

(1981). *The Age of Reconnaissance*. Berkeley: University of California Press.

Pinkowski, M. and M. Asch (2004). "Anthropology and Indigenous Rights in Canada and the United States: Implications in Steward's Theoretical Project." In A. Barnard, ed. *Hunter Gatherers in History, Archaeology, Anthropology*. Oxford: Berg.

Povinelli, E. A. (1998). "The State of Shame: Australian Multi-Culturalism and the Crisis of Indigenous Citizenship," *Critical Inquiry* (Winter): 575–610.

Quine, W. V. (1987). *Quiddities: An Intermittently Philosophical Dictionary*. Cambridge, MA: Belknap Press of Harvard University Press.

Ramirez, Renya K. (2007). *Native Hubs: Culture, Community, and Belonging in Silicon Valley and Beyond*. Durham, NC: Duke University Press.

Ramos, Alcida (2003). "'Comments' on Kuper's 'Return of the Native,'" *Current Anthropology,*, V. 44, No. 3: 397–398.

Rosaldo, Renato. (1989). *Culture & Truth: The Remaking of Social Analysis*. Boston: Beacon Press.

Rus, Jan (1994). "'Comunidad Revolucionaria Institucional': The Subversion of Native Government in Highland Chiapas, 1936–1968." In Gilbert Joseph and Daniel Nugent, eds. *Everyday Form of State Formation: Revolution and the Negotiation of Rule in Modern Mexico*. Durham, NC: Duke University Press.

Saugestad, Sidsel (2001). *The Inconvenient Indigenous: Remote Area Development in Botswana, Donor Assistance, and the First People of the Kalahari*. Uppsala: The Nordic Africa Institute.

(2008). "Beyond the 'Columbus Context': New Challenges as the Indigenous Discourse is Applied to Africa." In Henry Minde, ed. *Indigenous Peoples: Self-Determination, Knowledge, Indigeneity*. Delft: Eburon Academic Publishers.

Scott, James C. (1998). *Seeing Like a State: How Certain Schemes to Improve the Human Condition Have Failed*. New Haven, CT: Yale University Press.

Sena, Kanyinke (n.d.). "Report of IPACC's Mission to Tanzania to Visit the Hadzabe," mimeo, Cape Town, South Africa, Indigenous Peoples of Africa Coordinating Committee.

Shipek, Florence C. [as told to] (1968). *The Autobiography of Delfina Cuero – A Diegueno Indian*. Los Angeles, CA: Dawson's Book Shop.

Shipton, Parker (2003). "Legalism and Loyalism: European, African and Human 'Rights.'" In Dean, Bartholomew and Jerome M. Levi, eds. *At the Risk of Being Heard: Identity, Indigenous Rights, and Postcolonial Societies*. Ann Arbor: The University of Michigan Press.

South African San Institute (SASI) (2002). *Annual Report (January-December)*. Uppington: South African San Institute.

  (2008). *The Khomani-San, from Footnotes to Footprints; the Story of the Land Claim of the Khomani-San*. Uppington: South African San Institute.

Starn, Orin and Marisol de la Cadena, eds. (2007). *Indigenous Experience Today*. Oxford and New York: Berg.

Stephen, Lynn (2003). "Indigenous Autonomy in Mexico." In Bartholomew Dean and Jerome M. Levi, eds. *At the Risk of Being Heard: Identity, Indigenous Rights, and Postcolonial Societies*. Ann Arbor: The University of Michigan Press.

Stull, Donald (1990). "Reservation Economic Development in the Era of Self-Determination." *American Anthropologist*, V. 92, No. 1: 206–11.

Survival International (2009). "Bushman." Accessed May 2, 2009 at http://www.survival-international.org/tribes/bushmen

Sylvain, Renée (2002). "Land, Water, and Truth: San Identity and Global Indigenism," *American Anthropologist*, V. 1, No. 4: 1074–1085.

  (2005). "Disorderly Development: Globalization and the Idea of Culture in the Kalahari," *American Ethnologist*, V. 32, No. 3: 354–370.

Thompson, Ginger (2003). "Twee Rivieren Journal; Bushmen Squeeze Money From a Humble Cactus," New York *Times* (April 1). Accessed May 1, 2009 at http://www.nytimes.com/2003/04/01/world/twee-rivieren-journal-bushmen-squeeze-money-from-a-humble-cactus.html

Trouillot, Michel-Rolph (1991). "Anthropology and the Savage Slot. The Poetics and Politics of Otherness." In Richard Fox, ed. *Recapturing Anthropology. Working in the Present*. Santa Fe, NM: School of American Research Press.

Tsing, Anna (2007). "Indigenous Voice." In Orin Starn and Marisol de la Cadena, eds. *Indigenous Experience Today*. Oxford and New York: Berg.

Tuhiwai Smith, Linda (2007). "The Native and the Neo-Liberal Down Under: Neoliberalism and 'Endangered Authenticities.'" In Starn, Orin and Marisol de la Cadena, eds. *Indigenous Experience Today*. Oxford and New York: Berg.

Turner, V. (1967). *The Forest of Symbols: Aspects of Ndembu Ritual*. Ithaca, NY: Cornell University Press.

Turner, Victor (1995). *The Ritual Process: Structure and Anti-Structure* (first published in 1969). Piscataway, NJ: Aldine Transaction.

Warren, Kay B. and Jean E. Jackson, eds. (2002). *Indigenous Movements, Self-Representation and the State in Latin America*. Austin: University of Texas Press.

Weiner, James (1997). "Televisualist Anthropology: Representations, Aesthetics, Politics," *Current Anthropology*, V. 38, No. 2: 197–235.

  (1999). "Heritage and Tradition in the Hindmarsh Bridge Affair," *Journal of the Royal Anthropological Institute*, V. 5, No. 21: 193–210.

Wessendorf, Kathrin (2008). *The Indigenous World 2008.* Copenhagen: International Working Group for Indigenous Affairs [IWGIA].

Wolf, Eric R. (1968). *Peasant Wars of the Twentieth Century.* New York: Harper and Row.

Wynberg, Rachel (2005). "Rhetoric, Realism, and Benefit-Sharing: Use of Traditional Knowledge of Hoodia Species in the Development of an Appetite Suppressant," *Journal of World Intellectual Property,* V. 7, No, 6: 851–876.

4

Indigenous Peoples in Central Africa

The Case of the Pygmies

Quentin Wodon, Prospere Backiny-Yetna,
and Arbi Ben-Achour

INTRODUCTION

Four main criteria are usually used to define indigenous peoples: (1) they
are descendants of the original populations inhabiting their lands at the
time of conquest, and identified as such; (2) they speak a distinct native language and typically aspire to remain distinct culturally, geographically, and
institutionally rather than assimilate; (3) they have affinity and attachment
to their land; and (4) they tend to maintain distinct social, economic, and
political institutions within their territories (Martinez-Cobo, 1986, quoted
by Patrinos et al., 2007). These criteria emerge primarily from the body of
work examining indigenous peoples issues in Latin America.

In Africa, however, it is less easy to identify indigenous peoples than in
other regions such as Latin America because many ethnic groups could be
considered as belonging to native populations. Yet if there is one group that
does stand out as indigenous even according to those with vastly differ-
ing views on what exactly constitutes indigenous in the context of Africa,
it is the Pygmies. Using a range of different data sources, and based on
detailed country case studies by Backiny-Yetna and Wodon (2011a, 2011b)
and Ben-Achour et al. (2011), this chapter provides an analysis of the standards of living of the Pygmies living in Central Africa. As documented
among others in African Commission (2006), the Pygmies are found in
many different Central and Southern African countries (Angola, Botswana,
Burundi, Cameroon, Central African Republic [CAR], Gabon, Democratic
Republic of Congo [DRC], Namibia, Republic of Congo, Rwanda, Uganda,
and Zambia), but in this chapter, on the basis of data availability, we focus
on three countries: CAR, DRC, and Gabon.

The Pygmies are considered to be among the oldest inhabitants in Central
Africa, speaking different languages from the Bantu, the main ethnic group

of the region, especially in the DRC. Their seminomadic lifestyle has persisted largely unchanged for thousands of years, living from hunting, fishing, and gathering wild fruits and nuts. In the last two or three decades, however, under the influence of multiple factors, these populations have gone through a process of semi-sedentarization. More precisely, traditionally, the Pygmies in Central Africa have been closely attached to the rain forest. They were the "Forest People" (Turnbull 1961), and the forest was the source of their religion, livelihood, and protection. They used to lead a nomadic life in camps of thirty to forty families that maintained regular links and exchanges with each other. Their mostly egalitarian and horizontal society acknowledged the wisdom of elders who preserved the community's knowledge of plants, animals, ghosts, and spirits as well as their entire cultural heritage (rituals, music, dances, holy sites) and practices (pharmacopeia, hunting and fishing). Elders occupied prominent positions within the community and settled disputes. They lived in simple huts made out of leaves and branches.

This traditional lifestyle should not necessarily be equated with a life of poverty. It had its own dignity, its noblesse and coherence, and it is part of the universal heritage of humanity. Yet today, the traditional Pygmy lifestyle is in danger: As a population, they are losing what constitutes their identity and the richness of their culture and knowledge as a result of gradual sedentarization. Their access to the forest itself, as well as to the land that they cultivate, is increasingly at risk. In the DRC, their relationship with Bantu farmers – Sudanese, Nilotic – used to be described as harmonious (Ndaywel 1997), as the Pygmies managed to maintain a relative independence from the Bantu. The current situation presents a less idyllic picture of the relations between the two communities. Subjugation, a devaluation of their culture, denial of rights, looting, and violence are what numerous Pygmies are now subject to every day. Fieldwork conducted for this study suggests that many Pygmies are very poor and being exploited by the Bantu.

It is worth noting that the Pygmies are not the only indigenous population of the region. In the Central African Republic especially, the Mbororos, who descend from Peuhls living in the Sahel, may not strictly speaking be indigenous in the sense of the criteria cited earlier and used by the international organizations. Indeed they emigrated in CAR only about fifty years ago in search of new pastures. However, their minority status (they represent 1 percent of CAR's population, according to the 2003 population census), lifestyle, and deprivation could lead to their categorization as indigenous, and surely as vulnerable. However, as the analysis presented in this chapter shows, they tend to be less poor than the pygmies.

Evidence from Latin America suggests that in most countries, indigenous populations and ethnic minorities suffer from higher poverty levels compared to the national averages in the country they live (Hall and Patrinos, 2006). In Africa, however, good data to measure poverty and well-being among indigenous groups are scarce. In many cases, household surveys in the region do not include ethnic variables that facilitate such analysis. Even when this information is collected, the sampling methodology (i.e., lack of oversampling of minority groups) is not usually designed to provide enough observations to lead to robust conclusions relative to the living standards of these populations. In the DRC, for example, the nationally representative household survey of nearly 12,000 households implemented in 2004–2005 had only 29 households with a Pygmy household head. Because of this lack of data, most studies rely on ethnographic approaches, which are very useful but cannot necessarily provide robust national estimates.

The objective of this study is to draw together both quantitative and qualitative information to provide a diagnostic of the well-being of the Pygmies in Central Africa today, with material from three countries: the DRC, CAR, and Gabon. CAR is one of the poorest countries in the world. In 2008, the GDP per capita was only $300, and about two-thirds of the population lives in poverty. The nation is divided into more than eighty ethnic groups, each having its own language. The largest ethnic groups are the Baya (33 percent of the population), Banda (27 percent), Mandjia (13 percent), Sara (10 percent), Mboum (7 percent), M'Baka (4 percent), and Yakoma (4 percent). The Mbororos are estimated to account for 1 percent of the population, and the Pygmies for 0.3 percent, according to the 2003 population census.

The DRC is the third-largest country by area in Africa. GDP per capita was $184 in 2008, one of the lowest in the world, and household survey data suggests that more than seven in ten people live under the national poverty line. There are more than 200 African ethnic groups, of which the majority are Bantu (80 percent of the population). Other important groups include Sudanic-speaking groups in the north and northeast. Among the Bantu-speaking peoples, the major groups are the Kongo, or Bakongo, in the south; the Luba, or Baluba, in East Kasai and Katanga; the Mongo and related groups in the cuvette area; the Lunda and Chokwe in Bandundu and West Kasai; the Bemba and Hemba in Katanga; and the Kwango and Kasai in Bandundu. The four largest tribes – Mongo, Luba, Kongo (all Bantu), and Mangbetu-Azande (Hamitic) – make up about 45 percent of the total population. The Pygmies account for up to 1 percent of the population.

Gabon, by contrast, is an upper middle income country with an estimated GDP per capita of $8,085 in 2008. However, because inequality is high, so is the level of poverty; in 2005, one-third of the Gabonese lived under the national poverty line. There are more than forty ethnicities in Gabon. The largest ethnic group is the Fang, located in northern Gabon and southern Cameroon, including about 35 percent of the Gabonese population. The remainder of the Gabonese population is the Bantu, including the following ethnic groups: Benga, Beseki, Kombe, Mpongwe (3 percent), Baduma (16 percent), Eshira (10 percent), Okande (4 percent), Bakalai (7 percent), and Bakota (14 percent). The Pygmies are a small minority, distributed throughout Gabon, and are comprised of several different ethnic groups: the Baka and the Bekui in the north, the Bakoya in the northeast, the Barimba in the south, and the Baboongo in the southeast.

Given the lack of household survey data with representative samples of the Pygmy population, the data used for CAR and Gabon in this chapter come from the latest population census (*Recensement Général de la Population et de l'Habitat – RGPH*) carried out in each country. These censuses have basic information on household composition, education, and labor market at the individual level, as well as assets at the household level. A population census has the advantage of being exhaustive, giving the possibility of having enough observations to draw robust conclusions even on small segments of the population. On the other hand, information is more limited than in a survey. For example, no information on expenditure or income is typically collected through a census. Indirect techniques can nevertheless be used to conduct poverty or distributional analysis with census data by predicting the consumption level of households using poverty mapping. This is what we do in both Gabon and CAR.

The work on the DRC is more qualitative. Within Pygmy camps, information was obtained through individual interviews with key informants (Pygmies and non-Pygmies, with emphasis on the former), using open-ended questionnaires, focus groups with diverse members, including local authorities, women, elderly, and youth, and direct observation and open-ended group discussions (see Annex 1 for a description of the approach). Although a statistically representative sample for the analysis was not possible in the DRC at this stage, the (mostly qualitative) data collection was significant enough to obtain a purposive sample through which information and facts could be derived, analyzed, and extrapolated with an acceptable level of confidence, enhanced by the fact that the study covered all provinces where Pygmies are present (Kivu Sud, Kivu Nord, Maniema, Katanga, Kasai Oriental, Kasai Occidental, Equateur, Bandandu, and Province Orientale). In addition to qualitative data collection in Pygmy camps, data from the national "123" household survey were also used to compare key statistics between Pygmy and non-Pygmy populations. While the Pygmy sample in the 123 survey is small and thus not statistically representative, the results obtained from the survey analysis were very similar to the results obtained through the qualitative fieldwork, adding a degree of confidence in the validity of the results.

Overall, the Pygmy population in all three countries appears to be very poor. Children are not enrolled in schools and adult literacy is low. Health outcomes are weak, and vulnerability is high. In addition, the material from the qualitative work in the DRC suggests that many Pygmies perceive themselves negatively. This negative image is not only related to their poverty and a lack of access to goods and basic services, but also the result of certain patterns of behavior that are inherent aspects of their culture (type of housing, religious beliefs, rites and practices, etc.) and yet are considered "bad" by their neighbors. Although most Pygmies are willing to adapt to the changes around them while remaining culturally "Pygmy," the fieldwork shows that the Bantu, the state, and its institutions do not treat the Pygmies in a manner that allows them to make informed changes and adaptations to improve their general living conditions and live in harmony with their neighbors, while preserving their uniqueness (World Bank, 2009).

HOW MANY PYGMIES ARE THERE?

There is great uncertainty about the number of Pygmies living in Central Africa. This uncertainty can be illustrated in the case of the DRC. Researchers based in specific areas of the DRC have suggested that there may be between 100,000 and 250,000 Pygmies in the country as a whole. Other estimates, including those from the "Dynamique Pygmée," an advocacy group, mention up to 450,000 Pygmies. It is difficult to estimate the size of the Pygmy population because the only census ever undertaken in the DRC since independence was in 1984. It was updated by the Service National des Statistiques Agricoles (SNSA; statistical office) between 1990 and 1994. There are yearly administrative censuses but they have been subject to a number of distortions and do not typically have information on ethnicity.

Nongovernmental organizations (NGOs) involved in the preparation of a Pygmy development strategy for the DRC cooperated with authorities to estimate the percentage of Pygmies living in different areas as a proportion of the total population. These percentages were then applied to the overall population of the areas to estimate the size of the Pygmy population. In some cases, the numbers were directly estimated by Pygmy support

Table 4.1. *Documented Pygmy numbers for all provinces in the DRC*

Province	Number	% of total	Name	Lifestyle
Equateur	172,197	26%	Twa	Sedentary or semi-sedentary
Province Orientale	16,804	3%	Mbuti	Nomads in the process of sedentarization
Bandundu	56,210	8%	Twa	Semi-sedentary
Kasai Oriental	n.d	.	n.d	Nomads
Kasai Occidental	n.d		n.d	Nomads
Maniema	4,452	1%	Twa	Semi-sedentary
Katanga	320,930	48%	Twa	Sedentary
Nord Kivu	25,871	4%	Twa	Sedentary
Sud Kivu	63,600	10%	Twa	Sedentary
Total	660,064	100%		

Source: World Bank (2009).

organizations on the basis of their knowledge of the communities. The resulting overall estimates, provided in Table 4.1, suggest that there may be up to 660,000 Pygmies in the DRC – slightly more than 1 percent of the country's population. Although this is a more systematic effort than has been attempted before, the numbers remain estimates that cannot substitute for a proper census. In terms of geographic distribution, of the 147 territories of the DRC, 59 were identified as having at least one Pygmy community. But for 25 of those 59 districts, only very rough estimates of the number of the Pygmies could be obtained.

In the CAR and in Gabon, estimates of the number of the Pygmies can be obtained directly from the census data, where households are asked to state the ethnic group to which they belong. In the CAR, only 0.3 percent of the population declared itself as being Pygmy, and in Gabon, that percentage was also well below 1 percent (although there was a surprising sharp reduction in the number of Pygmies between the last two censuses). Still, in all three countries, the share of the total population considered as Pygmy seems to be at or below 1 percent. Pygmies are thus a small group in terms of their share of the overall population in all three countries, but given the large population of the DRC especially, they still represent a sizable group in absolute numbers.

POVERTY

Good data have up to now been lacking to assess the level of poverty among Pygmies, and to some extent the very concept of poverty as traditionally measured through the comparison of a consumption aggregate and a monetary poverty threshold is problematic, at least to some Pygmy groups. Indeed, the Pygmies' traditional nomadic lifestyle cannot be equated with poverty, as long as the outside conditions are favorable (i.e., good access to natural resources), but it does constrain their access to education and health care. However, once they abandon their traditional lifestyle and become sedentary, then their standard of living is often lower than for the rest of society. Hence, fieldwork and ethnographic studies have suggested a large gap between Pygmies and other groups in terms of ability to meet basic needs, assets, literacy, mortality, and morbidity, and clearly the Pygmies' monetary income is also lower than that of other groups. So far, however, little systematic quantitative evidence has been collected to compare both groups.

In the case of Gabon and CAR, poverty and welfare quintile estimates on Pygmies have been obtained by relying on poverty-mapping techniques, which help in estimating poverty for small, geographically defined population groups. Elbers et al. (2003) have shown how to construct poverty maps by combining census and survey data. The idea is straightforward. First, a regression of per capita or adult equivalent consumption is estimated using household survey data, limiting the set of explanatory variables to ones common to both the survey and the latest census. Second, the coefficients from that regression are applied to the census data to predict the expenditure level of each household in the census. Third, the predicted household expenditures are used to construct a series of poverty indicators for geographical population subgroups. Although the idea is simple, its implementation requires complex computations.

This poverty-mapping technique is used here to assess poverty levels among the Pygmies, because they are not well represented in the Gabon and CAR household surveys. Table 4.2 provides estimates of consumption per capita and poverty among Pygmies and nonindigenous populations in Gabon. The share of the population in poverty among Pygmies is twice that among non-Pygmies, and the differences are, in proportional terms, even larger for other poverty measures. In the CAR, similar data is provided in Table 4.3 by quintile of estimated per capita consumption. Again, Pygmies are much poorer, as they are much more likely to belong to the lowest quintiles of consumption.

In the case of the DRC, there is no national census, but at least some data are available from the "123" survey implemented in 2004 in Kinshasa and 2005 in the rest of the country to compare a range of indicators between Pygmies and the rest of the population. These data can be used to provide

Table 4.2. *Poverty and welfare indicators by ethnicity in Gabon*

	Poverty indicators			Per capita consumption (Fcfa per year)	
	Share of population in poverty	Poverty gap	Squared poverty gap	Average	Median
Gabon					
Pygmy	70.1	30.0	16.4	342,896	303,282
Non-Pygmy	32.7	10.7	4.9	760,399	587,879
All	32.8	10.7	4.9	760,067	587,589

Source: Authors' estimates.

Table 4.3. *Population share by quintile of per capita consumption, by ethnicity in CAR*

	Q1	Q2	Q3	Q4	Q5	Total
National						
Mbororos	46.7	14.0	13.1	11.6	14.6	100
Pygmy	89.7	6.2	2.4	0.9	0.8	100
Nonindigenous	21.0	18.7	20.1	20.1	20.1	100
All	21.4	18.6	20.0	20.0	20.0	100

Note: Fcfa = CFA (Communauté Financière Africaine) franc.
Source: Authors' estimates.

some idea of the standard of living of Pygmies (we use the term "idea" as the data are not strictly statistically representative of the Pygmy population due to the very small Pygmy sample size). Table 4.4 provides key results on poverty and selected other indicators. The 123 survey includes a total of 11,959 households, of which only 29 declared themselves as belonging to the Pygmy group. Using the expansion factors from the survey, this would mean that there would be 63,097 Pygmy individuals out of a total population of 54 million people (this is much smaller than the estimate of the Pygmy population in the DRC provided in the previous section, but remote groups are often underrepresented in national surveys). Statistics provided on the basis of only 29 households (and 110 individuals) observed in a survey are subject to caution, but nevertheless suggests picture of living conditions among the Pygmies.

The difference in poverty estimates between the Pygmies and the rest of the population is large. Poverty is measured in the DRC, as in other

Table 4.4. *Poverty and human development indicators in the national 123 household survey, DRC 2005*

	Number of households	Number of individuals	Weighted number of households	Weighted number of individuals	Share of rural population	Share of female population	Average age of individuals	Median age of individuals	Share of female-headed households
Non-Pygmies	11,930	64,454	10,240,496	54,190,264	70.0	50.4	20.9	16.0	17.1
Pygmies	29	110	19,828	63,097	95.0	51.6	26.7	24.0	6.6
All	11,959	64,564	10,260,324	54,253,361	70.1	50.4	20.9	16.0	17.0

	Average age of household head	Average household size	School enrollment rate (6–11 years)	Literacy rate (15+ years)	Labor force participation rate (15+ years)	Unemployment rate (15+ years)	Share working in informal sector	Poverty incidence (headcount)	Poverty gap	Squared poverty gap
Non-Pygmies	43.3	5.3	56.1	65.0	73.8	6.2	90.2	71.7	32.4	18.1
Pygmies	41.7	3.2	18.7	30.5	85.9	1.0	100.0	84.8	39.4	25.1
All	43.3	5.3	56.0	64.9	73.8	6.2	90.2	71.7	32.3	18.0

Source: Authors' estimates.

countries, by comparing a consumption aggregate with a poverty line that is meant to capture the cost of basic food and nonfood needs. Poverty is truly massive in the DRC: 71.7 percent of the population is estimated to be poor. Yet the proportion of the Pygmy population that is poor is even higher, at 84.8 percent. Measures of poverty that take into account not only the share of the poor, but also the distance separating the poor from the poverty line (such as the poverty gap) or the inequality among the poor (such as the squared poverty gap) also suggest very large differences between the Pygmies and the rest of the population. The data in Table 4.4 suggest that in the DRC, the Pygmy population is significantly poorer, less well educated, rural, and working more often in the informal sector than the rest of the population. Pygmies are hardworking, as suggested by very high rates of labor force participation, but they appear to be especially vulnerable despite that hard work.

The DRC qualitative work suggests that the main reasons for the impoverishment of the Pygmies are linked to their past, on the one hand, and to the characteristics of current Congolese society on the other. Historical reasons include submission to their Bantu neighbors, which is ingrained in the two communities' history of forced labor (paid or unpaid), abuse, and an internalized attitude by each of the two communities. From the Bantu side, it is a feeling of superiority and disdain for the Pygmies, and from the Pygmy side a feeling of inferiority and disregard for oneself, escapism and a passive attitude. The Pygmies are dependent on the Bantu for food as soon as resources become scarce. In addition, the transition is difficult from living a day-to-day life as hunter-gatherers to the foresight and planning necessary for successful sedentary agriculture. This is why most Pygmies have the mindset of a day laborer rather than one of a farmer, a mindset that promotes the search for a daily income as opposed to a long-term investment that could provide more food security (i.e., the long-term gain of larger fields vs. the short-term advantage of smaller parcels of land that are less time-consuming to maintain). Finally, there is a tendency of some Bantu to exploit Pygmy labor with no or low pay, which limits their access to public services such as health care or education, which cost money.

As noted in World Bank (2009), the loss of or limited access to natural resources as well as their gradual depletion is also affecting the Pygmies. This loss is caused by a range of factors including the proliferation of cut-and-burn agriculture on the Pygmies' traditional hunting territories; the nonrecognition of their customary rights of use; the dependence on Bantu landowners for access to any kind of natural resources including agricultural resources; the creation of wildlife reserves; logging concessions; artisanal logging in vital Pygmy territories; oil extraction in the Cuvette Centrale as well as the possible resumption of large-scale plantations (private Chinese and European projects currently under preparation); artisanal or industrial mining in the same territories; and demographic pressure. The Pygmies also suffer from a loss of identity and cultural heritage through religious proselytism and conformism with the Bantu or global society, the dissemination of contagious diseases their traditional medicine cannot heal, especially sexually transmitted diseases (STDs) but also tuberculosis; and the consumption of alcohol and cannabis, which has become a common phenomenon and exacerbates all of the previously mentioned problems. The combination of these factors is causing a loss of resources, a lack of food security, a lack of capacities, and a loss of cultural heritage for the Pygmies. The ongoing civil war in the DRC may also have contributed to the impoverishment and abuse of the Pygmies.

HUMAN DEVELOPMENT

Quantitative Evidence from CAR and Gabon on Education

The census data for the CAR and Gabon suggests that enrollment rates and educational attainment are much lower among the Pygmies than among other groups (see Tables 4.5a and 4.5b). In addition, the average years of schooling among indigenous adult populations in Gabon is 3 years for men and 2.8 years for women, versus 6.5 years for both genders in the nonindigenous population. In the CAR, the average number of years of schooling is 0.3 years for men and 0.1 year for women among indigenous groups, versus 2.8 years for men and 1.4 years for women among the nonindigenous. Regression analysis shows that being indigenous, controlling for other observable characteristics such as household composition, age, geographic location, and the like, leads to substantial and statistically significant gaps in education attainment. Indigenous children are also more likely to be older than nonindigenous children in any one grade. As a result of limited schooling, indigenous individuals are much more likely to be illiterate (see Tables 4.6a and 4.6b).

Qualitative Evidence from the DRC on Education and Health

The data presented earlier for the DRC suggests that the rate of school enrollment among children from six to eleven years of age is extremely low among Pygmies at 18.7 percent, versus 56.1 percent for the rest of the

Table 4.5a. *Gender and educational attainment (fifteen years and older) in Gabon*

	Indigenous			Nonindigenous			All
	Male	Female	All	Male	Female	All	
Still in school (%)	6.7	3.4	5	21.9	22.3	22.1	22.1
If not in school, highest achievement:							
None	66.4	67.4	66.9	14.1	21.4	17.7	17.8
Incomplete Primary	23.4	24.2	23.8	11.3	15.7	13.5	13.5
Complete Primary	7.4	1.4	4.3	13.3	16.3	14.8	14.8
Secondary	1	0.5	0.7	43.4	34.7	39.1	39
University	0.3	0	0.1	9.6	3.9	6.8	6.8

Source: RGPH 2003, Gabon.

Table 4.5b. *Gender and educational attainment (fifteen years and older) in CAR*

	Mbororo			Pygmy			Non indigenous			All		
	Male	Female	All	Male	Female	All	Male	Female	All	Male	Female	All
Still in school (%)	2.6	1.0	1.8	3.6	1.1	2.3	13.5	7.0	10.2	13.4	6.9	10.1
If not in school, highest achievement:												
None	93.8	97.3	95.5	86.3	93.6	90.1	41.3	66.1	53.9	41.9	66.4	54.4
Incomplete Primary	2.7	1.3	2.0	11.3	5.7	8.4	19.8	14.5	17.1	19.6	14.3	16.9
Complete Primary	1.3	0.5	0.9	1.5	0.2	0.9	12.4	6.7	9.4	12.2	6.6	9.3
Secondary	2.1	0.9	1.5	0.7	0.4	0.5	24.3	12.2	18.2	24.1	12.1	17.9
University	0.2	0.1	0.1	0.1	0.1	0.1	2.2	0.5	1.3	2.1	0.5	1.3

Source: RGPH 2003, CAR.

population. Only 30.5 percent of the Pygmies aged fifteen years or older are literate, versus 65.0 percent for the rest of the population. This is in part because the Pygmies only receive education that is provided on a community level as opposed to more traditional formal schooling. The fact that school enrollment rates are very low (especially for secondary education), despite the fact that most Pygmies are sedentarized and have been living close to Bantu villages for at least fifteen years, suggests that the Pygmies have limited access to public schools, even if they live close to Bantu villages. Those who live in camps or villages a little farther away rarely have access to schools at all and if they do, they are in poor condition.

Tale 4.6a. *Illiteracy rates in Gabon*

Age	Total population			Indigenous		
	Total	Male	Female	Total	Male	Female
10–14	17.6	18.5	16.7	93.8	92.9	94.7
15–19	7.1	6.5	7.8	75.8	77.4	74.6
20–24	8.7	8.3	9.1	82.2	73.9	89.1
25–29	11	11.6	10.5	92.2	86.4	95.2
30–34	12.2	13.4	11.4	89.6	76	96.2
35–39	14.2	15.1	13.8	95.9	95.5	96.1
40–44	17.1	16.8	17.3	97.8	94.4	100
45–49	21.7	17.9	23.4	88	71.4	94.4
50–54	33.6	20.9	39	94.4	85.7	96.6
55–59	53.1	29	61.6	92	33.3	100
60–64	71.9	42.6	80.3	100	100	100
65–69	80.6	53.9	87.4	100	100	100
Urban (aged 15–69)	12.6	10.5	14	77.6	60	86.3
Rural (aged 15–69)	32.3	19.5	39.5	89.8	84.2	92.9

Source: Authors' estimates.

Qualitative data from the DRC Pygmy strategy (World Bank 2009) suggest several reasons for low enrollment and literacy rates among Pygmies. Education is not free in the DRC. Even though teacher salaries are paid by the state (if schools are part of the *Education Nationale* and teachers are *conventionnés*, i.e., officially recognized by the state through ad hoc conventions), it is frequently the case that half or more of a school's teachers are paid by parents. Fieldwork shows that many Pygmy parents who aspire to give their children a good education do not have the means to pay for it. In addition, in both public and private schools, teachers' and Bantu children's attitudes toward Pygmy children are negative (rejection, denigration) because they do not have school uniforms, pens, or books, which "discourages the latter and is the cause for a grave inferiority complex" (DRC qualitative fieldwork). Qualitative fieldwork suggests that this inferiority complex has been internalized by some communities. The rather erratic school attendance of Pygmy children does not help either. Necessary trips to the forest for several days or weeks can occur at any time for all sorts of reasons vital to family livelihoods. Thus they frequently miss lessons, which makes it hard for them to succeed in school. Additionally, their parents and community members have received limited education themselves or are illiterate and do not speak the taught language, French. War, premature marriages, alcoholism, and cannabis addiction (of both parents and children) aggravate this. This lack of education is a major obstacle in terms of

Table 4.6b. *Illiteracy rates in CAR*

Age	Male				Female				All			
	Mbororos	Pygmy	Nonindigenous	All	Mbororos	Pygmy	Nonindigenous	All	Mbororos	Pygmy	Nonindigenous	All
10–14	79.9	89.9	55.2	55.5	82.5	90.8	62.9	63.2	81.1	90.3	58.9	59.3
15–19	75.9	88.7	42.9	43.3	83.1	91.7	60.2	60.5	79.7	90.3	52.0	52.4
20–24	73.0	82.6	40.9	41.3	83.8	93.4	61.4	61.7	79.0	88.4	51.6	51.9
25–29	74.6	88.8	40.0	40.4	85.8	93.2	63.9	64.2	80.8	91.3	51.9	52.3
30–34	77.0	89.9	39.4	39.9	86.6	95.9	66.6	66.9	82.1	93.0	52.6	53.1
35–39	75.9	89.4	39.7	40.2	87.7	96.4	68.9	69.2	82.1	93.0	54.3	54.6
40–44	74.0	92.1	40.7	41.3	87.3	96.5	72.7	72.9	80.2	94.2	56.6	57.0
45–49	74.2	92.4	41.2	41.7	88.9	94.0	76.9	77.1	80.1	93.1	59.1	59.3
50–54	77.8	93.1	46.7	47.2	90.1	94.9	83.1	83.2	83.0	94.0	65.6	65.8
55–59	79.4	94.9	54.1	54.5	87.7	100.0	87.1	87.2	82.2	97.4	71.1	71.3
60–64	81.8	96.7	65.4	65.7	91.8	95.3	90.5	90.5	85.8	96.1	79.2	79.3
65–69	83.2	93.6	70.2	70.4	91.4	95.1	91.5	91.6	86.0	94.4	82.1	82.2
Urban (aged 15–69)	54.2	75.4	23.6	23.7	64.5	79.0	44.7	44.8	59.4	77.3	34.2	34.3
Rural (aged 15–69)	77.3	89.9	55.6	56.0	87.3	94.9	82.8	82.9	82.3	92.5	69.6	69.9

Source: Authors' estimates.

leadership, relations with the administration and their environment, and access to basic education.

The Pygmies' health status and access to health services is also poorly documented, but results from fieldwork in the DRC suggest that the Pygmies do not have access to primary health care and mainly use traditional medicine; they are worse off than the Bantu whose access to primary health care is also poor, especially in the forest regions; and many diseases affect them more than other population groups, especially tropical parasitoses, STDs, tuberculosis, infectious diseases, respiratory diseases, and infantile infectious diseases. In addition, Pygmy women suffer from a higher mortality rate at birth. All of this owes partly to their lifestyle, especially to poor hygiene, consumption of unclean water, promiscuity, and smoke-infested houses, but also their exclusion from the health care system. They are less informed about diseases and their transmission than the Bantu, vaccination campaigns do not reach or target them, and they do not have access to health infrastructure or medication. These results are equally valid for nomadic, seminomadic, and sedentarized Pygmies.

Again, there are several reasons for the poor health outcomes observed among Pygmies. These include their geographic isolation, which limits access to health care and raises costs; malnutrition caused by monotone and poor diets for sedentary Pygmies; the predominance of cultural habits, some of which are guided by religious beliefs, as well as of other habits such as premature marriages, the consumption of alcohol, the lack of hygiene, giving birth within the camps, and a preference for their traditional medicine, and so forth. Although their traditional medicine is based on a rich pharmacopeia and their knowledge of medicinal plants used to be an advantage over the Bantu who would seek their medical help, it also has its limits, especially in combating diseases like AIDS or other STDs. Their high degree of poverty makes it impossible for them to pay for treatments or medication. In addition, their mistrust or fear of Bantu health care officials (and vice versa), as well as the contemptuous and discriminatory attitude of the latter (exclusion during the distribution of mosquito nets or the scheduling of vaccinations) and sexual abuse of Pygmy women, have contributed to poor health outcomes including the dissemination of STDs in Pygmy communities. The result of insufficient primary health care is a high infant mortality rate, particularly during birth, and a low life expectancy, especially compared to the Bantu. Again, although there are no official numbers or scientific studies to back up these findings, there is a clear consensus between both Bantu and Pygmies that health indicators are much worse for the Pygmies.

Table 4.7. *Labor force participation, unemployment, and unpaid work, Gabon and CAR*

	Gabon			CAR			
	Indigenous	Nonindigenous	All	Mbororos	Pygmy	Nonindigenous	All
Labor Force Participation Rate							
Male	71.4	50	50.1	81.1	70.9	74.4	74.5
Female	67.9	41.2	41.2	38.4	56.7	58.7	58.5
Unemployment Rate							
Male	2	14.1	14.1	4.6	7.8	9.7	9.7
Female	1.5	13.6	13.6	5.9	2.7	5	5
% Unpaid workers							
Male	12	3.5	3.5	8.7	3.7	4.1	4.2
Female	12.9	4.4	4.4	14.6	10.8	8.5	8.5

Source: Authors' estimates using RGPH 2003, CAR et RGPH 2003, Gabon.

LIVELIHOODS, LABOR MARKET PARTICIPATION, AND EMPLOYMENT

Quantitative Evidence from CAR and Gabon

Data are available in the Gabon and CAR census on labor force participation and employment (including for children), as well as on sector of employment. As shown in Table 4.7, labor force participation rates are higher among Pygmies (in large part due to a higher share of women willing to work), and unemployment is lower, probably in part because the Pygmies are so poor that they cannot afford not to work. The share of workers who are not paid for their work is also much larger among the Pygmies than the rest of the population, which contributes to higher levels of poverty. Tables 4.8a and 4.8b provide data on sectors of employment. The Pygmies tend to work more in agriculture than other groups, which is not surprising, and in the case of Gabon, a substantial share are employed by providing services to other households, including domestic work. The data also suggest that the incidence of child labor is significantly higher among Pygmies than among other groups. Thus, whereas the Pygmies are much poorer than other groups, they also seem to work harder according to the labor force data available (but we do not have data on time use and the number of hours worked).

Table 4.8a. *Employment by sector, Gabon*

	Indigenous	Nonindigenous	All
Gabon			
Agriculture	23.2	8.8	8.8
Mining/Manufacturing	0.0	3.6	3.6
Utilities/Construction	1.0	2.5	2.5
Commerce	0.2	4.8	4.8
Services to household	72.6	33.4	33.5
Household as employers	0.2	15.6	15.6
Other Services	2.7	31.3	31.2
All sectors	100.0	100.0	100.0

Source: Authors' estimates using RGPH 2003, Gabon.

Table 4.8b. *Employment by sector, CAR*

	Mbororos	Pygmy	Nonindigenous	All
Agriculture	80.8	95.3	76.4	76.5
Mining	1.5	1.6	2.7	2.7
Manufacturing	0.3	0.1	1.0	1.0
Utilities	0.0	0.1	0.1	0.1
Commerce	13.0	0.9	9.9	9.9
Services	4.4	2.1	9.9	9.9
All sectors	100.0	100.0	100.0	100.0

Source: Authors' estimates using RGPH 2003, CAR.

Qualitative Evidence from the DRC

The qualitative evidence from the DRC provides more information on the type of work and sources of livelihood of Pygmies. As mentioned earlier, the Pygmies used to lead lives of hunter-gatherers in the rainforest. They were nomadic and moved on to new hunting grounds as soon as they had used up the resources in a specific area. They also traded food with the Bantu such as agricultural products for their hunting, fishing, and gathering products. Pygmy sedentarization started with early colonization and this process was encouraged by the authorities and by NGOs supporting the Pygmies. Sedentarization is more generally the result of a number of factors: demographic pressure of both Pygmies and Bantu, which reduces the living space and creates a greater dependency on agriculture; the Pygmies' own aspirations to change their lives; and pressure from the

Bantu society, which is leading to a sociocultural homogenization (religious and behavioral).

Today, large parts of the sedentarized population are agriculturalists. They sometimes own small parcels of land, but mainly work as farm hands for the Bantu with whom they live. In the first stage of the "sedentarization cycle," the Pygmies offer labor to the Bantu. The cycle then continues with the creation of small fields as Pygmy groups permanently settle down in the periphery of Bantu villages, first at a distance (1 to 2 km), then closer. In the most advanced cases of sedentarization, Pygmies may have camps that are the same size as the Bantu's (for instance, in Bikoro). But agriculture is also a constraint that hinders the Pygmies from going too far away from their camps (for hunting or gathering) and therefore increases pressure on the closest forest. It is de facto turning into an "open" forest, to which everyone has access (Thomas and Bahuchet 1983). Consequently, the Bantu are increasingly hunting in these "open forests," which reduces their need for trading food with the Pygmies.

The level of sedentarization varies greatly from group to group. The Mbuti Pygmy of Province Orientale manage to leave their camps between one-third to two-thirds of the time over periods of several months. Others, for instance in the riverside villages of the Virunga Park, have completely ceased to be nomadic and rely entirely on agriculture, manual labor for the Bantu, and craftsmanship for income and food. Thomas and Bahuchet (1983) note that income opportunities are good for those Pygmy groups that still have the possibility to hunt, as the market for bush and game meat is particularly easy to access everywhere in the DRC.

Pygmies today in the DRC are often classified in three basic categories: nomadic, sedentary, or in the process of sedentarization (Table 4.1). The term "nomad" describes Pygmies who move in a certain hunting ground. Nomadic Pygmies can also be characterized using two other criteria: the predominance of hunting and gathering in their activities and for food procurement, and the fact that they do not have permanent camps close to Bantu villages and roads. By contrast, most sedentary Pygmies permanently live in villages that are constructed in a similar way to Bantu villages. They mainly farm – either their own land of which the size increases over time, or for Bantu agriculturalists. They depend entirely on agriculture for food supply. They may also hunt but this is no longer a determining factor in their diet. Between these two extremes, a process of sedentarization that is more or less advanced is underway (more or less time of the year spent in the forest, higher or lower dependence on its resources, migrating to live in the vicinity of mining activities to provide labor or bush meat for miners).

Table 4.1 suggests that today, the Pygmies in the DRC are mostly semi-sedentary or seminomadic and depend on agriculture at least as much as on hunting. Within the framework of this study, it was not possible to determine the number of true nomads, but it is very likely that they account for no more than 30,000 to 40,000 people – less than 10 percent of all Pygmies. It is equally difficult to establish the number of fully sedentarized Pygmies (those that have stopped hunting altogether). Still, these results modify the widespread image of Pygmies as forest nomads with limited contact with the Bantu and as generally keeping their distance from the outside world. In most cases, Pygmies live close to the Bantu and are in the process of becoming agriculturalists, craftsmen, laborers, or miners while maintaining activities linked to their old lifestyles at varying degrees. In certain cases their link to the forest is nearly or completely severed (as in Rutshuru, Masisi, and a large part of the Tanganyika district, Katanga province). The majority of Pygmies today are thus seminomads whose ties to a certain area depend on the possibilities of shorter or longer trips to the forest and on work opportunities (plantations, big agricultural campaigns, mining, etc.).

Whether they are nomadic, semi-sedentarized, or sedentarized, the Pygmies' income opportunities are bleak. Their labor is paid at a very low rate and often they are forced to work without payment. In the best cases, they receive about half of what a Bantu laborer would get paid, generating a monthly income of only $20 per household. Depletion of natural resources affects their main source of income: cut-and-burn agriculture that is spreading out further into the forests, logging that makes it impossible for them to farm and issues them a de facto useless hunting right (Forestry Code), artisanal mining, excessive hunting or fishing to which they often contribute to satisfy the demand for game meat (for miner households, logging camps, villages, and cities). Their lack of capital makes the utilization of the forest very difficult (artisanal logging, mining). They are incapable of obtaining official or customary rights of use (administrative procedures are too complicated for mining permits, objections of Bantu chiefs are prohibitive) and incapable of investing in the necessary equipment. In and around the National Parks, they are forced to become poachers and beggars, are often subject to bullying, and often lose all access to land. They are not very apt at farming and, given that they mostly tend to other people's fields, only own very small parcels of land that their "master" can harvest without their authorization. Wherever land is not abundant, they encounter difficulties getting access to it. Land is available in the Congo River basin and its margins, in the distant peripheries of the towns and cities, in the Kivu Mountains and Katanga savannahs, or wherever the population density is below fifty inhabitants per square kilometer, but they are the last ones to obtain parcels of land.

SOCIAL EXCLUSION AND LACK OF RIGHTS: THE CASE OF THE DRC

Abuse and Social Exclusion

In the rest of this chapter, our evidence is based on the DRC only because census data do not provide direct information on social exclusion and basic rights. As before, this summary of the existing qualitative evidence is based on World Bank (2009). According to the findings from the DRC fieldwork, many Pygmies claim to suffer from abuse. This includes forced labor and rape. In addition, their harvest is often stolen from their own fields, and their hunting and gathering equipment is seized. All this is a "custom," meaning that it is perceived as appropriate and normal. To try and resist it would equal a rebellion by the Pygmies and they could be tried by customary Bantu tribunals. Trials are usually to their disadvantage and punishments are often cruel. Many Bantu and some law enforcement agents find it normal to benefit from this imparallel treatment under the law. Reversing these mental schemes and behaviors is a complex undertaking and requires the recognition and affirmation of the Pygmies' human rights by the Bantu and the state. To date, Pygmies are often not considered to be "normal human beings" and this is the justification for the abuse that they suffer at the hands of the Bantu.

The social, political, and cultural domination of the Pygmies by the Bantu takes different forms. Some situations resemble slavery, such as when the Bantus speak of "their Pygmies"; the only factor that distinguishes this situation from slavery is that they cannot be bought or sold. Pygmies do not own the natural resources they exploit; they obtain access to these resources by the payment of a tribute. They only obtain farming land temporarily if it is abundant, while the Bantu owner retains the right to take their harvest. If selling the land in question or any other element related to it has to be negotiated, this is done without consulting the Pygmies. Although there are strong taboos that forbid sexual relations between members of the two communities (sanction of being dishonored), they are basically ignored or lifted in most provinces, especially within sedentarized communities. The consequences are often rape or imposed sexual relations from a very young age between Pygmy women and girls and Bantu men.

The archetypical Pygmy (as seen by many Bantu) has mainly negative characteristics: he is fearful, a liar, dirty, a thief, and the like. His positive characteristics include: a hard worker, good for doing the dirtiest and hardest work for free or cheap, knows nature very well, dances and sings very well, and is a good craftsman. But a Bantu would seldom sit down and eat with a Pygmy. The Pygmies' own culture is itself slowly vanishing under the influence of Bantu societal norms: religion, lifestyle, habitat, behavior. The Bantu, as the dominant majority, seldom accept the uniqueness of the Pygmies, and previous positive links between the two communities – such as links between rites and religious beliefs, the dependency on pharmaceutical knowledge, and trade of agricultural products against hunting produce, among others – are eroding.

All this is happening in a context where the Bantu lifestyle is highly appreciated by the Pygmies: They respect the Bantu and want to be like them. However, there also is a strong resistance against the Bantu culture, which might be a reflection of necessity: It is not easy for the Pygmies to totally resemble the Bantu. In some instances, the Pygmies see themselves as living in shame and "trying to hide" (their nudity for instance). They want to imitate the Bantu way of living with all of its attributes. Yet sedentarization is only very slowly resulting in the adoption of Bantu social norms by the Pygmies. When it comes to housing and hygiene, for instance, the Pygmies continue to build simple huts, even though the more solid clay Bantu houses they are imitating are literally right next door in the neighboring villages. It is not possible to invoke poverty or ignorance as reasons for the poor imitation of these houses: Building clay houses only requires unpaid, individual labor. Hygiene is another issue where the adoption of the existing Bantu norms should be easy but is not being done (and it is ostensibly for hygienic reasons that Pygmies are banished from the common wells, schools, etc.). Another example is the use of kitchenware: If the Pygmies own it, they save it for (foreign) visitors rather than using it themselves.

The Pygmies remain much attached to their ancient lifestyle, and poverty alone does not explain the preservation of this lifestyle. Their cultural model resists change for social reasons. By imitating others, they distance themselves from their own group – a source of tension both from within their own group and from the Bantu "masters." This leads to a more general point about the acculturation of the Pygmies. In past years, acculturation was strongly advocated to facilitate the Pygmies access to public services, for instance. However, this goal has become somewhat controversial, giving rise to the question of whether a more measured approach should be adopted, endorsing choice and alternatives to sedentarization, as well as the survival of cultural heritage. Still, change is taking place. The Pygmies are becoming more attracted to areas that offer opportunities, frequently around roads, rather than Bantu villages, because it is possible to find work there and sell products. Yet, they maintain a profound cultural identity to which they remain attached and preserve their beliefs, techniques, and cultural knowledge. Hence the process of progressive sedentarization by no means equates with integration into the Bantu society, where the Pygmies remain marginalized.

The traditional Pygmy culture is thus a threatened culture.[1] The majority of the Congo's Pygmies are in the process of acculturation, particularly under the influence of Christianization, which differs fundamentally from animist beliefs at the heart of Pygmy culture. Some observers have suggested that for many Pygmies, the Christian religion did not require them to discard their beliefs in their ancestors and the spirit of the rainforest, but this combination of belief systems might not be easy to maintain. The Bantu are apparently exerting pressure on the Pygmies to become their "Brothers in Christ." By contrast, Christian beliefs have had little impact on nomadic pygmies, for instance the Sankuru, who are widely scattered. Even for the sedentary Pygmies, however, animism remains important and animist rituals are widely accepted, from circumcision to initiation, birth and marriage rituals, as well as hunting rites such as calling the game.

Lack of Access to Land and Forests

The Pygmies' income depends entirely on their access to natural resources. The main cause of their gradual sedentarization is an increasingly limited access to these resources, as well as their general degradation, for instance the decreasing numbers of game and wildlife. Loss of access to these resources is the driving force behind their desire for better living conditions and income opportunities that proximity to Bantu settlements and roads provides. Paradoxically, their sedentarization leads to impoverishment and a deterioration of their living conditions.

[1] Traditional knowledge of nature is most advanced and conserved in nomadic communities. It is possible that poverty, which makes Pygmies use only their traditional medicine to treat ailments, is helping preserve their traditional medicine/pharmacopeia. Their music, however, is gradually disappearing from sedentary camps. Nomads have managed to preserve hunting techniques, whereas sedentary Pygmies, especially around the Virunga National Park and in Kalemie, hunt very rarely and their techniques are slowly being lost. On the other hand, arts and crafts such as pottery, braiding, and weaving are flourishing, and the Pygmies are known for the high quality of their craft work.

The Pygmies have their own customary rights of use for their forest "territories," but the Bantu, with whom they share these territories, do not recognize these customary rights. In fact, the concerned areas are actually owned by the Bantu, Sudanese, or Nilotic people according to their own customary law recognized by the state. The state does not recognize the customary rights of Pygmies. The "owners" of these territories may grant the Pygmies rights of use, as long as they do not conflict with their own interests or if they can benefit from the arrangement (e.g., by receiving tributes in the form of game meat, etc.). As soon as that changes, however, the Pygmies can be driven from the land; their customary rights of use are not legally binding and cannot be defended in court. And even if they had access to the legal system, Pygmies would be constrained by the power imbalance and their limited influence and experience with the legal system.

This is equally true for forest resources as well as access to soil and farmland. From one day to another, a Bantu "owner" can stop Pygmies from using "his" natural resources. Thus, in all areas where the demographic pressure increases or new economic opportunities arise – such as mining, artisanal or industrial logging, or plantations – the Pygmies are increasingly pushed off the land and compelled to work as underpaid day laborers. In terms of access to land, the Pygmies' situation does not differ from the situation of migrants of other ethnic groups who are quite numerous in the DRC. The significant difference between these two groups is that the Pygmies have been present in their territories for millennia. Another threat in terms of access to natural resources, which has arisen throughout the twentieth century, is the creation of national parks (e.g., the Virunga National Park). All human exploitation of natural resources, including hunting, is forbidden inside these parks, and thus entire Pygmy groups have been driven from their ancestral homeland and pushed back to the surrounding areas of the Park, becoming poachers in the eye of the law, without any compensation.[2]

Because the Pygmies are usually not considered to be the traditional owners of land or resources in the DRC, they have slowly lost their ancient rights

---

[2]   The Congolese Land Act (Loi Foncière), Bagajika, of 1973, which was amended and completed in 1981, stipulates that all the national territory belongs to the state. Concessionary dispositions, however, allow for private land ownership both in urban and rural areas. These clauses have recently been complemented with the Forestry Code (Code Forestier) and the Mining Code (Code Minier). Apart from these concessions (rural, urban, forest, and mines), customary law applies, even if the resources in question can be subject to concessions at all times. To date, no concessionary transaction has taken place in the DRC without the traditional owners receiving something in return for their land and therefore de facto selling their property. Usually land is bought from the customary owner and then registered as private property.

of use in the sense that they have been chased deeper into the forest or been invaded by or integrated into Bantu, Sudanese, or Nilotic societies. The forest itself has gradually been claimed and appropriated by the invaders. In these territories and within this legal framework, the Pygmies have thus only acquired or preserved rights of use that are linked to servitude. Every forest in the DRC has a customary owner who is not Pygmy. This owner can tolerate – and, for that matter, benefit from – Pygmy presence in "his" forest (for instance, as hunters and meat providers), but he can also use the forest for other purposes including concessions or conceding rights of use to other uses such as logging or mining rights). Customary owners do not have to consult the Pygmies at all, and the law does not require them to do so, even if the Pygmies have been residing in the forest long before them. This is also true for every other Congolese migrant who is settling down in an area he does not originate from: He can obtain rights of use from the customary owner for natural resources (land and forest), but these rights can be withdrawn unless he obtains a concessionary right recognized by the state.

The Pygmies thus live on the land of others, just like migrants. Their rights of use are always linked to the payments of returns to the customary owner. In addition, the customary rights of Bantu owners were initially merely clan rights for the operation of communal land. However, they have slowly turned into patrimonial rights for the chief and his lineage. The chief can make use of his rights as he wishes and dispossess himself and all the members of his clan (to their detriment) by selling "his" land. These patrimonial ties, which have been reinforced by the Land Act, are the cause of a large number of expropriations in DRC and have been the reason for many violent conflicts.

The Forestry Code does not distinguish between rights of use and customary property rights, a distinction which is crucial for customary law, because the state is the owner of the forest according to the Code. Thus, the Forestry Code recognizes customary rights of use but does not clarify how the custom defines them. Also, Article 37 outlaws all commercial activities, including hunting, in protected forests and production forests. The Forestry Code distinguishes between classified forests (which make up 15 percent of the national territory), protected forests, and production forests. The latter are part of the protected areas that have been made industrial concessions, either through tendering, conversion, or community concessions (by presidential decree). Hunting is forbidden in classified forests and agriculture is forbidden in forestry concession zones. Pygmies are basically forbidden to commercialize the products of their main activity, hunting, and they cannot farm in forest concessions, which they would need to do for their survival, because the noise from the engines chases away wildlife and makes hunting extremely difficult. Their only choice is to leave the area.

Another obstacle for the Pygmies is linked to the concept of "community forest concessions." This is where the notion of customary property resurfaces. Article 22 of the Code stipulates: "A local community may, upon request, obtain through a forest concession part of or an entire protected forest among the forests that are regularly owned under customary law. The modalities of the attribution of such a concession to a community are determined by presidential decree. The attribution is free." This article very clearly excludes any community forest concession to the benefit of the Pygmies simply because the Pygmies generally do not own forests according to customary law. The attribution by presidential decree politicizes the debate on a high political level and is an additional obstacle for the Pygmies.

It has to be emphasized that the zoning process is necessary prior to any new concession of forest territory (thus the necessary extension of the moratorium). Because of the Code, the Pygmies main source of income, hunting, is placed under surveillance and their main substitutive activity, agriculture, is forbidden in the concessions and protected areas. Two policy changes are critical. First, every zoning process should take Pygmy interests into consideration and reserve special areas for them for hunting and agriculture. The second policy area concerns the Forestry Code *cahier des charges*, the social responsibility and investments that logging companies have to make for local communities. It is important to ensure that the Pygmies will benefit from these investments and that their signature is required for the validation of each *cahier des charges*.

Lack of Institutional Representation

Pygmy participation in governance and administration is weak to nonexistent in the DRC. Contrary to the Bantu, whose villages are linked to *localités* recognized as administrative entities by the state, Pygmy camps are not. From the viewpoint of the administration, they are considered as hamlets in a Bantu, Sudanese, or Nilotic *localité*. To understand the difference, one has to come back to the different social structures and administrative history of the different components of Congolese society. Social organization in chiefdoms is a Bantu, Sudanese, or Nilotic institution. Today the division of the entire Congolese territory and the appropriation of land is based on chiefdoms, to the detriment of older forms of social organization such as that of the Pygmies. The colonial administration was built on the customary Bantu land division to create administrative districts, *groupements*, and chiefdoms or sectors. In the Congolese system, *groupements* are nearly always headed by representatives of the traditional chief, mostly of the chiefdom sectors. *Localité* chiefs are nearly always appointed by the *groupements* chiefs.

The customary and administrative systems are therefore closely intertwined. The chief of the *localité* could be the chief of a certain parcel of land, or the representative of the chiefdom, or *groupements* chief (being chief over land can be distinct from political chiefdom in some cases), or even a person nominated by the sector chief (who is not part of the customary hierarchy), but in this case that person is still linked to the customary system. The Pygmies, who never had and still do not have hereditary chiefs, are therefore excluded from the political and administrative system. However, the recognition of administrative interlocutors for the Pygmy communities is beginning to emerge. In some cases, the Bantu *localité* chiefs nominate representatives for the Pygmy neighborhoods, hamlets, or villages, and these representatives become de facto *localité* chiefs themselves. As such, they are the main contact person for the Pygmies, not only for liaison with the official Bantu *localité* chiefs, but also as a leader and a contact point with the outside world. Often, they already have a prominent position within their own communities, which is why they are acknowledged and accepted as representatives of the *localité* chiefs.

This *localité chiefdom* is not of a territorial nature; in other words, it is not associated with particular land rights or access to natural resources in specific areas. It is rather a position of leadership and representation. This process of delegation is also common for some nomadic pygmies or in areas where Pygmies live in greater numbers. In addition, the sector administration may recognize people who have been chosen by the communities themselves as *groupements* chiefs for several camps. Thus, nonhereditary and nonofficial administrative structures that are tied to communities and not land are gradually being put in place. These para-administrations, which have no control over land in terms of ownership and distribution, are nevertheless being mainstreamed and established through a double process of acknowledgment from above by the official administration and from below by Pygmy communities.

Representation of the Pygmies in the provision of public services is close to nonexistent, except in the "territories" of Equateur Sud (Bikoro, Ingende) where better educated and more numerous Pygmies have been able to overcome their "shyness" and the disdain of others and have representatives within the technical services. However, with a few exceptions, these Pygmy representatives do not have many responsibilities. Participation in Civil Society institutions is also very weak, including NGOs. The survey did not include Pygmy staff in NGOs supporting the Pygmies, but it is known that their numbers are very low. Pastors and clergymen charged with the Christianization of the Pygmies seldom belong to the Pygmy communities.

The Pygmies' participation in the most recent elections was high, which suggests that they are willing to be part of greater Congolese society and interested in exercising their electoral rights. The affirmation of their citizenship by the Independent Electoral Commission (and the Constitution) through the distribution of voting papers, as well as the act of voting itself, has been perceived as a recognition of their individual and communal citizenship and therefore has had a considerable political and psychological impact. Yet although the Pygmies are eager to vote, Pygmy candidates in elections are rare, even in areas where Pygmies are a majority. However, fieldwork suggests that several Pygmy candidates will be running for the sector elections in Katanga and Equateur Sud, which points to a gradual emergence of greater political awareness and desire to be active participants in the political process. Thus, although for now elections remain subject to manipulations and clientelism by Bantu politicians, Pygmy leaders are slowly emerging at the *localités* level, a trend that may continue in those districts with a proportionally high Pygmy population (more than 30 percent): the three Euquateur Districts and Mai Ndombe (Ingende, Bikoro, and Koro), Mambasa in Province Orientale, and Kalemie and Manono in the Tanganyika Nyunzu.

Lack of Citizenship and Registration

Formal identification in the DRC can only be received after obtaining a birth certificate and getting registered. This is a prerequisite to benefit from all rights linked to citizenship, like the right to vote. Pygmy births, marriages, and deaths are seldom registered in the nearest civil registry office; as a result, they are rarely legal citizens. Most IDs provided for administrative requirements are counterfeit in rural areas. This is also true for the Bantu, albeit to a lesser degree than for the Pygmies.

Fieldwork provides a number of possible explanations for the low Pygmy registration rates including the distance to the civil registry offices, poverty (fees have to be paid for the registration and stamp), and the attitude of civil servants who keep them at a distance from their offices. For example, the sector's civil registry offices are sometimes more than 100 kilometers away from Pygmy camps and villages. The territorial administration had originally established registration at the village level, by the *localité* chief.

A number of chiefs do it in certain provinces, sometimes even with a lot of diligence and rigor, but the practice is not widespread. Citizenship cannot be accorded, especially in rural areas, in an effective and reliable fashion if registrations are not done at the village level because many villages are too far away from sector offices. This in return increases the opportunity cost as well as the financial cost of registrations, which many poor families are not willing to pay. Data collected at village level could simply be transferred to the census agents at the sector level. Currently, however, registration is perceived as an additional tax by the population, which is why they try to evade it, and as an additional source of income for civil servants, which is why they do not have any interest in decentralizing it to *localité* chiefs. These factors make it difficult to increase the number of registrations and make the process more systematic. In addition, fieldwork has shown that there is mistrust toward what is perceived as "Bantu power", with the Bantus being associated with the agents of the state.

CONCLUSION

This chapter demonstrates that the Pygmies in Central Africa not only tend to live in extreme poverty, but also, via qualitative evidence, indicates they are often the victims of prejudice. Many aspects of the Pygmies' living conditions, which are directly linked to their traditional lifestyle, are considered by other groups such as the Bantu to be an example of a lifestyle that is "dedicated to suffering." Their hardiness is seen as an adaptation to a "life of shortages." They lack drinking water, sufficient and diversified food, solid houses that can protect them against bad weather, hygiene, commodities, and presentable clothes and shoes. The study also suggests that this negative image is increasingly becoming the way that the Pygmies see themselves too. They wish to make up for "their shortcomings" and when asked, individually or in groups, they respond that they want to be "like them" (the Bantu).

Thus, there is a fundamental ambiguity in the Pygmies' position toward their own culture and identity. This culture and identity is a symbol for archaism and often understood as the reason for their marginalization by many Bantu. At the same time, the Pygmies are also seen, and see themselves, to embody a valuable cultural heritage that should be protected and preserved. Their culture embodies one of the most original forms of human adaptation to the particular ecological conditions of the rainforest. They have a sophisticated knowledge of their environment and the possibilities for humans to adapt to it in a sustainable manner. They also have valuable cultural and artistic skills that are a major component of their countries' heritage.

It is clear that the Pygmies are in the process of an accelerated integration into the broader society through their sedentarization. As an unmanaged process with little input from the Pygmies themselves, their sedentarization to date has been intimately linked with their impoverishment, exploitation, and poor health and education outcomes. The challenge for minorities such as the Pygmy is to manage the process of their transformation in an increasingly global society. This, however, requires a degree of autonomy, empowerment, and education that the Pygmies lack. As the poorest group in some of the world's poorest countries (especially in the case of CAR and the DRC), they do not currently have the means or capacity to manage and benefit from the process of acculturation.

ANNEX 1: METHODOLOGY FOR THE QUALITATIVE ANALYSIS OF THE PYGMIES IN THE DRC

The qualitative and institutional analysis of the socioeconomic condition of the Pygmies in the DRC presented in this chapter is adapted from World Bank (2009), and this annex is adapted with minor modifications from the description of the methodology provided in World Bank (2009: 10–11). The DRC qualitative study followed a participatory approach to the collection of data, analysis, and diagnosis of the situation of Pygmy communities, and recommendations proposed to address the structural factors that contribute to their marginalization and vulnerability.

The study relied on information generated through: (1) an initial participatory consultation with key stakeholders; and (2) data collection in the nine provinces where Pygmy communities live (Kivu Sud, Kivu Nord, Maniema, Katanga, Kasai Oriental, Kasai Occidental, Equateur, Bandandu, and Province Orientale), including interviews with key informants and focus groups.

To collect field information, tables and frames were prepared, tested, and provided to surveyors who were trained and selected from within local NGOs working with Pygmy communities. Eleven frames (fiches) were prepared, covering: localization of Pygmy groups, administrative registration and identification of groups, administrative and political representation, electoral participation, living conditions, economic situation, access to health care, access to education, justice and security, cultural heritage, and relations with neighbors. The tables and frames were filled out in the field in a selected number of Pygmy camps in each of the nine provinces, then compiled and analyzed by a Kinshasa-based international consultant with support from two experts (one of which was a Pygmy) from OSAPY, a local NGO that coordinated the fieldwork.

The objectives of the field work were to: (1) validate and, if needed, adjust the information derived from the initial workshop; (2) identify the needs, concerns, objectives, and priorities of Pygmy communities in each province; (3) identify and prioritizing the causes of Pygmy impoverishment as seen by them; (4) identify and discuss mitigation measures as suggested by the Pygmies; and (5) make recommendations on how to address these issues and concerns.

Data and information were collected in a purposive sample of Pygmy camps based on their geographical location (in the forest, along a road, close to a city or a village) and status (sedentary, semi-sedentary, nomad). Within the Pygmy camps, information was obtained through individual interviews with key informants (Pygmies and non-Pygmies, with emphasis on the former), using open-ended questionnaires and discussions, focused discussions with diverse groups – including local authorities, women, elderly, and youth – and direct observation. Although it was not possible to carry out a statistically representative sample for this study (the total population is not known with precision and funding for the study was limited), coverage of all nine provinces and the selection criteria discussed earlier were significant enough to obtain a purposive sample to derive, analyze, and extrapolate data with an acceptable level of confidence.

The methodology used for the qualitative work in the DRC was thus a classic participatory approach that combined consultations at the lowest level and national validation workshops with expert input, thus ensuring relatively broad coverage and validation by relevant stakeholders. However, given the impossibility of surveying every Pygmy community, the involved NGOs had to call on their knowledge of Pygmy communities to fill out information gaps in the questionnaires. This affects to some extent the validity of the estimate of number of Pygmies, but also the analysis of issues confronting the Pygmies and the ensuing recommendations. Despite these limitations, the methodology and approach followed – especially the study's participatory nature – provide some assurances on the relevance and quality of the results obtained.

References

African Commission (2006). *Indigenous Peoples in Africa: The Forgotten Peoples?* Somerset, NJ: Transaction.

Backiny-Yetna, P., and Q. Wodon (2011a). "Pygmies in the Central African Republic: A Socio-Economic Diagnostic," mimeo, World Bank, Washington, DC.

(2011b). "Pygmies in Gabon: A Socio-Economic Diagnostic," mimeo, World Bank, Washington, DC.

Ben-Achour, M. A., Q. Wodon, and P. Backiny-Yetna (2011). "Pygmies in the Democratic Republic of Congo: A Socio-Economic Diagnostic," mimeo, World Bank, Washington, DC.

Elbers, Chris, Jean Olson Lanjouw, and Peter Lanjouw (2003). "Micro-Level Estimation of Poverty and Inequality." *Econometrica*, 71(1), 355–364.

Hall, G., and H. A. Patrinos (2006). *Indigenous Peoples, Poverty and Human Development in Latin America*. London: Palgrave Macmillan.

IRIN In-Depth (2006). *Minorities Under Siege: Pygmies Today in Africa*. Nairobi: United Nations.

Lewis, Jerome (2000). *The Batwa Pygmies of the Great Lakes Region*. London: Minority Rights Group.

Martinez-Cobo, J. (1986). "Study of the Problem of Discrimination against Indigenous Populations." United Nations Sub-Commission on the Prevention of Discrimination and the Protection of Minorities (UN Doc. E/CN.4/Sub.2/1986/7).

Ndaywel e Nzie (1997). *Histoire du Zaïre. De l'héritage ancien à l'âge contemporain*. Duculot: Louvain-la-Neuve.

Patrinos, H. A., E. Skoufias, and T. Lunde (2007). "Indigenous Peoples in Latin America: Economic Opportunities and Social Networks," World Bank Policy Research Working Paper 4227, Washington, DC.

Thomas, J. M. C. and S. Bahuchet (1983). *Encyclopédie des pygmées Aka: Techniques, langage et société des chasseurs-cueilleurs de la forêt centrafricaine (Sud-Centrafrique et Nord-Congo). I (1). Les Pygmées Aka*. Paris: Centre national de la recherche scientifique.

Turnbull, Colin M. (1961). *The Forest People: A Study of the Pygmies of the Congo*. New York: Simon & Schuster.

World Bank (2009). "Democratic Republic of Congo: Strategic Framework for the Preparation of a Pygmy Development Program," Report No. 51108–ZR, Washington, DC.

5

China

A Case Study in Rapid Poverty Reduction

Emily Hannum and Meiyan Wang

INTRODUCTION

This chapter investigates poverty and social welfare among China's minority groups. Focusing on the Zhuang, Manchu, Hui, Miao, and Uygur populations – China's five largest minority groups – as well as other minorities in the aggregate, this chapter begins by providing an introduction to the classification of ethnic groups in China. We consider the relationship of this classification scheme to the concept of indigenous populations, and develop working definitions of minority status and ethnic group for use in the chapter. We then discuss recent economic trends and introduce some of the main government policies targeted toward ethnic minorities. With this context established, we introduce the data employed in the chapter, namely the 2002 rural sample of the Chinese Household Income Project and recent censuses and surveys.

We then proceed to the main body of the chapter. We present empirical evidence about demographics and geography and investigate ethnic disparities in poverty rates, income and employment, educational access and attainment, health care, and access to social programs. We close with a summary of main findings and their implications for development activities in minority areas and for further policy research on ethnic stratification.

NATIONALITIES, ETHNIC GROUPS, AND THE CONCEPT OF INDIGENOUS POPULATIONS

We begin by providing background on the ethnic classifications used in this chapter. As in other countries, in China, concepts of ethnicity and the classification of ethnic groups have fluctuated dramatically over the course of history. The name used to refer to ethnic groups in China today, *minzu*

(民族), is a twentieth-century adaptation of the cognate Japanese term, *minzoku* (民族), and is often translated as "ethnic nation," "ethno-nation," or "nationality" (Gladney 2004). The particular categories in use today were largely set in place after the People's Republic of China was founded in 1949, as the State set out to identify and recognize as minority nationalities those who qualified among the hundreds of groups applying for national minority status. Decisions followed a Soviet model and were based on the "four commons": language, territory, economic life, and psychological makeup, meaning that ethnic minorities were identified as having common linguistic, economic, geographic, or cultural characteristics that distinguished them from the so-called Han majority population (Fei 1981, cited in Gladney 2004). Although scholars have debated the procedures for and aptness of some of the original official classifications, these classifications have become fairly set over time, with few new categories created in the ensuing years (Gladney 2004). Today, the Chinese government officially recognizes 55 minority nationalities (少数民族, *shaoshu minzu*), along with the Han majority nationality (汉族, *hanzu*), a "naturalized" category, and an unknown category that encompasses about 350 other ethnic groups not recognized individually (Wong 2000, p. 56). The officially designated minority population in China grew from 5.8 percent of the total in the 1964 census to more than 8 percent in 2000 (West 2004 and Table 5.1). China's minority populations are culturally and linguistically diverse, as suggested by the fact that they span the Sino-Tibetan, Indo-European, Austro-Asiatic, and Altaic language families (see Map 1 for an ethno-linguistic map of China).

Minzu categories do not map cleanly onto various notions of indigenous populations. Globally, the term "indigenous" is not one with a widely agreed-on definition. For purposes of illustrating disconnects between the "indigenous" concept and the concept of *minzu*, we will use one of several definitions proposed in a working paper by the UN Working Group on Indigenous Populations, and again in a report by the UN Development Group (Daes 1996, p. 22 and United Nations Development Group 2008, p. 9). This definition lists several elements "considered relevant to" the definition of indigenous by international organizations and legal experts (United Nations Development Group 2008, p. 9):

1. priority in time, with respect to the occupation and use of a specific territory;
2. the voluntary perpetuation of cultural distinctiveness, which may include the aspects of language, social organization, religion and spiritual values, modes of production, laws and institutions;

Table 5.1. *Percent minority by province, 2000*

Region	Province	Minority share (%)
National	—	8.41
North	Beijing	4.26
	Tianjin	2.64
	Hebei	4.31
	Shanxi	0.29
	Inner Mongolia	20.76
Northeast	Liaoning	16.02
	Jilin	9.03
	Heilongjiang	5.02
East	Shanghai	0.60
	Jiangsu	0.33
	Zhejiang	0.85
	Anhui	0.63
	Fujian	1.67
	Jiangxi	0.27
	Shandong	0.68
Central-South	Henan	1.22
	Hubei	4.34
	Hunan	10.21
	Guangdong	1.42
	Guangxi	38.34
	Hainan	17.29
Southwest	Chongqing	6.42
	Sichuan	4.98
	Guizhou	37.85
	Yunnan	33.41
	Tibet	94.07
Northwest	Shaanxi	0.49
	Gansu	8.69
	Qinghai	45.51
	Ningxia	34.53
	Xinjiang	59.39

Source: China Bureau of Statistics 2001, table 4-11.

3. self-identification, as well as recognition by other groups, or by State authorities, as a distinct collectivity; and
4. an experience of subjugation, marginalization, dispossession, exclusion, or discrimination, whether or not these conditions persist.

According to Michaud (2009, p. 37), no organizations from China are found on the list of members of the UN Forum on the World's Indigenous

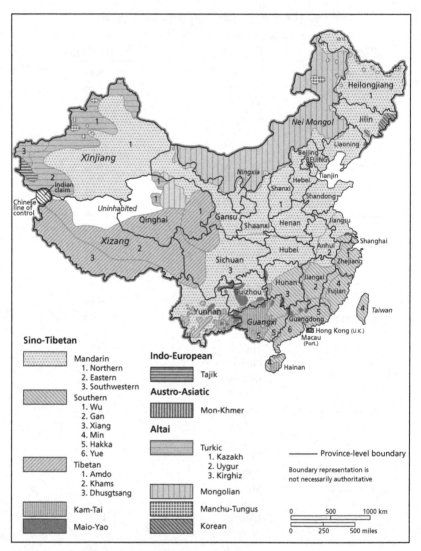

Map 1. Chinese linguistic groups, 1990.
Note: This map includes languages spoken by the Han majority.
Source: University of Texas Perry-Castañeda Library Map Collection, 1990.

People. While these circumstances may be due in part to a political reluctance to label minorities in this way, the notion of indigenous peoples is not
wholly appropriate for other reasons (Michaud 2009, p. 37). As Michaud
(2009, p. 37) writes of the highland groups of southwest China, one issue
is that many groups are not actually indigenous to the region where they

dwell today. More broadly, whereas members of some minority groups do meet the above elements of the definition of "indigenous," with the exception of the third point about official recognition on the preceding list, one could argue that some groups designated as ethnic minorities in China fail to meet the elements of the definition of indigenous populations. Conversely, some members of the group labeled as being part of the ethnic majority Han population, especially some rural members, could be argued to meet definitional elements. In fact, while the term for the majority, Han, has existed throughout history in China, Gladney (2004) has argued that the promulgation and widespread acceptance of an official Han label in the early twentieth century served a political purpose of unifying disparate sociocultural groups under a common national ethnic identity – groups with strong local identities and cultures and dialects as disparate as different romance languages.

Conceptually, there is room to debate the most appropriate boundaries with which to classify groups for the purpose of investigating issues of ethnicity or indigenous status. However, empirically, there is no option at present other than to employ the official *minzu* categories. To follow conventional English usage, we translate *minzu* categories as ethnic categories rather than ethno-nation or nationality categories. Where possible, we discuss particular ethnic groups, focusing on the largest ethnic minority groups – the Zhuang (Bouxcuengh) (壮族, *Zhuangzu*), the Manchu (满族, *Manzu*), the Hui (回族, *Huizu*), the Miao or Hmong (苗族, *Miaozu*), and the Uygur (sometimes also spelled Uighur, Uigur, or in transliteration of the Mandarin ethnonym, Weiwuerzu or Weizu) (维吾尔族, *Weiwuerzu*) – along with an "Other" category that encompasses all other groups than these and the Han majority. However, because of limited data sources on ethnic minorities and small sample sizes, and owing to the need for a parsimonious summary of ethnic differences, some of the chapter will compare minorities as a group to nonminorities as a group. Any summary statements about the overall situation of minorities will necessarily gloss over the cultural and socioeconomic diversity across, and of course also within, ethnic categories.

ECONOMIC HISTORY

Incomes in China have grown dramatically in recent decades, with mean household per capita income growing from 272 Yuan in 1981 to 990 Yuan in 2001 (at 1980 prices) (Ravallion and Chen 2007, table 1). Measured by the new international poverty standard of 1.25 USD per person per day, China's poverty headcount index dropped from 85 percent in 1981 to 27 percent in 2004, with rapid progress in the most recent period (World Bank 2009, p. iii; estimates using 2005 Purchasing Power Parity for China). Rates are much lower using China's official poverty line, but the reduction is similarly dramatic. At the same time, the impact of growth on the poor has been mitigated by rising inequality (Ravallion and Chen 2007). According to a recent World Bank report, estimates from national rural and urban household surveys indicate that the Gini index of income inequality rose from 30.9 percent in 1981 to 45.3 percent by 2003 (World Bank 2009, p. 33).

Importantly for the purposes of this chapter, patterns of growth, poverty reduction, and inequality have been uneven across regions. For example, using multi-province panel data, Goh, Luo, and Zhu (2009, p. 489) found that between 1989 and 2004, income in coastal provinces more than tripled, whereas income in inland provinces doubled. By 2004, mean per capita household income in inland provinces was barely two-thirds of the corresponding coastal province figure. Ravallion and Chen (2007, p. 31) found that coastal provinces had significantly higher trend rates of poverty reduction, compared to other provinces. Poverty is most severe in remote mountainous and minority areas (World Bank 2009).

The urban-rural dimension of inequality is also important, with estimates of the ratio of nominal mean urban income to rural income reaching as high as 3.3 by 2007 (World Bank 2009, p. 35). The income gap between rural and urban areas fell after the initiation of market reforms in 1978, then increased after the late 1980s, although when adjustments are made for inflation and for cost-of-living differences between rural and urban areas, the trend is less strong (Cai and Wang 2008, p. 61; World Bank 2009). However, urban-rural income ratios still increased significantly since the mid-1990s, and the absolute gap between urban and rural incomes widened tremendously (World Bank 2009, p. 35). Sicular et al. (2007, table 1) correct for a number of data limitations in earlier work that may have overstated the urban-rural gap and still estimate a substantial urban-rural income ratio in 2002, at 2.3. Other recent estimates indicate that household per capita incomes in urban areas have been roughly 2.5 to 2.7 times those in rural areas in recent years (Ravallion and Chen 2007; Cai and Wang 2008; World Bank 2009).

Like levels of income, the urban-rural gap in income has a spatial dimension. Goh, Luo and Zhu (2009, p. 489) found that the rural-urban gap in inland provinces was wider and rose faster than in coastal provinces. Similarly, Sicular et al. (2007) found that urban-rural income ratios in the western regions were higher – greater than 3 – than those in the center or eastern regions, at about two. Moreover, between 1995 and 2002, the urban-rural gap rose in the west and center but declined in the east, suggesting that those parts of China where poverty is most concentrated were falling farther behind, in relative terms (Sicular et al. 2007, pp. 101–102). As we discuss further in the section on demographics and geography, for those minority groups that live disproportionately in interior regions, rural areas, and remote and mountainous areas, even though growth and poverty reduction are likely to have ameliorated absolute economic disadvantage, patterns of inequality are likely to have perpetuated relative disadvantage.

POLICIES RELATED TO ETHNIC MINORITIES

Government policies that shape the rights and opportunities of official minorities are also important as context for understanding social and economic disparities by ethnic group. Being a member of a recognized ethnic minority in China implies a set of statuses somewhat different from those of nonminority members. One important element of minority status is access, at least for groups in some regions, to political representation through regional autonomy policies. According to a 2000 White Paper on minority policy in China (Information Office of the State Council of the People's Republic of China 2000, section 3), "Regional autonomy for ethnic minorities means that under the unified leadership of the state[,] regional autonomy is practiced in areas where people of ethnic minorities live in concentrated communities; in these areas[,] [instruments] of self-government are established for the exercise of autonomy and for people of ethnic minorities to become masters of their own areas and manage the internal affairs of their own regions."[1] There are several types of autonomous areas for ethnic minorities in China, established under different demographic circumstances, including autonomous regions, prefectures, counties, and

---

[1] The White Paper gives additional details on sources of these rights (Information Office of the State Council of the People's Republic of China 2000, section 3):

The Common Program of the CPPCC, adopted at the first CPPCC session on September 29, 1949 and serving as the country's provisional constitution, defined regional autonomy for ethnic minorities as a basic policy and one of the important political systems of the state. The Program for the Implementation of Ethnic Regional Autonomy of the People's Republic of China, issued on August 8, 1952, embodied overall arrangements for the implementation of regional autonomy for national minorities. The Constitution of the People's Republic of China adopted in 1954 and later amended and promulgated defines such autonomy as an important political system of state. The Law of the People's Republic of China on Ethnic Regional Autonomy, promulgated in 1984, contains systematic provisions on the political, economic and cultural rights and duties of ethnic minority autonomous areas.

townships (Information Office of the State Council of the People's Republic of China 2000, section 3). At the highest administrative level, there are five province-level autonomous regions: the Inner Mongolia Autonomous Region (内蒙古自治区, *Nei Menggu Zizhiqu*), founded in 1947; the Xinjiang Uygur Autonomous Region (新疆维吾尔自治区, *Xinjiang Weiwuer Zizhiqu*), founded in 1955; the Guangxi Zhuang Autonomous Region (广西壮族自治区, *Guangxi Zhuangzu Zizhiqu*), founded in 1958; the Ningxia Hui Autonomous Region (宁夏回族自治区, *Ningxia Huizu Zizhiqu*), also founded in 1958; and the Tibet Autonomous Region (西藏自治区, *Xizang Zizhiqu*), founded in 1965.

Autonomous areas have the right to self-government. The instruments of self-government of autonomous areas, as stipulated in the Constitution, are the people's congresses and people's governments of autonomous regions, autonomous prefectures, and autonomous counties (Information Office of the State Council of the People's Republic of China 2000, section 3). The Law on Ethnic Regional Autonomy specifies that all ethnic groups in autonomous areas shall elect appropriate numbers of deputies to take part in the people's congresses at various levels (Information Office of the State Council of the People's Republic of China 2000, section 3). Specifically, among the chairman or vice-chairmen of the standing committee of the people's congress of an autonomous area, there shall be one or more citizens of the ethnic group or groups exercising regional autonomy in the area concerned; the head of an autonomous region, autonomous prefecture, or autonomous county shall be a citizen of the ethnic group exercising regional autonomy in the area concerned, and the other members of the people's governments of these regions, prefectures, and counties shall include members of the ethnic group exercising regional autonomy, as well as members of other ethnic minorities, as far as possible. Instruments of self-government in autonomous areas have a series of designated rights and functions, which include legislative power, the power to "flexibly carry out, or halt the carrying out of, some decisions," the right to develop area economies and control local finances, the power to train and employ ethnic minority cadres (government officials), the power to develop education and minority cultures, the power to develop and employ local spoken and written languages, and the power to develop technological, scientific and cultural and undertakings (Information Office of the State Council of the People's Republic of China 2000, section 3). [2]

---

[2] The white paper also lays out a series of specific statements about rights (Information Office of the State Council of the People's Republic of China 2000, section 3):

The people's congresses of the autonomous areas have the right to enact regulations on the exercise of autonomy and separate regulations in light of local political, economic

Beyond policies on regional autonomy, the reform era dating from the late 1970s has seen the emergence of a growing network of laws intended to advance the interests of historically disadvantaged ethnic groups, with the intention of improving ethnic relations (Sautman 1999). Policies confer specific benefits on minority groups, including the heightened access to local political office already discussed, looser family-planning restrictions, educational benefits, and special economic assistance, including tax relief (Hoddie 1998, p. 120; Sautman 1999; Gladney 2004). These policies have contributed to a situation in which individuals have moved across ethnic boundaries over time to claim minority status – a phenomenon particularly pronounced in the early reform years immediately following the Cultural Revolution (Hoddie 1998; Gladney 2004, pp. 20–21).

Some of the most important incentives for claiming minority status have to do with family-planning policies and education policies. Fertility controls in China are less stringent for many minority groups than for the Han majority (Gladney 2004, p. 81). Gu et al. (2007) recently reviewed provincial fertility control policies in China, with a focus on provincial differences in the implementation of the one-child policy. The authors found that only five of China's thirty-one provinces, municipalities, and autonomous regions did not grant a second-child exemption to minority couples, reportedly defined as a couple in which at least one member belongs to a recognized minority group (see table 1, pp. 134–135). In all of the eleven provinces, municipalities, and autonomous regions where a third-child exemption was granted under some conditions, minority status was a criterion, although the details of the exemption varied considerably from place to place (see table 1, pp. 134–135).

and cultural characteristics. … If resolutions, decisions, orders and instructions from the higher-level state organs are not suited to the actual conditions of the autonomous areas, the organs of self-government of these areas may be flexible in carrying them out or may decide not to carry them out after approval by the higher state organs. … Organs of self-government of autonomous areas may independently arrange and manage local economic construction within the guidance of state planning, and formulate policies, principles and plans for their economic construction according to their local characteristics and requirements. The organs of self-government in the autonomous areas have trained a large number of minority cadres, technicians, management personnel and other specialized personnel and skilled workers in line with the needs of national construction and brought their roles in work into full play. … Organs of self-government of autonomous areas may decide their own local education programs, including the establishment of schools, the length of study, the forms of school running, course contents, language of instruction and procedures of enrollment and develop independently their own type of education based on their ethnic minority characteristics and within the state education policies and relevant laws. … Organs of self-government of autonomous areas make their own decisions concerning medical and health work.

In education, since the late 1970s, policy makers have supported the establishment of minority boarding schools and affirmative action policies for matriculation into colleges and universities, and subsidies for minority students (Lin 1997; Sautman 1999, p. 289; Ross 2006, p. 25). University admission quotas reserve spots only for minorities at universities, and minorities can be accepted with lower entrance scores on the Unified Examination for University Entrance (*gaokao*, 高考) (Clothey 2005, p. 396). In addition to these benefits, twelve national minority institutes and one national minority university have been established, dedicated specifically to the higher education of minority students (Clothey 2005, p. 396). Given the great demand for higher education, these benefits are highly prized and offer significant incentives for claiming minority status.

Although not a central element of incentives for claiming minority status, an additional set of important education policies have sought to address language of instruction issues critical for enhancing minority educational participation. The Chinese constitution has two provisions concerning language (Ma 2007, p. 15): Article 4 states that each ethnic group has the freedom to use and develop its own language and writing system, and Article 19 states that the national government will promote a common language to be used throughout the country. Article 6 of the Compulsory Education Law specifies that schools should promote the use of Mandarin (the national vernacular) (Ma 2007, p. 15). In a 1980 publication,[3] the Ministry of Education and the China State Ethnic Affairs Commission required that every ethnic group with a language and writing system should use that language for educational instruction, while also learning spoken and written Mandarin (Ma 2007, p. 15).

Regional and local governments shape the ways in which bilingual and multicultural education are incorporated into education across China (for a discussion of legislation from different regional and local governments in China, see Zhou 2005; for in-depth case studies of bilingual education in Yunnan and Sichuan, see Xiao 1998 and Teng 2002). Ma (2007, pp. 15–16, quoting Zhou Wangyun 1989, p. 31) states that when governmental educational authorities were planning and developing bilingual education, the principle they employed was consideration of the existing local language environment, along with social and economic development needs, pedagogical benefits, and preferences of residents. Scholars classify the modes of bilingual education in

---

[3] The publication is "Opinions Concerning Improving the Work of Minority Education" [关于加强民族教育工作的意见], Guanyu jiaqiang minzu jiaoyu gongzuo de yijian," cited in Ma 2007, p. 15.

China as falling into transition models (transitioning to Mandarin) or maintenance models (maintaining the origin language), with the determination between the two affected by the existence of a well-established writing system and the ethnic composition of local areas (Lin 1997; Teng 2002; Feng 2005, p. 534; see Ross 2006 for a discussion of language law in China).[4]

There are significant practical challenges to developing minority-language materials for instruction, especially for smaller minority groups and those without well-established writing systems. Important and obvious among these challenges are the human and economic resource constraints that pervade schools serving poor rural communities. Situations where there is no minority written language, or where there are multiple, non-Han ethnic groups attending the same school, present additional challenges. Another challenge to meaningful bilingual education is that of developing curriculum when instructional concepts do not exist in the minority language.[5] This practical linguistic challenge also represents an extreme example of the kind of cultural discontinuity that children from some minority groups may experience in the school system.

Despite these challenges, there is a significant commitment to minority language maintenance and bilingual education (Ross 2006; see CERNET 2005a, 2005b). The reform era dating from the late 1970s has seen support by policy makers for the increased use of several minority scripts in literacy education and for increased bilingual education, such that schools with a majority of minority language users can use minority languages as the primary medium of instruction (Ministry of Education 1986, Article 6: Ministry of Education 1995, Article 12; Lin 1997; Sautman 1999, p. 289; CERNET 2005a; Ross 2006, p. 25).[6] Candidates for nationalities institutes

[4] There is much contention surrounding what combination of languages of instruction best serves the needs of minority children (Feng 2005). A debate exists between prioritizing rapid immersion into Mandarin, as a prerequisite for educational advancement and economic mobility, or first language maintenance and development, thought to offer carryover effects on literacy in the second language, and valuable for promoting cultural diversity and cultural survival.

[5] We thank Professors Wang Jiayi and Xu Jieying at Northwest Normal University for helpful conversations that pointed out these challenges in curricular content in minority languages.

[6] The 1986 and 1995 laws emphasize popularization of Mandarin, as well as use of minority languages. For example, the 1995 law states, "The Chinese language, both oral and written, shall be the basic oral and written language for education in schools and other educational institutions. Schools or other educational institutions which mainly consist of students from minority nationalities may use in education the language of the respective nationality or the native language commonly adopted in that region. Schools and other educational institutions shall in their educational activities popularize the nationally common spoken Chinese and the standard written characters" (Article 12).

may sit the *gaokao* in their native language, although it is not clear that all minority languages are available as options (Clothey 2005, p. 396). Some applicants to minority region comprehensive universities and polytechnic institutes may also take the exam in their native language, and minority students may take higher-education courses in their region's main nationality language (Clothey 2005, pp. 397–398).

Many of the economic benefits accruing to minorities have to do with the fact that poverty-stricken minority areas have figured prominently in China's rural poverty alleviation initiatives. A key characteristic of national poverty alleviation efforts has been regional targeting – that poverty reduction funds from the government are targeted at defined regions and not directly at poor populations (Wang 2004, pp. 19–20). Counties remained the basic units for state poverty reduction investments until 2001 (Wang 2004, p. 19). The central government designated national poor counties, beginning in 1986, and required that provincial governments also designate and support with provincial funds "provincial poor counties" (Wang 2004, p. 22).

In principal, the standard for being selected as a nationally designated poor county was that the average net income per capita of all rural residents within the county was less than 150 Yuan in 1985, but less than one-third of designated counties actually met this standard (Information Office of the State Council of the People's Republic of China 2001, section IV; Wang 2004, p. 20). In part, the slippage in targeting was because of special treatment given to minority areas (Wang 2004, p. 20). For example, according to a White Paper on rural poverty reduction, the relief standard set for autonomous counties could be 200 Yuan to 300 Yuan (Information Office of the State Council of the People's Republic of China 2001, section IV). After the 1993 launch of the "Eight-Seven Poverty Reduction Plan (1994–2000)," which had the goal of eliminating absolute poverty by the end of the century, the government made adjustments to the designated poor county list (Wang 2004, p. 20). Among the 592 impoverished counties on the State's adjusted list, there were 257 ethnic minority counties, accounting for almost half of the total (Information Office of the State Council of the People's Republic of China 2001, section IV).

In addition to favoring autonomous regions and western provinces with large ethnic minority populations such as Yunnan, Guizhou, and Qinghai in allocating aid-the-poor funds, the central government has also arranged special funds such as the "Ethnic Minority Development Fund" to address specific problems facing minority areas (Information Office of the State Council of the People's Republic of China 2001, section IV). According to government reports, from 1994 to 2000, the State invested 43.253 billion Yuan in the Inner

Mongolia, Guangxi, Tibet, Ningxia, and Xinjiang Autonomous Regions, as well as Guizhou, Yunnan, and Qinghai provinces (Information Office of the State Council of the People's Republic of China 2001, section IV). During one or two years during the Eight-Seven Plan, poverty alleviation credit funds for six relatively economically developed coastal provinces (Guangdong, Fujian, Zhejiang, Jiangsu, Shandong, and Liaoning) were pooled for use among the central and western regions where the poverty problems were more severe (Government of China 1993). The plan also specified that in nationally designated old military base areas, minority areas, and border areas, new businesses could have a three-year delay in paying taxes, or pay only partial taxes (Government of China 1993). Minority areas remained a focus of poverty alleviation and development strategies in the most recent plan, the "Poverty Reduction Compendium, 2001–2010," in which village targeting was proposed, although key poverty reduction counties were still designated and the counties would still exercise overall administration of poverty reduction funds (Government of China 2001; Wang 2004, p. 24).

DATA USED

In the remainder of this chapter, we assess available evidence about the socioeconomic circumstances of ethnic minorities in China. To do so, we draw on four sources of data. The first source, referred to hereafter as the 1990 Census, is a 1 percent micro-sample of the 1990 China population census data. The second data source, referred to hereafter as the 2000 census, is a 0.95 per thousand micro-sample of the 2000 China population census data. The third source of data, referred to hereafter as the 2005 mid-censal survey or mini-census, is a 20 percent micro-sample of the 2005 China 1 percent population-sampling survey data. For these three data sources, we dropped collective households from the sample and only analyzed family households. These sources cover all provinces. The 1990 and 2000 census forms were very limited and do not contain information on earnings. The 2005 mini-census does contain earnings information.

The fourth source of data employed here is the 2002 Rural Chinese Household Income Project survey data, referred to hereafter as the 2002 CHIP. The 2002 CHIP rural sample is a multistage sample that covers twenty-two provincial level administrative units of China: Beijing, Hebei, Shanxi, Liaoning, Jilin, Jiangsu, Zhejiang, Anhui, Jiangxi, Shandong, Henan, Hubei, Hunan, Guangdong, Guanxi, Chongqing, Sichuan, Guizhou, Yunnan, Shaanxi, Gansu and Xinjiang. Sampled households are located in 961 villages located in 120 different counties (Gustafsson and

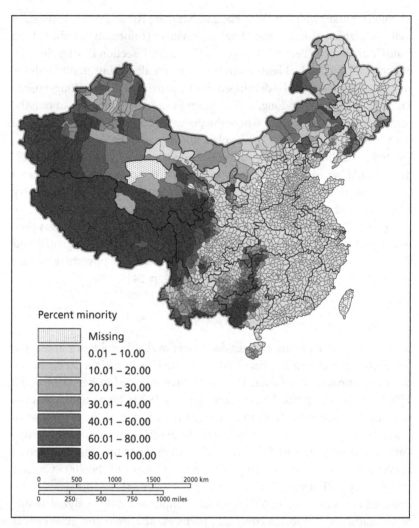

Map 2. Distribution of the minority population by county-level administrative units, 2000.
Source: West 2004, map 1.

Ding 2006, p. 5).[7] In addition to household questionnaires, village questionnaires were administered to cadres.

---

[7]   Gustafsson and Ding (2008, p. 7) provide a useful description of the sample for the rural 2002 CHIP: "The sample was drawn from the large sample used by [the National Bureau of Statistics] in its annual household survey covering around 67,000 households. This sample is selected in a multi-stage procedure to be representative at the province level and each province statistical bureau is responsible for samples at the village level. At the village level,

Table 5.2. *National poverty county status in minority*
and nonminority villages (two definitions)

	Village is minority area[1]		50%+ of village households are minority[2]	
	No	Yes	No	Yes
Village in National Poverty County (percent yes)	19.8	36.9	21.2	32.0

[1] Pearson: Uncorrected chi2(1) = 21.0908.
[2] Pearson: Uncorrected chi2(1) = 7.2336
Source: CHIP 2002 Village Data.

DEMOGRAPHICS AND GEOGRAPHY

We turn next to a discussion of demographics and geography. In certain parts of China, minorities constitute a much larger proportion of the population than their national share of 8 percent, and demographic differences across China's regions and urban-rural divide are significantly related to patterns of socioeconomic advantage and disadvantage by ethnic group. There are three interrelated dimensions of geography – region, urbanicity, and topography – that provide critical context for thinking about ethnic differences in many dimensions of social welfare. First, for many groups, ethnic differences in social welfare indicators are tied closely to China's regional economic disparities, meaning coast-interior and interprovincial economic disparities. Many ethnic groups reside in the interior western parts of the country. As Table 5.1 and Map 2 illustrate, minorities are most heavily represented in the strategic, resource-rich periphery in portions of the northeast, central-south to southwest, and northwest (Schein 1997, p. 71–72). In 2000, the Autonomous Regions – Tibet, Xinjiang, Guangxi, Ningxia, and Inner Mongolia – along with the provinces of Qinghai (青海), Guizhou (贵州), and Yunnan (云南), contained the most county-level units with minority population shares exceeding 40 percent (West 2004). These regions and provinces are among the poorest in terms of rural household income (West 2004). Among villages sampled in the rural 2002 Chinese Household Income Project (CHIP) survey, about one-fifth of nonminority villages were in nationally designated poor counties, compared to about one-third of minority villages (see Table 5.2).

a probability sample of ten households is selected. The rural households are asked to keep detailed records of their expenditures as well as provide information on their income. A large number of assistant enumerators aid the households in keeping good accounts and in checking the information."

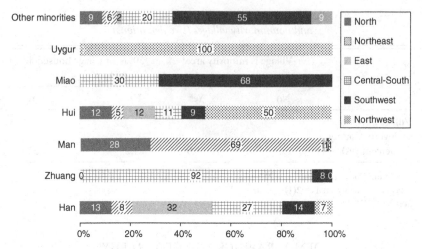

Figure 5.1. Regional distribution of ethnic groups, 2000.
Source: 2000 census.

However, the scope and nature of the disparity in geographic location compared to the Han population varies considerably across specific ethnic groups. Figure 5.1, based on the 2000 census, depicts the distribution by ethnic group across China's macro-regions. Distributions are shown for the Han population, for each of the five largest minority groups, and for other minorities, as a group. About 59 percent of the Han population is in the east and central south, with just 14 percent and 7 percent in the poor regions of the southwest and northwest, respectively. The picture is quite different for minorities. Nearly all Zhuang live in the central-south region (92 percent), the location of the Guangxi Zhuang Autonomous Region, with the remainder living in the southwest (8 percent). Nearly all Manchus live in the north (28 percent) and northeast regions (69 percent); virtually all Miao live in the central-south (30 percent) and southwest (68 percent); and virtually all Uygurs (close to 100 percent) live in the northwest, the vast majority in their home Autonomous Region. Fully half of all Hui, who are among the most dispersed of ethnic groups, live in the northwest, and 55 percent of other minorities live in the southwest.

As noted earlier, the urban-rural breakdown is also an important element of inequality, with household per capita incomes in urban areas far outpacing incomes in rural areas in recent years (Cai and Wang 2008). Minorities, as a group, are less urbanized than the Han population. Figure 5.2 illustrates this point by showing urbanization by ethnic group and year, based on the 2000 census and the 2005 mid-censal survey.

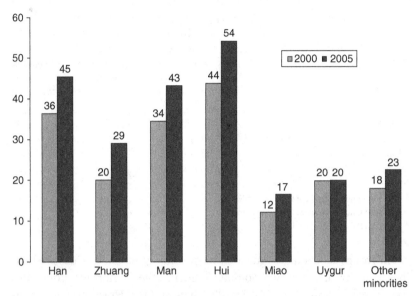

Figure 5.2. Urbanization rate by ethnic group and year.
Note: Definition of urban is that in operation at the time of the census or survey.
Source: 2000 census micro-sample and 2005 mid-censal survey.

Figure 5.2 also shows two important exceptions among the largest ethnic minority groups. One exception is the Manchus, descendants of the ruling class of the last imperial dynasty, the Qing Dynasty. Manchus tend to live in the more industrialized north and northeast, and their degree of urbanization approximates that of the Han. Manchus are a highly assimilated group, most of whom do not speak the Manchu language. This point is related to the fact that Manchus were among the groups with the highest rate of reclaiming minority status (moving from nonminority to minority status) in the 1980s (Hoddie 1998; West 2004, table 1).

The second exception is the Hui, sometimes known as ethnic Chinese Muslims to distinguish them from other Muslim ethnic groups of Turkic, Persian, and Mongolian descent. Hui are said to be descendents of Middle Eastern merchants, emissaries, soldiers, and traders who began coming to China as early as the Tang and Song Dynasties (618 A.D. to 1279 A.D.) and intermarried with local populations (Lipman 1998, p. 25; Gladney 2004, p. 161). Hui are among the most urbanized ethnic groups in China, as well as being highly dispersed across the country (Poston and Shu 1987, p. 25). Gladney (2004) has suggested that because the category "Hui" has been defined mainly based on religion, it encompasses groups with very different geographical ties and cultural practices.

Table 5.3. *Village topography in minority and nonminority*
villages (two definitions)

	Village is minority area[1]		50%+ of village households are minority[2]	
	No	Yes	No	Yes
Flat	49.0	52.3	49.6	46.8
Hilly	33.2	9.4	32.7	9.7
Mountainous	17.8	38.3	17.7	43.5
Total	100	100	100	100

[1] Pearson: Uncorrected chi2(2) = 49.6457.
[2] Pearson: Uncorrected chi2(2) = 53.4936.
Source: CHIP 2002 Village Data.

All groups except the Uygur, a Turkic Muslim group that resides predominantly in Xinjiang, an Autonomous Region in the far northwest of China, were notably more urbanized in 2005 than in 2000. However, the continuing low levels of urbanization among the Zhuang, but especially among the Miao, Uygur, and "Other" categories, suggest the disadvantaged context, in terms of infrastructure and economic opportunities, faced by these groups.

Finally, and related to the regional and urbanization differences already mentioned, minorities are more likely to live in more isolated, remote villages with difficult topography and poor infrastructure. In villages surveyed as part of the 2002 CHIP, minority villages were about twice as likely as nonminority villages to be located in mountainous areas – 38 percent to 44 percent of minority villages, depending on definition, were reported to be in mountainous areas (see Table 5.3). Related to these topographical differences, minority villages sampled in the 2002 CHIP tended to be more isolated: further from seats of government and transportation; more recently electrified; and more likely to still lack telephone access (see Table 5.4; for a detailed description of economic differences across minority and nonminority villages, see Gustaffson and Ding 2006). As becomes clear in the following discussions, regional and urban-rural inequalities and village remoteness and isolation are important pieces of contextual information in interpreting ethnic differences in poverty, income, and social welfare outcomes.

POVERTY AND INCOME DISPARITIES

We turn now to a discussion of poverty and income, in which we draw on survey data from the 2002 CHIP rural sample. There is no official urban

Table 5.4. *Village isolation in minority and nonminority villages (two definitions)*

	Village is minority area		50%+ of village households are minority	
	No	Yes	No	Yes
Village distance...				
from Nearest County Seat (km)*	22.5	33.7	23.0	33.2
from Nearest Township Government (km)*	4.6	6.9	4.7	7.1
from Nearest Transportation Terminal (km)*	5.0	7.6	5.0	7.6
Electricity available...*				
before 1969	30.3	15.4	30.2	14.4
1970–1979	36.1	26.8	36.0	27.2
1980–1989	26.0	31.5	25.7	32.8
1990–1998	6.7	14.1	6.6	14.4
after 1999	1.0	10.7	1.4	9.6
not yet	0.0	1.3	0.0	1.6
Telephone available...*				
before 1969	19.5	14.1	19.6	12.8
1970–1979	11.1	9.4	11.4	7.2
1980–1989	12.2	4.0	11.8	4.8
1990–1998	34.2	20.1	33.5	24.0
after 1999	19.7	36.2	19.4	38.4
not yet	3.3	16.1	4.2	12.8

* Significantly different at 05 level for both typologies of minority village.
Source: CHIP 2002 village data.

poverty line in China, and different instruments are used to measure household income in rural and urban areas, so we restrict our analyses to the rural sample. The CHIP data are the only publicly available data source that has reasonable coverage of minority areas and comprehensive measures of household income. However, the CHIP data in 2002 do have some limitations for our purposes. They cover twenty-two provinces out of thirty-one and do not cover some significant minority areas, including the Ningxia Hui, Tibet, and Inner Mongolia Autonomous Regions.

Earlier analyses of CHIP data (Khan 2008, cited in Gustafsson and Ding 2008) have shown that rural poverty decreased dramatically between 1995 and 2002. However, majority-minority differences in poverty remain substantial. Table 5.5 shows the official rural poverty line, official rural poverty headcount indices, and the same measures calculated from the 2002 rural CHIP data.

Table 5.5. *Rural poverty lines and headcount estimates,*
Han vs. minority population

Line	RHS Total	CHIP 2002 Total		Han		Minority	
(Yuan)	Percent	Percent	N	Percent	N	Percent	N
Using Official Poverty Line							
1998 635	4.6	6.4	36,685	5.6	31,898	11.5	4,787
1999 625	3.7	4.8	36,710	4.2	31,923	8.8	4,787
2000 625	3.4	4.1	37,373	3.6	32,339	7.4	5,034
2001 630	3.2	4.4	37,362	3.7	32,328	8.8	5,034
2002 627	3.0	3.7	37,913	3.5	32,613	5.4	5,300
Using Low Income Line							
2000 — (875)	—	11.3	37,373	9.9	32,339	20.5	5,034
2001 872 (881)	9.7	10.6	37,362	8.9	32,328	21.4	5,034
2002 869 (878)	9.2	9.8	37,913	8.9	32,613	15.2	5,300

Notes: RHS=Rural Household Survey; CHIP=Chinese Household Income Project Survey. The low-income line for 2000 was not available in RSONBS 2004, so lines adapted for use with CHIP data by Gustafsson and Ding (2008), shown in parentheses, are used to calculate CHIP-based head-counts in this table. Italicized CHIP estimates indicate that information collected prior to 2000 may have been collected retrospectively – the documentation in the data source is not clear. Further, the valid sample drops for those years. These numbers should be treated with some caution.
Sources: Rural Survey Organization of the National Bureau of Statistics (RSONBS) 2004; Gustafsson and Ding 2008; CHIP 2002.

The CHIP data contain household total income and size for the years from 1998 to 2002, for households that were part of the rural household survey for those years. In the 2002 CHIP, 99 percent of the cases with valid data for 2002 also have valid data for the years 2000 and 2001; numbers are slightly lower for the earlier years for which data were collected and data from these years should be viewed with caution, as they may have been collected retrospectively. The upper panel shows poverty rates using the official poverty lines for each year, and the lower panel shows poverty rates using somewhat higher "low income" lines available for 2000 onward. By both measures, minorities in the rural CHIP sample have been roughly twice as likely as their Han counterparts to be in poverty until the most recent year, 2002, in which they were about 1.5 times as likely to be in poverty, according to the official poverty line, and slightly more than 1.5 times according to the higher low-income line. In 2002, by the lower official poverty line, about 3.5 percent of the Han sample was below the poverty line, compared to about 5.4 percent of the minority sample. Using the higher low-income line, the corresponding numbers were 8.9 percent for the Han sample and 15.2 percent for the minority sample. Gustafsson and Ding's (2008) analysis of the 2002 rural CHIP showed, moreover, that using the low-income line, almost one-third of ethnic minorities experienced poverty during the three years from 2000 to 2002, whereas the fraction experiencing poverty among the ethnic majority was only about half as high.

Can we generalize about ethnic differences or year-to-year changes from these estimates? Table 5.6 shows estimates, standard errors, and 95 percent confidence intervals[8] for the headcount measures shown in Table 5.5, as well as for the other Foster-Greer-Thorbecke[9] indices measuring depth of poverty – the poverty gap ratio and the squared poverty gap. Confidence intervals for the headcount index do not overlap for Han and minorities within any year. Comparing 2002 to 1998, headcount indices do not overlap for Han or minorities, suggesting a significant reduction in poverty between those years. If we focus instead on 2000 as the initial year for comparison, which may be warranted for data reasons described earlier, the confidence interval does not overlap for minorities but does for the Han, suggesting that poverty was significantly reduced between 2000 and 2002 for minorities only between these years.

For the additional poverty measures shown in Table 5.6, different stories emerge. The poverty gap ratio, signifying the mean shortfall from the poverty line (counting the nonpoor as having zero shortfall) expressed as a percentage of the poverty line, ranges from 2.8 percent in 1998 to 2 percent in 2002 for minorities, and from 1.5 percent to 0.9 percent for the Han subsample. The decline is not monotonic for minorities, and confidence intervals for most years have some overlap. The indicator for minorities is about twice that for the Han in most years. Confidence intervals for the Han and minorities never overlap.

---

[8] An important caveat is that the CHIP sample is a subsample of a larger Rural Household Survey sample, and the dataset does not include sufficient documentation to incorporate sample design effects in these calculations. A second caveat is that the year-to-year observations may not be fully independent. These caveats suggest that some caution is due in interpreting confidence intervals.

[9] These measures are the headcount index, the poverty gap ratio, and the squared poverty gap. They are calculated as $P_\alpha = (1/n)^* \Sigma_{i=1,q} [(z-y_i)/z]^\alpha$, where P is the poverty indicator, $\alpha=0$ for the headcount index, 1 for the poverty gap ratio, and 2 for the squared poverty gap ratio. Z is the poverty line, y_i is the income for person i, and q is the number of people who are poor.

Table 5.6. *Foster-Greer-Thorbecke (FGT) indices, standard errors, and confidence intervals (CI), rural CHIP sample, 2002*

Poverty Measure	Year	Han				Minority			
		Proportion	SE	CI Lower	CI Upper	Proportion	SE	CI Lower	CI Upper
Headcount									
	1998	*0.056*	*0.001*	*0.053*	*0.058*	*0.115*	*0.005*	*0.106*	*0.124*
	1999	*0.042*	*0.001*	*0.040*	*0.044*	*0.088*	*0.004*	*0.080*	*0.096*
	2000	0.036	0.001	0.034	0.038	0.074	0.004	0.067	0.081
	2001	0.037	0.001	0.035	0.039	0.088	0.004	0.081	0.096
	2002	0.035	0.001	0.033	0.037	0.054	0.003	0.048	0.060
Poverty Gap									
	1998	*0.015*	*0.000*	*0.015*	*0.016*	*0.028*	*0.002*	*0.024*	*0.031*
	1999	*0.012*	*0.000*	*0.011*	*0.013*	*0.023*	*0.002*	*0.020*	*0.027*
	2000	0.010	0.000	0.009	0.010	0.021	0.001	0.018	0.024
	2001	0.010	0.000	0.009	0.011	0.024	0.001	0.021	0.027
	2002	0.009	0.000	0.008	0.010	0.020	0.001	0.017	0.023
Squared Poverty Gap									
	1998	*0.007*	*0.000*	*0.007*	*0.008*	*0.013*	*0.001*	*0.011*	*0.015*
	1999	*0.006*	*0.000*	*0.005*	*0.006*	*0.012*	*0.001*	*0.010*	*0.014*
	2000	0.005	0.000	0.004	0.005	0.010	0.001	0.008	0.012
	2001	0.005	0.000	0.004	0.005	0.011	0.001	0.009	0.014
	2002	0.005	0.000	0.004	0.005	0.012	0.001	0.010	0.015

Notes: Measures are calculated using official poverty lines. Estimates, standard errors, and confidence intervals are calculated using the SEPOV routine in Stata. Available sampling documentation for the CHIP data precludes incorporating adjustments for the sample design. Italicized CHIP estimates indicate that information collected prior to 2000 may have been collected retrospectively – the documentation in the data source is not clear. Further, the valid sample drops for those years. These numbers should be treated with some caution. Sample sizes are as shown in Table 5.5.

The squared poverty gap measure, which measures the squared distance from the poverty line among the poor and measures the severity of poverty, is also about twice as high for minorities as for the majority, with nonoverlapping confidence intervals by ethnic category. There is little evidence of a consistent time trend. Point estimates diminish slightly among the Han; confidence intervals for most years overlap for both groups.

Overall, the evidence available in the CHIP data suggests that minorities remain more likely to be in poverty than the Han, but rates of poverty have declined for minorities. For those who are poor, the poverty gap and squared poverty gap measures suggest that minorities are likely to be poorer, and there is little evidence of a clear trend in depth of poverty.

What factors contribute to higher rates of poverty among ethnic minorities? Geography plays an important role. It is important to reiterate that these figures pertain to rural China alone. If the urban population were included here, observed majority-minority differences in poverty rates would be exacerbated because minority groups are much more likely to live in rural areas. Within rural areas, important contextual differences exist between Han and minority populations. As noted earlier, minority villages are more likely to be poor, to be in mountainous settings, and to be isolated; they are also located in different regions of China. These geographic differences may also be related to differences in opportunities for educational attainment, the acquisition of other individual characteristics with implications for income, and the context within which to translate human capital into income.

We estimate a series of logit models[10] of poverty status, conducted at the household level using the rural CHIP 2002 sample, to investigate factors contributing to the minority-majority gap in poverty status.[11] We define a minority household as one in which the household has any members who report minority status. These models confirm a significant minority-majority gap in a baseline model in which only demographic characteristics of the household head are controlled (minority status, age, age squared, and sex). Models also suggest that although education and other household characteristics contribute to the ethnic gap in poverty, a key story comes from community context. Accounting for whether households are in national poverty counties reduces the coefficient on minority status considerably, and accounting for topography of the community where the household is

---

[10] Full empirical tables for this analysis and all other regression analyses described in this chapter can be found in the extended report, "Ethnicity, Socioeconomic Status, and Social Welfare in China," available at http://works.bepress.com/emily_hannum/25

[11] Logistic regression models estimate the log-odds (or logit) of the presence of a condition, such as poverty status, as a function of series of independent variables:

$logit(\pi_i) = \ln\left(\frac{\pi_i}{1-\pi_i}\right) = \beta_0 + \beta_1 x_{1i} + ... \beta_k x_{ki}$, where i indexes individuals, π is the probability

of a positive outcome (in this case, an impoverished household), $x_1 - x_k$ are variables of interest, and β_0 to β_x are parameters to be estimated.

Variables included in this analysis fall into three categories: (1) demographic (minority household [yes or no]; household head age and age squared; household head gender); (2) human capital (years of education of the best-educated household member, cadre in the household [yes or no]; person with migration experience in the household [yes or no]); (3) geographic context (in national poverty county [yes or no]; topography [flat, hilly mountainous]; distance from county seat [kilometers]; distance from nearest township government [kilometers]; as well as dummies for macro-region of China. In this analysis, we first estimate a base model containing only minority status and demographic characteristics of the head of household. Next, we add education and other household human capital characteristics to the base, to identify the effects of accounting for human capital composition of minority and nonminority households. Next, we add community measures to the base, again to investigate the impact on the coefficient associated with minority status once these compositional differences are accounted for. Finally, we add all individual, household, and community characteristics, and macro-region dummy variables, to most completely control for differences in community composition.

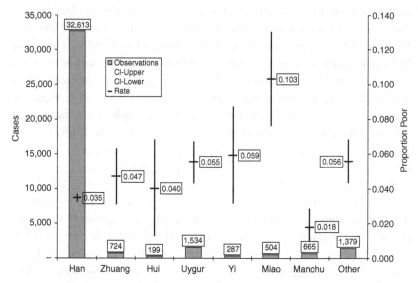

Figure 5.3. Rural poverty headcount, cases, and confidence interval bounds by ethnic group, CHIP 2002.
Source: 2002 rural CHIP.

located renders the minority-majority gap coefficient statistically insignificant. Minority status is insignificant in subsequent specifications, in which more geographic variables are included. This finding is consistent with Gustafsson and Ding's (2008) conclusion that ethnic differences in poverty can be attributed in large part to differences in regional distribution, given that poverty in rural China is concentrated in the western region and villages with low average income.

This insight is also consistent with patterns of variability in poverty across individual ethnic groups. Small sample sizes preclude any detailed analysis of this issue here. However, Figure 5.3 shows a descriptive result – poverty headcounts, observations, and upper and lower bounds of confidence intervals, disaggregated by ethnic category, with data for the Han, the five largest minority groups, and an 'other' category for remaining groups. The Yi, another southwestern ethnic group, are included as an individual group in the CHIP questionnaire, and are included in this figure as well.

The Manchu population, residing in the relatively developed north and northeast, has the lowest poverty rates of any group in the sample, including the Han, with a confidence interval that does not overlap with the Han. Point estimates for all other groups are higher than for the Han; for some groups, substantially so. However, sample sizes for individual ethnic groups are small, and confidence intervals in some cases wide, and for this reason, estimates cannot be distinguished statistically from those of the Han. This is true for the Zhuang, Hui, and Yi. The Uygur, Miao, and "Other" categories show higher rates and nonoverlapping confidence intervals, with the Miao highly disadvantaged at more than 10 percent poor, using the official poverty line. Virtually all of the Uygur live in Xinjiang; the Miao are also highly concentrated in the central-south and southwest. As described earlier, the Uygur and the Miao are also among the least urbanized of ethnic groups.

We are able to look with a bit more refinement at economic disparities by considering household income differences between minorities and the majority population using the CHIP data. In the aggregate, the per capita household income for rural minorities is about 1,850 RMB – about 69 percent of that the Han, at 2,691 RMB. We perform a series of household-level regression analyses of logged per capita income, following a parallel modeling strategy and definition of minority households to that described for the poverty status analysis.[12] Our baseline model of logged per capita income, containing only demographic characteristics of the head, shows a substantial penalty of approximately 34 percent for minority households. Accounting for differences in education of the best-educated household member and other household characteristics reduces the penalty to about 30 percent. Here, as in the poverty models, the role of geography is important. Without controlling for any household characteristics, adding to the baseline an indicator of whether the village of residence is in a nationally designated poverty county reduces the penalty from 34 percent to 24 percent; adding controls for topography and then isolation reduce it a bit further. Adding both household and community controls brings the penalty down to 17 percent. This specification doubles the explanatory power of the model (as reflected in the r-squared measure) to about 12 percent, compared to just about 6 percent for models with only household controls. Finally, to illustrate the importance of regional distribution, incorporating a series of dummy variables for region of residence eradicates the penalty for minority status and brings the percent of variation explained up to 16 percent.

LABOR MARKET ANALYSIS: INCOME, EMPLOYMENT, AND OCCUPATIONAL ATTAINMENT

For those who are employed, individual income differences by minority status are also of interest. Table 5.7 shows average monthly and hourly

[12] These models are household-level regression models of logged per capita income. Variables included and the modeling sequence used are identical to those described in note 11 to this chapter.

Table 5.7. *Average income of the adult population by ethnic group, 2005*

	Monthly income (Yuan)			Hourly income (Yuan)		
	Urban	Rural	Total	Urban	Rural	Total
RMB:						
Han	842	386	574	4.44	2.18	3.12
Zhuang	604	266	359	3.14	1.43	1.90
Manchu	793	390	545	4.38	2.43	3.20
Hui	806	319	550	4.31	1.76	3.00
Miao	639	253	313	3.28	1.35	1.65
Uygur	693	236	310	3.95	1.35	1.76
Other minorities	714	282	367	3.80	1.55	2.00
As a Percent of Corresponding Han Income:						
Zhuang	72	69	63	71	66	61
Manchu	94	101	95	99	111	103
Hui	96	83	96	97	81	96
Miao	76	66	55	74	62	53
Uygur	82	61	54	89	62	56
Other minorities	85	73	64	86	71	64

Source: 2005 mid-censal survey.

income, overall, in urban and in rural areas, as reported by individuals in the 2005 mid-censal survey. Looking first at totals, we see a pattern that has emerged already: The Hui and the Manchu, more urbanized and less concentrated in poor parts of the country than other minority groups, receive incomes (in hourly or monthly terms) roughly comparable to those enjoyed by the Han population. The Zhuang and "Other" groups receive slightly less than two-thirds the income of the Han; the Miao and Uygur receive slightly more than half the income of the Han. A substantial fraction of the income penalty for most groups can be attributed to differences across rural and urban areas. Within urban areas, the Zhuang receive 71–72 percent of the income of the Han; the Miao, 74–76 percent; and the Uygur and "Other" categories, 82–89 percent. In rural areas, the Manchu again earn comparably to the Han, but the rural Hui population experiences a penalty not seen in the urban or overall figures: They earn 81–83 percent of the income of the Han. Rural Zhuang, Miao, and Uygur earn about two-thirds the income of the Han, and other minorities earn slightly less than three-fourths.

Both location of residence and gaps in income are also tied to the kinds of work people are able to secure. Table 5.8 shows occupational composition

Table 5.8. *Occupational composition of the adult population by ethnic group and residence status, 2005*

	Head of Government, Party, Industrial Unit	Professional & Technical	Clerical & Related	Business Service	Agriculture & Aquatic	Production, Transport Equipment Operators	Other
Urban							
Han	3.03	13.11	8.07	24.05	25.05	26.28	0.41
Zhuang	1.53	12.72	7.52	23.78	34.79	18.62	1.03
Manchu	4.23	14.64	7.73	23.40	26.23	23.55	0.23
Hui	3.19	13.18	9.79	28.90	21.80	22.86	0.28
Miao	1.73	12.88	7.37	17.22	36.85	23.32	0.62
Uygur	2.63	19.41	7.63	18.98	39.24	11.83	0.28
Other minorities	2.82	16.01	8.39	16.67	38.24	17.47	0.39
Total	*3.02*	*13.21*	*8.08*	*23.87*	*25.51*	*25.90*	*0.41*
Rural							
Han	0.59	3.85	0.59	4.16	80.17	10.52	0.11
Zhuang	0.14	2.25	0.20	1.93	92.00	3.44	0.04
Manchu	0.45	2.46	0.81	3.64	82.49	10.12	0.04
Hui	0.24	4.11	0.36	4.21	83.73	7.17	0.16
Miao	0.12	3.58	0.44	1.38	90.08	4.24	0.16
Uygur	0.33	2.52	0.66	3.27	90.10	3.06	0.05
Other minorities	0.29	4.30	0.99	1.86	89.27	3.25	0.05
Total	*0.56*	*3.83*	*0.61*	*3.94*	*81.19*	*9.78*	*0.11*
Total							
Han	1.60	7.69	3.69	12.40	57.35	17.05	0.24
Zhuang	0.53	5.14	2.23	7.97	76.18	7.64	0.31
Manchu	1.90	7.15	3.47	11.25	60.83	15.29	0.11
Hui	1.65	8.43	4.86	15.97	54.23	14.64	0.22
Miao	0.37	5.01	1.50	3.81	81.91	7.16	0.23
Uygur	0.70	5.20	1.77	5.75	82.05	4.45	0.09
Other minorities	0.79	6.60	2.45	4.78	79.22	6.05	0.11
Total	*1.54*	*7.56*	*3.58*	*11.87*	*59.02*	*16.19*	*0.23*

Source: 2005 mid-censal survey.

175

of the adult population by ethnic group and residence status, based on the 2005 mid-censal survey. Looking first at the overall numbers, it is clear that the Manchu and Hui are again exceptional among the largest minority groups. Relative to the Han, these groups are comparably (or even favorably) distributed across high-status categories of head of government, party, or industrial unit; professional and technical jobs; and clerical, service, and sales jobs. All other groups are underrepresented among these kinds of jobs and in labor jobs, and overrepresented in agriculture. In urban areas, the underrepresentation of these groups in nonagricultural jobs is generally much less pronounced than in rural areas.

We investigate further income disparities, first using the CHIP rural sample. We conduct regression analyses of logged individual wage income, meaning income from primary and secondary jobs, for those reporting income ages twenty-one and older.[13] Here, the penalty for minority status in the baseline model containing only minority status, age, age squared, and sex was about 58 percent. Accounting for education and other human capital characteristics brings the number down to about 50 percent and more than doubles the explanatory power of the model, although it is still small, at about 7 percent of variance explained. A substantial amount of the remaining penalty has to do with differences in occupational sector and occupational category; with these factors incorporated, the penalty drops to about 36 percent and the percent of variance explained rises to 19 percent. Adding variables for community characteristics reduces the minority penalty to about 16 percent and increases the explanatory power of the model to about 22 percent. Finally, in these models, if we account for regional differences in income levels with the addition of a series of macroregion dummy variables, we eradicate the significance of the minority status coefficient and increase the r-squared measure slightly, to 24 percent.

We also calculate the percent of the Han-minority disparity due to endowment differences. These numbers are estimated by running a series of models containing the same variables separately for the minority and

---

[13] We perform an analysis of logged individual wage income, meaning income from primary and secondary jobs, for those reporting income ages twenty-one and older. Variables were demographic (minority or majority, age, age squared, sex); human capital (years of education, cadre status [yes or no], migration experience [yes or no]); job characteristics (dummy variables for occupational category and occupational sector); community characteristics (poverty county, topography, distance from county seat and township government); and regional location (dummy variables for macro-region). We first estimate a baseline model with demographic characteristics to obtain an overall estimate of the minority penalty, then incorporate other sets of variables in turn to identify the degree to which these other factors may contribute to the minority penalty.

majority subsamples, then implementing a regression (Oaxaca) decomposition of the difference in income. The decomposition results show that just 7–8 percent of the gap in income can be attributed to differences in education and other indicators of "human capital" – cadre status and migration experience. The difference due to endowments rises to 13 percent if we account for differences in the types of jobs people are able to secure (which are likely to be related to where people live). Adding community controls raises the percent due to endowments to 30 percent. Adding regional dummies raises the percent to about 52 percent (and in the pooled model, as noted, the coefficient for ethnic minority status turns insignificant with the addition of macroregion controls).

Access to wage employment in rural areas is itself an important piece of the picture of differentials in economic welfare by ethnic group. We perform a logistic regression analysis, at the individual level, of whether individuals report wage income from a primary or secondary job.[14] Here, overall, minorities' odds of reporting employment wages at all are 56 percent lower than those of Han Chinese (based on model 1, with only minority status, age, age squared, and sex included). Substantial reductions in the minority penalty are achieved less by accounting for human capital differences and more by accounting for differences in community context and region of residence. Odds of wage employment for minorities are 46 percent lower than for the Han when we add community characteristics to a model containing demographic and human capital measures, and 25 percent lower when we account for regional location.

We next perform an analysis of logged income using data from the 2005 mid-censal survey, with separate models for urban and rural areas.[15] These are parallel to the models estimated using the CHIP data, although the measurement of income is slightly different in the two data sources, and the sample coverage differs. Our goal in analyzing the 2005 data is to investigate urban-rural differences rather than to compare the scope of the minority wage penalty across the two surveys. In the 2005 analysis, we see an overall

---

[14] These models predict the log-odds of reporting wage income from a primary or secondary job (see note 11 to this chapter for the formula for a logit model). Variables included and the sequence of models here are identical to those in the logged wage income models described in note 13 to this chapter.

[15] We estimate a baseline model containing only minority status, age, and age squared. We next add education, then job characteristics (sector and occupational category dummy variables), and finally province of residence (a series of dummies for provinces). We perform parallel analyses on the combined urban-rural sample, and then separately for urban and rural areas.

minority penalty of about 15 percent in models including only minority status, age, age squared, and sex. The penalty is reduced slightly with the inclusion of controls for education and job type. The penalty drops to just 5 percent when we account for geography with the addition of province dummies.

Importantly, in urban areas, the minority penalty in the 2005 data is smaller, about 8 percent, overall. Accounting for education and job type does not reduce the penalty at all – in fact, the penalty is about 10 percent with these factors included. The penalty drops to just 3 percent when we account for geographic differences, with controls for province. In contrast, in rural areas, the overall minority penalty stands at about 24 percent. It drops almost imperceptibly to 23 percent with controls for educational composition and to 17 percent with controls for job type, but again, the big drop, to 7 percent, comes with controls for province. These results underscore again the role of geography: Ethnic disparities in income are smaller in urban than in rural areas. Accounting for human capital and job type does not do much in urban areas to explain the gap; in rural areas, job type matters a little. In both cases, penalties really drop, however, by accounting for province of residence.

EDUCATIONAL ACCESS AND ATTAINMENT BY ETHNIC GROUP

The Importance of Educational Attainment

In recent decades, education has become closely tied to earnings (Yang 2005; Zhang et al. 2005; Zhao and Zhou 2007). Analysis of data from National Bureau of Statistics surveys show rapid increases in economic returns to a year of education in urban China: returns nearly tripled during the period from 1988 to 2003, rising from 4.0 percent to 11.4 percent (Zhang and Zhao 2007, table 14.2). In rural areas, by the year 2000, an additional year of education increased wages by 6.4 percent among those engaged in wage employment, and education is becoming the dominant factor that determines whether rural laborers are successful in finding more lucrative off-farm jobs (Zhao 1997; de Brauw et al. 2002; de Brauw and Rozelle 2007).

In our analysis of logged wages using the 2002 rural CHIP data (described in the preceding section), we find returns ranging from 6 percent to 10 percent for those who report income, depending on specification, and our models of wage employment indicate that each additional year of schooling is associated with an 8–9 percent increase in the odds of working for income.[16] Our analysis of logged income in the 2005 mid-censal survey implies somewhat lower returns of 4 percent in rural areas among those with wage income, and returns of 6–8 percent in urban areas. It is important to acknowledge structural constraints facing minorities: The geographic context and other factors such as potential discrimination may shape ability to translate education into income. Yet, for those reporting wage income, when we implement separate regressions of logged wage income by minority status, gender, and urban-rural residence, we find that returns to education may, if anything, be higher among minorities than among the Han Chinese, especially in rural communities.[17] Thus, it is reasonable to say that those who lack access to schooling face barriers to economic mobility.

Educational Attainment in the Total Population

We next consider educational attainment trends by ethnic group in the national population. At the base of the educational system, expansion is very evident across groups. Figure 5.4 shows national illiteracy rates by ethnic group and year. In 1990, the Miao had the highest illiteracy rates, at 44 percent, followed by the "other" category, at 40 percent, the Hui, at 35 percent, and the Uygur, at 28 percent. The figure for the Zhuang was 24 percent, and for the Han, 23 percent. The Manchus had the lowest rate, at just 12 percent. By 2005, the ordering was similar but the rates much lower: Illiteracy rates among the Miao were 26 percent; among "Other," 24 percent; among Hui, 19 percent, and among Uygur, Zhuang, and Han, 11 percent. The rate among the Manchu population had dropped to 5 percent in 2005. Much of the literacy reduction happened between 1990 and 2000.

At the top of the educational distribution, there is also evidence of significant expansion. Figure 5.5 shows percent college-educated by ethnic group and year. In 1990, just 1.59 percent of the Han population was college-educated. For the Manchu and Hui populations, the figures were slightly higher, at 2.11 percent and 1.72 percent. The figure was 1.42 percent among the Uygur. The figures were less than 1 percent for other groups: 0.8 percent for the "Other" category, 0.51 percent for the Miao, and 0.41 percent for the Zhuang. Substantial expansion occurred between 1990 and 2000,

---

[16] These percentages are obtained by the formula 100*({exp[b]}-1), where b is the coefficient for years of education.

[17] To obtain these results, we modeled logged wage income for all, as well as by minority status, gender, and urban-rural status. Variables included in the estimations were years of education, years of experience, and years of experience squared.

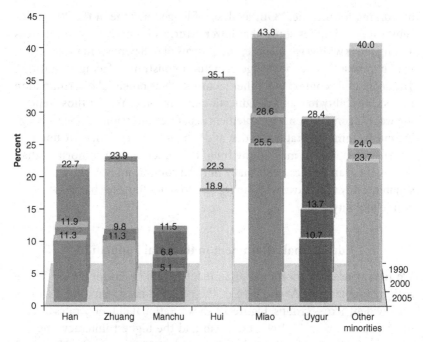

Figure 5.4. National percent illiterate by ethnic group and year, adult population.
Sources: 1990 and 2000 census public-use micro-samples; 2005 mini-census.

and again between 2000 and 2005, such that by the latter year, the figure was 8.46 percent for the Hui, 7.54 percent for the Manchu, 6.42 percent for the Han, and 6.27 percent for the Uygur. For other groups, the figure was 4.26 percent for the "Other" category, 3.93 percent for the Zhuang, and 2.85 percent for the Miao. Interestingly, the Hui have both elevated illiteracy rates and elevated college-educated rates. This is likely related to the bifurcation of the relatively urbanized Hui population between its urban and disadvantaged rural components.

Table 5.9 shows the full educational distribution by year and ethnic group, and confirms the picture of upgrading in educational attainment for all groups. In 1990, the modal educational category was the illiterate category for the Hui, Miao, and "Other" groups and the primary category for the Han, Zhuang, and Uygur groups. Only the Manchu population had a modal category of junior high school. By 2005, the Han, Zhuang, and Hui, along with the Manchu population, had this modal category; the Miao, Uygur, and "Other" categories had primary school as the modal category (for Uygurs, this was nearly a tie). No groups continued to have illiteracy as the modal category.

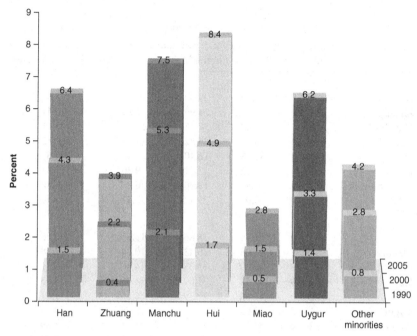

Figure 5.5. National percent college-educated by ethnic group and year, adult population
Sources: 1990 and 2000 census public-use micro-samples; 2005 mini-census.

Compulsory Education Policy and Exclusion in Rural Communities

The pattern of continued disadvantage paired with substantial improvements in access is also visible when considering the outcome of exclusion from compulsory education. A report produced at the Northwest Normal University Center for the Educational Development of Minorities indicated that by the end of 2002, there were 431 counties across China that had not universalized the nine-year cycle of compulsory education (Wang, Jiayi 2006b, p. 1).[18] Among these counties, 372 were in the western regions, and among these 372 counties, 83 percent were counties where minorities lived. In Gansu Province at the end of 2004, twenty-three counties, constituting 20.71 percent of the provincial population, had not universalized nine years of compulsory education (Wang, Jiayi 2006b, p. 1). Among these, fifteen

---

[18] According to the same source, more than sixty counties had not universalized primary education (Wang 2006b, p. 1).

Table 5.9. *Educational composition of the adult population
by ethnic group in 1990, 2000, and 2005*

	Illiterate	Primary	Junior high	Senior high	College and higher
			1990		
Han	22.73	34.99	29.99	10.70	1.59
Zhuang	23.97	43.37	24.90	7.36	0.41
Manchu	11.54	35.63	37.25	13.47	2.11
Hui	35.17	25.69	26.82	10.60	1.72
Miao	43.83	33.75	16.40	5.50	0.51
Uygur	28.46	43.32	17.51	9.30	1.42
Other minorities	40.08	33.46	18.90	6.77	0.80
Total	*23.49*	*35.03*	*29.43*	*10.51*	*1.54*
			2000		
Han	11.99	31.14	38.86	13.65	4.36
Zhuang	9.87	41.08	36.43	10.34	2.28
Manchu	6.88	30.09	43.35	14.38	5.31
Hui	22.39	27.50	31.09	14.09	4.93
Miao	28.65	42.40	21.79	5.65	1.51
Uygur	13.72	43.03	29.11	10.75	3.39
Other minorities	24.02	38.28	25.37	9.44	2.89
Total	*12.59*	*31.66*	*38.10*	*13.38*	*4.27*
			2005		
Han	11.31	27.17	40.41	14.69	6.42
Zhuang	11.35	35.96	38.67	10.09	3.93
Manchu	5.16	25.44	47.58	14.28	7.54
Hui	18.99	26.32	31.13	15.11	8.46
Miao	25.55	40.50	24.43	6.66	2.85
Uygur	10.73	37.57	37.14	8.29	6.27
Other minorities	23.74	37.03	26.40	8.57	4.26
Total	*11.94*	*27.83*	*39.65*	*14.28*	*6.30*

Sources: 1990 and 2000 census public-use micro-samples; 2005 mid-censal survey.

were national minority counties, out of a total of just twenty-one minority counties in the province.[19]

Consistent with these reports, census data show that minorities have been disproportionately vulnerable to exclusion from achievement of the national goal of a nine-year cycle of compulsory education. At the same

[19] The source uses the term "minority counties" (少数民族县, *shaoshu minzu xian*), but this does not appear to mean minority autonomous counties.

Table 5.10. *Indicators of "exclusion": Percent not enrolled and less than junior high school attainment by year and residence status, ages sixteen to twenty-one*

	1990	2000			2005		
	Total	Total	Urban	Rural	Total	Urban	Rural
Among all	42.4	16.3	6.0	21.3	9.6	4.5	13.2
Among males	34.9	13.7	5.7	17.5	8.3	3.9	11.3
Among females	49.9	19.1	6.4	25.5	11.0	5.0	15.1
Among Han	40.7	13.4	5.6	17.6	7.5	4.0	10.1
Among Han males	33.2	10.9	5.3	13.8	6.2	3.4	8.3
Among Han females	48.4	16.2	5.9	21.8	8.8	4.5	12.0
Among minority	59.6	38.2	12.6	44.5	28.2	11.6	33.9
Among minority males	53.4	34.7	11.6	40.0	26.4	10.7	31.6
Among minority females	65.9	42.3	13.6	49.8	30.1	12.4	36.3

Sources: 1990 and 2000 census public-use micro-samples; 2005 mid-censal survey.

time, their absolute level of vulnerability has lessened over time. Table 5.10 shows the percent excluded: not currently enrolled and with less than a junior high school attainment among those ages sixteen to twenty-one, tabulated by different characteristics. In 1990, 60 percent of minority youth fell into this category. By 2000, the figure was down to 38 percent. By 2005, it had fallen to 28 percent. Exclusion was higher among minority women than men (66 percent excluded for women in 1990 versus 53 percent excluded for men), but the downward trend was the same, and by 2005, the difference between men and women among minorities was just a few percentage points (30 percent for women versus 26 percent for men). The problem of exclusion was much higher in rural communities throughout the years, although minorities in 2005 were about three times as likely as the Han to be excluded in both urban and rural areas.

Whereas the absolute level of exclusion has dropped precipitously among minorities, their *relative* vulnerability to exclusion has intensified as exclusion has dropped even faster among nonminorities. In 1990, minorities were about 1.5 times as likely as Han to be excluded. By 2005, they were about 3.8 times as likely. The point of rising relative vulnerability is also made in Table 5.11, which shows the percent of total youth ages sixteen to twenty-one with given characteristics and the percent of excluded youth ages sixteen to twenty-one with given characteristics. Among all youth in 2005, about 10 percent were minority, but among excluded youth, about 30 percent were minority. Fifteen years earlier, when many more youth overall were excluded, the overrepresentation of minorities among excluded youth

Table 5.11. *Indicators of "exclusion": Percent with each characteristic among all and among "excluded" by year, ages sixteen to twenty-one*

	1990		2000		2005	
	Among excluded	Among all	Among excluded	Among all	Among excluded	Among all
Percent rural	—	—	87.82	67.17	81.03	59.11
Percent minority	12.11	8.6	26.66	11.33	30.09	10.25
Percent female	58.47	49.63	56.06	47.78	56.84	49.86
Percent region north	7.86	10.72	9.09	13.72	9.07	13.71
Percent region northeast	5.96	8.79	7.38	9.08	8.28	7.87
Percent region east	27.72	28.09	17.03	26.91	16.31	26.34
Percent region central-south	26.19	26.78	24.28	28.91	20.67	29.89
Percent region southwest	23.79	17.83	29.32	13.3	32.51	13.36
Percent region northwest	8.48	7.79	12.9	8.09	13.16	8.82

Sources: 1990 and 2000 census public-use micro-samples; 2005 mid-censal survey.
Notes: Excluded=not enrolled and less than junior high school attainment. 1990 figures are not broken down by residence status because of large differences in definition of urban between 1990 and 2000.

was much less pronounced: about 9 percent of all youth were minority, as were about 12 percent of excluded youth. Ironically, China's dramatic successes in basic educational expansion have had the consequence that those currently excluded from the system are much more dissimilar from the general population than was the case fifteen years ago – they are now much more likely to be poorer, to reside in hard-to-reach isolated regions, and, as shown in Table 5.11, to be members of ethnic minority groups.

The Context of Education for Minority Children

What factors might present educational barriers for minority children? Minorities' higher likelihood of living in impoverished remote areas mean that children from minority groups are disproportionately susceptible to the kinds of problems of rural poverty faced by children, regardless of ethnicity, in poor rural areas. Such problems include severe finance problems and difficulty recruiting and retaining sufficient numbers of qualified, effective teachers (Wang, Jiayi 2006a, pp. 2–3).

On average, minority children also face somewhat different family contexts from their Han counterparts. Table 5.12 presents evidence from the 2002 rural CHIP data about family circumstances of compulsory-education-aged children. Compared to rural Han children, rural minority children were much less likely to live in a house with a phone or to live in

Table 5.12. *Household characteristics, children ages seven to sixteen*

	Han	Minority	N
Telephone Access(%)			
Has Telephone	39.9	15.5	2,544
Lacks Telephone, but Telephone Available in the Village	55.6	64.3	4,015
No Telephone in House or Village	4.5	20.2	492
Building Materials are…(%)			
Concrete Framework	30.1	8.90	1,889
Brick or Stone	55.9	43.8	3,813
Clay and Straw	8.7	32.6	874
Other	5.3	14.7	479
Economic Indicators			
Average Household Per Capita Income, 2001	2,319	1,507	7,056
Proportion Below Poverty Line	0.04	0.11	7,056
Household Member Characteristics (Means)			
Years of Education, Best-Educated Member	8.92	8.21	7,056
Cadres in Household	0.19	0.12	7,056
Migrants in Household	0.29	0.15	7,056

Source: CHIP 2002.

a home made with better-quality (brick or concrete) materials. About 11 percent of rural minority children were below the poverty line, compared to just about 4 percent of rural Han children, and rural minority children's household incomes, on average, were slightly less than two-thirds of the figure reported for Han children. Minority children came from households that were slightly less educated and were less likely to have cadres or migrants as household members.

Of course, family disadvantages do not apply across the board. Table 5.13 shows family characteristics for compulsory-education-aged children from national census data. There is a general trend of upgrading in head-of-household and spouse education, as well as movement out of agricultural occupations, but there is still considerable variability along these lines by 2005. In 2005, the most educated Manchu population showed 9 years of education for heads of household and 8.41 years for spouses; both of these figures outpaced corresponding Han averages. The least-educated Miao population had less than 7 years as the average for heads of household and just 4.7 years for spouses. With the exception of the Manchu group, all groups had less education than the Han group. About 59 percent of Han children

Table 5.13. *Family circumstances of children ages seven to sixteen, by ethnic group and year*

Year	Family Characteristic	Han	Zhuang	Manchu	Hui	Miao	Uygur	Other
1990	Mean Head of Household's Education	6.6	6.5	7.7	5.2	4.7	5.3	4.8
	Mean Spouse's Education	4.6	4.2	6.4	3.4	2.0	5.0	2.8
	Mean Household Size	4.9	6.0	4.6	5.5	5.7	6.4	5.8
	Head of Household's Occupation (%)							
	Head of Government, Party, Industrial Unit	3.2	1.2	5.0	3.3	1.4	3.7	2.1
	Professional & Technical	4.6	2.7	6.9	4.7	2.8	6.6	3.7
	Clerical & Related	1.6	0.7	2.7	2.0	0.6	2.4	1.0
	Business Service	4.2	1.8	4.9	5.9	1.0	4.4	1.5
	Agriculture & Aquatic	73.8	90.9	65.9	69.8	91.1	74.2	87.9
	Production, Transport Equipment Operators & Related	12.3	2.4	14.3	14.1	2.8	8.4	3.6
	Other	0.0	0.0	0.0	0.0	0.0	0.0	0.0
2000	Mean Head of Household's Education	8.3	8.3	8.7	7.1	6.5	6.4	6.8
	Mean Spouse's Education	7.2	7.1	7.9	5.3	4.1	6.2	5.3
	Mean Household Size	4.3	4.7	3.9	4.8	4.7	5.5	4.8
	Head of Household's Occupation (%)							
	Head of Government, Party, Industrial Unit	2.1	0.9	3.4	2.9	0.8	1.1	1.7
	Professional & Technical	3.8	2.7	5.3	4.8	1.4	4.5	3.2
	Clerical & Related	2.4	1.2	2.9	4.1	1.0	1.6	1.9
	Business Service	7.5	3.3	7.6	11.2	2.1	5.0	3.0
	Agriculture & Aquatic	69.2	85.8	64.2	61.0	90.8	81.7	84.4
	Production, Transport Equipment Operators & Related	14.7	5.5	16.3	15.6	3.6	5.7	5.4
	Other	0.0	0.3	0.0	0.1	0.0	0.1	0.0

2005							
Mean Head of Household's Education	8.4	8.2	9.0	7.0	6.8	6.7	6.6
Mean Spouse's Education	7.4	6.8	8.4	5.4	4.6	6.8	5.3
Mean Household Size	3.4	3.5	3.1	3.9	3.7	4.3	3.9
Head of Household's Occupation (%)							
Head of Government, Party, Industrial Unit	1.9	0.4	2.7	2.3	0.7	1.0	1.2
Professional & Technical	6.3	5.4	6.2	6.4	6.2	3.8	5.8
Clerical & Related	2.9	2.1	3.6	3.9	1.4	1.6	2.8
Business Service	10.5	6.7	9.1	12.0	2.9	6.4	3.9
Agriculture & Aquatic	58.8	76.5	57.2	59.1	81.2	81.3	78.5
Production, Transport Equipment Operators & Related	19.0	8.4	20.8	16.0	7.2	5.5	7.5
Other	0.2	0.2	0.2	0.1	0.2	0.0	0.1

Sources: 1990 and 2000 census public-use micro-samples; 2005 mid-censal survey.

188   *Hannum and Wang*

came from households where the head of household was employed in agriculture, with very similar figures for the Manchu and Hui children. More than three-fourths of Zhuang children and children in the "Other" category came from households where the head was employed in agriculture, as did more than 81 percent of Uygur and Miao children. Thus, on average, rural minority children are residing in poorer households with slightly less education than their rural Han counterparts.

Looking nationally at individual ethnic groups, much disparity across minority groups is present. The family contexts of Manchu children are more advantaged than those of the Han. Overall, head-of-household and spouse education gaps are narrowing, but children other than the Hui and Manchu continue to reside in households headed by individuals with high levels of occupational divergence from the Han.

Enrollment and Attainment in the Compulsory-Education Ages

Do these contextual differences across groups matter for enrollment? Figure 5.6 shows enrollment rates among seven- to sixteen-year-olds in 1990, 2000, and 2005. The figure makes clear that enrollment rates are rising and cross-group enrollment disparities are declining over time. In 1990, enrollment rates ranged from a low of 57–58 percent among the Miao and "Other" categories to 65 percent among the Hui, to 68 percent among the Uygur, to 75 percent among the Zhuang, to 78 percent among the Han, to a high of 84 percent among the Manchu. By 2005, the range was from a low of 84 percent among the "Other" category to percentages in the high 80s for Uygur, Miao, and Hui, to 90 percent for the Manchu, 92 percent for the Zhuang, and 93 percent for the Han.

Table 5.14 shows enrollment rates among seven- to sixteen-year-olds tabulated by residence status[20] and census year. For all groups residing in urban areas, enrollment exceeded 90 percent by 2000, with the exception of the Uygurs. In contrast, in rural areas, in 2000, enrollment rates ranged from 76 percent for the "Other" category to nearly 90 percent for the Han. However, the variability is dropping over time: By 2005, rural rates ranged from a low of 82 percent among the Hui to 92 percent among the Han.

---

[20] Research has indicated that it is primarily in rural contexts where minority educational disadvantage is concentrated. Connelly and Zheng's (2007) analysis of 2000 census data showed that that those minority children who can muster the resources to get through middle school, within urban or rural areas, enjoyed slightly *better* chances of going on to high school, compared to their Han counterparts (p. 87).

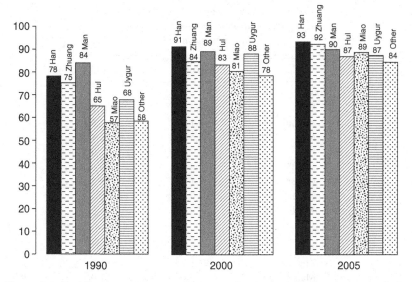

Figure 5.6. Enrollment rates among seven- to sixteen-year-olds by year and ethnic category.
Sources: 1990 and 2000 census public-use micro-samples; 2005 mini-census.

We perform a series of logistic regression analyses of enrollment among seven- to sixteen-year-olds using the 2005 mid-censal survey data.[21] Results show significant minority penalties that are reduced in models that control for human capital in the household, but also when controls for province are incorporated. Models for urban areas show a minority-Han odds ratio of enrollment of about 0.62 in the baseline model (with only minority status, age, age squared, and sex); the rural models show a lower corresponding odds-ratio of about 0.35. These patterns are consistent with findings that disparities are lower in urban areas, and that regional differences are critical for understanding ethnic disparities.

In the 2002 rural CHIP data, the rate of enrollment among seven- to sixteen-year-olds does not differ significantly between Han and minority children, although minority children in this age group are progressing through education at a slower pace. The difference between the rural mid-censal survey enrollment results and the CHIP enrollment results likely has

---

[21] See note 11 to this chapter for the formula for a logistic regression model. We estimate the log-odds of enrollment among seven- to sixteen-year-olds with a base model (minority status, age, age squared, sex), a model adding controls for head of household's and spouse's education in years, and a model controlling for province of residence with a series of dummy variables. We estimate these models for the whole sample, for the urban sample, and for the rural sample.

Table 5.14. *Enrollment rates among seven- to
sixteen-year-olds by year, ethnic group,
and urban-rural status*

	Urban	Rural
2000		
Han	94.5	89.7
Zhuang	94.1	82.6
Man	94.6	86.1
Hui	91.9	78.0
Miao	91.5	79.6
Uygur	87.1	88.2
Other	92.0	75.5
Total	*94.3*	*88.5*
2005		
Han	94.6	92.3
Zhuang	94.1	91.4
Man	93.5	87.0
Hui	92.3	82.2
Miao	92.6	87.8
Uygur	87.3	87.3
Other	91.8	81.9
Total	*94.4*	*91.3*

Notes: 1990 figures are not presented because of large
changes in the definition of urban between 1990 and 2000.
Sources: 2000 census public-use micro-sample; 2005 mid-
censal survey.

to do with sample coverage differences – the CHIP survey covers twenty-
two province-level units and does not include three Autonomous Regions,
Ningxia, Inner Mongolia, and Tibet, which tend to have the worst educational indicators. The census covers all province-level units.

The rural CHIP data, unlike the mid-censal survey data, allow us to look
directly at years of schooling attained, to gain a summary measure of progress through the school system. Overall, minorities are about a half-year
behind Han children in attainment and are less likely to have made the
transition to junior high school (about two-thirds of minority children
have done so, compared to more than three-fourths of Han children) (see
Table 5.15). We also perform a regression analysis of models of attainment estimated using the rural CHIP data.[22] Here, we find that, net of age

[22] We regress years attained among seven- to sixteen-year-olds using five specifications. We
begin by estimating a baseline specification with only demographic variables: minority

Table 5.15. *Rural enrollment and attainment,*
children ages seven to sixteen

	Enrolled Students		Attainment		JHS+ (13+)	
	Proportion	N	Years	N	Proportion	N
Total	0.89	7,056	5.51	7,056	0.77	3,771
By Minority Status						
Han	0.90	5,959	5.58	5,959	0.79	3,220
Minority	0.89	1,097	5.11	1,097	0.66	551

Source: CHIP 2002.

composition effects, minority children are about a third of a year behind in attainment (0.29 years), but this figure drops to 0.158 years once household income is accounted for, and down to less than a tenth of a year (and only marginal significance) with controls for other dimensions of family socio-economic status (education of the best-educated member in the household; whether there is a cadre in the household; and whether there is a migrant in the household, although the latter measure is not significant). Adding controls for village poverty status, village topography, and village isolation reduces the coefficient to insignificance.[23]

HEALTH CARE

Data with which to assess national health care disparities by ethnic group are hard to come by. Self-rated health measures of the sort typically available in surveys show few differences by ethnic category in China. Table 5.16 shows measures of health reported in the 2005 survey and the 2002 CHIP survey, with slightly different wording of questions. In the 2002 rural CHIP data, about 7 percent of Han and about 8 percent of minority people were reported as having bad or very bad health. In 2005, about nine out of ten

status, age, age squared, and gender. We add sequentially a series of other control variables to examine the impact on the coefficient for minority status. First, we add dummy variables for household income quintile in the preceding year, and then other household socioeconomic status indicators (years of schooling of the most educated member, and whether or not there are cadres or people with migration experience in the household). We then add community context measures (whether or not the village is in a designated poverty county, topography, distance from county seat and township government) and controls for macro-region.

[23] However, models that account further for regional differences yield estimates of a significant minority penalty of 0.179 years.

Table 5.16. *Reported health status by ethnic group, adult population (percent)*

| | 2002 CHIP, Rural | | | | | |
	Very Healthy	Healthy	So-so	Bad	Very bad	N
Majority	19.9	59.3	13.9	5.1	1.6	22,289
Minority	21.0	56.3	14.2	6.5	1.7	3,308

| | 2005 Mid-Censal Survey, National | | |
	Healthy	Basically Can Maintain Regular Living/Work	Cannot Regularly Work or Cannot Live Alone	N
Han	90.8	5.6	3.1	1,735,041
Zhuang	91.8	5.3	2.1	19,463
Manchu	90.6	5.1	4.0	14,047
Hui	91.3	5.4	3.0	21,024
Miao	91.1	4.7	3.8	12,503
Uygur	89.5	7.4	2.4	15,004
Other	90.3	5.3	3.9	116,255
Total	90.8	5.5	3.2	1,933,337

Sources: 2002 CHIP; 2005 mid-censal survey.

individuals from all groups reported being healthy, and about 2 to 4 percent reported not being able to complete daily tasks or live alone. In this latter group, no clear pattern emerges: The groups with the highest percentages falling into this category include the wealthy, urbanized Manchus as well as the impoverished, rural Miao and the "Other" category. However, self-rated health measures are not very good proxy measures of health care access, given the potential for those with greater access to health care to be more aware of their problems.

It is well established that the rural health service infrastructure is less well developed than that in urban areas. Moreover, within rural villages, the health service infrastructure is less well developed in minority villages than nonminority villages. Table 5.17 shows village health facilities in minority and nonminority villages, from the 2002 rural CHIP village sample. By official definition, 26 percent of minority villages, but only 7 percent of nonminority villages, lacked health facilities. Using the 50-percent-of-households definition, corresponding figures were 20 percent and 9 percent, respectively.

Differences in infrastructure, related to the geographic disparities already discussed, likely contribute to very different health circumstances

Table 5.17. *Village health facilities in minority*
and nonminority villages (two definitions)

| | Village is minority area* | | 50%+ of village households are minority** | |
	No	Yes	No	Yes
No clinic	7.4	25.5	8.6	20
Village-collective	9.8	10.7	10	9.6
Branch township hospital	18.5	19.5	18.2	20
Private	63.5	42.3	62.2	48.8
Other	0.9	2	1	1.6
Total	100	100	100	100
Cases	810	149	828	125

*chi2(4) = 51.4842 Pr = 0.000
**chi2(4) = 17.9169 Pr = 0.001
Source: CHIP 2002 village data.

across ethnic groups. Little recent national data or research is available on health care access or health problems by ethnic group. A number of studies of maternal and infant and child health have been completed in Yunnan, however. Using data from Yunnan's population censuses and provincial health department, Li et al. (2008) analyzed infant mortality rates and life expectancies for the national population, the Yunnan Han population, and the largest minority groups in Yunnan. Results showed that in 2000, the national infant mortality rate was 26.9 per 1,000 live births for China; it was 53.6 per 1,000 for Han in Yunnan; and it was 77.7 per 1,000 for the 22 largest minority nationalities in Yunnan, despite improvements in health status indicators since 1990. Disparities in life expectancy at birth between China as a whole and some minority nationalities also remained striking: National life expectancy in 2000 was 71.4 years, compared to 57.2 years for some minorities in Yunnan (it was 64.5 years for the 22 groups studied as a whole). The maternal mortality ratio in Yunnan is about twice the national average (56.2 per 100,000 live births), and in remote mountainous regions, the rate is five times higher (Li et al. 2007). Earlier work in Yunnan conducted by Li et al. (1999) showed that belonging to the Miao, Yi, and Hani ethnic groups, compared with the Han, was associated with an increased risk of stunting for children.

In addition to the previously mentioned studies, which speak to a general unmet need for health care among some ethnic minority groups,

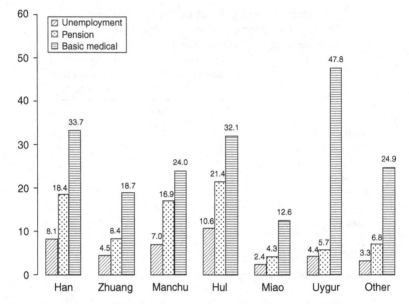

Figure 5.7. Access to social insurance programs by ethnic category, 2005.
Sources: 2005 mini-census.

recent evidence has indicated that members of some ethnic minorities in China have been particularly vulnerable to HIV/AIDS (for example, Choi, Cheung, and Jiang 2007; Zhang et al. 2007; Zhang et al. 2008). Overall, more than 30 percent of the reported HIV/AIDS cases in China are among ethnic minorities – a much higher proportion than their representation in the general population (Deng et al. 2007). Three of the five highest prevalence provinces in China are western provinces with large minority populations, namely Yunnan Province, the Xinjiang Uygur Autonomous Region, and the Guangxi Zhuang Autonomous Region (Grusky et al. 2002). These findings indicate significant health care needs and access gaps for some ethnic groups.

ACCESS TO SOCIAL SERVICES AND PROGRAMS

Finally, we discuss access to social programs among ethnic minorities. Figure 5.7 shows access to social welfare services by ethnic group for the adult population, excluding students, in 2005. Looking first at unemployment insurance, Figure 5.7 shows that this benefit is available to very few members of any ethnic group: Just 8 percent of the Han population has access, along with about 7 percent of the Manchu and about 11 percent of

Table 5.18. *Access to social insurance programs by ethnic group and residence*
status, adult population, excluding students, 2005 (percent)

	Unemployment		Pension		Basic Medical	
	Insurance		Insurance		Insurance	
	Urban	Rural	Urban	Rural	Urban	Rural
Han	16.3	1.0	34.9	3.9	42.8	25.6
Zhuang	13.2	0.8	23.2	1.9	29.0	14.2
Manchu	15.5	0.6	34.5	3.5	33.7	16.6
Hui	18.0	1.0	36.4	1.8	39.2	22.8
Miao	10.4	0.7	18.9	1.2	25.8	9.9
Uygur	14.6	1.7	17.9	2.6	38.4	50.2
Other	11.5	0.9	22.3	2.2	35.4	21.7
Total	16.1	1.0	34.4	3.7	42.4	25.2

Source: 2005 mid-censal survey.

the Hui. Rates are less than 5 percent for all other groups. Rates of access
to pension insurance are a little higher for some groups, with slightly less
than one in five Han people having pension insurance. Once again, the corresponding figure is only slightly lower for the Manchu and slightly higher
for the Hui. It is about 8 percent for Zhuang, 7 percent for the "Other"
group, 6 percent for Uygurs, and just 4 percent for the Miao. Thus, with the
exceptions of the Hui and Manchu, other minority groups have access to
pensions at less than half the rates of the Han. The story for health insurance is a little different: about half of Uygurs have access to health insurance, as do about one-third of Han and Hui, about one-fourth of Manchu
and "Other," 19 percent of Zhuang, and 13 percent of Miao. We were unable
to find research to explain the high rate among the Uygurs; it likely has
to do with policies specific to the Xinjiang Uygur Autonomous Region, as
nearly all Uygurs live there.

In general, social welfare services are associated with urban residence
(see Table 5.18). This pattern is most pronounced for unemployment insurance. Among urban dwellers, rates of unemployment insurance ranged
from a low of about 10 percent among the Miao, to about 12 percent among
members of the "Other" category, to 13 percent among the Zhuang, to 15–16
percent among the Uygur and Manchu, to 16 percent among the Han, to a
high of 18 percent among the Hui. Among rural dwellers, rates were below
2 percent for all groups. Pension insurance was available to more than one-
third of Han, Hui, and Manchu urban dwellers, 23 percent of Zhuang urban

dwellers, 22 percent of "Other" urban dwellers, 19 percent of urban Miao, and 18 percent of urban Uygurs. Rates never rose higher than 4 percent for any rural group.

The story is slightly different for health insurance, in that rural access is higher than for other social insurance programs. However, the kind of health insurance that exists in rural areas – the Rural Cooperative Medical Scheme – tends to reimburse costs at a much lower rate than urban health insurance schemes. Among urban dwellers, basic medical insurance rates are highest among the Han, at 43 percent, and range downward to a low of 29 percent among the Zhuang and 26 percent among the Miao. Among rural dwellers, the range is from a high of 50 percent among Uygurs, to 22–26 percent among the Hui, Han, and "Other" categories, to 14–17 percent among the Zhuang and Manchu, to less than 10 percent for the Miao. Here again, the Uygur case is unusual in that rural coverage rates are higher than urban rates.

Thus, having access to social services – unemployment, pension, and health insurance – is not the typical experience for any ethnic group. For unemployment and pensions, the familiar pattern of higher levels of access for more urbanized Han, Hui, and Manchu populations and lower levels of access for all other groups recurs here. In addition, the importance of residence is clear when urban and rural residents are considered separately: variability is much lower within urban/rural categories, and levels of access across categories are much different. For health insurance, Uygurs are added to the groups with high levels of access, and rural access rates are higher than urban rates. However, this finding is difficult to interpret, as the basic health insurance often available in rural areas is much more minimal than many urban plans.

CONCLUSIONS AND POLICY IMPLICATIONS

This chapter investigates social welfare among China's officially designated minority groups. Five main findings emerge. First, poverty rates are dropping among minorities, but minorities as a group remain disadvantaged in economic terms. Minorities are more likely to be poor: Even restricting the analysis to rural areas, minorities are 1.5 to 2 times more likely to experience poverty than their Han counterparts. More than one in ten rural minority children were below the official poverty line, compared to about one in twenty-five rural Han children, and rural minority children's household incomes were slightly less than two-thirds of the figure reported for Han children. In rural areas, minorities have less access to wage employment than the Han and make less money when they do engage in wage employment; household income is also significantly lower among ethnic minorities in rural areas. Income gaps are also striking in the national population.

Second, all groups have experienced educational expansion in recent decades. Disparities exist in attainment and enrollment among school-aged children. In the 2005 mid-censal survey, significant enrollment differences persisted across ethnic groups. In the rural CHIP sample, which covered fewer Autonomous Regions, differences were found not in enrollment but in attainment. Importantly, whereas the last fifteen years have seen striking reductions in levels of exclusion from compulsory education among minority youth, their overrepresentation among excluded youth has intensified as the school system has expanded.

Third, provision of health care stands out as a potentially crucial element of an improved poverty alleviation strategy for disadvantaged ethnic minorities, and is an issue about which more detailed evidence is needed. Evidence from the rural CHIP village data indicates that minority areas, on average, have less-developed health care infrastructures. Existing research on maternal and child health from Yunnan indicates that health care access is a substantial problem for rural minorities, but we have little evidence about the national situation. More work is needed to gain a broad-based understanding of the nature of general health disparities by ethnic group. A number of studies on the emerging HIV/AIDS epidemic in China show that ethnic minorities are highly overrepresented among those affected, and that some of the hardest-hit provinces – Yunnan, the Guangxi Zhuang Autonomous Region, and the Xinjiang Uygur Autonomous Region – are those with large ethnic minority populations.

Fourth, less urbanized ethnic groups have less access to important safety nets – unemployment and pension insurance – than do the more urbanized Han, Hui, and Manchu populations. For health insurance, good quality insurance is tied to urban residence. Within rural areas, Miao, Zhuang, and Manchu populations have low access to health insurance, with just one in ten Miao reporting access.

Fifth, across many of the outcomes considered here, geography plays an important role in patterns of ethnic advantage and disadvantage. More urbanized groups, and groups not disproportionately resident in poor regions, tend to have much smaller disparities compared to the Han population, and sometimes even have advantages relative to the Han population. Majority-minority disparities in income diminish when household and individual characteristics are taken into account, but also notably diminish when geographic differences are taken into account. Enrollment gaps tend to be smaller in urban areas, and accounting for region and province reduces gaps. Health infrastructure is less developed in minority than in nonminority communities, and access to social safety nets also has clear geographic gradients.

Our findings suggest three policy implications. First, relatively poor access to health care and health insurance among many rural minority ethnic groups points to a potential source of vulnerability to poverty. Catastrophic medical spending is a critically important precipitant of transient poverty in rural China (Liu and Hsiao 2001; Kaufman 2005; Wang, Zhang and Hsiao 2005). One recent study found that medical spending raised the number of rural households living below the poverty line by 44.3 percent (Liu, Rao, and Hsiao 2003). The government has responded to concerns about impoverishment due to health shocks, along with other concerns, with an ambitious health care reform agenda that sought to provide insurance coverage to 100 percent of the population by 2010 (Yip and Hsiao 2008). Assuring insurance coverage that supports real, affordable access to decent quality care in impoverished minority communities would provide an important contribution toward helping families avoid falling into poverty.

Second, under conditions of scarce resources, poverty alleviation interventions should be targeted using information about overlapping dimensions of advantage and disadvantage. There is a great diversity of socioeconomic circumstances *within* ethnic categories, associated with location of residence. High levels of socioeconomic disadvantage occur at the intersection of minority status, rural status, and impoverished community status. Information on county and village-level remoteness and impoverishment, in conjunction with information about the culture and history of particular communities, could be used to focus scarce development funds on the most disadvantaged members of ethnic minority groups. In the case of China, this suggestion is workable, as China has a long record of regional poverty targeting at the county level and, more recently, at the village level (Wang 2004).

Third, and related to the second point, poverty alleviation efforts targeted at individuals in poor communities are most likely to be successful if paired with community development initiatives. As poverty alleviation strategies and educational expansion strategies have reached ever more people and places in China, disadvantaged minority groups are increasingly concentrated in situations of multiple disadvantage, where poor infrastructures and impoverished communities heavily shape individual economic opportunities and social welfare outcomes (World Bank 2009).

Continued efforts to improve health care access and educational opportunities for members of disadvantaged ethnic groups are needed, but these interventions alone may not have the same impact in highly isolated rural communities as they would in communities with better-developed economies, or better communication and transportation ties to the urban areas. Projects that build up communication and transportation infrastructure will enhance ties to outside markets and labor markets and, by extension, to remittances that have become such important sources of economic development in many of China's rural communities. In addition, policies or development projects that stimulate or support sustainable businesses and entrepreneurial activities – whether these are culturally tied, such as cultural tourism or marketing of cultural products, or ecotourism, or marketing of local agricultural products, or the development of local industries – can also maximize the impact of improved communication and transportation infrastructures. Tax incentives are an example of existing policy that supports this goal. Cultivating sustainable businesses and entrepreneurial activities within communities is a critical part of the equation, as improving ties to the outside may otherwise lead to an exodus of the young, more educated workforce.

There is, however, an important caveat to be considered in designing policies or initiatives to develop minority communities. There may be tensions between economic development goals – poverty alleviation, educational expansion, development of communications and transportation infrastructure, and even expansion of health care access – on the one hand and maintaining cultural integrity on the other. There may be vast differences of opinion about the priority attached to these different goals by global, national, and local stakeholders, in particular development policies or projects.[24] These are issues that are likely to loom large in determining the success of development efforts, but about which we have little information at present. They are often highly sensitive issues, and may be best assessed via field methods in the context of particular projects.

In addition to policy recommendations, our analysis suggests some directions for data collection that could support more informative policy research. At present, limited empirical data precludes many important lines of inquiry on the topic of ethnic stratification. The available data sources with sufficient sample sizes and suitable geographic coverage to study majority-minority differences on any indicator are limited, and data

---

[24] In thinking about this issue, we benefited from discussions with Professor Wang Jiayi at Northwest Normal University and participants in the Oxford China Seminar.

sources that could permit the study of issues of individual ethnic groups even more so. To obtain a reasonable portrait of ethnic stratification in China, there is a dire need for better data. The key issue is sample coverage. This problem could be addressed if regularly occurring national surveys were purpose-designed with minority oversamples for selected groups, or by use of focused surveys that employed sample designs aimed at coverage of minority areas.

Aside from sample coverage, a second problem is topical coverage. At present, all large-scale data sets that might be employed to address questions of ethnic disparities in welfare come from multiuse household surveys focused on economic and demographic data. Surveys that also encompassed better measures of health care access and experiences and use of social programs would be helpful. In addition, much work on other dimensions of social inequality in China, and work on ethnic disparities in other countries, encompasses attitudes and subjective experiences of inequality as well as socioeconomic variables. This sort of data would also help us better understand ethnic stratification in China.

Finally, the measurement of ethnicity should be as detailed as possible. Binary concepts of minority status or indigenous status are useful for developing summary measures, but results presented here make clear that these concepts tell only part of the story and provide insufficient information for designing and implementing interventions. Of course, more detailed classification schemes come at a cost in terms of making comparative summary statements, but they are likely to provide a more comprehensive picture of the complicated nature of ethnic disparities and a more valid indicator of strategies that might ameliorate disadvantages faced by particular groups.

References

Cai, Fang and Meiyan Wang. 2008. "A Counterfactual Analysis on Unlimited Surplus Labor in Rural China." *China & World Economy* 16:51–65.

China Data Center. N. D. "2000 Total Han Population (Map C205)." Ann Arbor: University of Michigan. Retrieved March 13, 2009 at http://chinadatacenter.org/chinageography/MapDisplay.asp?FigureNumber=c.205

China Education and Research Network (CERNET). 2005a. "Bilingual Teaching Promoted in Ethnic Minority Regions." Retrieved July 7, 2006 at http://www.edu.cn/20050523/3138247.shtml

　　2005b. "China Protects Endangered Ethnic Languages." Retrieved July 7, 2006 at http://www.edu.cn/20050530/3139079.shtml

Choi, Susanne Y. P., Y. W. Cheung, and Z. Q. Jiang. 2007. "Ethnicity and Risk Factors in Needle Sharing among Intravenous Drug Users in Sichuan Province, China."; *AIDS Care* 19:1–8.

Clothey, Rebecca. 2005. "China's Policies for Minority Nationalities in Higher Education: Negotiating National Values and Ethnic Identities." *Comparative Education Review* 49:389–409.

Connelly, Rachel and Zhenzhen Zheng. 2007. "Enrollment and Graduation Patterns as China's Reforms Deepen, 1990–2000." Pp. 81–92 in *Education and Reform in China*, edited by Emily Hannum and Albert Park. London and New York: Routledge.

Daes, Erica-Irene A. 1996. "On the Concept of "Indigenous People" (Working Paper by the Chairperson-Rapporteur)." *United Nations Economic and Social Council Working Paper* E/CN.4/Sub.2/AC.4/1996/2:1–22.

de Brauw, Alan, Jikun Huang, Scott Rozelle, Linxiu Zhang, and Yigang Zhang. 2002. "The Evolution of China's Rural Labor Markets during the Reforms." *Journal of Comparative Economics* 30:329–353.

de Brauw, Alan and Scott Rozelle. 2007. "Returns to Education in Rural China." Pp. 207–223 in *Education and Reform in China*, edited by Emily Hannum and Albert Park. London and New York: Routledge.

Deng, Rui, Jianghong Li, Luechai Sringernyuang, and Kaining Zhang. 2007. "Drug Abuse, HIV/AIDS and Stigmatisation in a Dai Community in Yunnan, China." *Social Science & Medicine* 64:1560–1571.

Fei, Xiaotong. 1981. *Toward a People's Anthropology*. Beijing: New World Press.

Feng, A. 2005. "Bilingualism for the Minor or the Major? An Evaluative Analysis of Parallel Conceptions in China." *International Journal of Bilingual Education and Bilingualism* 8:529–551.

Gladney, D. C. 2004. *Dislocating China: Muslims, Minorities, and Other Subaltern Subjects*. Chicago: University of Chicago Press.

Government of China. 1993. "Eight-Seven Poverty Reduction Plan (1994–2000) [国家八七扶贫攻坚计划(1994–2000年)]."

2001. "Poverty Reduction Compendium, 2001–2010 [中国农村扶贫开发纲要(2001–2010年)]."

Griffin, Keith and Renwei Zhao. 1988. "Chinese Household Income Project 1988" [Computer File]. New York: Hunter College. Academic Computing Services [Producer], 1992. Ann Arbor, MI: Inter-University Consortium for Political and Social Research [Distributor], 1993. Doi:10.3886/ICPSR09836.

Grusky, O., H. Liu, and M. Johnston. 2002. "HIV/AIDS in China: 1990–2001." *AIDS and Behavior* 6:381–393.

Gu, Baochang, Feng Wang, Zhigang Guo, and Erli Zhang. 2007. "China's Local and National Fertility Policies at the End of the Twentieth Century." *Population and Development Review* 33:129–148.

Gustafsson, Bjorn and Sai Ding. 2006. "Villages Where China's Ethnic Minorities Live." *Institute for the Study of Labor (IZA) Discussion Paper* 2418:1–41.

2008. "Temporary and Persistent Poverty among Ethnic Minorities and the Majority in Rural China." *Institute for the Study of Labor (IZA) Discussion Paper* 3791:1–31.

Hoddie, M. 1998. "Ethnic Identity Change in the People's Republic of China: An Explanation using Data from the 1982 and 1990 Census Enumerations." *Nationalism and Ethnic Politics* 4:119–141.

Information Office of the State Council of the People's Republic of China. 2000. "National Minorities Policy and its Practice in China." Beijing: Information Office of the State Council of the People's Republic of China. Retrieved March 31, 2009 at http://www.china.org.cn/e-white/4/

2001. "The Development-Oriented Poverty Reduction Program for Rural China." Beijing: State Council. Retrieved April 24, 2009 at http://www.china.org.cn/e-white/fp1015/index.htm

Kaufman, Joan. 2005. "China: The Intersections between Poverty, Health Inequity, Reproductive Health and HIV/AIDS." *Development* 48:113.

Khan, Azizur R. 2008. "Growth, Inequality and Poverty: A Comparative Study of China's Experience in the Periods before and After the Asian Crisis." Pp. 145–181 in *Inequality and Public Policy in China*, edited by B. Gustafsson, S. Li, and T. Sicular. Cambridge: Cambridge University Press.

Li, J., C. Luo, R. Deng, P. Jacoby, and N. d. Klerk. 2007. "Maternal Mortality in Yunnan, China: Recent Trends and Associated Factors." *BJOG: An International Journal of Obstetrics & Gynaecology* 114:865–874.

Li, Jianghong, Chun Luo, and Nicholas d. Klerk. 2008. "Trends in Infant/Child Mortality and Life Expectancy in Indigenous Populations in Yunnan Province, China." *Australian and New Zealand Journal of Public Health* 32:216–223.

Li, Yan, Guangping Guo, Anping Shi, Yuping Li, Tokie Anme, and Hiroshi Ushijima. 1999. "Prevalence and Correlates of Malnutrition among Children in Rural Minority Areas of China." *Pediatrics International* 41:549–556.

Lin, J. 1997. "Policies and Practices of Bilingual Education for the Minorities in China." *Journal of Multilingual and Multicultural Development* 18:193–205.

Lipman, Jonathan N. 1998. *Familiar Strangers: A History of Muslims in Northwest China.* Seattle: University of Washington Press.

Liu, Y. and W. C. Hsiao. 2001. "China's Poor and Poor Policies: The Case of Rural Health Insurance." Conference on Financial Sector Reform in China, Cambridge, MA, Harvard School of Public Health.

Liu, Y., K. Rao, and W. C. Hsiao. 2003. "Medical Expenditure and Rural Impoverishment in China." *Journal of Health, Population, and Nutrition* 21:216–222.

Ma, Rong. 2007. "Bilingual Education for China's Ethnic Minorities." *Chinese Education and Society* 40:9–25.

Michaud, Jean. 2009. "Handling Mountain Minorities in China, Vietnam and Laos: From History to Current Concerns." *Asian Ethnicity* 10:25.

Ministry of Education. 1986. "People's Republic of China Law on Compulsory Education." Beijing: Ministry of Education. Retrieved April 2, 2009 at http://www.edu.cn/20050114/3126820.shtml

People's Daily. 2007. "China's Rural Poverty Elimination Drive Stalls in Minority Habitats." Retrieved March 2, 2009 at http://english.people.com.cn/90001/90776/90882/6307788.html

Perry-Castañeda Library Map Collection. 1990. "Chinese Linguistic Groups 1990." Austin: University of Texas. Retrieved March 13, 2009 at http://www.lib.utexas.edu/maps/middle_east_and_asia/china_ling_90.jpg

Poston, Dudley L., Jr. and Jing Shu. 1987. "The Demographic and Socioeconomic Composition of China's Ethnic Minorities." *Population and Development Review* 13:703–722.

Ravallion, Martin and Shaohua Chen. 2007. "China's (Uneven) Progress Against Poverty." *Journal of Development Economics* 82:1–42.

Ross, Heidi. 2006. "Where and Who Are the World's Illiterates: China." UNESCO: Global Monitoring Report China Country Study.

Sautman, Barry. 1999. "Ethnic Law and Minority Rights in China: Progress and Constraints." *Law and Policy* 21:284–314.

Schein, Louisa. 1997. "Gender and Internal Orientalism in China." *Modern China* 23:69–98.

Teng, Xing. 2002. "Bilingual Society and Bilingual Education of the Yi Ethnic Minority of the Liangshan Yi Ethnic Minority Autonomous Prefecture in China Amid Cultural Changes – History, Present Situation, Problems, and Analysis." *Chinese Education and Society* 35:65.

United Nations Development Group. 2008. "United Nations Development Group Guidelines on Indigenous Peoples' Issues." February:1–53.

Wang, Hong, Licheng Zhang, and William Hsiao. 2006. "Ill Health and Its Potential Influence on Household Consumptions in Rural China." *Health Policy* 78:167–177.

Wang, Jiayi 2006a. "农村中小学实施素质教育的几个问题 (Implementing Education for All-Around Development [Quality Education] in Rural Secondary and Primary Schools: Several Issues.)" Lanzhou, China: Northwest Normal University Center for the Educational Development of Minorities, Ministry of Education Humanities and Social Sciences Research Base. Consultation Report 2006 (1). Retrieved June 15, 2006 at http://www.nwnu.edu.cn/mzjy/jdzxbg/zxbg6.doc

2006b. "素质教育的实施与民族地区教育发展 (Implementation of All-Around Development Education [Quality Education] and Educational Development in Minority Areas)." Lanzhou, China: Northwest Normal University Center for the Educational Development of Minorities. Retrieved June 14, 2006 at http://www.nwnu.edu.cn/mzjy/chengg/cg9.htm

Wang, Sangui. 2004. "Poverty Targeting in the People's Republic of China." Tokyo: Asian Development Bank Institute Discussion Paper No. 4. Retrieved April 24, 2009 at http://www.adbi.org/files/2004.01.04.dp004.poverty.china.pdf

West, Loraine A. 2004. "Demographic and Socioeconomic Status of China's Minority Ethnic Population: Any Closing of the Gap?" Paper presented at the Annual Meeting of the Population Association of America, April 1–3, 2004, Boston, MA. Session 110: Racial and Ethnic Differences in Schooling: International Contexts:1–30.

Wong, David W. S. 2000. "Ethnic Integration and Spatial Segregation of the Chinese Population." *Asian Ethnicity* 1:53–72.

World Bank. 2009. *From Poor Areas to Poor People: China's Evolving Poverty Reduction Agenda*. Washington, DC: World Bank.

Xiao, Hong. 1998. "Minority Languages in Dehong, China: Policy and Reality." *Journal of Multilingual and Multicultural Development* 19:221–235.

Yang, Dennis T. 2005. "Determinants of Schooling Returns during Transition: Evidence from Chinese Cities." *Journal of Comparative Economics* 33:244–264.

Yip, Winnie and William C. Hsiao. 2008. "The Chinese Health System at A Crossroads." *Health Affairs* 27:460–468.

Zhang, Junsen and Yaohui Zhao. 2007. "Rising Schooling Returns in Urban China." Pp. 248–259 in *Education and Reform in China*, edited by Emily Hannum and Albert Park. London and New York: Routledge.

Zhang, Junsen, Yaohui Zhao, Albert Park, and Xiaoqing Song. 2005. "Economic Returns to Schooling in Urban China, 1988 to 2001." *Journal of Comparative Economics* 33:730–752.

Zhang, Li, Junling Zhu, Baoling Rui, Yuanzhi Zhang, Lijiang Zhang, Lu Yin, Yuhua Ruan, Han-Zhu Qian, and Yiming Shao. 2008. "High HIV Risk among Uigur Minority Ethnic Drug Users in Northwestern China." *Tropical Medicine & International Health* 13:814–817.

Zhang, Yuanzhi, Hua Shan, Jennifer Trizzino, Yuhua Ruan, Geetha Beauchamp, Benoît Mâsse, Jun Ma, Yuan Gu, Yixin He, Baoling Rui, Jun Wang, Katharine Poundstone, Yan Jiang, J. Brooks Jackson, and Yiming Shao. 2007. "Demographic Characteristics and Risk Behaviors Associated with HIV Positive Injecting Drug Users in Xinjiang, China." *Journal of Infection,* 54:285–290.

Zhao, W. and X. Zhou 2007. "Returns to Education in China's Transitional Economy: Reassessment and Reconceptualization." Pp. 224–247 in *Education and Reform in China,* edited by Emily Hannum and Albert Park. London and New York: Routledge.

Zhao, Yaohui. 1997. "Labor Migration and Returns to Rural Education in China." *American Journal of Agricultural Economics* 79:1278.

Zhou, M. 2005. "Legislating Literacy for Linguistic and Ethnic Minorities in Contemporary China." *Current Issues in Language Planning* 6:102–121.

Zhou, Wangyun. 1989. "'Tan Sichuan Minzu Diqu De Jiaoyu Tixi Wenti' [A Discussion of Problems in the Education System in Minority Areas of Sichuan]." Pp. 18–38 in *Zhongguo Minzu Jiaoyu Luncong (Collected Essays on Ethnic Education),* vol. 4, edited by Hongtao Chen and Zhuqun Meng. N.A.: N.A.

6

India

The Scheduled Tribes

Maitreyi Bordia Das, Gillette H. Hall, Soumya Kapoor, and Denis Nikitin

INTRODUCTION

Tribal groups or *Adivasis* in India are considered to be the earliest inhabitants of a country that experienced diverse waves of invaders and other settlers over thousands of years, making it difficult to identify the precise origin of today's tribal peoples from a purist's perspective. The term *Adivasi* is commonly translated as "indigenous people" or "original inhabitants" and literally means "Adi (earliest time)" and "vasi (resident of)." The state and discourse in India, however, reject the term "indigenous peoples" as it is considered "divisive, undermining the unity of the Indian nation."[1] Furthermore, it is the government's official position that all citizens of India are indigenous.[2] The government instead recognizes most *Adivasis* under the Constitutional term "Scheduled Tribes" (see Annex 1). The Constitution Order 1950 declared 212 tribes located in 14 states of India as Scheduled Tribes (STs).[3] The government of India today identifies 533 tribes, with 62 of them located in the state of Orissa.[4] To many, therefore, any aggregate analysis of STs is meaningless because it is impossible to aggregate these diverse groups of peoples. That being understood, this analysis is an attempt

---

[1] Anthropologist G. S. Ghurye, as quoted in Chopra, Suneet. 1988. "Revolt and Religion: Petty Bourgeois Romanticism." *Social Scientist*, 16(2), Four Decades of Economic Development (February): 60–67.

[2] Burra, Neera. 2008. *The Political Economy of Tribals in the Context of Poverty and Social Exclusion.* New York: World Bank (draft).

[3] The terms "*Adivasi*" and "Scheduled Tribe" are not coterminous. There are more "*Adivasi*" or "tribal" communities (635) than Scheduled Tribes. For purposes of this chapter, we use the term ST for tribal groups in India, as this is the category officially used while collecting data in the country. In India, however, the terms *Adivasis* or tribals are used interchangeably with STs.

[4] http://www.tribal.nic.in/index1.html

to use the available data to understand what happened to this artificially and statistically "homogenized" group over time.

Social stratification in India is primarily determined by the fourfold *varna* system commonly known as the caste system.[5] STs do not strictly fall within this Hindu caste hierarchy because they have traditionally lived in forest areas, away from mainstream village life, and have distinct (often considered non-Hindu) cultural and religious practices and social mores. Although "Scheduled Castes (SCs) and Scheduled Tribes" is sometimes said in the same breath, they are distinct social categories. Whereas STs do not face ritual exclusion in the form of untouchability, as do the SCs or *Dalits*, when exclusion is defined more broadly in terms of being "prevent(ed)... from entering or participating" or "being considered or accepted,"[6] STs fit squarely within the conception of excluded people. The major difference in the development status of the SCs and STs is that whereas the former lived among but were segregated socially and ritually from the main-stream and from upper-caste groups, the latter were isolated physically, and hence socially (Béteille, 1991), although the degree of "isolation" remains in question.[7]

Over time, geographic isolation of STs, primarily in remote forest and hilly tracts, has manifested in relative and oftentimes absolute deprivation, which has periodically surfaced in the starkest manner, reported widely in the press. Kalahandi district in the state of Orissa has long been a metaphor for starvation due to reports dating back to the 1980s. The Melghat area in the state of Maharashtra has similarly surfaced in the press, especially dur-ing the monsoon season, when migrant STs return for transplanting rice on their subsistence plots of land, household food stocks are depleted, and cash to purchase food is scarce.

There is a wealth of ethnographic data on deprivation of the STs. National research and activist organizations have also conducted microlevel surveys of households facing chronic food shortage and brought them before the public gaze. For example, a 2005 survey of ST areas in two Indian states

---

[5] The caste or varna system comprises Brahmins or the priestly class at the top, followed by Kshatriyas or the martial caste, Vaishyas or traders, and finally the Shudras – the large category of manual workers who often engage in ritually "polluting" work. Of the Shudras, many are erstwhile untouchables. Untouchability is illegal, but Scheduled Castes (or the untouchables) continue to suffer varying degrees of subordination and segregation in Indian society, depending on the region of the country.

[6] Encarta Online Edition.

[7] Anthropological literature suggests that tribals are in more ways integrated into the "main-stream" than is recognized. There is considerable evidence on tribes emulating traditions of the caste system and influencing them (Sinha 1958).

found that 99 percent of the sampled ST households faced chronic hunger, one-quarter faced semi-starvation during the previous week, and not a single household had more than four of ten assets from a list that included such basic items as "a blanket," "a pair of shoes," or "a radio" (Center for Environment and Food Security, 2005). The discourse on ST deprivation is rich and interdisciplinary, but most often it is based on small area studies such as the ones mentioned earlier. This evidence, although compelling, has limited statistical validity and generates results limited to one tribe, village, or state. The purpose of this chapter is to present a comprehensive and nationally representative picture of the nature of poverty and the evolution of socioeconomic indicators among India's ST population as compared to national trends for the two intervening decades between 1983 and 2004–2005 – a period of rapid growth of the national economy.

There are six sections in this chapter. The next section sums up India's track record on growth and poverty reduction in recent decades and policies that have been put in place by the Indian state to safeguard and promote the welfare of STs. The third section describes the data sources and methodology used for analysis. The fourth section presents overall trends in poverty and employment, health, and education indicators for the period from 1983 to 2005 – a time when India as a whole registered dramatic progress – disaggregated by STs and other social groups. The fifth section discusses briefly the underlying processes that explain deprivation of STs. These include poor physical access to services; increasing alienation of STs from their traditional lands; low voice and participation in political spaces; and poor implementation of public assistance/poverty reduction programs, which affects the STs disproportionately because they dominate the ranks of the poor and the disadvantaged. The final section concludes and summarizes the discussion.

INDIA'S RAPID GROWTH AND POLICIES RELATED TO SCHEDULED TRIBES

India achieved rapid economic growth in the decade of the 1990s, so much so that it is now considered a "star performer" among other economies in the world – developed and developing – next to China. Growth rates of GDP for the twenty-year period between 1980 and 1999 averaged about 5.8 percent per annum, accelerating further at the turn of the century to 8.5 percent in 2003–2004, driven by continued growth in the service sector and improved performance of industry (Virmani 2005; World Bank 2006b).

While there has been considerable debate about poverty estimates during this period,[8] it is clear that growth facilitated reduction in poverty. Using official poverty lines and consumption data from the National Sample Survey, the World Bank's latest Poverty Assessment for India estimates that poverty headcount levels declined from 45.6 percent in 1983 to 27.5 percent in 2004–2005 (World Bank 2011). What is not clear is whether the pace of poverty reduction *increased* as growth accelerated. There have also been concerns about the extent to which the fruits of growth have been shared equally. The gap between rural and urban areas reportedly widened in the 1990s as did the wedge between rich and poor people, particularly in urban centers (World Bank 2011).

More worryingly, perhaps, structural inequalities defined by caste and tribe remained salient (World Bank 2011). Although there appear to be some cracks in caste-based occupational hierarchies, glass walls and ceilings were still difficult to break through (Das and Dutta 2007). Health and education indicators also improved but not enough to bridge the gap between SCs and STs on one hand and the rest of the population on the other. The STs fared the worst, lagging behind because of their physical location.

The Indian state's response to the vulnerability among STs has been proactive and has strong constitutional backing. Schedule V of the Indian Constitution identifies special privileges for those areas where the majority of the population belongs to STs. Schedule VI is different in that it applies special privileges to tribals who reside in the northeastern states of India. Here, tribal groups are the majority in states that have been founded on tribal status. Many of the residents converted to Christianity and obtained Western education and jobs. While tribes in the northeastern states represent less than 20 percent of the total ST population, the entire northeast has been isolated from the development process mainly because of the geographical and cultural isolation of these areas. On the other hand, in areas where STs are a minority or the Schedule V areas located within other states, tribal peoples are among the most impoverished and marginalized. Both Schedule V and VI underscore the area-based approach the state has followed in addressing tribal issues.

Several well-known state-sponsored commissions have recommended greater voice for STs in their own development, and underscore the importance of land and forests in this process. Of late, the state has legislated to acknowledge the "rights" of ST areas by taking them further toward self-rule.

[8] For a summary of issues, see Deaton and Kozel (2005).

In 1996, the Indian Parliament also passed the Panchayats Extension to Scheduled Areas Act (PESA), 1996. The Act covers nine Schedule V states of Andhra Pradesh, Chhattisgarh, Gujarat, Himachal Pradesh, Jharkhand, Madhya Pradesh, Maharashtra, Orissa, and Rajasthan and, instead of individuals, recognizes and stresses traditional community rights over natural resources. PESA gives power over matters like sale of non-timber forest produce, acquisition of land, and so forth to the tribal *gram sabhas* – village assemblies – instead. Similarly, in the context of mining, PESA gives a large role to gram sabhas, which need to be consulted for environmental clearance. The recent Forest Rights Act and the Tribal Rights Act go further in adopting a rights-based perspective and acknowledging the preeminent rights of STs to natural resources.

In parallel, there are earmarked development funds both from the central government and the states that flow to tribal areas through a special budgetary instrument called the "tribal sub-plan" (TSP). STs also have quotas in public employment, with 7.5 percent seats in all government and quasi-government jobs (which form the major part of all regular salaried jobs) reserved for them. They have similar quotas in public educational institutions and, according to the seventy-third amendment to the Indian constitution, have reserved seats in local governments as well. However, enforcement of these far-reaching laws and policies has been weak for a variety of reasons, as discussed later in this chapter.

DATA AND METHODOLOGY

The analysis contained in this chapter draws primarily on the Indian National Sample Survey (NSS). The NSS allows trends in socioeconomic indicators to be examined over three rounds conducted in 1983, 1994–1995, and 2004–2005, and is considered to be one of the most reliable data sources for socioeconomic indicators in India. The survey covers both rural and urban areas, and data from it are highly regarded and widely used for planning purposes in India. Given that the STs comprise about 9 percent of the total NSS sample and somewhat less of the national population according to the census (see Table 6.1), all analysis is weighted to make the results nationally representative. In addition, the chapter draws on health and education indicators from the Indian census; three rounds of the Indian National Family Health Survey (NFHS 1992–1993, 1998–1999, and 2005–2006); and the Reproductive Child Health Survey (RCH) II (2005).

Evidence on poverty and labor market outcomes for STs draws on analysis undertaken for the 2011 *World Bank India Poverty Assessment Report*.

Table 6.1. *Share of Scheduled Tribes in total population, 1951–2001*
(population in millions)

Census years	Total population	Population of STs	ST %
1951	361.1	19.1	5.29
1961	439.2	30.1	6.85
1971	548.2	38.0	6.93
1981	685.2	51.6	7.53
1991	846.3	67.8	8.10
2001	1028.6	84.3	8.19

Source: http://www.tribal.nic.in/index1.html

The poverty analysis uses India's official national poverty lines, which are calculated separately for each state, and within each state for urban and rural areas (see Annex 2). They are defined using the Consumer Price Index for Agricultural Laborers (CPIAL) in rural areas and Consumer Price Index for Industry Workers (CPIIW) in urban areas. Defined in real terms and regularly updated to account for inflation, these poverty lines follow the Expert Group Method (Government of India, 1993) that applies weights to food and nonfood components of expenditure to mimic the consumption patterns of households around the poverty line. The strengths and limitations of this methodology are discussed at some length in the literature (see, for example, Deaton, 2003, 2008).

OVERALL TRENDS

Demographic Profile

According to the 2001 census, India had 84.3 million ST members, comprising 8.1 percent of the total population of the country (Table 6.1). As the table suggests, the share of STs in total population remained fairly stable, particularly in the ten-year period between 1991 and 2001.

The main distinguishing demographic feature that differentiates STs from the rest of the Indian population is the degree to which they inhabit rural or urban areas. India as a whole has been urbanizing at a fairly rapid pace – the share of the population in urban areas has risen from roughly one-quarter to one-third of the population between 1993 and 2005 (Table 6.2). Among the STs, on the other hand, the proportion living in urban areas has held fairly constant over this period – at roughly 10 percent of the population – with the vast majority still living in rural areas. Even though socioeconomic conditions among tribal people living in urban areas are measurably better

Table 6.2. *Basic demographic characteristics, Scheduled Tribes and total population, 1993–2005*

	Scheduled Tribes			Other			Total population		
	1993	1998	2005	1993	1998	2005	1993	1998	2005
Male, %	50.6	50.5	49.7	50.8	50.8	50.0	50.8	50.8	49.9
Age	23.8	24.2	24.7	24.8	25.5	26.5	24.7	25.4	26.4
Household size	5.7	5.4	5.0	5.9	5.6	5.0	5.9	5.6	5.0
Urban, %	9.9	10.8	10.3	27.9	28.1	32.8	26.3	26.4	30.8
Observations	61,839	66,834	72,459	452,988	446,834	457,607	514,827	517,379	534,161

Source: NFHS, various years.

than for those in rural areas, the ST population remains overwhelmingly concentrated in rural areas.

Trends in Poverty Reduction and Distribution of Wealth

India is widely considered a success story in terms of poverty reduction. In just two decades, the national poverty rate has been cut almost in half, from 45.6 percent in 1983 to 27.5 percent in 2004–2005. All social groups have contributed to the decline, including the STs among whom poverty was reduced from 63.3 percent to 43.8 percent in the intervening period. However, the pace of poverty decline among STs as a whole has been slower than it has been among other social groups, including SCs (Table 6.3). Thus in 2004–2005, almost half of the ST population remained in poverty (44 percent), whereas nationwide the poverty rate reduced almost to one-quarter of the population (27.5 percent).

When a relatively impoverished group registers slow progress in poverty reduction, it can be useful to explore changes in other poverty measures – particularly those that examine "poverty gap" and "poverty severity." Calculations for the P1 "Poverty Gap"[9] (Table 6.4) not only show a relatively high poverty gap for STs in 1983 (0.21) compared with both SCs (0.18) and the national average (0.13), but also a smaller decline in that gap (49 percent) between 1983 and 2004–2005 with respect to both SCs (56 percent) and the population average (57 percent). STs, however, do as well as SCs in urban areas, registering an almost equivalent decline in poverty gap, albeit lower than the average for the urban population (48 percent)

---

[9] The poverty gap or depth of poverty is also referred to as the FGT P_1 index and measures the average distance between household consumption and the poverty line.

Table 6.3. *Trends in poverty incidence (Headcount Index), 1983–2005 – Scheduled Tribes are poorer than other social groups*

Location	Social Group	1983	1993–1994	2004–2005	% change between 1983 and 2005
Rural	Scheduled Tribe	63.9	50.2	44.7	–30
	Scheduled Caste	59.0	48.2	37.1	–37
	Others	40.8	31.2	22.7	–44
	All	46.5	36.8	28.1	–40
Urban	Scheduled Tribe	55.3	43.0	34.3	–38
	Scheduled Caste	55.8	50.9	40.9	–27
	Others	39.9	29.4	22.7	–43
	All	42.3	32.8	25.8	–39
Total	Scheduled Tribe	63.3	49.6	43.8	–31
	Scheduled Caste	58.4	48.7	37.9	–35
	Others	40.5	30.7	22.7	–44
	All	45.6	35.8	27.5	–40

Notes: Headcount indices are in average normalized form.
Source: Estimates based on Consumption Expenditure Survey (CES) of respective NSS rounds.

Table 6.4. *Trends in poverty gap (FGT P_1 Index), India, 1983–2005 – slower decline in poverty gap for Scheduled Tribes*

Location	Social Group	1983	1993–1994	2004–2005	Percent change between 1983 and 2005
Rural	Scheduled Tribe	21.2	12.2	10.7	–50
	Scheduled Caste	18.7	11.7	7.5	–60
	Others	11.1	6.7	4.1	–63
	All	13.6	8.4	5.5	–59
Urban	Scheduled Tribe	17.4	12.4	10.9	–37
	Scheduled Caste	16.8	14.1	10.4	–38
	Others	11.0	7.2	5.2	–52
	All	11.9	8.3	6.2	–48
Total	Scheduled Tribe	20.9	12.2	10.7	–49
	Scheduled Caste	18.4	12.2	8.1	–56
	Others	11.1	6.8	4.4	–60
	All	13.2	8.4	5.7	–57

Notes: FGT – Foster, Greer and Thorbecke; FGT P_1 indices are in average normalized form.
Source: See Table 6.3.

Table 6.5. *Trends in poverty severity (FGT P_2 Index), India, 1983–2005 – slower decline in poverty severity for Scheduled Tribes*

Location	Social Group	1983	1993–1994	2004–2005	Percent change between 1983 and 2005
Rural	Scheduled Tribe	9.5	4.3	3.7	−61
	Scheduled Caste	8.2	4.1	2.2	−73
	Others	4.6	2.1	1.1	−76
	All	5.8	2.8	1.6	−72
Urban	Scheduled Tribe	7.2	5.0	4.7	−35
	Scheduled Caste	7.1	5.6	3.8	−46
	Others	4.5	2.6	1.8	−61
	All	4.9	3.0	2.2	−56
Total	Scheduled Tribe	9.4	4.3	3.8	−60
	Scheduled Caste	8.0	4.3	2.5	−68
	Others	4.6	2.3	1.3	−72
	All	5.6	2.8	1.8	−68

Notes: FGT P_2 indices are in average normalized form.
Source: See Table 6.3.

Similarly, there are higher "poverty severity"[10] rates in 1983 and slower declines among the STs compared with the population average and even the SCs. In this case, the exception for STs in urban areas disappears (Table 6.5).

The relatively slower decline in poverty among the STs has increased their concentration in the poorest deciles. Table 6.6 draws from the NFHS data and gives a distribution of STs across population deciles using a wealth index.[11]

[10] Poverty severity (or the FGT P_2) index measures the severity of poverty, accounting for the fact that under FGT P_1, an income transfer from two households beneath the poverty line would register no change in the index.

[11] Each household asset is assigned a weight (factor score) generated through principal components analysis, and the resulting asset scores are standardized in relation to a normal distribution with a mean of zero and standard deviation of one [...]. Each household is then assigned a score for each asset, and the scores are summed for each household; individuals are ranked according to the score of the household in which they reside." Specifically, wealth index is based on the following 33 assets and housing characteristics: household electrification; type of windows; drinking water source; type of toilet facility; type of flooring; material of exterior walls; type of roofing; cooking fuel; house ownership; number of household members per sleeping room; ownership of a bank or post-office account; and ownership of a mattress, a pressure cooker, a chair, a cot/bed, a table, an electric fan, a radio/transistor, a black and white television, a color television, a sewing machine, a mobile telephone, any other telephone, a computer, a refrigerator, a watch or clock, a bicycle, a motorcycle or scooter, an animal-drawn cart, a car, a water pump, a thresher, and a tractor. (IIPS and Macro International, 2007, p. 43)

Table 6.6. *Distribution of Scheduled Tribes across deciles (Wealth Index),
1993–2005: Scheduled Tribes are concentrated in the poorest wealth deciles*

	Share of Scheduled Tribes in Population, by Deciles			Distribution of Scheduled Tribes Population across Deciles		
	1993	1998	2005	1993	1998	2005
Poorest Decile	0.223	0.217	0.251	0.253	0.245	0.297
2	0.132	0.148	0.167	0.149	0.167	0.198
3	0.106	0.118	0.120	0.120	0.134	0.142
4	0.108	0.123	0.081	0.122	0.139	0.096
5	0.099	0.091	0.065	0.113	0.102	0.077
6	0.081	0.061	0.048	0.091	0.069	0.057
7	0.052	0.052	0.037	0.059	0.059	0.044
8	0.035	0.035	0.031	0.040	0.039	0.037
9	0.030	0.031	0.027	0.034	0.035	0.031
Richest Decile	0.017	0.015	0.017	0.020	0.017	0.021

Notes: The wealth index is a factor score based on ownership of assets.
Source: NFHS.

Recalling that STs represent roughly 8 percent of national population, the results show that in 1993 STs were over-represented in the poorest decile (22 percent of the decile population) and under-represented in the wealthiest decile (1.7 percent). By 2005, their share in the poorest decile had risen to 25 percent, signifying a widening wealth gap between STs and the rest of the population (Table 6.6, first three columns).

Taking the entire ST population and allocating it across deciles shows a similar worsening of the distribution, only more starkly (Table 6.6, last three columns). In 1993, 25 percent of those belonging to a Scheduled Tribe fell into the poorest wealth decile. By 2005, this figure had risen to 30 percent. Further, whereas 52 percent of the ST population fell into the poorest three deciles in 1993, this figure had risen to 64 percent by 2005.

In sum, it is clear that not only are the STs poorer than any other group; their concentration among the poorest has become more severe over time. Their initial consumption levels are so far below the poverty line, and they have such limited assets, that marginal gains made by them in the past two decades have resulted in relatively few households among them crossing over the threshold successfully.

These results need to be qualified: There is considerable variation in poverty outcomes by state and even within STs. A look at poverty trends by state indicates that the marginal gains made by STs in the aggregate seem to

Table 6.7. *Poverty incidence is higher in states with a high proportion of Scheduled Tribes (percent)*

	1983		1993–1994		2004–2005	
	STs	All	STs	All	STs	All
Assam	48	42	41	41	12	21
Gujarat	58	33	31	24	33	17
Madhya Pradesh	72	50	60	42	57	38
Maharashtra	63	44	53	37	54	31
Orissa	86	66	71	49	75	47
Rajasthan	63	39	44	27	32	21
Jharkhand	73	60	68	55	53	42
Chhattisgarh	59	50	53	44	54	41
All India	63	46	50	36	44	28

Notes: States that had 10% or greater ST population in 1983.
Source: Indian National Sample Survey.

be further offset by highly unequal results across states (Table 6.7). In states with high tribal populations (about 10 percent of the state's total population), ST households exhibited poverty rates that were higher than across the nation as a whole in 2004–2005 (with the exception of Assam). The highest poverty rates recorded for tribal groups were in Orissa, with the tribal population in the state registering a headcount ratio of 75 percent in 2004–2005 – an *increase* of about 6 percent from 1993–1994 levels. Tribals in rural areas in Orissa were particularly worse off, with poverty levels among the group declining at a slower pace (13 percent) during the 1983–2005 period compared with a decline of 44 percent for other groups (non-SCs and non-STs). Tribals in rural areas in Madhya Pradesh, Maharashtra, Rajasthan, Jharkhand, and Chhattisgarh also recorded far lower declines in poverty than other groups.

Are STs relatively homogenous in the way poverty has declined for them in the aggregate? Or is there intragroup variation in poverty for STs over time? Figure 6.1 gives the Growth Incidence Curves (GIC) for STs nationwide, and then broken down by rural and urban areas. These graphs indicate the growth rate in expenditure over two points in time (1993 and 2004) at each percentile of the expenditure distribution. They show that among the ST population nationwide, expenditures grew more rapidly at the higher end of the expenditure distribution than in the lower end. The urban-rural breakdown shows that the phenomenon actually only holds true in urban areas, and may in part be explained by particularly large

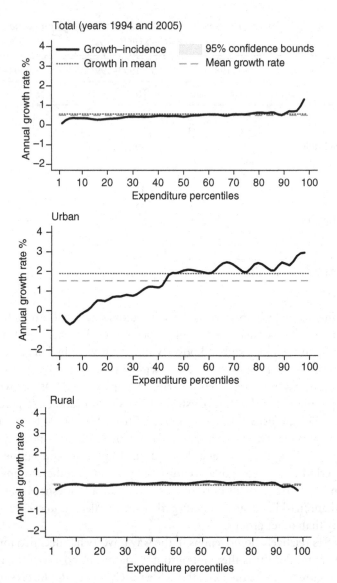

Figure 6.1. Scheduled Tribe expenditures grew more rapidly at the higher end of the expenditure distribution between 1994 and 2005.

Source: World Bank. 2011. *India Poverty Assessment Poverty Report*; estimates based on Consumption Expenditure Survey (CES) of respective NSS rounds.

income gains among those with access to and benefits from reserved jobs. This result may also explain why poverty among STs in urban areas has fallen relatively quickly.

Correlates of Poverty

What factors are associated with the higher incidence of poverty among the STs?

Table 6.8 gives sample means for a series of household characteristics. It highlights several distinct features of ST households. Across both rural and urban samples, ST households tend to be smaller and younger, with more children age zero-to-six years than non-ST households. However, there are several dissimilarities across the ST urban and rural samples, particularly with respect to the characteristics of the head of household. Urban ST heads of household are likely to be better educated and have regular wage employment. In contrast, in rural areas, the majority of ST heads of household can be found in agricultural self-employment, mostly working as subsistence farmers. The incidence of female headship is also higher among STs in urban areas; in fact, more than even urban, non-ST households.

To further investigate correlates of poverty, we ran a probit multivariate regression of poverty headcount on a number of household characteristics, separately for rural and urban areas. The results of this multivariate analysis reveal interesting insights (not shown here). First, whereas education of the head of household is associated with lower poverty among all households, the poverty-reducing effect of higher education (secondary and beyond) is less pronounced among STs. This result holds only for rural areas, however; in urban areas, being educated above the secondary level has a greater poverty-reducing effect on STs. Second, rural female-headed ST households are significantly more likely to be poor than their non-ST peers, but this effect disappears in urban areas – where the incidence of female headship among STs is also higher. Third, employment as a rural agricultural laborer is associated with greater poverty among non-STs, but not among STs, perhaps because they have access to subsistence land. In urban areas, however, employment as a casual laborer has a positive and statistically significant association with poverty among ST households. This mostly captures ST migrant laborers in urban India. Finally, land ownership is associated with lower poverty among all groups with the exception of urban STs; this last point may be moot, however, because very few STs own land in urban areas.

Table 6.8. *Sample means: Urban and rural ST households differ, particularly in characteristics of the household head (HH)*

	RURAL			URBAN		
	ST	Non-ST (including OBC/SC)	Non-ST (excluding OBC/SC)	ST	Non-ST (including OBC/SC)	Non-ST (excluding OBC/SC)
Poverty headcount	0.447	0.261	0.175	0.342	0.256	0.161
Household size	5.845	6.128	6.162	5.312	5.614	5.517
Proportion of HH members 0–6 years old	0.177	0.161	0.144	0.137	0.123	0.109
Proportion of HH members 60+ years old	0.056	0.076	0.086	0.046	0.072	0.085
Age of HH head	44	46	48	42	46	48
HH head's education level						
No education	0.593	0.432	0.313	0.292	0.198	0.126
Below primary	0.126	0.113	0.109	0.077	0.078	0.061
Primary	0.213	0.304	0.356	0.298	0.314	0.281
Secondary	0.055	0.120	0.170	0.236	0.252	0.293
Post-secondary	0.013	0.030	0.052	0.097	0.157	0.241
Female HH head	0.064	0.077	0.073	0.114	0.083	0.077
Household's most important source of income:						
Rural areas						
Agricultural self-employment	0.429	0.393	0.489	n.a.	n.a.	n.a.
Nonagricultural self-employment	0.068	0.177	0.177	n.a.	n.a.	n.a.
Agricultural labor	0.336	0.238	0.141	n.a.	n.a.	n.a.
Other labor	0.115	0.103	0.076	n.a.	n.a.	n.a.
Other	0.053	0.090	0.117	n.a.	n.a.	n.a.
Urban areas						
Regular wage employment	n.a.	n.a.	n.a.	0.427	0.394	0.421
Self-employed	n.a.	n.a.	n.a.	0.274	0.435	0.454
Casual labor	n.a.	n.a.	n.a.	0.220	0.114	0.057
Other	n.a.	n.a.	n.a.	0.078	0.057	0.068
Area of agricultural land owned	3,085	1,345	2,741	252	210	269

Note: OBC stands for "Other Backward Castes" and "SC" stands for Scheduled Castes.
Source: NSS 2004–2005.

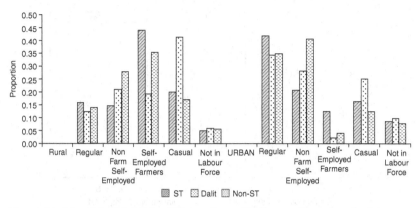

Figure 6.2. Most Scheduled Tribe (ST) men in rural India are self-employed subsistence farmers: 2004–2005.
Source: Das 2008.

These results are consistent whether using region or state controls in the models. An OLS regression testing how these factors are correlated with consumption yields consistent results.

Employment

The labor market profile of ST households and workers is distinct from that of any other social group. The large majority of ST households in rural areas own at least subsistence land and so, when they cannot get benefits from job quotas, either because of lack of education or lack of access to information about vacancies, they have subsistence agriculture to fall back on. Land and forests are indeed the default source of their livelihood. This is very different from the situation of SC households that have very low access to land, are overrepresented in casual wage employment, and are underrepresented in self-employment. About 44 percent of ST men, compared to 35 percent of men from the general category and only 19 percent from the SC category, are self-employed subsistence farmers in rural areas. ST men are also less likely to take up non-farm self-employment in rural areas compared to men from the SC and general category (see Figure 6.2).

Das (2006) finds a premium to being an ST in urban areas where formal jobs are concerned. ST men have a 4 percent higher likelihood of being in regular salaried jobs compared to non-ST men. Further, salaries paid to ST regular workers are at par with or higher than non-STs as indicated by the shift of the earnings distribution to the right for ST workers compared to that of non-STs (see left panel of Figure 6.3). Interestingly, the earnings

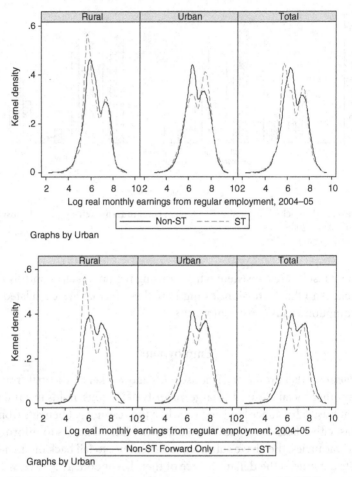

Figure 6.3. Scheduled Tribe members earn more than non–Scheduled Tribe members when employed in high-paying, regular, urban jobs.
Note: Log real monthly earnings from regular employment, 2004–2005, adjusted for regional differences in cost of living
Source: NSS 2004–2005

distribution of ST workers in urban areas is more or less similar to that of non-ST workers at the bottom quantiles, but it is higher at the top quantiles. These unexpectedly high earnings are likely driven by ST elites in administrative jobs or second- and third-generation beneficiaries of such reservation, who may later have entered other salaried jobs (those at the higher end of the urban expenditure distribution in Figure 6.1).[12]

[12] For more details, see Das and Dutta (2007).

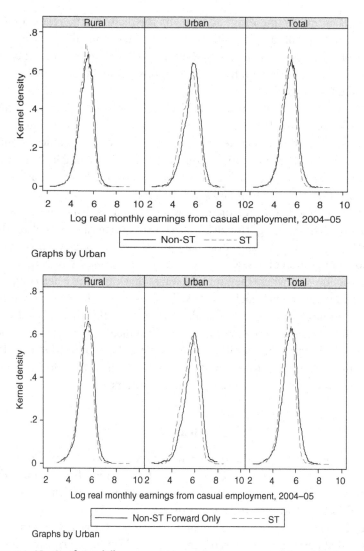

Figure 6.4. No significant differences exist in earnings among casual, low-skilled workers.
Note: Log real monthly earnings from regular employment, 2004–2005, adjusted for regional differences in cost of living.
Source: NSS 2004–2005.

However, given the predominantly agrarian focus of ST households, these numbers on wages capture only a small proportion of STs. Also, if SCs and Other Backward Classes (OBCs) are excluded, the difference between earnings of regular ST workers and workers from forward classes (read: general caste) in urban areas is not significant (right panel of Figure 6.3), which is an interesting result on its own. The picture is therefore a mixed one for the overall sample, with the non-STs having an advantage at lower levels of earnings (consistent with their higher earnings in rural areas) and STs having an advantage at higher levels (consistent with their higher earnings in urban areas).

With respect to wages from casual labor, the differences are more subtle. This is because casual workers are largely a homogenous pool of low-skilled workers. Thus, the kernel density plots do not reflect significant differences – the earning distribution is only slightly more favorable for non-STs (Figure 6.4). Excluding OBCs and SCs from the non-ST group clarifies the trend for higher non-ST earnings in urban areas.

This does not take away from the low level of wages that casual ST workers are paid. In fact, wages for all ST casual workers (in rural as well as urban areas) are the lowest among all social groups. Surveys often do not capture seasonal migration of STs, who move to cities as manual labor employed in construction sites where they are paid wages that are lower when compared to wages paid to other social groups. There is a large body of literature – mainly ethnographic and from small area surveys – that focuses on distress migration of STs. Mosse et al. (2002), for instance, emphasize the importance of addressing the conditions under which STs migrate. Moreover, lack of earnings data for self-employed persons prevents us from looking more closely at the earnings of self-employed ST farmers.

Health

Drawing on three rounds of the NFHS, this section provides a closer look at trends in basic health indicators and outcomes for STs as compared to other groups. Results show that STs in 1992 had significant deficits in access to health care. And even though trends are improving – in some cases at a faster-than-average pace – the size of deficits was so large at the start of the period that persistent and sizeable gaps remain. Thus in nearly every health outcome – whether child mortality, malnutrition, immunization, contraception, pregnancy or maternal care – STs continue to exhibit worse outcomes vis-à-vis the national average and in comparison to non-SC/STs. STs in urban areas do better on virtually every indicator than their counterparts in rural areas. This is partly because of better access to health care[13] and

---

[13] Lack of access to health facilities in rural areas is evident from the fact that 12 percent of rural women in the NFHS 2005 sample cited prohibitive distance as a reason for not using a health facility for their last birth within the last five years. In contrast, only 6 percent of urban women said so.

partly because there are larger numbers of STs in the higher wealth quantiles who live in cities and towns compared to villages.

Although the tables in this section show the large gap between STs and the "rest," the latter – that is, the nontribal category – is extremely diverse. Caste membership, for instance, exercises huge influence over outcomes, and SCs in many areas are as vulnerable as STs. Most analyses for India report findings by SC and ST status and then for the rest of the population. Consistent with this chapter's focus uniquely on STs, we report results for ST and non-STs and show that despite the fact that the non-ST category is so heterogeneous, STs still do worse than everyone else. Annex 3 disaggregates key health outcomes by different social groups. Results show that whereas SCs remain below par on most indicators such as maternal health, the STs are worse off than even the SCs, which makes the gap between them and the rest all the more alarming.

Child mortality and malnutrition. India's child health indicators have shown considerable improvement between 1992 and 2005, with infant mortality declining from 78 to 57 deaths per 1,000 live births and under-five mortality declining by roughly one-third over the intervening period (from 109 to 74 deaths per 1,000 live births). However, under-five mortality among tribal children remains startlingly high (at 96 deaths per 1,000 live births). In fact, mortality of tribal children starts off on par with that of non-tribals, but gets rapidly worse in rural areas by the time the children are five years old (Table 6.9). Maharatna (1998, 2000) has documented the more sustainable practices that STs follow and that historically have kept rates of fertility and mortality among them lower than the national average, and how this began to change as tribals had to give up their traditional practices. The existing pattern of excess mortality of tribal children is in keeping with ethnographic and media reports and data from administrative records, and remains one of the starkest markers of tribal deprivation in India.

Numbers for under-five mortality rates differ across states. With the exception of Maharashtra and Gujarat, most states with a large proportion of ST populations[14] show higher than average under-five mortality rates. Of these, Chhattisgarh, Jharkhand, Orissa, and Madhya Pradesh are particularly worse off, with under-five mortality rates exceeding 90 per 1,000 live births (Table 6.10).

Das et al. (2010) decompose child mortality by age and make a set of policy recommendations. First, consistent with the aforementioned results, a disproportionately high number of child deaths are concentrated among STs, especially in the one-to-five age group and in those states and districts

---

[14] States that had 10 percent or greater ST population in 1983.

Table 6.9. *Infant mortality rates are similar across the population, but by age five, ST children are at significantly greater risk of dying*

Deaths per 1,000 births	Neonatal Mortality (NN)	Post-neonatal Mortality (PNN)	Infant Mortality $(1q_0)$	Child Mortality $(4q_1)$	Under-five Mortality $(5q_0)$
Urban					
Scheduled Tribes	29	14.8	43.8	10.4	53.8
All urban	28.5	13	41.5	10.6	51.7
Rural					
Scheduled Tribes	40.9	23	63.9	38.3	99.8
All rural	42.5	19.7	62.2	21	82
India					
Scheduled Tribes	39.9	22.3	62.1	35.8	95.7
All India	39	18	57	18.4	74.3

Notes: Mortality indicators are in deaths per 1,000 births. Neonatal mortality (NN) – probability of dying in the first month of life; post-neonatal mortality (PNN) – probability of dying after the first month of life, but before the first birthday; infant mortality $(1q_0)$ – probability of dying before the first birthday; Child mortality $(4q_1)$ – probability of dying between the first and fifth birthdays; and under-five mortality $(5q_0)$ – probability of dying before the fifth birthday.
Source: IIPS and Macro International (2007), pp. 181–182.[15]

where there is a high concentration of STs. Thus any effort to reduce child morality in the aggregate will have to focus more squarely on lowering mortality among the STs. Second, the gap in mortality between ST children and the rest really appears after the age of one. In fact, before the age of one, tribal children face more or less similar odds of dying as other children. However, these odds significantly reverse later. This calls for a shift in attention from infant mortality in general to factors that cause a wedge between tribal children and the rest between the ages of one and five. Third, the analysis goes contrary to the conventional narrative of poverty being the primary factor driving differences between mortality outcomes. Instead, the authors find that breaking down child mortality by age leads to a much more refined picture. Tribal status is significant even after controlling for poverty.

Malnutrition and child mortality are highly correlated, and malnutrition in India is widespread, with 48 percent of Indian children showing signs of long-term malnutrition (stunting or deficit in height-for-age), 24 percent

[15] These tables replicate NFHS published data on infant mortality rates: Our own calculations produced results that were slightly different with those presented in Table 6.9. Given that the reason for the discrepancy could not be ascertained, we rely on the published NFHS results.

Table 6.10. *Under-five mortality is higher in states
with high proportion of Scheduled Tribe members*

Deaths per 1,000 births	Under-five mortality ($5q_0$)
Assam	85.0
Gujarat	60.9
Chhattisgarh	90.3
Jharkhand	93.0
Madhya Pradesh	94.2
Maharashtra	46.7
Orissa	90.6
Rajasthan	85.4
All-India	74.3

Notes: Mortality indicator is in deaths per 1,000 births. Under-five mortality ($5q_0$) – probability of dying before the fifth birthday.
Source: National Family Health Survey, 2005–2006.

of severe stunting, and 42 percent of being underweight.[16] According to the 2007 World Development Indicators, only two countries have higher proportions of underweight children (based on the same standards): Bangladesh and Nepal (World Bank 2007a). In fact, child malnutrition is much higher in India than it is in Burundi, Niger, or Afghanistan.

Even worse than the population averages are outcomes for ST children, among whom 53 percent are stunted, 29 percent are severely stunted, and 55 percent are underweight. Interestingly, the gap between the ST children and those from other groups appears within the first ten months of birth and persists – with some variations – throughout early childhood. The rise in severe wasting among ST children during the first ten months of life is particularly alarming (Figure 6.5).

States with large ST populations have had frequent public outcry over what are called "malnutrition deaths." Child deaths usually cluster around periods of seasonal stress like drought, when household food supplies are low and employment dries up, or during the monsoon when remote

[16] Malnutrition is usually measured along three dimensions: stunting (deficit in height-for-age), wasting (deficit in weight-for-height), and underweight (deficit in weight-for-age). Stunting reflects long-term effects of malnutrition, whereas wasting measures the current nutritional status of the subject – that is, his/her food intake immediately prior to the survey. The underweight indicator is a combination of the former two and captures both long-term and short-term effects of deficient food intake. A child is considered to be malnourished with respect to each of these measures, if his/her indicator falls below -2 standard deviations from the median (defined for 2006 WHO international reference population). Falling below -3 standard deviations signals severe malnutrition.

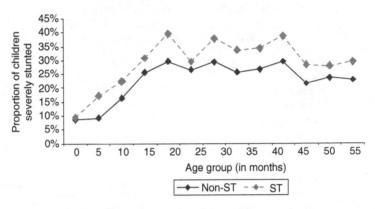

Height-for-age (children 0–59 months old), 2005–2006

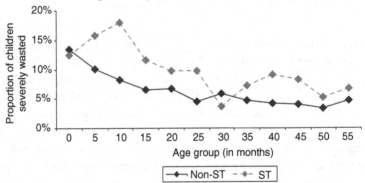

Weight-for-height (children 0–59 months old), 2005–2006

Figure 6.5. More Scheduled Tribe children are severely stunted and wasted within the first ten months of their birth.
Source: National Family Health Survey.

communities are cut off from communication and transport. Public-interest lawsuits have been filed on behalf of families that lost their children,[17] and state governments have been repeatedly directed by the courts to take remedial action. Governments have undoubtedly become more vigilant on this issue than they were before, but serious problems in service delivery continue to exist.

Malnutrition and high mortality among ST children have two likely main causes: extreme poverty among ST households and poor access to health care (Rao 2008). This section focuses on health indicators that may be driven by these two causes, such as poor immunization coverage, high

[17] See for instance, Sheela Barse v/s State of Maharashtra 1993.

Table 6.11. *The gap between Scheduled Tribes and others persists in immunization outcomes, as well*

	Urban			Rural			Overall		
	ST	Other	Total	ST	Other	Total	ST	Other	Total
Percent of children with all basic** vaccinations									
1992–1993	36	51	51	24	32	31	25	37	35
1998–1999	43	57	57	22	39	37	25	43	41
2005–2006	52	58	58	30	40	39	32	45	44
Change 1993–2006, %	*45*	*13*	*13*	*27*	*25*	*25*	*30*	*22*	*23*
Percent of children with at least one of the basic** vaccinations									
1992–1993	79	84	84	56	67	66	58	71	70
1998–1999	85	95	95	75	86	85	76	88	87
2005–2006	94	97	97	89	95	94	89	95	95
Change 1993–2006, %	*19*	*15*	*15*	*57*	*41*	*43*	*53*	*34*	*35*

Notes: Children 12 to 23 months old born to ever married women, 15 to 49 years old.
** Basic vaccinations include three rounds of polio 1–3 and DPT1–3, BCG, measles;
Source: NFHS.

incidence and inadequate treatment of illnesses, and poor maternal health indicators.

Immunization coverage: Vaccine-preventable diseases and other (mainly waterborne and vector-borne) diseases are an important proximate cause of mortality among ST children. Complications arising from each or any of these – such as post-measles pneumonia – create a web of morbidity and malnutrition that children find difficult to fight off. While there has been an overall improvement in immunization coverage this section finds that although improvements have been larger in magnitude for STs, absolute proportions are still low and gaps between ST and non-ST children remain high, especially in rural areas.

Immunization coverage is measured using two indicators – *breadth* of coverage (percentage receiving any basic vaccination) and *intensity* or *quality* of coverage (percentage receiving all basic vaccinations). Analysis using the NFHS data suggests that both indicators registered substantial improvement between 1992 and 2005, especially among STs, thus narrowing the differential between ST and non-ST populations (Table 6.11). At the all-India level, among the twelve-to-twenty-three-month-olds born to ever married women in the age group between fifteen and forty-nine years, the proportion that received any of the basic vaccines expanded by about 35 percent. The corresponding increase for ST children was 53 percent. The intensity of coverage expanded more slowly – 23 percent for all India and 30 percent for STs. This is not surprising given that improvements in intensity of coverage are considerably more difficult to bring about, insofar as they are more costly and require a more coordinated immunization policy.

However, a disaggregated analysis suggests that despite the gains made, immunization rates among STs remained consistently below those recorded for other groups including the SCs and OBCs, for all types of vaccinations (see Table 6.3A, Annex 3). For instance, even though coverage for the polio vaccine (polio 0) more than quadrupled to 30 percent among ST children in the age group of twelve to twenty-three months, it was still lower than the coverage reported among their SC counterparts (47 percent in 2005). The persistence of this gap is mostly due to the extremely poor immunization coverage among ST children to begin with.

Illness of ST children – Prevention and treatment: Disparities also remained in treatment of illness for ST children three years of age and younger, compared with other children, although the incidence of disease varied only slightly. The gap was more acute in the treatment of acute respiratory infections (ARIs). Only about half of ST children, compared with 67 percent of non-ST children, were taken to a health facility for treatment for fever or cough in 2005. The latter were also more likely to be taken to a health facility for treatment of diarrhea, compared with ST children. Whereas SC and OBC children were less likely to receive treatment in health facilities than the upper castes, ST children registered the lowest rates of access to qualified medical assistance (see Table 6.3B, Annex 3).

Maternal Health. Existing literature confirms that malnutrition is intergenerational, passed on from mother to child. Evidence on stunting and wasting in the first ten months of birth for ST children suggests that inequities in children's health can be attributed, to an extent, to the disparities in health of their mothers. Overall, in India, maternal health continues to be an intractable problem, despite improvements over the last couple of decades. Even though improvements for ST women occurred at a faster pace than those for other women, the low base from which the former started has driven their low levels. Moreover, gaps between ST and other women in a range of indicators related to access to care continue to be wide. For instance, the proportion of ST women going for prenatal visits or using contraception remained lower than the population average or the average for women belonging to other social groups. The comparisons with SC and OBC women are particularly instructive. Fifty-five percent of ST women in the 2005 NFHS reported having ever used contraception, compared with 63 percent of SC women and 62 percent of OBC women and the all-India figure of 65 percent. In comparison to SCs and OBCs, a relatively smaller proportion of ST women reported three or more prenatal visits (40 percent compared with 44 percent for SC women and 48 percent for women from the OBC

Table 6.12. *Scheduled Tribe children are less likely to be treated for illnesses (percent)*

	Urban			Rural			Overall		
	ST	Other	Total	ST	Other	Total	ST	Other	Total
Diarrhea
1992–1993	0.118	0.105	0.105	0.113	0.119	0.119	0.114	0.116	0.115
1998–1999	0.229	0.194	0.196	0.209	0.185	0.188	0.211	0.187	0.189
2005–2006	0.134	0.121	0.122	0.124	0.122	0.123	0.125	0.122	0.122
Taken to health facility for diarrhea
1992–1993	0.535	0.692	0.686	0.497	0.600	0.589	0.500	0.620	0.609
1998–1999	0.602	0.787	0.778	0.525	0.644	0.628	0.534	0.680	0.664
2005–2006	0.678	0.662	0.662	0.578	0.609	0.606	0.588	0.624	0.620
Fever or cough
1992–1993	0.256	0.263	0.263	0.273	0.274	0.274	0.271	0.271	0.271
1998–1999	0.479	0.438	0.440	0.461	0.436	0.439	0.463	0.436	0.439
2005–2006	0.235	0.242	0.241	0.227	0.261	0.257	0.228	0.256	0.253
Taken to a health facility for fever or cough
1992–1993	0.694	0.771	0.768	0.527	0.633	0.621	0.540	0.666	0.654
1998–1999	0.559	0.602	0.600	0.409	0.499	0.488	0.425	0.524	0.514
2005–2006	0.772	0.749	0.750	0.534	0.642	0.631	0.558	0.669	0.660

Note: Children under 3 years old of ever married women, 15 to 49 years old; health facilities exclude pharmacies, shops, any traditional treatments. All numbers to be read as proportion of children.
Source: NFHS.

group – see Table 6.3C, Annex 3). ST women also remained less likely to receive prenatal care from doctors. Only one-third received such care in 2005 as compared to the population average of 49 percent (Table 6.13). Worse, the proportion of ST women to have received such care actually declined marginally from 1998 levels (from 35 percent to 32 percent).

In the case of home-based births too, 80 percent of ST women, compared to about 60 percent of all women in India, tend to give birth at home. In fact, the incidence of home births declined at a much slower pace for ST women than it did for others between 1998 and 2005 (at 4 percent, compared to a decline of 10 percent for all India). Most women, not just ST women, in the NFHS 2005 sample say it is not necessary to go to a health facility for childbirth. Interestingly, exploratory multivariate analysis based on RCH II data for institutional delivery (controlling for a range of household and individual characteristics including receipt of prenatal care, as well as supply-side variables like availability of doctor and distance to health facility) shows that STs and Christians (the majority of whom are STs, mainly

Table 6.13. *Despite gains, maternal health indicators for ST women remain below par (percent)*

	Urban			Rural			Overall		
	ST	Other	Total	ST	Other	Total	ST	Other	Total
Number of children*									
1992–1993	2.94	2.84	2.85	3.15	3.19	3.19	3.13	3.10	3.10
1998–1999	2.89	2.70	2.70	3.16	3.07	3.08	3.13	2.97	2.98
2005–2006	2.58	2.51	2.51	3.17	2.97	2.99	3.11	2.82	2.84
Women currently using contraception*									
1992–1993	0.406	0.483	0.481	0.300	0.356	0.350	0.310	0.391	0.384
1998–1999	0.492	0.548	0.546	0.346	0.430	0.421	0.362	0.463	0.454
2005–2006	0.571	0.625	0.624	0.457	0.525	0.518	0.469	0.558	0.551
Women ever used any contraception*									
1992–1993	0.486	0.583	0.580	0.348	0.426	0.418	0.361	0.470	0.460
1998–1999	0.585	0.659	0.656	0.424	0.509	0.500	0.441	0.551	0.541
2005–2006	0.663	0.732	0.731	0.535	0.623	0.614	0.548	0.659	0.650
Women who reported prenatal visit during first trimester**									
1992–1993	0.305	0.417	0.413	0.151	0.213	0.206	0.164	0.263	0.253
1998–1999	0.449	0.564	0.559	0.189	0.280	0.269	0.214	0.347	0.334
2005–2006	0.577	0.632	0.630	0.295	0.370	0.361	0.322	0.441	0.430
Women who reported three or more prenatal visits**									
1992–1993	0.495	0.679	0.673	0.273	0.393	0.380	0.292	0.463	0.447
1998–1999	0.601	0.713	0.708	0.250	0.390	0.375	0.284	0.466	0.449
2005–2006	0.707	0.738	0.737	0.374	0.435	0.428	0.405	0.518	0.507
Women for whom prenatal care provider: doctor**									
1992–1993	0.568	0.727	0.722	0.191	0.349	0.332	0.223	0.441	0.421
1998–1999	0.650	0.770	0.765	0.318	0.435	0.422	0.350	0.514	0.498
2005–2006	0.765	0.762	0.762	0.275	0.414	0.398	0.322	0.509	0.491
Women for whom prenatal care provider: midwife/nurse**									
1992–1993	0.110	0.159	0.157	0.093	0.148	0.142	0.094	0.151	0.145
1998–1999	0.232	0.248	0.247	0.172	0.197	0.195	0.178	0.209	0.206
2005–2006	0.293	0.299	0.299	0.374	0.385	0.384	0.367	0.361	0.362
Women giving birth at home**									
1992–1993	0.577	0.401	0.407	0.937	0.818	0.831	0.906	0.716	0.734
1998–1999	0.392	0.332	0.335	0.877	0.730	0.746	0.829	0.636	0.655
2005–2006	0.379	0.291	0.295	0.841	0.668	0.688	0.797	0.565	0.588
Women who received assistance in giving birth from a doctor**									
1992–1993	0.321	0.498	0.491	0.057	0.156	0.145	0.080	0.240	0.225
1998–1999	0.391	0.577	0.569	0.120	0.249	0.235	0.147	0.326	0.309
2005–2006	0.504	0.649	0.644	0.166	0.297	0.282	0.198	0.393	0.374
Women who received assistance in giving birth from a midwife/nurse**									
1992–1993	0.394	0.520	0.516	0.093	0.197	0.185	0.119	0.276	0.261
1998–1999	0.562	0.598	0.597	0.141	0.273	0.258	0.182	0.350	0.333
2005–2006	0.355	0.433	0.430	0.141	0.256	0.243	0.162	0.305	0.291

Notes: *Ever married women, 15 to 49 years; ** Ever married women who gave birth in the last 3 years (in reference to the last pregnancy or birth).
Source: NFHS.

Table 6.14. *Educational attainment (1983–2005): Scheduled
Tribes still lag far behind the rest (percent)*

	Urban			Rural			Overall		
	Other	STs	Total	Other	STs	Total	Other	STs	Total
No education									
1983	29	46	29	61	78	63	52	75	54
1993–1994	23	35	24	51	70	53	43	67	45
2004–2005	17	26	17	40	56	42	33	53	35
*Below primary**									
1983	10	10	10	10	9	10	10	9	10
1993–1994	9	10	9	11	10	11	11	10	11
2004–2005	7	7	7	11	12	11	10	12	10
Completed primary									
1983	16	14	16	13	7	12	14	7	13
1993–1994	13	14	13	12	8	12	12	9	12
2004–2005	12	11	12	14	12	14	13	12	13
Any Post-primary									
1983	45	30	44	17	6	16	24	8	23
1993–1994	55	41	54	26	12	24	34	15	32
2004–2005	63	55	63	35	20	34	44	23	42

Notes: 15–49 year old individuals; (*) Includes individuals who are literate but have no formal schooling;
Source: NSS.

in the northeastern states), compared to upper-caste Hindus, were the only groups that had a lower likelihood of giving birth in health centers (World Bank, 2006a).

Education

Gains in education have been considerable in India between 1983 and 2005. The proportion of individuals with no education dropped from 54 percent to 35 percent and post-primary attainment nearly doubled from 23 to 42 percent. STs too have shared in the gains, recording almost equivalent or more improvements (Table 6.14). Educational inequalities by caste and tribal status are well recognized, but there has been a convergence in educational outcomes between STs and others over time. Although a differential still persists, it has narrowed over the 1983–2005 period, in particular among younger age cohorts in terms of the proportion with no education, indicating that ST children today fare better in the acquisition of basic education than their parents did (Figure 6.6).

Das, Hall, Kapoor, and Nikitin

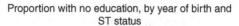

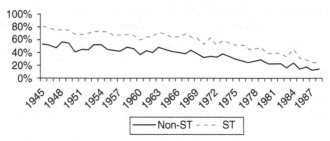

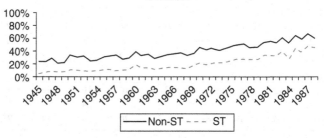

Figure 6.6. More Schedule Tribe members now have some education, but gaps are still large after primary level.
Source: NSS.

However, these findings need to be nuanced by the unequal results across regions and by differences according to the *level* of post-primary education attained. More than half of the ST population in rural areas (56 percent) remained uneducated in 2004–2005 (Table 6.14). In urban areas, however, there was a slight convergence in literacy levels between the STs and the rest of the population. In 2004–2005, about one-quarter among STs were illiterate, in comparison to 17 percent among the rest of the urban population.

Even within the category of post-primary attainment, the improvement registered was at lower levels of education (secondary), not at the college level. Finally, as with other outcomes, the starting point of STs was so low that even with gains similar to the rest of the population, a lower proportion of STs was literate or had attained post-primary education than other groups. For instance, only 8 percent of STs had post-primary schooling in 1983. The

Table 6.15. *Age-grade distortion is higher among*
Scheduled Tribe children (percent)

	Scheduled Tribes	Other	Total
Grade 1	30	27	27
Grade 2	31	25	26
Grade 3	33	28	28
Grade 4	35	24	25
Grade 5	34	29	29
Total	33	27	27

Notes: Percent of students more than one year older than the
appropriate age-for-grade.
Source: NFHS 2005.

numbers had nearly tripled by 2005 – much more than the increase recorded by other groups, yet not enough to meet their levels of attainment.

Yet another qualifier to the gains made by STs is the issue of age-grade distortion. Analysis using the NFHS data[18] suggests that nearly 27 percent of elementary school students in India are two or more years behind the expected grade level for their age (Table 6.15). Among STs, the proportion of children falling behind is somewhat higher than the national average (33 percent). The problem is more extensive in rural schools than in urban schools – a difference of five percentage points between ST and non-ST children compared to a one percentage point difference in urban areas. The greater age-grade distortion for ST children may partly be the result of poor quality or virtually nonexistent education facilities in remote ST habitats.

The triple disadvantage: Tribe, gender, and place of residence. No analysis of education outcomes for ST groups in India is complete without highlighting the low levels of educational attainment among ST women. Even among the youngest age cohort, now emerging from their prime schooling years (ages fifteen to twenty-one), ST women attain an average of just four years of education. In comparison, non-ST women in this age group attain nearly seven years of education (Figure 6.7). Worse, in terms of the number of years, the gap between ST men and women has actually widened. Among

[18] The NSS data has the advantage of greater sample size, but none of the available rounds of the NSS data (until 2005–2006) contain information on current enrollment in specific grades, which makes it impossible to calculate age-grade distortion at specific grade levels. By contrast, the 2005–2006 NFHS dataset contains data on grades. Similarly, Figure 6.7 uses the NFHS data on the number of completed years of schooling, which is not available in the NSS.

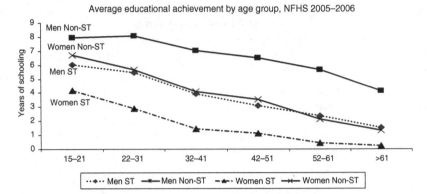

Figure 6.7. Scheduled Tribe women are at a significant disadvantage compared to non–Scheduled Tribe women and Scheduled Tribe men: They are in school for fewer years. *Source*: National Family Health Survey.

older-age cohorts, the gap is roughly 1.5 years, but among the fifteen-to-twenty-one age-cohort, the male-female gap is two years (with male STs in this category attaining an average of six years of education).

ST women in rural areas are particularly worse off, as they are beset by a triple disadvantage: identity, gender, and place of residence. Poor access to schools in remote regions implies that only one in three ST women in rural areas is literate and one in eight has attained post-primary education (NSS, 2004–2005). Meanwhile, ST women in urban areas seem to benefit significantly from better physical access to schools, with more than half completing post-primary education. Not all are better off, however. There appear to be wide inequalities even among urban ST women, with one-third of them illiterate in 2004–2005.

Regardless of tribal status, gender is an important factor in age-grade distortion in primary schools, with girls reporting *lower* overall age-grade distortion than boys (except among rural non-ST children), perhaps because boys tend to be taken out of school to work in family farms and businesses more often than girls. This pattern stands in contrast to the lower overall educational attainment among women (Figure 6.7). Thus, girls face the challenge of *access* to schooling rather than falling behind once already enrolled.

WHAT EXPLAINS POOR OUTCOMES FOR SCHEDULED TRIBES IN INDIA?

Why are ST outcomes – on child mortality, maternal health, or enrollment rates – poorer than that of any other group? The government's response to this question is usually that poverty among STs is to blame. There may be some truth to this assertion. Consistent with this argument, multivariate analysis using the RCH II data also finds that the relationship between infant or child mortality and tribal (or indeed caste) status vanishes when controlling for wealth quintile and distance to nearest health care facility (World Bank, 2006a). Other variables associated with children's mortality are mother's characteristics including education, number of prenatal visits, birth order of child, and distance to the nearest town.

That the effect of poverty trumps the effect of ST status is corroborated by other recent analyses. Jose and Navaneetham (2008) analyze malnutrition levels in women over the seven years between 1998–1999 and 2005–2006, based on the National Family Health Survey. Their findings suggest that while social disadvantage (membership to an SC or ST group) is associated with increased malnutrition among women, economic disadvantage has a greater impact. Poor women from almost all social groups report higher malnutrition than others. In another study on the progress of the millennium development goals in Orissa, the World Bank finds that while child and infant mortality rates are higher among the Scheduled Tribes, they are largely a function of poverty (lower levels of income and assets), low levels of education, and poor access/utilization of health services (World Bank 2007b). Even among STs, there is evidence of a strong socioeconomic gradient in health, with those in the bottom quintiles having a higher odds ratio for mortality compared to those in the top fifth of the wealth distribution (Subramanian et al. 2006). Analysis of enrollment rates using NSS data suggests that while ST children are at all times less likely to enroll in schools than non-ST children (even after controlling for wealth), the gap widens for poorer households.[19] That is, the difference in the predicted probability of current school enrollment for ST and non-ST children varies with the position of the household in the expenditure distribution – it is 8 points for households in the poorest quintile but only 3 points for households in the wealthiest quintile.

Therefore, poor health and education outcomes may in some sense result from high poverty. But poverty is, in turn, endogenous to each of these outcomes, such that the argument becomes tautological. *Perhaps the critical question then is not why mortality rates or malnutrition levels*

---

[19] We ran probit regressions using the NSS 2004–2005 data. Current enrollment (primary or secondary) among seven- to fourteen-year-olds was treated as the dependent variable. The model controlled for the usual predictors, such as age, gender, household size, place of residence, household head's education, log monthly real expenditure per capita, and social group membership. State controls were also added.

*are higher among ST children, but why poverty among STs is higher or why
ST households are food-insecure.* Why do development projects not reach
them? There are multiple factors that contribute, but a few specific ones
lie at the root of poor outcomes for STs. These include (but are not limited
to) poor physical access to services, widespread removal from their traditional lands and forests, poor enforcement of legislation meant to protect their interests, lack of collective voice, and poor implementation of
government programs aimed to assist them (although the last is not particular to tribal regions). Together, they explain the complex web of deprivation in which tribal people in India find themselves (see Xaxa 2001).
Each of these factors merits a separate analysis, well beyond the physical
constraints of this chapter. However, the next section summarizes the key
issues for each, highlighting the core institutional factors that account for
tribal deprivation.

Centrality of Land and Natural Resources in
Explaining Poor Outcomes

The relationship of STs to land is beyond that of subsistence cultivation
and extends to the use of forest products and their dependence on natural resources for a livelihood. This is evident given that about 60 percent
of India's forest cover lies in the 187 tribal districts covered by the Fifth
and Sixth Schedules of the Constitution (Forest Survey of India Report,
2003). Estimates from Orissa indicate that one-fifth to one-half of annual
income of tribal households comes from Non-Timber Forest Products
(NTFPs). Many NTFP (e.g., kendu leaves) are of high value and are prone
to commercial exploitation. Their sale is usually governed by a complex
set of rules and regulations, and tribal rights activists allege that the state
and middlemen work toward keeping the tribals' share of the profits low.
Although there have been efforts to devolve the procurement and marketing of NTFPs to gram sabhas,[20] the lack of capacity of gram sabhas
in these areas has meant that middlemen may have benefited more than
tribal people.

   In addition to their tenuous hold over NTFPs, the STs in India have also
been gradually losing access to their traditional lands – a process referred to
as alienation. The largest form of alienation from traditional land has taken

[20] Orissa, for instance, has devolved the procurement and marketing of sixty-nine NTFPs;
the Gram Sabha is a village assembly of which each resident of the village is a member.

place as a result of state acquisition of land for development. The tenth Five-Year Plan of India noted that between 1951 and 1990, 21.3 million people were displaced, of which 40 percent – or 8.5 million – were tribal people (Burra, 2008).

Proactive Legislation but Poor Enforcement

In addition to the policies described to safeguard the welfare of STs (second section of this chapter), India has had an active program of land reform, albeit with patchy implementation. Moreover, legislation prevents ST land from being "alienated," but this can act as a double-edged sword. It may mean that tribals cannot sell their land to nontribals even when they want to. But land grabbing takes place regardless – through marriage or through fraud by contractors/lenders as a means to recover debt from STs. ST indebtedness is another important reason for lands being handed over to moneylenders, often through fraudulent transactions. Mander (2002) estimates that nearly 46 percent of land transfers in Jhabua (Madhya Pradesh) in the 1970s were to repay loans. The issue of fake ST certificates has also acquired very sensitive political ramifications. Despite the publicized Supreme Court case of a student named Madhuri Patil who fraudulently received an ST certificate, indicating herself as Mahadeo Koli (an ST) when in fact she was a Hindu Koli (OBC),[21] such cases continue to come to light.

One of the most important pieces of legislation in the last decade has been PESA. It is unique in being in consonance with customary laws, focusing more on tribal hamlets based on culture rather than revenue villages. Several steps have been taken to operationalize PESA – state amendments and rules have been passed, and monitoring is underway. However, it is widely believed that PESA has not been implemented in spirit. Most recently, another Act – the Scheduled Tribes and Other Traditional Forest Dwellers (Recognition of Forest Rights) Act, 2006 (known variously in common parlance as the Forest Rights Act or the Tribal Rights Act) – recognizes the preeminent rights of tribals on forest land. Both PESA and the Tribal Rights Act fundamentally question the power relations between ST and non-ST areas and peoples and purport to transfer greater power to the former. It is the politics of this power sharing that is at the crux of poor implementation and needs to be taken on squarely at the political level.

[21] Kumari Madhuri Patil vs. Addl. Commissioner [1994] RD-SC 445 (September 2, 1994).

Poor Implementation of Government Programs

Legislative instruments have gone hand in hand with special programs for vulnerable groups and areas, especially for tribals. However, the implementation of programs and enforcement of laws has been very weak. The public administration and activist literature documents the challenges in implementing programs in tribal areas. There are both supply-side and demand-side challenges and often the two are mutually reinforcing.

One of the key issues in scheduled areas is poor physical access. In most states in India, STs are physically isolated, concentrated in certain regions and districts and in hilly and forested areas that make communication and access to services difficult even in normal circumstances. Poor coverage of all weather roads makes transportation in emergencies virtually impossible, even if health centers were attended by medical personnel. There is also a deep-rooted cultural chasm and mistrust between the largely nontribal health providers and the tribal residents (Bharat et al. 2003; Pallavi 2004). Migration of STs during the lean season to cities and towns makes the task of health surveillance for prenatal care or immunization or growth monitoring of children even more difficult. Finally, although administrators realize the value of recruiting local residents as field-level medical personnel, it is often impossible to find even secondary-educated ST women who can fill the positions of nurses or female health workers. As a result, the positions either remain vacant or are filled by nontribal, nonresident providers.

The Integrated Child Development Services (ICDS) program provides an illustration of implementation challenges that impede maximum impact. The program aims to improve the nutritional status of preschool children, pregnant women, and lactating mothers, particularly those belonging to the poorest of the poor families and living in disadvantaged areas. It also has a component of early childhood education. Program incidence across expenditure quintiles in 2004–2005 shows that while it does benefit a substantial proportion of the ST population (14.1 percent of tribal children), it also reaches the better-off quintiles (NSS, 2004–2005). More than one-fifth of children in the third and fourth quintile of tribal households receive benefits. The scheme also benefits 8.7 percent of tribal children in the richest quintile. These issues of targeting and program performance have been in the policy discourse for several years, but issues of monitoring, gaps in targeting, and political interference are significant roadblocks. Other programs are challenged with similar problems (see Box 1).

Box 1. *Missing Hostels*

Among its several programs to encourage education among disadvantaged groups, the government of India has formulated schemes
for providing hostel facilities to SC and ST students. The expenditure
under the scheme is shared on 50:50 basis between the Centre and
State Governments.

In an audit report of such facilities covering the period 2001–2006
in the state of Jharkhand, the state department was allocated a sum
of Rs. 120 million and Rs. 250 million to spend on constructing and
maintaining hostels for Scheduled Caste and Scheduled Tribe children
respectively between 2001 and 2006. The department spent only 40
per cent of the allocation amount for SCs and 28 per cent of the allocation amount for STs. The State Government sanctioned construction of 184 hostels (78 for SCs and 106 for STs) over the intervening
period. Of these, 71 hostels (SC- 32 and ST- 39) were incomplete in
August 2006. The department never monitored the construction.
Moreover, the site selection was not need based. For instance, one tribal hostel constructed at a cost of Rs. 6 million in the state's capital –
Ranchi – was eventually handed over to a college, without any basic
facilities like electricity, drinking water supply, beds and manpower
to run it. Tribal hostels that were found in a running state were usually overcrowded, accommodating at times about 90 students in 3–4
rooms. In other sites, hostels constructed were found to be occupied
by outsiders – police constables, and at times the offices of government agencies themselves. (CAG report for Jharkhand, 2006)

Strong Protest Movements But Limited Voice in Decision Making

Legislation and other special provisions for enhanced voice of ST groups
have worked in consonance with strong movements from below. Tribal
movements against the state predate the British, and STs have historically
been assertive of their rights over land and forests. In the recent period,
tribal action has not translated into better integration of their voice in decision making. Both SCs and STs have faced political disadvantages in the past,
but the former have been more effective in claiming political representation

and power. The SCs have nationally known political parties and leaders who can represent their claims in the wider political system. STs, on the other hand, despite enabling legislation, seem to have become increasingly marginalized. Banerjee and Somanathan (2007), for instance, show that between 1971 and 1991, fewer education and health facilities were available in parliamentary constituencies with ST concentrations.

Many, including Guha (2007) and Xaxa (2001), have maintained that disparities between STs and non-STs are largely related to low collective voice of the former and low accountability to them by the ruling elites. Restricted to remote villages, in no state of India are the STs in majority.[22] They can influence election results in only a few isolated districts. In contrast, the SCs form a considerable share of total population in several states, and therefore can play a decisive hand in influencing voting results (Guha 2007). Thus the concerns of the STs remain marginal in the national context on the one hand, and on the other, there are increasingly violent insurgent movements in tribal areas. A recent Planning Commission report (Government of India, 2008) links these movements squarely to underdevelopment and marginalization of STs.

CONCLUSIONS

This chapter draws attention to some of the issues in the deprivation of ST groups in India. It is by no means a comprehensive analysis, but the national picture it paints is sobering. It highlights the differences in outcomes between STs and other groups – even the SCs.

Our analysis leads to three important conclusions. First, it suggests that the pace of poverty reduction has been considerably slower for the STs than it has been for other social categories, the SCs included. There is also considerable heterogeneity in poverty outcomes by state and within STs. States where STs comprise more than 10 percent of the total population register headcount poverty rates that are higher than the national average. Similarly, within STs, those in lower deciles of the expenditure distribution do worse, registering lower growth in expenditure than those in the upper deciles.

Second, even though the STs saw significant gains in indicators of health, some of which improved at rates faster than the population average, such gains were not sufficient to bridge the gap between the STs and the rest.

---

[22] Even in states like Jharkhand and Chhattisgarh, which have considerable tribal populations, roughly two-third of the population is nontribal.

Under-five mortality of children remains a stark marker of deprivation of STs in India, with nearly 96 ST children dying for every 1,000 births, compared with an under-five mortality of 74 per 1,000 births for non-ST children. Interestingly, no differences were found in neonatal mortality outcomes among ST children and the rest, suggesting that the former were more at risk as they grew up. This finding is supported by alarming figures on malnutrition for ST children – nearly 53 percent were reported to be stunted (had lower height for age) and 29 percent were reported to be severely stunted in 2005.

Third, despite improvement in educational attainment, literacy levels among STs remained at an abysmally low level of 47 percent of ST population in 2005–2006, compared with 67 percent for others – an indication of the former's considerably lower starting point. There were differences by region and by gender. STs in rural areas were usually worse off, as were women, especially on educational attainment.

- During a period of relative prosperity for India as a whole, poverty among STs has declined slower than for other groups and particularly slowly in states that have large proportions of ST populations.
- Health and education outcomes among STs, while showing faster progress in some respects than for the rest of the population, are still very poor. Convergence with other groups has occurred in only a small number of areas, notably at lower levels of education and in immunization coverage.
- Excessive mortality among ST children continues to be the starkest marker of tribal disadvantage and has its roots in a number of complex processes that exclude STs in general.
- A number of laws and programs are in place to address the special disadvantages of STs, but their implementation is poor.
- The limited voice of STs in public decision making and their alienation from land and forests are central to their continued exclusion from progress and development.

ANNEX 1

The term "Scheduled Tribes" first appeared in the Constitution of India. Article 366 (25) defined Scheduled Tribes as "such tribes or tribal communities or parts of or groups within such tribes or tribal communities as are deemed under Article 342 to be Scheduled Tribes for the purposes of this constitution." Article 342, which is reproduced below, prescribes procedure to be followed in the matter of specification of Scheduled Tribes.

Article 342 Scheduled Tribes

The President may, with respect to any State or Union territory, and where it is a state, after consultation with the Governor there of by public notification, specify the tribes or tribal communities or parts of or groups within tribes or tribal communities which shall, for the purposes of this constitution, is deemed to be Scheduled Tribes in relation to that state or Union Territory, as the case may be. Parliament may by law include in or exclude from the list of Scheduled Tribes specified in a notification issued under clause(1) any tribe or tribal community or part of or group within any tribe or tribal community, but save as aforesaid, a notification issued under the said clause shall not be varied by any subsequent notification.

Thus, the first specification of Scheduled Tribes in relation to a particular State/ Union Territory is by a notified order of the President, after consultation with the State governments concerned. These orders can be modified subsequently only through an Act of Parliament. The above Article also provides for listing of Scheduled Tribes State/Union Territory wise and not on an all India basis.

The criterion followed for specification of a community, as Scheduled Tribes are indications of primitive traits, distinctive culture, geographical isolation, shyness of contact with the community at large, and backwardness. This criterion is not spelt out in the Constitution but has become well established. It subsumes the definitions contained in 1931 Census, the reports of first Backward Classes Commission 1955, the Advisory Committee (Kalelkar), on Revision of SC/ST lists (Lokur Committee), 1965 and the Joint Committee of Parliament on the Scheduled Castes and Scheduled Tribes orders (Amendment) Bill 1967 (Chanda Committee), 1969.

In exercise of the powers conferred by Clause (1) of Article 342 of the Constitution of India, the President, after Consultation with the State Governments concerned have promulgated so far 9 orders specifying the Scheduled Tribes in relation to the state and union territories. Out of these, eight are in operation at present in their original or amended form. One order namely the Constitution (Goa, Daman & Diu) Scheduled Tribes order 1968 has become defunct on account of reorganization of Goa, Daman & Diu in 1987. Under the Goa, Daman & Diu reorganization Act 1987 (18 of 1987) the list of Scheduled Tribes of Goa has been transferred to part XIX of the Schedule to the Constitution (Scheduled Tribes) Order, 1950 and that of Daman & Diu II of the Schedule of the Constitution (Scheduled Tribes) (Union Territories) Order, 1951.

ANNEX 2

Annex 2. Table 1. *Official poverty lines of India, 2004–2005 (Rupees/month)*

	Rural	Urban
States		
Andhra Pradesh	293.0	542.9
Arunachal Pradesh	387.6	378.8
Assam	387.6	378.8
Bihar	354.4	435.0
Chhattisgarh	322.4	560.0
Delhi	410.4	612.9
Goa	362.3	665.9
Gujarat	353.9	541.2
Haryana	414.8	504.5
Himachal Pradesh	394.3	504.5
Jammu & Kashmir	391.3	553.8
Jharkhand	366.6	451.2
Karnataka	324.2	599.7
Kerala	430.1	559.4
Madhya Pradesh	327.8	570.2
Maharashtra	362.3	665.9
Manipur	387.6	378.8
Meghalaya	387.6	378.8
Mizoram	387.6	378.8
Nagaland	387.6	378.8
Orissa	325.8	528.5
Punjab	410.4	466.2
Rajasthan	374.6	559.6
Sikkim	387.6	378.8
Tamil Nadu	351.9	547.4
Tripura	387.6	378.8
Uttar Pradesh	365.8	483.3
Uttarakhand	478.0	637.7
West Bengal	382.8	449.3
Union Territories (UT)		
Andaman & Nicobar	351.9	547.4
Chandigarh	466.2	466.2
Dadra & Nagar Haveli	362.3	665.9
Daman & Diu	362.3	665.9
Lakshadweep	430.1	559.4
Pondicherry	351.9	547.4
All India	356.3	538.6

Source: Planning Commission.

ANNEX 3

Annex 3. Table 1. *Gap between Scheduled Tribes and others persists
for all types of immunization (percent)*

	ST	SC	OBC	Other	Total
Year = 1998					
BCG	0.599	0.710	0.735	0.781	0.733
Polio 0	0.074	0.157	0.233	0.174	0.180
Polio 1	0.739	0.835	0.880	0.860	0.849
Polio 2	0.662	0.787	0.827	0.808	0.796
Polio 3	0.470	0.605	0.646	0.645	0.620
DPT 1	0.569	0.694	0.739	0.783	0.729
DPT 2	0.483	0.645	0.677	0.727	0.670
DPT 3	0.372	0.551	0.588	0.637	0.578
Measles	0.343	0.491	0.523	0.596	0.526
All basic vaccinations	0.245	0.393	0.422	0.461	0.413
Any of the basic vaccinations	0.760	0.859	0.903	0.884	0.873
Year = 2005					
BCG	0.722	0.757	0.758	0.851	0.782
Polio 0	0.299	0.466	0.458	0.589	0.484
Polio 1	0.874	0.914	0.941	0.942	0.929
Polio 2	0.808	0.881	0.901	0.901	0.888
Polio 3	0.654	0.765	0.812	0.805	0.785
DPT 1	0.660	0.739	0.737	0.832	0.758
DPT 2	0.543	0.639	0.636	0.765	0.666
DPT 3	0.422	0.515	0.524	0.665	0.554
Measles	0.469	0.559	0.554	0.699	0.590
All basic vaccinations	0.324	0.392	0.402	0.549	0.436
Any of the basic vaccinations	0.892	0.940	0.957	0.956	0.947

Note: Children 12–23 months old of ever married women, 15 to 49 years old.
Source: NFHS.

Annex 3. Table 2. *Scheduled Tribe children are less likely to be treated for illnesses like diarrhea, fever, and cough (percent)*

	ST	SC	OBC	Other	Total
Survey year = 1998					
Diarrhea over last two weeks	0.211	0.195	0.181	0.188	0.189
Received no medical treatment for diarrhea	0.417	0.273	0.284	0.257	0.286
Taken to health facility for diarrhea	0.534	0.670	0.671	0.693	0.664
Fever over last two weeks	0.315	0.293	0.278	0.305	0.295
Cough over last two weeks	0.384	0.355	0.346	0.353	0.354
Had fever/cough over last two weeks	0.463	0.437	0.423	0.447	0.439
Received no medical treatment for fever/cough	0.459	0.324	0.308	0.273	0.314
Taken to health facility for fever/cough	0.425	0.494	0.530	0.535	0.514
Survey year = 2005					
Diarrhea over last two weeks	0.125	0.120	0.130	0.112	0.122
Received no medical treatment for diarrhea	0.336	0.304	0.333	0.253	0.306
Taken to health facility for diarrhea	0.588	0.618	0.589	0.684	0.620
Fever over last two weeks	0.150	0.172	0.165	0.191	0.173
Cough over last two weeks	0.180	0.199	0.193	0.234	0.205
Had fever/cough over last two weeks	0.228	0.249	0.241	0.282	0.253
Received no medical treatment for fever/cough	0.415	0.269	0.278	0.248	0.278
Taken to health facility for fever/cough	0.558	0.651	0.658	0.695	0.660

Note: Children 0–35 months old of ever married women, 15 to 49 years old.
Source: NFHS.

Annex 3. Table 3. *Despite gains, maternal health indicators for ST women remained below par, even by comparison with SC peers (percent)*

	ST	SC	OBC	Other	No caste/ tribe	Total
Survey year 1998						
Three or more prenatal visits	0.284	0.383	0.469	0.512	0.486	0.449
First prenatal visit during first trimester	0.214	0.263	0.339	0.407	0.343	0.334
Currently use contraception	0.362	0.416	0.438	0.516	0.417	0.454
Ever use contraception	0.441	0.494	0.509	0.621	0.543	0.541
Know of a modern method of contraception	0.965	0.988	0.991	0.991	0.986	0.988
Location of last birth (home)	0.830	0.730	0.634	0.579	0.651	0.655
Birth assisted by doctor	0.350	0.428	0.494	0.580	0.563	0.498
Birth assisted by midwife/ nurse	0.178	0.220	0.220	0.197	0.184	0.206
Survey year 2005						
Three or more prenatal visits	0.405	0.443	0.482	0.631	0.527	0.508
First prenatal visit during first trimester	0.322	0.359	0.420	0.540	0.426	0.430
Currently use contraception	0.469	0.539	0.531	0.605	0.569	0.551
Ever use contraception	0.548	0.631	0.619	0.723	0.763	0.650
Know of a modern method of contraception	0.970	0.992	0.993	0.994	0.992	0.991
Location of last birth (home)	0.797	0.650	0.599	0.439	0.640	0.587
Birth assisted by doctor	0.322	0.412	0.470	0.642	0.550	0.492
Birth assisted by midwife	0.367	0.417	0.356	0.321	0.411	0.362

Notes: Ever-married women (15–49 years) who gave birth in last 3 years. Statistics refer to last birth.
Source: NFHS.

References

Banerjee, A. and R. Somanathan. 2007. "The political economy of public goods: Some evidence from India." *Journal of Development Economics*, 82(2): 287–314.

Béteille, A. 1991. *Society and Politics in India: Essays in a Comparative Perspective.* London School of Economics Monographs on Social Anthropology. New Delhi: Oxford University Press

Bharat, S., Patkar, A., and Thomas, D. 2003. *Mainstreaming Equity and Access into the Reproductive and Child Health Program.* London: Department for International Development (DFID) Health Systems Resource Centre

Burra, N. 2008. "The political economy of tribals in India in the context of poverty and social exclusion." Paper prepared for the India Poverty Assessment Report (2009).

Centre for Environment and Food Security. 2005. *Political Economy of Hunger in Adivasi Areas.* New Delhi: CEFS.

Comptroller and Auditor General of India (CAG). 2006. *Report* for the State of Jharkhand. New Delhi: CAG

Das, M. 2006. "Do traditional axes of exclusion affect labor market outcomes in India?" South Asia Social Development Discussion Paper No. 3. Washington, DC: World Bank.

2008. "Minority status and labor market outcomes: Does India have minority enclaves?" Policy Research Working Paper 4653. Washington, DC: World Bank.

Das, M. and P. Dutta. 2007. "Does caste matter for wages in the indian labor market?" Draft Paper, World Bank.

Das M., S. Kapoor, and D. Nikitin. 2010. "A closer look at child mortality among adivasis in India." World Bank Policy Research Working Paper 5231. Washington, DC: World Bank.

Deaton, A. 2003. "Prices and poverty in India, 1987–2000." *Economic and Political Weekly*, January 25–31: 362–368.

2008. "Price trends in India and their implications for measuring poverty." *Economic & Political Weekly*, February 9: 43–49.

Deaton, A. and V. Kozel. 2005. *The Great Indian Poverty Debate.* London: MacMillan.

Forest Survey of India. 2003. *State of Forest Report.* New Delhi: Ministry of Environment and Forests, Government of India

Government of India. 1993. *Report of the Expert Group on Estimation of Proportion and Number of Poor.* New Delhi: Planning Commission.

2008. *Development Challenges in Extremist Affected Areas: Report of an Expert Group to Planning Commission.* New Delhi: Planning Commission. Accessed April 2009 at http://planningcommission.nic.in/reports/publications/rep_dce.pdf

Guha, R. 2007. "Adivasis, Naxalites and Indian democracy." *Economic and Political Weekly*, 42(32): 3305–3312.

International Institute for Population Sciences (IIPS) and Macro International. 2007. *National Family Health Survey (NFHS-3), 2005–06: India, Volume I.* Mumbai: IIPS.

Jose, S. and K. Navaneetham. 2008. "A factsheet on women's malnutrition in India." *Economic and Political Weekly*, August 16: 61–67.

Maharatna, A. 1998. "On tribal fertility in late nineteenth and early twentieth century India." Working paper No 98.01, Harvard Centre for Population and Development Studies. Cambridge, MA: Harvard University.

2000. "Fertility, mortality and gender bias among tribal population: An Indian perspective." *Social Science and Medicine*, 50:1333–1351.

Mander, H. 2002. "Tribal Land Alienation in Madhya Pradesh: The Problem and Legislative Remedies." In *Land Reforms in India: Issues of Equity in Rural Madhya Pradesh*, ed. P. Jha. New Delhi: Sage Publications.

Mosse, David, Gupta, Sanjeev, Mehta, Mona, Shah, Vidya, Rees, Julia, and Team, KRIBPProject. 2002. "Brokered livelihoods: Debt, labour migration and development in tribal western India." *Journal of Development Studies*, 38(5): 59–88.

Pallavi, A. 2004. "Why their kids are dying." *India Together* (September 2004). http://www.indiatogether.org/2004/sep/adv-dyingkids.htm

Rao, V. S. 2008. *Malnutrition, An Emergency: What It Costs the Nation*. New Delhi: Council for Advancement of People's Action and Rural Technology.

Sinha, S. 1958. "Tribal cultures of peninsular India as a dimension of little tradition in the study of Indian civilization." *The Journal of American Folklore*, Vol. 71(281): 504–518.

Subramanian S. V., Davey Smith, G., and Subramanyam, M. 2006. "Do socioeconomic differences account for the Indigenous and non-indigenous health divide in India? A population-based cross-sectional study." *PLoS Medicine*, 3(10, e421): s86–s95.

Virmani, A. 2005. "Policy regimes, growth and poverty in India: Lessons of government failure And entrepreneurial success!" Working Paper 170, Indian Council for Research on International Economic Relations, New Delhi.

World Bank. 2006a. Exploratory analysis of the health status of social groups from RCH II data. Work in progress.

2006b. *Inclusive Growth and Service delivery: Building on India's Success*. New Delhi: World Bank and MacMillan.

2007a. *World Development Indicators 2007*. Washington DC: World Bank.

2007b. *Achieving the MDGs in India's Poor States: Reducing Child Mortality in Orissa*. New Delhi: World Bank.

2011. *India Poverty Assessment Report*. New Delhi: World Bank.

Xaxa, V. 2001. "Protective discrimination: Why scheduled tribes lag behind scheduled castes." *Economic and Political Weekly*, 36(29): 2765–2772.

7

Laos

Ethnolinguistic Diversity and Disadvantage

Elizabeth M. King and Dominique van de Walle

INTRODUCTION

Laos (officially, the Lao People's Democratic Republic) is one of Southeast Asia's poorest countries and probably also the region's most ethnically diverse. Its population of 5 million has four broad ethnolinguistic families: the Lao-Tai (67 percent of the population), the Mon-Khmer (21 percent), Hmong-Lu Mien (8 percent), and the Chine-Tibetan (3 percent). These categories further subsume 49 distinct ethnicities and some 200 ethnic subgroups (World Bank 2006b).[1]

There are pronounced disparities in living standards across these ethnolinguistic groups, with some groups faring much worse than others. The groups are geographically dispersed and sometimes categorized not by their linguistic family but rather by whether they live in the country's lowlands, midlands, or highlands. Many live in ethnically homogeneous villages. The historically politically, economically, and socially dominant Lao-Tai are the primary residents of urban areas, and also live in the high-density, agriculturally productive lowland areas around Vientiane and the Mekong corridor. The Mon-Khmer people, whose presence in present-day Lao PDR predates all the other groups, typically live in midland rural areas of the north and south. The Hmong-Lu Mien people are found in the uplands and high mountains in the north, and the Chine-Tibetan are located in the northern highland areas.

---

[1] There are several ethnic classification systems in Lao PDR, and depending on the system used, the number of ethnic groups vary from about 50 to more than 200 (Pholsena 2006). An alternative classification that is commonly used is based on geographic location. Hence, Tai-Kadai is called *Lao Loum* or Lao people of the valleys; Mon-Khmer are *Lao Theung* or the Lao people of the hillsides, and Tibeto-Burman and the Hmong-Mien are the *Lao Soung* or Lao people of the highlands.

Lao PDR is a predominantly rural country: In 2003, agriculture contributed 48 percent of the country's gross domestic product and employed 80 percent of its labor force (World Bank 2006a). Rural Lao-Tai households are often engaged in the cultivation of lowland irrigated paddy-rice. In contrast, non-Lao-Tai households typically practice subsistence-oriented semi-permanent or shifting agriculture in ways adapted to their specific agro-ecological environments; they grow upland rice, often supplemented by corn and, in many more isolated areas, poppy (Ireson and Ireson 1991; Evrard and Goudineau 2004).[2] Many are also reliant on the collection of forest products and, although often blamed for deforestation, they are also negatively affected by encroaching commercial logging by the government and military for whom this has become a profitable source of foreign exchange (Ireson and Ireson 1991). Some non-Lao-Tai minority groups are still seminomadic, moving to new areas when their lands are depleted, but others have become sedentary. They often live in areas with limited access to transport infrastructure, marketing opportunities, and social services, and many have low levels of human development outcomes, have no tradition of literacy, and do not speak Lao, the official national language.

Significant geographic variations in living standards and by elevation, as well as a desire on the part of the government to assimilate the non-Lao-Tai, have encouraged the government to promote various types of poor-area programs. Since the late 1980s, there have been efforts to resettle highland villagers in lowland "focal" areas where basic public services such as schools and health facilities already exist, or can be more efficiently and cheaply provided (Cohen 2000; Evrard and Goudineau 2004). Since 2003, the government has also had a program that focuses interventions on 72 out of 143 total districts, identified as "priority districts."

Observers have claimed that these programs have failed and even worsened the welfare of relocated households due to a lack of support and infrastructure necessary to adapt to the new and foreign environments. Many have succumbed to diseases, such as malaria, to which they have no resistance (Cohen 2000). Indeed, it has been argued that the government is more interested in resettling and assimilating the ethnic groups into Lao-Tai culture than in raising their living standards per se (Ireson and Ireson 1991; Baird and Shoemaker 2007).[3]

---

[2] In 1998, 45% of the country's villages were dependent on swidden agriculture for their livelihoods (State Planning Committee and National Statistical Center 1999).

[3] "Resettlement, then, is a strategy for the development of ethnic minorities that was conceived by lowland Lao and is carried out by Lao and culturally assimilated ethnic minority men. While forest land use and resettlement policy is only one aspect of development for government personnel, it is a life and death issue for minorities. Projects so far have been

This chapter examines various aspects of the living standards of Lao PDR's ethnic minority groups relative to that of the historically dominant Lao-Tai ethnolinguistic group. The analysis draws primarily on data from the Lao Expenditure Consumption Survey of 2002–2003 (LECS3), a nationally representative household survey that covered 8,100 households. Unlike the earlier surveys, this survey collected information on ethnic group affiliation of household members. It also collected an array of demographic and socioeconomic information about the sample's households, including measures of consumption, household assets, household size, education levels, and health status of household members, utilization of public services, and employment and time use. Because of data inadequacies, we undertook consistency checks on the data related to consumption, schooling, health, employment and time use, and other background information on households and individuals. The checks include (but are not limited to) cross-checking the responses to related questions and verifying responses against response codes and skip patterns. We use the data for the survey questions that pass these tests and discard the responses to questions that do not, or avoid using the survey information altogether; in particular, employment, labor force participation, and health cost data appear to have problems.

For our analysis we also use data from a school survey module that was added to the LECS3. The module was applied to all the primary schools in the same LECS3 survey villages; it collected data on a variety of school characteristics, including information on individual teachers and the school head.[4] About 80 percent of children in the sample live in a village with a primary school. In cases where there was no primary school in the village, the most attended school and the second-most attended school outside the village were surveyed, provided these schools were located in villages contiguous to the sample village.

clumsy, culturally insensitive efforts to attract upland minorities to an area by constructing physical structures such as roads, schools, clinics, or dams, but which include few or no programmatic activities such as agricultural extension, training or public health outreach. Donor agency and government personnel administer resettlement resources according to their conception of what is good for the minorities or for national development goals. Thus, resettlement becomes another means by which ethnic minorities are Laoized as they are 'developed'" (Ireson and Ireson 1991, pp. 935–936).

[4] The primary school module was developed by Elizabeth King, Keiko Miwa, and Dominique van de Walle. The principal respondent of the questionnaire was the school principal, responding to questions about personal and educational characteristics as well as about the facilities in the school and its physical condition, its parent-teacher association, school fees, and other school characteristics. All teachers in the sample schools were also interviewed to elicit individual characteristics, including educational attainment, teaching experience, and activities as a teacher.

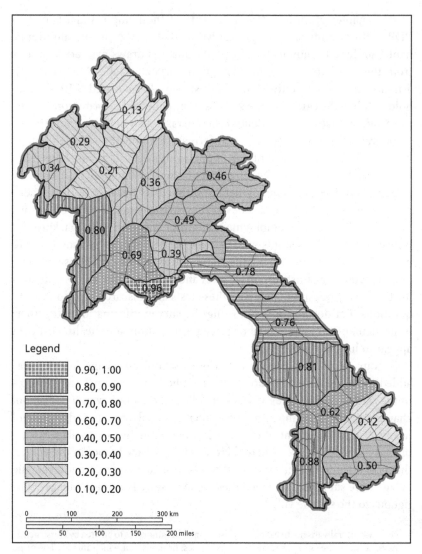

Figure 7.1. Share of Lao PDR population in the majority Lao-Tai ethnicity, by province. *Source*: LECS3 2002–2003.

For simplicity, we classify the population into just two ethnic groups – the Lao-Tai (henceforth referred to as LT) and the non-Lao-Tai (NLT). Just 3 percent of survey households (264 of 8,092) have both LT and NLT members, but three-fourths of these mixed households are in urban areas. These mixed households are classified as LT if there are at least as many LT as NLT members. Moreover, given that the NLT ethnic groups predominantly live in rural areas and so have small urban sample sizes, we either do not show them under the urban category or simply focus on rural areas. The maps in Figure 7.1 show the provincial distribution of the LT population alongside the average altitude of provinces, demonstrating that the LT population tends to reside in the lowlands and midlands as compared with the NLT population.

POVERTY PROFILE

Throughout the chapter, we use real household per capita consumption expenditures to measure overall living standards. This measure includes the value of consumption from own production and imputed housing costs. It accounts for spatial price differences across the urban and rural areas of four regions: Vientiane, North, Center, and South.

In 2002–2003, one-third of Lao PDR's population was poor, but the incidence of poverty was substantially higher for the NLT than for the LT at 50.6 and 25.0 percent, respectively (Table 7.1).[5] In general, urban areas were less poor than rural areas; specifically, poverty was lowest in the urban areas of the highlands (14.4 percent) and highest in the rural highlands (45.2 percent). Among urban areas, the midlands had the top incidence of poverty (37.7 percent). These patterns are repeated for the LT and NLT populations except that, interestingly, the incidence of poverty was slightly higher for the NLT in the rural lowlands (55.1 percent) than in the highlands (50.0 percent). The urban midlands deserve special mention as the NLT have a headcount index of 63 percent in those areas, the highest poverty incidence among either ethnic group in urban or rural areas. There is also a deep pocket of poverty among the LT residing in the urban midlands, albeit much smaller at 27.3 percent. Both the depth and severity of poverty as measured by the poverty gap index and the squared poverty gap mirror the patterns for the headcount index.

Comparing the characteristics of LT and NLT households and the places where they live, along most dimensions the LT have, on average, more favorable attributes than the NLT.[6] They have more education: 5.4 years of schooling versus 2.9 for heads of household (predominantly male), and 3.7 years versus 1.1 for their spouses. They have better access to basic social and economic infrastructure. Nationally, 61 percent of the LT live in villages with electricity versus 22 percent of the NLT; 86 percent and 21

---

[5] We use the government's poverty line, which is based on the cost-of-basic-needs method and incorporates spatial price differences (Richter et al. 2005).

[6] See Appendix Table 1 for a comparison along a fuller list of household characteristics.

Table 7.1. *Poverty by ethnicity, urban/rural, and elevation*

	Urban			Rural			Total		
	Lao-Tai	Non-Lao-Tai	Total	Lao-Tai	Non-Lao-Tai	Total	Lao-Tai	Non-Lao-Tai	Total
Lowlands									
Poverty headcount (%)	15.85	36.98	17.19	28.42	55.07	33.62	23.83	52.56	28.18
Poverty gap (%)	3.15	6.85	3.38	5.70	15.46	7.61	4.77	14.27	6.21
Poverty severity (%)	0.96	1.83	1.01	1.64	5.83	2.45	1.39	5.27	1.98
No.	6,665	700	7,365	12,948	4,130	17,078	19,613	4,830	24,443
Midlands									
Poverty headcount (%)	27.29	62.59	37.73	28.11	49.44	36.24	27.96	51.13	36.48
Poverty gap (%)	5.94	16.90	9.18	7.79	13.15	9.83	7.46	13.63	9.73
Poverty severity (%)	1.78	6.17	3.08	3.35	4.60	3.83	3.07	4.80	3.71
No.	830	490	1,320	4,477	3,019	7,496	5,307	3,509	8,816
Highlands									
Poverty headcount (%)	12.78	18.39	14.37	30.27	50.01	45.17	28.33	49.51	43.91
Poverty gap (%)	2.32	2.04	2.24	7.35	12.79	11.45	6.79	12.62	11.08
Poverty severity (%)	0.76	0.47	0.68	2.64	4.52	4.06	2.43	4.46	3.92
No.	316	168	484	3,413	12,383	15,796	3,729	12,551	16,280
Total									
Poverty headcount (%)	16.84	43.79	19.58	28.60	51.13	37.71	24.97	50.62	33.56
Poverty gap (%)	3.39	9.83	4.04	6.33	13.50	9.22	5.42	13.24	8.04
Poverty severity (%)	1.03	3.21	1.25	2.10	4.85	3.22	1.77	4.74	2.77
No.	7,811	1,358	9,169	20,838	19,532	40,370	28,649	20,890	49,539

Source: LECS 2002–2003.

percent of LT reside in places with primary and lower secondary schools, respectively, compared to 79 percent and 5 percent of NLT; and 17 percent versus 7 percent have health posts in their villages. These patterns persist after controlling for income: Similar disadvantages appear for the NLT relative to the LT when we examine only the poor or even the non-poor among them. However, there are a few reversals for the urban NLT, more of whom live in places with upper secondary schools, hospitals, and health posts.

The receipt of remittances, whether from other parts of Laos or abroad, is quite low at 3.2 percent of the population nationally, or 2.7 percent of all households. But this proportion varies with living standards and by urban and rural location (Figure 7.2). The well-off LT population, whether residing in urban or rural areas, is more likely to receive remittances. At the highest consumption levels, more than 30 percent of them receive remittances; at the poorest levels, around 10 percent do. The likelihood of receiving remittances rises with consumption also for the urban NLT, up to a maximum of about 10 percent among the richest people. There is no such economic gradient for the rural LT; the incidence of remittances for them hovers around 2–5 percent across the entire distribution. Because of this pattern in remittances, they exacerbate both consumption and interethnic inequality.

We investigate the differences in living standards among ethnic groups in Lao PDR. Following the literature, we estimate the relationship between household welfare, measured as household per capita consumption, and a set of household and community endowments captured by geographic variables (Ravallion and Wodon 1999; van de Walle and Gunewardena 2001).[7] Household characteristics include the log of household size and demographic composition variables: shares of children of different gender in the zero-to-six and seven-to-sixteen age brackets; shares of male and female adults (age seventeen to fifty-five); and the share of elderly, which is the left-out variable. Household demographics may not be exogenous, because family members can choose to cohabit or not and because fertility is at least partly a behavioral outcome. Ideally, we would also like to control for whether household members speak Lao, irrespective of their ethnicity, but this information is not available. However, recognizing that per capita household expenditure may be an imperfect measure of welfare, the

---

[7] We estimate the statistical relationship between the log of per capita expenditures of households and their household characteristics and geographic or locational variables using multivariate regression analysis. The analysis is undertaken separately for each of the four gender-ethnic groups.

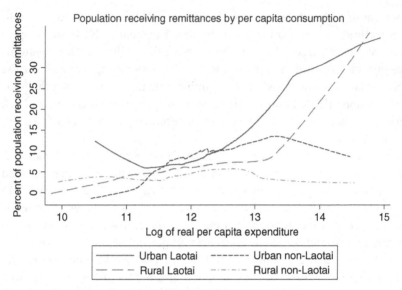

Figure 7.2. Incidence of remittances by per capita consumption.
Source: LECS 2002–2003. Remittances are received either in kind or cash, from Laos or abroad.

inclusion of demographic controls help account for differences in welfare at given expenditures per person. Such heterogeneity might arise through likely economies of scale in consumption or differences in needs for different age groups.

We include a dummy variable for whether or not the household receives remittances from abroad. This too is likely to be endogenous to living standards, but the arguments for including this variable outweigh those for leaving it out. We expect this variable to reflect unobserved attributes of the household such as those related to social networks that may be crucially important to welfare.

A few explanatory variables describe the head of household: age, age squared, and gender. Household human capital is assumed to be exogenous to current consumption and is measured as a series of dummy variables for the highest education level of the household member who has completed the most formal schooling, allowing us to measure the incremental returns to extra levels of schooling. There are eight possible levels: no schooling (the left-out level); some primary school; completed primary school (five years); some lower secondary; completed lower secondary (three years); some upper secondary school; completed upper secondary school; vocational education or university education.

Given that the vast majority of rural households rely on agriculture for their livelihoods, we would have liked to include controls for each household's access to land, both amounts and quality, but the data on this front are weak. The LECS3 asks only whether the household has access to or owns land and its value if the land were to be sold; however, the responses do not seem reliable. Furthermore, given how widespread swidden cultivation still is for many households in the uplands, it is not clear that these data would mean much.

Finally, we include a full set of variables identifying the villages in which the households live, as well as whether those villages are located in the highlands or lowlands (as opposed to the left-out midlands category). In this particular setting we expect that location is largely exogenous and has a direct effect on living standards; we also expect the village effects to help deal with the potential bias from unmeasured factors that are common within a village. Apart from government resettlement programs to focal ("priority") sites, mobility in rural areas appears to be limited. Villages are small and the village effects should adequately capture differences in inter-village access to land and education, local infrastructure, geo-environmental attributes, prices, and other community level factors. This helps deal with the likely correlation between the included variables – notably education – and location. Without geographic fixed effects, a bias is probable.[8]

Table 7.2 presents the results for the entire sample and separately for the two ethnic groups by urban and rural location.[9] We find that the structure of returns to household characteristics is not the same for the LT and NLT groups, so the following discussion focuses on the disaggregated ethnic- and location-specific regressions (columns 2 to 5).[10] Because the urban NLT sample includes only 213 households, the coefficients for that sample may be less precisely estimated.

A larger household size significantly reduces per capita consumption for all groups. Controlling for household size, demographic composition

---

[8] Research has shown the importance of controlling for geographic fixed effects in similar settings in neighboring countries. See Jalan and Ravallion (2002) for Southwest China and van de Walle and Gunewardena (2001) for Northern Vietnam. In all regressions, we estimate the standard errors using the Huber-White correction for heteroscedasticity, and we correct for cluster sampling of households within villages using the robust cluster option in STATA.

[9] Summary statistics for the included variables are given in Appendix Table 2.

[10] Chow tests reject the null hypothesis that the parameters are the same for the different groups when geographic fixed effects are excluded ($F = 3.37$ (59, 536)). Tests also reject the same models for the urban LT and NLT ($F = 3.37$ (20, 106)) and for the rural LT and NLT ($F = 4.66$ (21, 432)).

Table 7.2. *Determinants of living standards*

Variables	(1) All	(2) Urban Lao-Tai	(3) Urban Non-Lao-Tai	(4) Rural Lao-Tai	(5) Rural Non-Lao-Tai
Log household size	-0.502***	-0.561***	-0.538***	-0.533***	-0.423***
	(0.017)	(0.046)	(0.173)	(0.026)	(0.023)
Lao-Tai household	0.095***				
	(0.028)				
Share of male adults, 17 to 55	0.101*	0.017	0.093	0.210**	0.058
	(0.057)	(0.165)	(0.328)	(0.087)	(0.081)
Share of female adults, 17 to 55	0.110*	0.076	0.441	0.147*	0.027
	(0.062)	(0.187)	(0.350)	(0.088)	(0.085)
Share of males aged 6 to 16	-0.113**	-0.096	0.123	-0.044	-0.272***
	(0.053)	(0.161)	(0.474)	(0.072)	(0.080)
Share of females aged 6 to 16	-0.134**	-0.108	-0.058	-0.051	-0.301***
	(0.053)	(0.165)	(0.596)	(0.071)	(0.071)
Share of boys aged 0 to 5	-0.335***	0.026	0.381	-0.425***	-0.453***
	(0.060)	(0.201)	(0.651)	(0.087)	(0.082)
Share of girls aged 0 to 5	-0.392***	-0.464**	0.623	-0.431***	-0.443***
	(0.059)	(0.208)	(0.676)	(0.092)	(0.076)
Male head of household	0.125***	0.158***	0.124	0.106**	0.124**
	(0.028)	(0.055)	(0.195)	(0.043)	(0.048)
Age of head of household	0.014***	-0.0005	0.100**	0.017***	0.011***
	(0.003)	(0.011)	(0.042)	(0.004)	(0.004)
Age of head of household, squared/1,000	-0.137***	0.002	-0.977**	-0.165***	-0.114**
	(0.029)	(0.110)	(0.417)	(0.040)	(0.049)
Most educated member has:					
Some primary	0.059***			0.089	0.048**
	(0.022)			(0.057)	(0.024)
Completed primary	0.116***	0.037	0.032	0.161***	0.093***
	(0.024)	(0.079)	(0.113)	(0.058)	(0.027)

(continued)

Table 7.2 (continued)

Variables	(1) All	(2) Urban Lao-Tai	(3) Urban Non-Lao-Tai	(4) Rural Lao-Tai	(5) Rural Non-Lao-Tai
Some lower-secondary	0.120***	0.069	−0.033	0.167***	0.094***
	(0.026)	(0.080)	(0.159)	(0.058)	(0.032)
Completed lower-secondary	0.181***	0.150**	0.028	0.229***	0.141***
	(0.027)	(0.070)	(0.128)	(0.060)	(0.036)
Some upper-secondary	0.177***	0.128	0.096	0.245***	0.077
	(0.033)	(0.090)	(0.122)	(0.063)	(0.055)
Completed upper-secondary	0.230***	0.178**	0.210	0.271***	0.213***
	(0.032)	(0.078)	(0.160)	(0.063)	(0.071)
Vocational training	0.303***	0.243***	0.543***	0.362***	0.201**
	(0.033)	(0.084)	(0.161)	(0.063)	(0.079)
University	0.418***	0.374***	0.430***	0.502***	0.212
	(0.051)	(0.099)	(0.144)	(0.096)	(0.210)
Received remittances from abroad	0.208***	0.375***	0.138	0.128**	0.192***
	(0.043)	(0.105)	(0.195)	(0.053)	(0.067)
Highlands	−0.698***	0.175***	0.460**	0.762***	−0.211***
	(0.029)	(0.033)	(0.171)	(0.076)	(0.024)
Lowlands	0.222***	−0.556***	0.489	0.042	0.105
	(0.019)	(0.045)	(0.547)	(0.076)	(0.076)
Constant	11.996***	12.992***	9.477***	11.783***	12.229***
	(0.067)	(0.285)	(1.142)	(0.096)	(0.103)
Observations	8063	1382	213	3497	2971
R-squared	0.558	0.368	0.551	0.538	0.583

Notes: Estimates are obtained by OLS regression on log of real per capita expenditure. Robust standard errors in parentheses are clustered at village level. *** $p<0.01$, ** $p<0.05$, * $p<0.1$. Village dummies are included but not reported for ease of presentation. The omitted categories are the share of elderly (55 and older), no education for the most-educated member, and the midlands. For the urban samples, no and some primary education are omitted due to small number of observations in the "no education" category. We tried a version that included size squared and the dependency ratio but found they added no explanatory power.
Source: Lao PDR Expenditure & Consumption Survey, 2002–2003.

appears to be of less consequence to living standards in urban than in rural areas. One surprising exception is the significant negative coefficient of the share of infant and toddler girls but not of boys in the same age bracket for the urban LT. Why the effect of small children on per capita consumption would differ by gender is not obvious. Children of that age typically require considerable care, as is implied by the negative coefficients for both sexes in rural areas. A possible explanation is that urban LT households consume more and invest in very young sons more than they do in young daughters. Studies have examined the hypothesis that a strong son preference may lead parents to provide inferior care for daughters in terms of food allocation, prevention of diseases and accidents, and treatment of sick children (Arnold et al. 1998). Some studies have found little evidence of discrimination against girls in feeding, but other studies conclude that the discriminatory behavior might depend on the number and sex composition of surviving children (e.g., Mishra et al. 2004 on India).

In rural areas and relative to the elderly group omitted from the regression, more prime-age LT adults, whether male or female, are associated with significantly higher living standards. This is not the case for the NLT for whom the returns to prime-age adults are not significantly different from the returns to elderly adults. However, a larger share of members between the ages of six and sixteen exerts a negative effect not found for the LT. For both rural ethnic groups, a larger share of small children is negatively related to per capita consumption expenditures. Male headship tends to have a significant positive effect as does the age of the head of household with turning points in the late forties and early fifties.

Controlling for other characteristics, there are significant, large returns to education, although the pattern of returns differs across the groups. In urban areas, returns to lower levels of education are not significantly different from the returns to no or some primary schooling for the NLT, whereas the LT get significant returns from the completion of lower and upper secondary schooling. The picture is quite different in rural Laos, where there are pronounced and significant returns to schooling at all levels, although the completion of a schooling level tends to do more for consumption than having only completed part of the level. Still, the returns tend to be larger and more consistently statistically significant for the LT. For example, the relation between per capita consumption and level of schooling of the most educated household member having completed primary school is 10 percent of original consumption for the NLT versus 17 percent for the LT.

Completion of lower secondary school results in a per capita expenditures increase of 15 percent for the rural NLT and 26 percent for the rural LT. The returns to vocational education are strongest for the urban NLT and those to university are strongest for the rural LT.

The regressions also attest to powerful geographic effects on living standards. The village fixed effects (not shown in Table 7.3) are overwhelmingly significant and have strong explanatory power, almost doubling each regression's explanatory power. As in similar settings in Vietnam (van de Walle and Gunewardena 2001), the returns to education are substantially overestimated for the rural disadvantaged minority groups as well as for the rural LT groups when geographic fixed effects are not accounted for. This result probably reflects geographic differences in the supply (and quality) of education services. Places with better endowments and hence higher living standards are also the places where households will tend to invest more in education. If both the amounts of education and its quality are higher in places where living standards are also higher, then not accounting for quality will tend to overestimate the returns to education. For both groups, then, the returns to schooling depend on where they live. Furthermore, even controlling for village effects, the coefficients on whether the household lives in the highlands relative to the midlands are highly significant. The lowlands dummy has a significant (and negative) effect on living standards only for the urban LT.

Receiving transfers from abroad significantly raises consumption for all groups except the urban NLT. Strikingly, in rural areas, receipt of remittances reduces inequality between the LT and NLT because relatively more NLT households receive remittances, but as we saw earlier, the households receiving remittances remain few.

EDUCATION: CONVERGENCE, WITH PERSISTENT DIFFERENCES

In the following sections, we turn to the schooling levels of the ethnic groups in Lao PDR. Investments in education are one of the best hopes for improving the lifetime prospects of a child – even a child from a poor family – and for Lao PDR, we see both progress and persistence in schooling inequalities. First, we describe the historical trend in education levels. Because higher mortality rates in older ages might affect average schooling years, we limit the age range to between eighteen and sixty years. Second, we focus on recent education outcomes.

EDUCATIONAL PROGRESS OVER TIME

To derive historical changes without long time-series data, we examine the differences in the average completed years of schooling of adults of different ages.[11] Comparing urban and rural populations, LT and NLT, as well as males and females, we find a steady increase in educational attainment over the last forty years for all groups and important relative changes among those population groups (Figure 7.3). In general, progress was significantly higher for the LT than for the NLT. One notable finding is that, in both urban and rural areas, LT women showed the largest improvement. In urban areas, LT women rose to equal the average schooling years of LT men; in rural areas, LT women narrowed the gap with LT men to slightly more than a year and overtook NLT men some twenty years ago. In contrast, there is no sign of any gender convergence between men and women in the NLT groups. Although rural NLT women lag furthest behind, NLT men also perform badly in comparison to the LT. Indeed, there are signs of divergence between ethnic groups, with a widening schooling gap between the rural LT and NLT.

The average completed years of schooling started from a low base of 2 years nationally around 1960, and increased to 5.5 years – an annual rate of increase of 0.08 of a school year, or 1 full school year every 12.5 years. Educational attainment was higher throughout for urban populations (3.9 years increasing to 8.2 years in 2002–2003) and lower for rural populations (1.6 to 4.6 years in 2002–2003). Among all gender and ethnolinguistic groups, rural NLT women have the least schooling during the period, as well as the smallest yearly gain over the last 40 years – just 0.04 of a school year per year. Even among those in the youngest birth cohort, these women had 6.6 fewer years of schooling than urban LT men, the group with the most schooling. The urban-rural distinction is, of course, evolving over time as a result of rural-urban migration and the upgrading of rural areas to urban ones, so this makes the urban progress over the period all the more impressive but may also account for the relative stagnation in the literacy rate in recent years.

The overall increase in years of schooling translates into higher literacy, defined as the ability to read and write.[12] Plotting the literacy rate against

[11] The average years of schooling attained is defined as highest grade completed rather than the actual number of years enrolled in school. Due to grade repetition, the highest grade attained can imply fewer years of schooling than the number of years actually spent in school. We have no separate information on grade repetition from the surveys.

[12] The answers given to questions about whether one can read and whether one can write correspond almost perfectly across individuals. For this reason we aggregate the two into one measure of literacy. Note also that there are two possible measures of literacy – whether one can read and write with or without difficulty. When we define literacy more

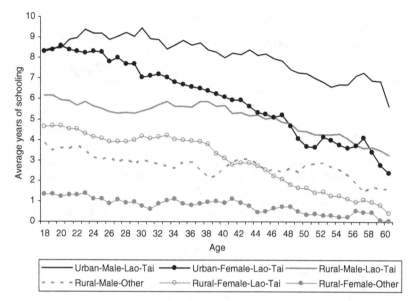

Figure 7.3. Average years of schooling, by age, gender, and ethnolinguistic group, 2002–2003.
Note: Data for urban non-Lao-Tai are not plotted because of small sample size. Graphs have been smoothed using three-year moving averages. Because the number of observations dwindles with age due to mortality, only data for those up to age 60 are plotted.
Source: LECS3, 2002–2003.

age, we see that urban LT men have the highest literacy rate, upward of 90 percent (Figure 7.4). The continuous increase in schooling years of urban LT women shows up in a sharp rise in their literacy rate from more than thirty years ago, leading to a convergence in the literacy rates of male and female eighteen-year-olds. In rural areas, LT men have become more literate, but they have been overtaken by urban LT women. Rural LT women also have surpassed rural NLT men, but rural NLT women continue to have the lowest literacy rate, reaching only 30 percent for the youngest cohorts.

CURRENT EDUCATION PATTERNS

Lao PDR's school cycle starts with five years at the primary level, followed by three years each at the lower and upper secondary levels.[13] Some students go

strictly as being able to read and write without difficulty, literacy rates drop significantly, especially for poor groups.
[13] Preprimary school can play an important role in preparing children intellectually, psychologically, and socially for entering primary school, but in Laos, few children attend preprimary school, perhaps reflecting the high fees and low supply of those facilities. In our

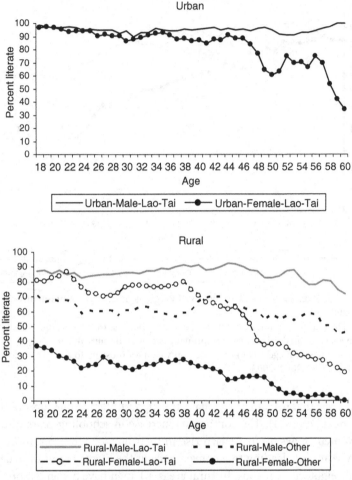

Figure 7.4. Literacy rates, by age, gender, and ethnolinguistic group, 2002–2003.
Note: Data for urban non-Lao-Tai are not plotted because of small sample size. Graphs have been smoothed using three-year moving averages. Because the number of observations dwindles with age due to mortality, only data for those up to age 60 are plotted. *Source*: LECS3, 2002–2003.

directly from primary or lower-secondary school to teacher training or vocational training, which may take an additional year or two; alternatively, some graduate from the upper-secondary level to a university education. Ideally, a student enters primary school at age six and finishes university education at age twenty-two.[14]

sample, only 11% of all children aged ten to eighteen ever attended kindergarten, although there is a large difference between urban and rural children (24.9% versus 5.4%).

[14] Currently, a bachelor's degree course at the University of Lao is five years.

To assess school enrollment numbers, we use three different measures: age-specific enrollment rates for three different age groups (six to ten, eleven to thirteen, and fourteen to sixteen), which correspond to the official age groups for the first three education cycles; net enrollment rates for the three education cycles; and gross enrollment rates for the three cycles.[15] The net enrollment and gross enrollment rates would be equal if all enrollees in a school cycle belonged only to the official age group. However, high rates of grade repetition and entry into school spread out over several ages result in the gross enrollment rate greatly exceeding the net enrollment rate. We emphasize this point because many children in Lao PDR begin the primary cycle later than the prescribed entry age of six, entering instead only at age nine or ten; correspondingly, children remain in the primary cycle until their middle to late teens.[16] Rural children enter school, if ever, later than do urban children, and so a larger percentage of them – male or female, poor or nonpoor, and LT or NLT – are still at the primary level even in their late teens.[17]

Likewise, the net enrollment and age-specific enrollment rates would be equal if students of a particular age group were enrolled only in the official school cycle for that age group; again, grade repetition and late entry lead to these rates being unequal. Because of late entry into school relative to the official start age for school, especially in rural areas, gross and net enrollment rates based on the official school ages can give a misleading picture of schooling in the country. In Lao PDR, among children in the official primary school-age group (ages six to ten), the gross enrollment rate was 114.9 percent and the net enrollment rate 70.4 percent, according to LECS3 (Table 7.3).[18] The difference between the two rates indicates that

---

[15] See Appendix 1 for a definition of these measures.

[16] LECS3 includes a question asking respondents about their age of starting school, so this information is not a computed age of entry.

[17] However, the average age at which children start school has declined markedly over time. In 2002–2003, nearly 80% of those aged ten entered school by age eight; by comparison, just slightly more than 20% of those aged eighteen did so.

[18] We examined the reliability of the LECS3 schooling data and various enrollment definitions. Our estimates of enrollments include children who were on vacation during the survey, who also stated that they were going to return to school the following year. We also use information on whether those vacationing children were in school previously and had completed at least one year. If so, then we considered them as enrolled; if they had not attended school previously, then even if they reported an intention to attend school the following school year, we considered them as not enrolled. In the broader education literature, parental aspirations or expectations about their children's schooling are considered (at least) partial information about schooling outcomes. The percentages of children on vacation but expected to return to school are higher in urban than in rural areas. Because of this pattern, the aggregate enrollment rates are inflated when considering the children on vacation. In general, they were higher by some ten percentage points, depending on location. However, when we disaggregate enrollment rates by urban and rural residence,

Table 7.3. *Enrollment rates, by school cycle and age group*

| | School cycle (Corresponding official age group) | | |
	Primary level (6–10)	Lower-secondary level (11–13)	Upper-secondary level (14–16)
Age-specific participation	71.8	82.6	60.6
Net enrollment	70.4	22.7	13.4
Gross enrollment	114.9	58.6	30.9
Observations	7,616	4,394	3,886

Notes: (a) Missing enrollment data are treated as missing. See also note 19 to this chapter for discussion of data on enrollment. (b) All estimates are population-weighted. (c) see Appendix 1 for detailed definitions of enrollment categories.
Source: LECS3, 2002–2003.

many primary school students are either younger or older than the official ages for the cycle, which is six to ten years. It is much less likely that the enrollees are younger than six, so the explanation must be that about half of primary school students are older than ten. The age-specific enrollment rate for the six-to-ten age cohort was 71.8 percent, indicating that only 1.4 percent of the children attending school in this age group are enrolled in another school cycle, most likely at the lower-secondary level. At older ages, as children fall behind in their schooling, this gap between the net enrollment rate and the age-specific rate widens.

Enrollment drops off sharply after the primary cycle. At the lower-secondary level, the overall net enrollment of those ages eleven to thirteen was just 22.7 percent, the gross enrollment was 58.6 percent, and the age-specific enrollment rate was 82.6 percent. The much larger age-specific enrollment rate indicates that the majority of children ages eleven to thirteen attend school, but most are still at the primary level. A similar picture emerges at the upper-secondary level: the net enrollment rate was 13.4, the gross enrollment rate was 30.9, and the age-specific enrollment rate was 60.6. Thus, each enrollment rate measure paints a very different picture for Lao PDR.

The enrollment rates also mask wide variation by gender, ethnolinguistic affiliation, and residence. The patterns in these differences are clear: Urban children are more likely to be in school than rural children, LT children are more likely to be in school than NLT children, boys are more likely to be in school than girls, and nonpoor children are more likely to be in school

this discrepancy is not quite as large. If all the children on vacation during the survey are considered as not enrolled, enrollment rates are greatly understated.

than poor children. By looking across all these groups at once, we note more extreme disparities, indicating that multiple sources of disadvantage compound inequalities. Taking poverty into account as well as gender, ethnicity and residence, age-specific participation rates for children ages six to ten range from 43.2 percent for poor NLT girls in rural areas to 92.5 percent for nonpoor LT boys and girls in urban areas – an immense difference (Table 7.4). Differences between these two groups are also large with respect to gross enrollment rates (70 versus 132.7 percent) and net enrollment rates (42.6 versus 89.4 percent). Hence, although Lao PDR has achieved significant progress in closing education gaps over the past decades, reducing education inequalities is still a huge challenge that policy and the economy must address.

As one would expect, the group inequalities at the secondary levels are even larger than at the primary level. The net enrollment rate at the lower-secondary level ranges from a low of 4.7 percent for rural NLT girls to a high of 45.0 percent for urban LT boys – a tentuple difference (Table 7.5). At the upper-secondary level, the range is even wider: The overall net enrollment ranges from 1.6 percent for rural NLT girls to a high of 23.8 percent for urban LT boys (Table 7.6). These net enrollment rates, however, do not capture the proportion of youth who are actually in school in either of the two secondary cycles. To illustrate this point, consider that although only 4.7 percent of rural NLT girls ages eleven to thirteen are enrolled in lower-secondary schools, 59.0 percent of them are actually in school, though most are probably still in primary schools. Similarly, although only 1.6 percent of rural NLT girls ages fourteen to sixteen are enrolled in upper-secondary schools, 31.1 percent of them attend school, most being in either primary schools or lower-secondary schools. These large gaps are a result of children starting primary school much later than the official entry age of six, and of some failing and repeating grades. In settings where these phenomena are frequent, age-specific enrollment rates, instead of gross or net enrollment rates, provide a helpful outlook into schooling outcomes.

Introducing the poverty dimension adds to the overall picture of large education inequalities. The net enrollment rate at the lower-secondary level among the poor rural NLT children is just 1.9 percent for girls and 3.9 percent for boys, as compared with 7.6 percent and 10.5 percent for nonpoor rural NLT girls and boys, respectively. The gross enrollment rates at this level are also low for poor rural NLT children – just 8.9 percent for girls and 20.0 percent for boys – but these indicate that at least three times the number of these youth are actually continuing on to the lower-secondary level, albeit at ages older than thirteen. By comparison, poor rural LT youth are enrolled in secondary schools at significantly higher rates. For example,

Table 7.4. *Primary school enrollment rates, by residence, gender, ethnolinguistic group, and poverty status*

| | Urban | | | | Rural | | | | | | Total |
| | Lao-Tai | | Total | | Lao-Tai | | Non-Lao-Tai | | Total | | |
	Male	Female	Male	Female	Male	Female	Male	Female	Male	Female	
TOTAL											
Age-specific enrollment (6–10)	89.6	91.8	88.3	90.1	79.4	79.6	56.0	49.4	69.7	66.3	71.8
Net enrollment	87.0	90.4	85.6	88.6	77.8	77.7	55.1	48.7	68.4	65.0	70.4
Gross enrollment	130.6	132.3	133.36	130.4	126.0	122.0	104.3	83.7	117.0	105.2	114.9
Observations	462	430	567	537	1,700	1,571	1,612	1,629	3,312	3,200	7,616
NONPOOR											
Age-specific enrollment (6–10)	92.5	93.6	91.4	92.3	85.9	85.4	62.7	57.2	78.4	75.8	80.4
Net enrollment	89.4	92.2	88.1	91.0	84.0	83.3	61.5	56.5	76.6	74.1	78.5
Gross enrollment	128.8	131.4	131.2	130.6	134.1	129.6	113.1	96.1	127.3	118.2	124.7
Observations	367	349	418	399	1,138	1,020	735	708	1873	1,728	4,418
POOR											
Age-specfic enrollment (6–10)	78.9	84.5	78.8	83.1	65.5	68.1	50.1	43.2	57.2	54.1	58.4
Net enrollment	77.9	83.2	78.1	81.1	64.7	66.8	49.5	42.6	56.5	53.1	57.6
Gross enrollment	137.7	136.2	139.9	129.6	108.7	107.1	96.8	74.0	102.2	88.4	99.7
Observations	95	81	149	138	562	551	877	921	1,439	1,472	3,198

Notes: (a) Missing enrollment data are treated as missing. See also note 19 to this chapter for discussion of data on enrollment. (b) The denominator for the net and gross enrollment rates is the number of children aged 6 to 10. (c) All estimates are population-weighted.
Source: LECS3, 2002–2003.

Table 7.5. *Lower-secondary school enrollment rates, by residence, gender, ethnolinguistic group, and poverty status*

| | Urban | | | | Rural | | | | | | Total |
| | Lao-Tai | | Total | | Lao-Tai | | Non-Lao-Tai | | Total | | |
	Male	Female	Male	Female	Male	Female	Male	Female	Male	Female	
TOTAL											
Age-specific enrollment (11–13)	94.6	91.3	94.1	91.1	89.6	83.3	76.5	59.0	84.8	74.6	82.6
Net enrollment	44.7	42.8	40.6	41.3	22.5	25.0	7.1	4.7	16.9	17.7	22.7
Gross enrollment	108.1	91.9	101.9	91.2	69.9	53.9	29.1	14.7	54.9	39.9	58.6
Observations	350	347	428	395	999	1,017	751	804	1,750	1,821	4,394
NONPOOR											
Age-specific enrollment (11–13)	96.0	92.3	95.3	91.9	90.1	86.0	79.5	66.2	87.2	80.5	86.4
Net enrollment	49.5	47.5	45.9	46.5	26.0	29.3	10.5	7.6	21.8	23.3	28.7
Gross enrollment	120.9	96.6	114.6	96.2	77.8	62.6	38.8	20.6	67.2	51.0	71.3
Observations	280	284	324	309	732	716	355	393	1,087	1,109	2,829
POOR											
Age-specific enrollment (11–13)	89.4	86.8	90.2	88.0	88.2	76.3	73.7	51.9	80.3	64.1	74.7
Net enrollment	25.9	21.6	23.0	21.7	12.4	13.7	3.9	1.9	7.8	7.8	10.1
Gross enrollment	58.2	70.3	59.5	72.7	46.7	31.5	20.0	8.9	32.2	20.1	32.1
Observations	70	63	104	86	267	301	396	411	663	712	1,565

Notes: (a) Missing enrollment data are treated as missing. See also note 19 to this chapter for discussion of data on enrollment. (b) The denominator for the net and gross enrollment rates is the number of children aged 11 to 13. (c) All estimates are population-weighted.
Source: LECS3, 2002–2003.

Table 7.6. *Upper-secondary school enrollment rates, by residence, gender, ethnolinguistic group, and poverty status*

| | Urban | | | | Rural | | | | | | Total |
| | Lao-Tai | | Total | | Lao-Tai | | Non-Lao-Tai | | Total | | |
	Male	Female	Male	Female	Male	Female	Male	Female	Male	Female	
TOTAL											
Age-specific enrollment (14–16)	81.1	74.6	81.5	73.8	67.4	51.7	57.8	31.1	64.2	44.3	60.6
Net enrollment	23.8	32.0	23.2	30.5	11.9	11.1	3.2	1.6	9.1	7.7	13.4
Gross enrollment	68.4	57.6	66.8	54.6	30.6	25.1	7.6	2.59	23.0	17.0	30.9
Observations	371	385	429	438	887	848	627	657	1,514	1,505	3,886
NONPOOR											
Age-specific enrollment (14–16)	85.6	75.8	85.5	76.0	71.7	56.7	65.5	31.0	70.2	49.8	66.5
Net enrollment	26.1	33.6	26.2	32.9	13.1	13.3	4.6	3.0	11.1	10.5	16.6
Gross enrollment	74.0	60.8	73.4	59.6	33.9	29.1	11.1	4.1	28.4	22.4	38.1
Observations	308	317	342	340	656	625	293	323	949	948	2,579
POOR											
Age-specific enrollment (14–16)	58.8	68.9	64.3	65.3	54.6	37.5	50.6	31.2	52.6	34.2	47.0
Net enrollment	12.3	24.2	10.4	21.4	8.3	4.9	2.0	0.3	5.1	2.5	5.9
Gross enrollment	40.6	42.4	39.1	35.9	20.7	13.6	4.3	1.1	12.4	7.0	14.5
Observations	63	68	87	98	231	223	334	334	565	557	1,307

Notes: (a) Missing enrollment data are treated as missing. See also note 19 to this chapter for discussion of data on enrollment. (b) The denominator for the net and gross enrollment rates is the number of children aged 14 to 16. (c) All estimates are population-weighted.
Source: LECS3, 2002–2003.

Table 7.7. *Net primary school enrollment rates, by residence, gender, and ethnolinguistic group (percent)*

	Urban			Rural			Total		
	Male	Female	Total	Male	Female	Total	Male	Female	Total
Lao-Tai	87.0	90.4	88.6	77.8	77.7	77.8	80.1	80.8	80.4
Observations	462	430	892	1,700	1,571	3,271	2,162	2,001	4,163
Mon-Khmer	70.4	69.5	70.0	55.7	53.0	54.3	56.4	53.8	55.1
Observations	47	57	104	952	978	1,930	999	1,035	2,034
Chine-Tibetan	84.0	91.3	87.1	35.9	30.2	33.3	41.9	36.4	39.4
Observations	19	15	34	195	177	372	214	192	406
Hmong-Iu Mien	81.7	79.4	80.6	62.2	46.7	54.4	64.0	49.3	56.7
Observations	36	32	68	434	430	864	470	462	932
Other	–	–	–	36.1	32.4	33.8	36.3	35.9	36.1
Observations	3	3	6	31	44	75	34	47	81
Total	85.6	88.6	87.0	68.4	65.0	66.7	71.6	69.1	70.4
Observations	567	537	1,104	3,312	3,200	6,512	3,879	3,737	7,616

Notes: (a) Missing enrollment data are treated as missing. See also note 19 to this chapter for discussion of data on enrollment. (b) The official age range for primary education is 6 to 10. (c) All estimates are population-weighted.
Source: LECS3, 2002–2003.

12.4 and 13.7 percent of boys and girls, respectively, are enrolled at the lower-secondary level, percentages that are higher even than those of nonpoor rural NLT youth. These gaps are wide also when comparing the nonpoor rural youth: LT youth are more than twice as likely to be enrolled in lower-secondary schools as NLT youth.

The numbers for the NLT population hide considerable heterogeneity across the minority groups that make up the NLT ethnic category. Focusing on just the net enrollment rates at the primary education level, we see that some subgroups fare much worse than others (Table 7.7). For example, in the rural population, compared to LT boys aged six to ten, of whom 77.8 percent were enrolled in primary schools, the net enrollment rate was 55.7 percent for Mon-Khmer boys and 35.9 percent for Chine-Tibetan boys. Among rural girls, compare 77.7 percent for LT girls with 53.0 percent for Mon-Khmers and 30.2 percent for Chine-Tibetans. In urban areas, ethnolinguistic differences are not significant except for Mon-Khmer children whose lower enrollment rates were much lower than those of other groups, but the limited size of the NLT urban sample weakens such comparisons.

Education inequalities are evident in the extreme by the proportion of youth who have never attended school. For this, we look at a slightly older group, because school entry is typically late. Overall, 10 percent of children

Table 7.8. *Children aged ten to sixteen who have never attended school (percent)*

	Urban				Rural						Total
	Lao-Tai		Total		Lao-Tai		Non-Lao-Tai		Total		
	Male	Female	Male	Female	Male	Female	Male	Female	Male	Female	
Total	1.9	1.8	2.1	2.2	3.8	6.0	17.2	34.3	8.6	16.3	10.0
Observations	839	830	992	954	2,253	2,200	1,678	1,770	3,931	3,970	9,847
Nonpoor	0.9	1.5	1.1	1.7	2.1	4.2	13.8	28.4	5.2	10.9	6.2
Observations	682	681	769	740	1,641	1,565	787	849	2,428	2,414	6,351
Poor	6.1	3.1	5.5	4.3	8.5	10.6	20.4	39.8	14.7	25.8	18.0
Observations	157	149	223	214	612	635	891	921	1,503	1,556	3,496

Notes: Urban non-Lao-Tai estimates are not shown due to the small number of observations. All estimates are population-weighted.
Source: LEC3, 2002–2003.

ages ten to sixteen had never attended school in Laos, but there are notable differences in this proportion by gender and ethnicity as well as by urban-rural residence. In rural areas, 34.3 percent of NLT girls and 6.0 percent of LT girls had never attended school. The corresponding numbers for rural boys are 17.2 percent and 3.8 percent – truly immense differences even within rural areas (Table 7.8). Poverty further accentuates the gaps, even just among girls: In rural areas, 39.8 percent of NLT girls and 10.6 percent of LT girls from poor families have never attended school, as compared with 28.4 percent of NLT girls and 4.2 LT girls from nonpoor families. The challenge of just getting children to enter school is obviously still a crucial challenge for Lao PDR – and it is plainly evident that efforts to remedy this should be targeted to minority children from poor rural households.

ACCESS AND QUALITY OF SCHOOLS

The availability of schools within a reasonable distance from the household has been shown to be an important determinant of whether or not a student goes to school (see Orazem and King 2008 for a review of the literature).[19] As noted earlier, nationally, 84 percent of the population lives in a village with a primary school, but this proportion varies across

[19] Beside availability, other supply factors are also expected to influence that decision and, according to educators, whether students learn or not. Studies have focused on measurable indicators such as the pupil-teacher ratio, educational background and work experience of teachers, the availability of textbooks and learning materials, and the physical condition of school buildings as indicators of school quality. Others have also used the performance of students on standardized tests (controlling for their socioeconomic background and innate ability) as a measure of school quality.

population groups, with LT households more likely to have access than NLT households. In both urban and rural areas, this measure of school supply does not necessarily mean that children residing in a village without a school do not have access to a primary school as they may attend school in neighboring villages. In urban areas, perhaps because of better means of transportation, children are more likely to attend school in the next village or locality.

Our survey of primary schools in the same villages as LECS3 sample households provides detailed information about the schools that children were attending.[20] The data show that rural schools are far more likely to have multigrade classrooms than urban schools. Nearly half of rural LT households and 66 percent of rural NLT households have schools that have multigrade classrooms (Table 7.9). In such classrooms, the teacher has to impart lessons to students of widely different ages and grades – a very challenging job to do well. By comparison, only 8 percent of urban LT households have schools that have multigrade classrooms. This immense difference between urban and rural schools probably reflects an imbalance in the deployment of teachers among provinces and schools, resulting in an oversupply of teachers in some areas and severe undersupply in others.[21]

Balancing teacher supply is not just about getting the numbers right, however. The quality of schools depends on who the teachers are and how well prepared they are to teach, and so the distribution of teacher characteristics matters also. In urban areas, less than one-third of teachers are men; the opposite is true in rural areas, where teaching probably represents a coveted opportunity for wage employment for better-educated men. LT children are taught predominantly by LT teachers (93 percent in urban areas and 79 percent in rural areas), whereas a much smaller proportion of NLT children are taught by LT teachers. This pattern suggests that schools tend to rely on local teachers, especially in rural areas. This has pros and cons: Because local teachers are more likely to stay on, teacher attrition is going to be less of a problem; because local teachers know the local language and customs, they are likely to be better able to communicate with students and parents; but because local teachers in NLT areas may themselves have limited facility in the majority language, they may not be adequately effective in teaching their students the national curriculum.

---

[20] The school survey was fielded at the same time as the LECS3. As explained earlier, if a village did not have a school at the time of the survey, the closest school that village children attended was covered by the survey.

[21] This deployment issue is partly a result of a quota system that requires newly trained teachers to return to their home district after training, thus restricting mobility and the capacity of the school system to balance teacher supply.

Table 7.9. *Mean characteristics of accessible primary schools,*
by residence and ethnolinguistic group (percent)

	Urban		Rural		Total	
	Lao-Tai	Non-Lao-Tai	Lao-Tai	Non-Lao-Tai	Lao-Tai	Non-Lao-Tai
School						
complete primary school	8.9	9.8	8.0	3.9	8.2	4.4
with multigrade classrooms	8.0	14.9	46.9	65.6	37.0	61.4
Teachers:						
Male	27.5	26.0	65.6	76.7	64.8	72.5
Lao-Tai	93.0	46.6	78.9	29.5	72.9	40.9
Schooling (years)	10.1	9.9	9.8	9.4	9.9	9.4
Experience (years)	14.6	12.5	12.6	9.5	13.1	9.8
Facilities:						
with electricity	68.6	32.6	33.8	25.4	42.7	26.0
with drinking water	53.1	13.1	7.8	2.8	19.4	3.6
with student toilet	70.4	33.7	21.0	14.2	33.6	15.8
with library	21.1	20.3	9.5	7.7	12.4	8.8
with phone line	43.7	22.8	12.4	5.1	20.4	6.6
with principal's room	74.3	60.1	32.4	10.4	43.1	14.5
with teachers' room	61.2	42.5	23.5	11.9	33.2	14.4
Classrooms:						
permanent	43.7	32.1	28.4	21.3	32.4	22.0
with blackboard	92.2	97.8	88.4	90.3	89.4	90.9
without leaky roof	76.1	72.6	73.9	72.0	74.4	72.0
Each student has desk	95.2	94.2	93.9	80.8	94.2	81.9

Source: LECS3, 2002–2003.

The education and experience of the average teacher are highest in urban areas for the LT and lowest in rural areas for the NLT, although the gap is not so large. On average, urban teachers have ten years of schooling and about twelve to fifteen years of experience; teachers in schools accessible to NLT children in rural areas have, on average, nine years each of schooling and experience in schools. The latter may well reflect the more recent expansion of schools in areas where the rural NLT live.

Finally, based on a set of school characteristics, the schools that are accessible to children from urban households and LT households are better equipped than the schools accessible to rural and NLT populations.[22]

---

[22] Past studies on Asian countries have found that distance to school deters enrollment (Anderson, King, and Wang 2002 for Malaysia; Maliki 2005 for Indonesia), tuition reduces enrollment (Behrman and Knowles 1999 for Vietnam), and having more educated teachers increases enrollment (World Bank 2005 for Cambodia).

The disparities are smaller with respect to the basic inputs of classrooms with blackboards and functioning roofs, but much greater with respect to whether the school has electricity or drinking water. On average, the large majority of households, urban or rural, have access to primary schools that have classrooms with blackboards and about three-fourths have schools that have non-leaking roofs. In urban areas, 69 percent of LT households have access to schools with electricity, whereas in rural areas, only 34 percent of LT households do; and in both urban and rural areas, it is much worse for NLT households than LT households.

Using a multivariate analysis (described later in the chapter), we find that multigrade schools are associated with lower enrollment rates and that children who have access to a complete primary school are 25 percent more likely to be enrolled. Better school infrastructure – as measured by the availability of electricity, the existence of desks for each student, and the physical condition of classrooms (as measured by the proportion of classrooms with non-leaky roofs) – also promotes enrollment, although this association is considerably weaker than having a complete school without multigrade classrooms. The distance from the primary school to a city or to a lower-secondary school and the average time it takes for a student to walk from home are negatively related to enrollment, supporting further that school supply matters.

Determinants of School Enrollment

Here we examine the determinants of schooling in Lao PDR using a set of individual and household data that reflect the factors discussed earlier using multivariate regression analysis. We estimate a model with individual, household, community, and school variables for the two subgroups based on ethnolinguistic affiliation, and then for more disaggregated samples based on all three characteristics at the same time. We find striking differences in the normalized coefficients of the probit model, estimated as marginal effects, between LT and NLT children (Table 7.10). Indeed, Wald tests reject equality of the models across these groups.

In addition to gender, urban-rural location, and ethnolinguistic affiliation, the regressions include measures of household welfare (proxied by consumption expenditures), parental education, the age-gender composition of the household, and village and school characteristics.[23] However,

---

[23] The elasticity of demand for schooling with respect to household income or expenditure can be larger than in developed countries. For example, elasticities reported (or derived from reported estimates) by Bhalotra and Heady (2003) for Pakistan and Handa (2002) for Mozambique are near or greater than 1.

Table 7.10. *The probability of attending school for rural children ages six through fifteen, by gender and ethnolinguistic group, 2002–2003*

Independent Variable	Rural male Lao-Tai dF/dx	Rural female Lao-Tai dF/dx	Rural male non-Lao-Tai dF/dx	Rural female non-Lao-Tai dF/dx
A. Child/Household Characteristics				
Log of per capita consumption	0.06 (3.14)	0.08 (4.47)	0.08 (2.42)	0.07 (1.55)
Log household size	0.01 (0.32)	−0.02 (0.76)	−0.01 (0.14)	−0.01 (0.13)
Age 7	0.10 (6.68)	0.08 (3.87)	0.19 (5.99)	0.19 (3.86)
Age 8	0.13 (9.68)	0.12 (7.44)	0.23 (7.33)	0.30 (7.50)
Age 9 to 11	0.20 (13.06)	0.20 (11.17)	0.40 (12.61)	0.45 (10.55)
Age 12	0.13 (9.59)	0.13 (7.19)	0.29 (11.12)	0.32 (6.57)
Age 13	0.13 (9.12)	0.10 (4.92)	0.28 (10.12)	0.26 (4.57)
Age 14 and up	0.11 (7.29)	0.04 (1.44)	0.25 (7.42)	0.17 (2.87)
Share of male adults, 17 and up	0.05 (0.41)	−0.28 (2.42)	−4.3e-03 (0.02)	−0.74 (2.89)
Share of males aged 6 to 16	−0.04 (0.41)	−0.28 (3.41)	−0.24 (1.30)	−0.75 (3.80)
Share of females aged 6 to 16	−0.02 (0.24)	−0.28 (3.35)	−0.24 (1.53)	−0.48 (2.43)
Share of boys aged 0 to 6	0.09 (0.95)	−0.35 (3.22)	−0.34 (1.78)	−0.45 (2.30)
Share of girls aged 0 to 6	−0.13 (1.15)	−0.25 (2.22)	−0.07 (0.38)	−0.64 (3.15)
Child is first- or second-born	−0.02 (1.17)	−0.02 (1.09)	0.02 (0.74)	0.03 (0.81)
Birth order is missing	−0.02 (0.57)	−4.4e-03 (0.16)	−0.08 (1.55)	−0.09 (1.82)
Male head of household	– –	– –	0.60 (2.30)	0.07 (0.18)
Age of head of household	−4.2e-03 (1.02)	3.8e-03 (0.79)	−0.01 (1.68)	0.01 (1.49)
Age of head of household, squared	4.6e-05 (1.10)	−3.5e-05 (0.69)	1.3e-04 (1.57)	−1.3e-04 (1.18)
Child is disabled	−0.10 (1.47)	−0.37 (2.97)	−0.03 (0.32)	−0.03 (0.28)

Independent Variable	Rural male Lao-Tai dF/dx	Rural female Lao-Tai dF/dx	Rural male non-Lao-Tai dF/dx	Rural female non-Lao-Tai dF/dx
Male head/spouse's years of schooling	0.01 (3.84)	1.1e-03 (0.38)	0.02 (3.21)	0.02 (2.90)
Female head/spouse's years of schooling	0.01 (2.80)	0.02 (5.83)	0.01 (1.47)	0.02 (2.44)
B. School Characteristics				
Electricity	0.02 (0.56)	0.06 (1.73)	0.07 (0.48)	0.26 (1.58)
Complete and not multigrade	0.19 (9.04)	0.23 (8.27)	0.30 (4.79)	0.46 (5.32)
Each student has desk	−0.02 (0.61)	−1.3e-03 (0.03)	0.11 (2.30)	0.08 (1.12)
Share of leaky classrooms	−0.04 (1.85)	−0.04 (2.06)	−0.06 (1.16)	−0.07 (1.30)
Share of male teachers	0.02 (0.97)	−0.06 (2.37)	−0.07 (1.55)	−0.10 (1.39)
Share of Lao teachers	0.02 (0.62)	0.02 (0.52)	0.04 (0.74)	0.12 (2.09)
Teachers' years of schooling	3.5e-03 (0.62)	−0.01 (1.13)	−3.9e-03 (0.55)	0.01 (0.57)
Official principal	−0.03 (0.41)	−0.20 (2.71)	0.10 (0.63)	0.05 (0.20)
Principal is male	−0.02 (0.35)	0.11 (2.16)	−0.03 (0.29)	0.11 (0.99)
Principal is a Lao	−0.01 (0.50)	1.5e-03 (0.04)	−0.02 (0.31)	−0.25 (2.37)
Principal's years of schooling	5.8e-04 (0.10)	5.0e-03 (0.98)	−0.02 (1.41)	−0.01 (0.52)
Km to closest city	−2.6e-04 (1.73)	−3.6e-04 (2.21)	−1.2e-03 (3.70)	−5.8e-04 (1.10)
Km to closest paved road	3.2e-04 (1.58)	−5.9e-06 (0.02)	1.0e-03 (2.29)	1.3e-04 (0.22)
Km to closest lower-secondary school	−1.4e-03 (2.37)	−9.4e-04 (1.63)	−9.8e-04 (1.38)	−1.8e-03 (1.36)
Tuition fees are compulsory	0.02 (0.93)	0.02 (0.90)	0.03 (0.83)	0.08 (1.54)
Exam fees are compulsory	−0.03 (1.66)	0.01 (0.65)	−0.03 (0.71)	−2.9e-03 (0.05)
Mean walking time to school	5.2e-05 (0.19)	1.2e-04 (0.43)	−8.9e-04 (2.70)	1.3e-04 (0.18)

(*continued*)

Table 7.10. (*continued*)

Independent Variable	Rural male Lao-Tai dF/dx	Rural female Lao-Tai dF/dx	Rural male non-Lao-Tai dF/dx	Rural female non-Lao-Tai dF/dx
C. Village Characteristics				
High altitude lands	–1.8e-03	–0.06	–0.04	–0.01
	(0.09)	(2.23)	(0.87)	(0.12)
Priority 1 districts	0.01	0.03	0.06	0.01
	(0.30)	(1.21)	(1.59)	(0.25)
Priority 2 districts	–0.04	–0.05	–0.04	0.01
	(1.49)	(1.50)	(0.62)	(0.06)
Number of observations	2749	2686	1832	1955
Pseudo R^2	0.25	0.33	0.27	0.24

Note: A full set of province rural dummies are included in all regressions but not shown for ease of presentation. Z statistics based on standard errors corrected for heteroskedasticity and clustering at the village level are given in parentheses.
Source: LECS3, 2002–2003.

we highlight only the regression results that pertain to ethnic differences. To aid interpretation, we transformed the estimated probit coefficients into marginal effects, evaluated at the means. Standard errors in all estimated regressions have been corrected for heteroscedasticity and clustering at the village level.

The results confirm the inequalities across ethnolinguistic groups documented earlier: NLT children (except for Mon-Khmers) are significantly less likely to attend school than LT children, and this relative disadvantage is largest (by 20 percent) for Chine-Tibetans.[24] These results emerge even when controlling for household expenditures, which measure the family's ability to incur schooling costs, and also for a host of household, school, and community characteristics.[25] Interactions between province and urban-rural

[24] The results confirm that enrollment rates peak at ages nine to eleven and decline thereafter. A disability lowers a child's probability of attending school by 13%. Household size does not matter for enrollment, but the composition of the household does. Controlling for household size, the higher is the proportion of household members under six or six to sixteen years of age, the lower is the probability that a child is in school. This negative association (of 15%–24%) is largest with respect to the share of under-six children. One interpretation of these results is that they capture the effect of schooling costs – both direct and opportunity – on families with more children. Surprisingly, even the number of adult men relative to adult women in the household is negatively associated with school enrollment, albeit with less statistical significance.

[25] All else being equal, increasing log per capita consumption of the household by one unit – increasing the level of consumption by a factor of almost three – increases the probability

location – thirty-eight residence dummy variables in all – capture geographical variation and heterogeneity not captured by other included variables, including an area's ability to supply schools and the local demand for an educated labor force.[26] Although a strict urban-rural dichotomy is seldom an accurate representation of economic difference across areas, our results indicate that urban areas are associated with higher enrollment, controlling for other characteristics. Furthermore, the altitude of the village measures the specific effect of living in highland areas where schools tend to be of lower quality and are more difficult to reach. Even controlling for ethnolinguistic affiliation, residing in highland villages is associated with a 7 percent lower probability of being enrolled.

Disaggregating the full sample by urban-rural residence yields some striking effects that suggest that keeping the geographic samples together hides important differences between them. Highlighting the results that pertain to ethnolinguistic grouping, we find that only the Chine-Tibetan children are significantly less likely to be enrolled in school as compared with the LT children. Disaggregating by gender, we find significant ethnolinguistic differences are more pronounced for girls than for boys. Compared with boys, girls from the Chine-Tibet group are much less likely to be in school than those from the LT group. Living in the highlands or a priority district has a greater (negative) effect on girls, indicating that girls' enrollment is more highly correlated with the household's living standard and the economic value of schooling in the community.

Finally, we estimate the same probit models separately for each of four groups defined by residence, gender, and ethnolinguistic affiliation.[27] Several differences among the four groups are noteworthy:

- Breaking down the rural sample reveals that the demographic composition variables are significant only for girls and that the size of the

---

of a child going to school by 6 percent. The probit regression of schooling on per capita expenditures (and no other regressors) gives a highly significant (z-stat = 11.2) estimated coefficient of 0.21 – more than three times the size of the partial regression coefficient including the controls. Controlling for other observable characteristics, however, this coefficient falls, suggesting a considerably lower importance of living standards for achieving universal primary school enrollment. Related to the expenditure variable is the completed education level of the household head and his or her spouse, but having controlled for household expenditures, these education variables are probably measuring parental preferences for schooling. We expect more educated parents to value their children's schooling more highly – indeed, child enrollment is associated positively with parents' education, albeit at a weaker level than expenditures.

[26] With one exception, we obtained positive coefficients for the urban-province variables; with two exceptions, we obtained negative coefficients for the rural-province variables.

[27] For the rural subgroups, Wald tests reject the hypothesis that the models for boys and for girls are equal within the Lao-Tai population (chi²(55) = 234.7, probability>chi² = 0.0000)

coefficients for these variables is far larger for NLT girls than for LT girls. The results strongly suggest that girls' enrollment is reduced by household demands on their time – school-age girls are expected to substitute for adult women caring for younger children and performing chores. The coefficient of the share of girls ages six to sixteen is somewhat smaller than the other coefficients, perhaps indicating that the presence of other school-age girls diminishes the burden on any one school-age girl in the household.

- School-age girls are the only subgroup for whom per capita household consumption has an insignificant effect on the probability of going to school.

- Disability has a considerably larger (and significant) negative effect on enrollment for rural LT girls than for other subgroups.

- Having a complete primary school without multigrade classrooms in the village is the school attribute that has the largest and most consistently significant positive effect on enrollment across the models. Disaggregating the samples reveals that among the rural groups, the effect is largest for the NLT, partly reflecting the greater shortage of such schools faced by rural NLT children. This effect is larger for girls, possibly because of a greater reluctance to send girls outside the village to attend school due to risk and cost.

- Living in a highland village has a significant negative effect on enrollment only for rural LT girls. Having controlled separately for school supply conditions that partly measure the cost of schooling, this result suggests that girls' enrollment is also responsive to the perceived returns to education, which are likely to be low in the rural highlands.

HEALTH

In this section, we turn to patterns regarding health status, illness and disability, and health service utilization. We are interested in health indicators over the life span, but we do not have panel data on any one individual. Instead, we assume that the current average health status at different ages in the population approximates the health profile and the corresponding health care needs in the country. The health status of current children may be a poor predictor

or within the non-Lao-Tai group (chi^2(55) = 322.6, probability>chi^2 = 0.0000). The tests also reject equality of models among the rural ethnolinguistic groups for girls (chi^2(57) = 4126.5, probability>chi^2 = 0.0000) and for boys (chi^2(57) = 6760.2, probability>chi^2 = 0.0000). For the urban subgroups, the tests reject equality of models for boys and girls (chi^2(57) = 1795.8, probability>chi^2 = 0.0000). The urban sample includes too few observations to disaggregate by ethnolinguistic group.

of the health status of future children because of future improvements in, say, public health, but the health status of young children today could serve as predictors of the future (adult) health concerns in a country.[28]

The LECS3 collected information on a number of health-related factors, including self-reported health status, long-term and temporary illness, and the use of health services.[29] Self-reported measures of health are typically used in behavioral models, but their validity has been questioned because they may bring reporting biases that are systematically associated with the respondent's background characteristics. Given that self-reported health reflects perceived health, it may measure something different from actual health, such as a person's belief that she or he can competently cope with a challenging physical situation. For the LECS3, there was only one respondent for the household questionnaire, which may have attenuated this reporting bias but could have introduced measurement error because the respondent may have not had accurate information about another household member's health status.

SELF-REPORTED HEALTH STATUS

The survey asked the respondents to rate their health status as "very good," "good," "average," "bad," and "very bad."[30] Transforming these responses into a dichotomy of "bad health status" and "not bad health status," the graphs in Figure 7.5 show that people feel a worsening of their health status with age; at the maximum, about one-fifth reported that they were in bad health at age sixty, compared with 5 percent at age thirty.[31] Starting with the top graph,

---

[28] Alderman and Behrman (2006) reviewed studies that show that low birthweight significantly affects later life outcomes in developing countries. Also, infections in very young children can have deleterious long-run consequences; inflammations early in life can lead to the development of atherosclerosis (Finch and Crimmins 2004). A study by Phimmasone et al. (1996) documents significant differences in "the prevalence of both stunting and wasting when comparing subgroups of children: urban children are less stunted and wasted than rural children, children of the lowland majority less than children of ethnic minorities, and children whose mothers had completed primary education less than children whose mothers had never been to school" (p. 5)

[29] The survey questions considered in this analysis are along the following lines: How would you evaluate your health? Do you have any long-term illness, disability, or permanent mark from an accident? Does this affect your ability to work/go to school or conduct other daily activities?

[30] Respondents were also asked to compare their health status with the health status of others. We do not show these results because they are very similar to the responses to the question about rating their health status.

[31] To help discern the patterns, we use STATA's "lowess" command to smooth the curves; this is a nonparametric estimate using moving averages. For each distinct value of x it produces a fitted value y by running a regression in a local neighborhood of x, giving more weight to points closer to x. The size of the neighborhood is called the *bandwidth;* we use 0.4 throughout this chapter, one-half the command's maximum smoothing.

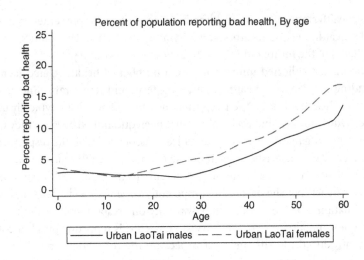

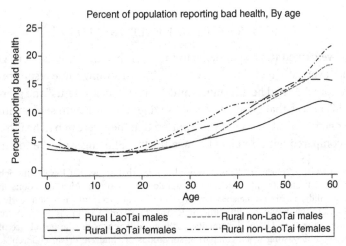

Figure 7.5. Self-reported health status over four weeks prior to survey.
Notes: Because of the small NLT urban sample, we have omitted the NLT curves. Graphs
have been smoothed using STATA's "lowess" smoothing command with a bandwidth of
0.4. Because the number of observations dwindles with age due to mortality, only data
for those up to age 60 are plotted.
Source: LECS3 2002–2003.

Table 7.11. *Determinants of self-reported health status*

	Health status is bad	Health status is worse compared to others
Log of real per capita expenditure	−0.0036***	−0.0073***
	(0.0012)	(0.0014)
Age	0.0006***	0.0009***
	(0.00004)	(0.00005)
Have long-term illness, disability, or permanent mark from an accident	0.304***	0.343***
	(0.023)	(0.024)
Have temporary health complaints in four weeks prior to survey	0.151***	0.158***
	(0.009)	(0.010)
Age x Long-term illness	−0.0004***	−0.0004***
	(0.00009)	(0.0001)
Age x Temporary illness	−0.00021***	−0.00025***
	(0.00007)	(0.00008)
Female	0.0049***	0.0031**
	(0.0012)	(0.0014)
Lao-Tai	−0.0033**	−0.0019
	(0.0013)	(0.0015)
Urban	−0.0035**	−0.0052***
	(0.0015)	(0.0018)
Observations	46975	46979
Pseudo R-squared	0.342	0.324

Note: Estimates are obtained with dprobit regression for the population 0 to 60 years old. Standard errors are in parentheses. *** $p<0.01$, ** $p<0.05$, * $p<0.1$.
Source: LECS3, 2002–2003.

we see a notable difference between males and females in the LT urban residents, with women being more likely to report bad health than men from adolescence. In fact, urban men, regardless of ethnolinguistic affiliation, are less likely to report being in bad health when compared with the rural population (not shown in the graph). As the bottom graph shows, in rural areas, from about age twenty, LT men, like LT men in urban areas, are less likely to report bad health than rural women in general and also less likely than NLT men to do so, although this divergence occurs at a later age than twenty.

We estimate a regression of self-reported health status against reported illness and disability and a few background characteristics as a simple check on whether or not self-reported health status is related to specific health complaints (Table 7.11). First, using our two measures, we find that living standards are negatively associated with the probability of being in bad health. We also find that self-reported bad health is positively associated with age, although the size of the association is quite small when we control for the existence of a health problem, implying that aging alone does not have a huge effect on the self-perception of own health status. Having an illness or disability – whether a long-term condition or a temporary problem – however, is strongly associated with self-reported health. Those people with a long-term illness or disability were 30 percent more likely to report being in bad health; those who had suffered a temporary illness four weeks prior to the survey were 15 percent more likely to do so. Women were more likely to report being in bad health, whereas the LT and urban residents were less likely to be in bad health. As with age, these associations are small in magnitude once the existence of a long-term or a temporary health problem has been taken into account. We also examine gender-ethnicity interaction terms, but they are not statistically significant.

PATTERNS IN ILLNESS AND DISABILITY

LECS3 obtained separate data on long-term illness and disability and temporary health problems. We continue to examine age curves because they suggest life cycle patterns in health problems and show differences in such patterns across population groups.

Among children under fifteen years of age, less than 5 percent are reported to be afflicted with long-term illness and disability. This prevalence rate increases with age, and by age sixty, 10–15 percent of the population is reported to have long-term adverse health conditions (Figure 7.6). There are no distinct differences across population groups during early childhood; beyond early adulthood, the prevalence rates diverge. The patterns that emerge are that the prevalence rates for the rural males and females are higher than those for urban males and females. Focusing on rural areas, NLT men have a higher prevalence of long-term illness or disability than LT men, especially after age forty (middle graph). The pattern among rural women is not as clear.

The age pattern of the incidence of temporary illness (during the four weeks prior to the survey) is quite different from that of the prevalence of long-term ailment or disability. Its distinct V-shape is not surprising: Early childhood diseases such as diarrhea, fevers, and common respiratory illness likely account for the high incidence of temporary health problems from birth (an incidence rate of 20–30 percent) (Figure 7.7). This incidence falls until early to late adolescence (below 10 percent) before it starts to rise and reach about 25 percent at age sixty as the effects of aging manifest themselves.

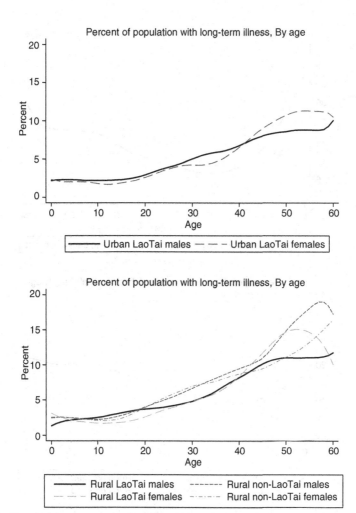

Figure 7.6. Prevalence of long-term illness or disability.
Notes: Graphs have been smoothed using STATA's "lowess" smoothing command with a bandwidth of 0.4. Because the number of observations dwindles with age due to mortality, only data for those up to age 60 are plotted.
Source: LECS3 2002–2003.

There is more divergence in the rate of temporary health illness across population groups than in the prevalence of long-term illness or disability. In the simple dichotomies by gender, residence and ethnolinguistic affiliation, we find that the incidence of temporary health problems is higher among females than males from late adolescence, among rural than urban

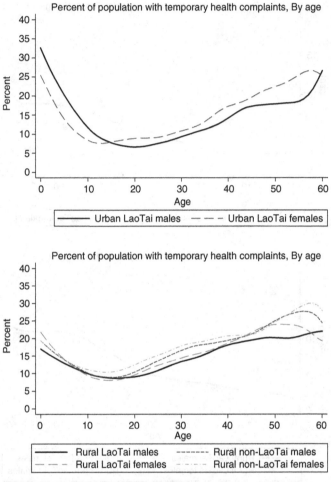

Figure 7.7. Incidence of temporary health problems over four weeks prior to survey.
Notes: Graphs have been smoothed using STATA's "lowess" smoothing command with
a bandwidth of 0.4. Because the number of observations dwindles with age due to mortality, only data for those up to age 60 are plotted.
Source: LECS3 2002–2003.

residents from late adolescence, and among the NLT than LT people from
childhood. Combining the gender, residence, and ethnolinguistic groupings, we find that in rural areas, male LT have the lowest incidence and
female NLT have the highest incidence of temporary health problems, but
the curves diverge only after childhood. In urban areas, focusing on just
the LT population, an interesting pattern is that urban boys have a higher

incidence of temporary health problems than urban girls, but as in rural areas, from adulthood, the incidence rates for men are lower than those for women.

The number of days of primary activity (such as work or school) missed as a result of illness is a common measure of the severity of illness; but because this measure reflects not only the severity of illness but also the opportunity cost of missed days of work or school, its interpretation is not straightforward. For the same illness, one person might continue to work whereas another might stop. Keeping this in mind, we see that similar to illness prevalence, this variable tends to increase with age, although this pattern seems quite unstable for urban LT males. In rural areas, due to illness, very young children miss primary activities for an average of five days over a four-week period, and sixty-year-olds miss six to ten days of activities over the same period. There are no clear differences across the population groups, except that NLT males tend to report fewer missed days of their primary activity from early adolescence compared with LT males or females. This is striking given that NLT males are the likeliest to report illness or disability.

HEALTH SERVICE UTILIZATION

We examine the percentage of the population reporting illness who sought care or treatment at a health facility or provider four weeks prior to the survey.[32] Focusing first on utilization rates by age, in urban areas, these rates start at about 25 percent for LT infants of both sexes and then drop as these children get older (Figure 7.8). At all ages in rural areas, there is a significant difference between the LT and NLT populations: On average, LT males and females are about ten percentage points likelier to seek treatment when ill than the NLT population, indicating perhaps both limited access to and demand for services within the NLT population. There is no clear gender difference as we see among the urban LT population, but if one considers only a two-way disaggregation by gender and ethnolinguistic affiliation, a more defined life cycle pattern emerges for females than for males – although only for the LT population. Women's utilization rates increase after age ten and eventually reach their peak during their childbearing and childrearing ages (and exceed those of men) before declining just as men's utilization rates start to rise around age fifty.

---

[32] The question pertains to public and private facilities or providers, as well as traditional healers.

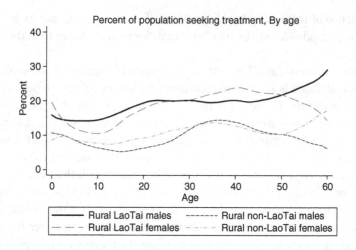

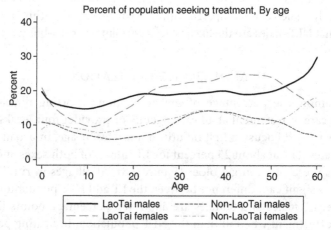

Figure 7.8. Demand for treatment at a health facility or provider.
Notes: Graphs have been smoothed using STATA's "lowess" smoothing command with a bandwidth of 0.4. Because the number of observations dwindles with age due to mortality, only data for those up to age 60 are plotted.
Source: LECS3 2002–2003.

Summing up the group differences with respect to health, LT males tend to report the best health status, have the lowest prevalence of illness or disability, and are likelier to seek treatment when ill than any of the NLT groups. By comparison, rural NLT females are the likeliest to report being in bad health, have the highest incidence of temporary health problems, and, like NLT males, are less likely to seek treatment when ill than the LT groups. NLT men are not far off from NLT women in terms of illness rates, but they miss fewer days of primary activity when they are sick than any LT group in rural areas.

TIME USE AND CHILD LABOR

Child labor is a topic that has received much attention recently because of concerns about human rights violations and also because of its potentially adverse long-run effect on child development, in particular on schooling and health status (Edmonds 2008). The LECS3 survey allows us to examine not only whether a child is employed for pay, but also what work activities a child engages in. The survey contains a time use module covering all household members; unfortunately, the module was applied only to members aged ten years and older, so the possibility that children below ten might be working cannot be explored. Table 7.12 shows the average number of hours per day spent on various activities for children (ages ten through sixteen). For comparison, Table 7.13 shows time use by adults aged seventeen through fifty-five. Each table is broken down by gender, urban and rural location, and ethnolinguistic affiliation.

A few caveats related to measurement are worth noting; these measurement problems are common to most, if not all, time use studies. First, the reporting of time use is always tricky because of imperfect recall; because an adult respondent might not be aware of the activities of all household members, especially by those who spend time outside the home; and because of joint activities – that is, activities that are undertaken simultaneously (e.g., caring for a child while cooking). The LECS3 mitigates the problem of imperfect recall by using as the reference period the "last 24 hours" prior to the survey, and prods the respondent about time spent on specific activities. Second, time use is highly seasonal and so a short recall period and a survey conducted once will not capture the variation in time use during the year for a specific individual. For example, children are in school for only part of the week and only part of the year. However, this is less of an issue when looking at sample averages across individuals or households. The LECS3 sampling design and the interview schedule, whereby households from a given geographic area are interviewed at different times of the year, reduces the problems related to the seasonality of incomes and many activities. Third, as with all household surveys, children who live outside the home are going to be missing. If those children reside outside the home for work or schooling purposes, then the data obtained from children remaining at home are likely to underestimate work and school hours of children.

Table 7.12. *Time use of children (excluding those on vacation) aged ten to sixteen, by gender, poor/nonpoor status, and ethnicity (hours per day)*

Activity	Lao-Tai									Non-Lao-Tai								
	Nonpoor			Poor			Total			Nonpoor			Poor			Total		
	Male	Female	Total	Male	Female	Total	Male	Female	Total	Male	Female	Total	Male	Female	Total	Male	Female	Total
Urban																		
Sleeping, eating, and personal care	11.5	11.3	11.4	11.5	11.4	11.5	11.5	11.3	11.4	11.4	12.2	11.7	11.4	10.6	11.0	11.4	11.5	11.4
Leisure time	4.0	3.4	3.7	4.4	3.9	4.2	4.1	3.5	3.8	3.9	3.9	3.9	4.0	4.1	4.0	3.9	4.0	3.9
School	5.5	4.9	5.2	4.5	4.6	4.5	5.3	4.8	5.1	5.9	5.5	5.7	4.6	3.6	4.1	5.4	4.7	5.1
Total work	2.0	3.6	2.8	2.7	3.3	3.0	2.1	3.6	2.8	1.9	2.0	1.9	3.5	4.9	4.1	2.5	3.2	2.8
Work as employed	0.4	0.3	0.3	0.5	0.4	0.4	0.4	0.3	0.4	0.0	0.0	0.0	0.4	0.0	0.2	0.1	0.0	0.1
Own business work	0.2	0.5	0.4	0.1	0.3	0.2	0.2	0.5	0.3	0.1	0.0	0.1	0.0	0.0	0.0	0.1	0.0	0.1
Agricultural work	0.5	0.5	0.5	0.7	0.5	0.6	0.6	0.5	0.5	0.5	0.2	0.4	1.6	2.2	1.9	0.9	1.0	1.0
Home production	0.9	2.3	1.5	1.4	2.1	1.7	1.0	2.3	1.6	1.2	1.9	1.5	1.5	2.7	2.1	1.3	2.2	1.7
Travel, Other	1.0	0.9	0.9	0.9	0.9	0.9	1.0	0.9	0.9	1.0	0.5	0.8	0.6	0.8	0.7	0.8	0.6	0.7
Rural																		
Sleeping, eating, and personal care	11.6	11.5	11.6	11.8	11.6	11.7	11.6	11.6	11.6	11.6	11.5	11.5	11.8	11.5	11.7	11.7	11.5	11.6
Leisure time	3.9	3.7	3.8	4.2	3.7	4.0	4.0	3.7	3.9	3.9	3.2	3.5	4.5	4.0	4.3	4.2	3.7	3.9
School	4.9	4.1	4.5	3.8	3.0	3.4	4.6	3.8	4.2	3.7	2.4	3.0	2.5	1.8	2.1	3.1	2.1	2.6
Total work	2.7	3.8	3.2	3.2	4.9	4.1	2.8	4.1	3.5	3.4	5.1	4.3	3.8	4.8	4.3	3.6	5.0	4.3
Work as employed	0.1	0.1	0.1	0.2	0.1	0.1	0.1	0.1	0.1	0.0	0.1	0.1	0.1	0.0	0.1	0.1	0.0	0.1
Own business work	0.1	0.2	0.1	0.0	0.1	0.1	0.1	0.1	0.1	0.1	0.1	0.1	0.0	0.0	0.0	0.0	0.0	0.0
Agricultural work	1.2	1.5	1.3	1.5	1.8	1.7	1.3	1.6	1.4	1.3	2.1	1.7	1.6	1.9	1.8	1.4	2.0	1.7
Home production	1.3	2.1	1.7	1.5	2.9	2.2	1.3	2.3	1.8	2.1	2.9	2.5	2.0	2.9	2.5	2.1	2.9	2.5
Travel/Other	0.9	0.8	0.9	1.0	0.8	0.9	1.0	0.8	0.9	1.4	1.8	1.6	1.4	1.8	1.6	1.4	1.8	1.6

Note: Population includes all children aged 10 to 16 not on vacation. Schooling includes time spent on homework. Home production includes time spent on cooking, washing/cleaning, collecting wood and water, shopping, care for children/elderly, handicraft/weaving, sewing, textile care, construction, and hunting/fishing.
Source: LECS3, 2002–2003.

Table 7.13. *Time use of adults aged 17 to 55, by gender, poor/nonpoor status, and ethnicity (hours per day)*

| | Lao-Tai | | | | | | | | | Non-Lao-Tai | | | | | | | | |
| | Nonpoor | | | Poor | | | Total | | | Nonpoor | | | Poor | | | Total | | |
Activity	Male	Female	Total	Male	Female	Total	Male	Female	Total	Male	Female	Total	Male	Female	Total	Male	Female	Total
Urban																		
Sleeping, eating, and personal care	11.1	10.8	10.9	11.1	10.9	11.0	11.1	10.8	11.0	11.2	10.9	11.0	11.1	10.9	11.0	11.2	10.9	11.0
Leisure time	3.7	3.2	3.4	4.1	3.6	3.9	3.8	3.3	3.5	3.8	3.4	3.6	4.3	2.8	3.6	4.0	3.1	3.6
School	0.9	0.5	0.7	0.6	0.4	0.5	0.8	0.5	0.7	0.8	0.3	0.6	0.6	0.1	0.4	0.8	0.2	0.5
Total work	7.1	8.5	7.8	7.1	8.3	7.7	7.1	8.5	7.8	6.5	8.7	7.6	7.4	9.5	8.5	6.9	9.0	8.0
Work as employed	2.8	1.3	2.0	2.9	1.0	1.9	2.8	1.3	2.0	1.9	1.0	1.4	1.6	0.6	1.1	1.8	0.8	1.3
Own business work	2.0	2.9	2.5	1.2	1.8	1.5	1.9	2.8	2.3	1.5	2.6	2.0	1.6	1.5	1.6	1.5	2.2	1.9
Agricultural work	1.1	0.8	0.9	1.7	1.2	1.5	1.2	0.8	1.0	1.6	1.2	1.4	2.4	2.2	2.3	1.9	1.6	1.8
Home production	1.3	3.5	2.4	1.3	4.3	2.8	1.3	3.6	2.5	1.5	3.9	2.8	1.7	5.2	3.4	1.6	4.4	3.0
Travel, Other	1.2	0.9	1.1	1.1	0.8	1.0	1.2	0.9	1.1	1.5	0.8	1.2	0.6	0.7	0.6	1.2	0.8	1.0
Rural																		
Sleeping, eating, and personal care	11.4	11.2	11.3	11.4	11.4	11.4	11.4	11.3	11.3	11.5	11.3	11.4	11.4	11.4	11.4	11.5	11.4	11.4
Leisure time	3.9	3.4	3.6	3.7	3.0	3.4	3.8	3.3	3.6	3.2	2.4	2.8	3.3	2.6	3.0	3.3	2.5	2.9
School	0.4	0.3	0.3	0.3	0.2	0.2	0.4	0.2	0.3	0.2	0.1	0.2	0.2	0.1	0.2	0.2	0.1	0.2
Total work	6.6	8.0	7.3	6.8	8.4	7.7	6.7	8.1	7.4	6.4	8.0	7.2	6.3	7.6	7.0	6.4	7.8	7.1
Work as employed	0.7	0.2	0.5	0.5	0.1	0.3	0.7	0.2	0.4	0.3	0.1	0.2	0.2	0.1	0.1	0.2	0.1	0.2
Own business work	0.8	0.9	0.8	0.2	0.2	0.2	0.7	0.7	0.7	0.2	0.2	0.2	0.1	0.1	0.1	0.2	0.1	0.1
Agricultural work	3.2	2.9	3.0	3.9	3.2	3.6	3.4	3.0	3.2	3.7	3.6	3.6	3.3	3.3	3.3	3.5	3.4	3.5
Home production	1.8	4.0	2.9	2.2	4.8	3.6	1.9	4.2	3.1	2.3	4.1	3.2	2.7	4.2	3.5	2.5	4.2	3.4
Travel/Other	1.7	1.1	1.4	1.8	1.0	1.4	1.7	1.1	1.4	2.6	2.1	2.3	2.8	2.3	2.5	2.7	2.2	2.4

Note: Home production includes time spent on cooking, washing/cleaning, collecting wood and water, shopping, care for children/elderly, handicraft/weaving, sewing, textile care, construction, and hunting/fishing.

Source: LECS3, 2002–2003.

The time use of school-age children suggests that the ethnic and gender inequalities are likely to persist in the near future. Rural children attend fewer hours of school than urban children (Table 7.12). The length of the school day is prescribed, so this lower average reflects the fact that more children in rural than in urban areas are out of school. However, among rural children, it is NLT children who spend the least time at school per day (2.6), especially girls (2.1 hours versus 3.1 hours for the boys). In this group, poor girls spend even less time at school, 1.8 hours per day on average, again reflecting their lower rate of enrollment. Instead, they spend an average of five hours each day working both on agriculture and on home production: collecting wood and water and looking after younger siblings and elderly family members.

In urban Laos, poor NLT girls also work harder than any other group at 4.9 hours a day on average, but our sample size is too small to support a strong statement about this. Otherwise, the biggest differences across urban children appear to be in the composition of their work hours. NLT children spend more of their non-home production-related working time on agricultural production, whereas their LT counterparts are likelier to be employed for a wage or on a family business. Within each ethnolinguistic group, gender differences are relatively clear and there appears to be an economic gradient.

Adults work an average of six to eight hours within a twenty-four-hour period. Because home production work can total as many as five hours, the total work hours for women exceed that of men, with the largest gap (about two hours) being among urban NLT men and women (Table 7.13). As expected, most of the non-home production work in rural areas is in agriculture, whereas it tends to be in wage and self-employment in urban areas. However, in both urban and rural areas, the LT engage in more off-farm work than do the NLT. Focusing on just the rural population, on average, both LT men and women work more hours than NLT men and women when we exclude time spent on "travel" and "other" from this total. Travel could be work-related and it could be not; it is unclear what "other" refers to. If this time is considered also as work, then rural NLT women work the most, followed by LT women, NLT men, and LT men, in that order. For all groups, there is a clear economic gradient: Poor women work many more hours than men do, and they also work more than nonpoor women, but this difference derives mainly from home production. Consistent with the work patterns, LT men have the most leisure hours and NLT women have the least; and although leisure hours converge as per capita consumption rises, this convergence does not include NLT women.

CONCLUSIONS

The household survey evidence discussed here confirms that despite a clear narrowing in disparities in literacy and completed schooling among ethnolinguistic groups in Lao PDR, non-Lao-Tai (NLT) ethnolinguistic minority groups are disadvantaged in numerous respects relative to the Lao-Tai (LT) majority. Whereas one in four LT lives in poverty, one in two among the NLT does so. NLT adults continue to have fewer years of completed formal schooling and their children are less likely to attend school, partly because they have poorer access to schools and to schools that have adequate instruction. A larger share of the NLT population lives in villages that have no health facilities at all. They predominantly live in isolated rural highland areas far from public services and basic infrastructure services. Similar to the rural LT households, rural NLT households are primarily farmers, but by and large they derive livelihoods from cultivating less productive lands in harsher upland areas and rely much more on forest products as an income source than do the rural LT households. They have successfully adapted their agricultural and livelihood practices to survive in such environments.

Amid the previously presented litany of disadvantages of the NLT relative to the LT, it is important to recognize that the somewhat arbitrary aggregation of households into LT and NLT ethnolinguistic groups hides a clearer picture of disparities. Some among the NLT ethnic groups are considerably worse off in many respects than others. Among them, those who live in rural areas are typically more disadvantaged, although we also noted some deep pockets of urban poverty as well. Finally, an important dimension of further disadvantage is gender. NLT adult women and girls lag behind NLT men in numerous ways. Disadvantage is felt along all these dimensions in varying degrees. This fact must be front and center when thinking about policies to redress inequalities and raise living standards for all.

Existing government policies focus on providing access to basic services, land tenure, and agriculture. Some of these policies require that highland NLT households abandon their villages and environments and resettle in lowland "focal" areas where it is easier to supply public services and they can engage in more productive paddy wet-rice cultivation. These relocation policies are also promoted as ways to safeguard forests and the environment by putting an end to swidden agriculture. However, many observers have been critical of the policies, their underlying assumptions, and their results. Critics note that in practice, the relocation areas are typically already occupied by LT who have made claims on much of the productive land and resent the incoming households and the associated pressure on resources (Cohen 2000; Evrard and Goudineau 2004; Rigg 2006; Baird and Shoemaker 2007). The infrastructure and social services are often inadequate, resulting in a decline in living standards, and NLT households have had trouble adapting to the new environments and creating livelihoods there. They also face health problems such as malaria that were not common in the highlands.

Policies that promote a LT-centric development approach are not likely to be broadly successful. The results of this study cast doubt on this approach. Our regressions of household per capita consumption suggest that the underlying models of living standards and human development are structurally different across the groups. This in turn suggests that to be successful, policies aimed at raising welfare levels must be tailored to each group's specific needs and capabilities. Looking forward, our study suggests that policies must also address female disadvantage to ensure that future generations of NLT have better human capital. Failure to do so may well mean that existing disparities and the currently high poverty levels found among the NLT ethnolinguistic minorities will be reproduced in the next generation.

APPENDIX 1: THREE EDUCATION ENROLLMENT RATES

The following equations define three commonly used enrollment measures and indicate how they are related:

$$\text{Age-specific Enrollment Rate}_j = (\Sigma_{i=1,2,3}\text{Enrolled}_j^i)/\text{Population}_j$$
$$\text{Net Enrollment Rate}_i = \text{Enrolled}_j^i/\text{Population}_j$$
$$\text{Gross Enrollment Rate}_i = (\Sigma_{j=6-10,11-13,14-16}\text{Enrolled}_j^i)/\text{Population}_j$$

where j refers to one of three age groups (6–10, 11–13, 14–16), and i pertains to one of three school cycles (1=primary level, 2=lower-secondary level, 3=upper-secondary level). In principle, j could include any age group older or younger than the three age groups specified here, and i could include a preschool cycle and the university level. We define the age-specific enrollment rate of children of age j to pertain to any school enrollment, irrespective of grade or cycle, and the gross enrollment rate in school cycle i to include all students in that cycle, irrespective of age.

Appendix Table 1. Basic household and population characteristics by urban/rural residence, ethnicity, and poor/nonpoor status, 2002–2003

		Urban			Rural			Total		
		Lao-Tai	Non-Lao-Tai	Total	La-Tai	Non-Lao-Tai	Total	La-Tai	Non-Lao-Tai	Total
Total										
Household characteristics										
school years of head of household	Mean	6.9	5.3	6.7	4.7	2.7	3.9	5.4	2.9	4.6
	SD	4.1	3.7	4.1	3.3	2.8	3.2	3.7	3	3.7
school years of head of household's spouse	Mean	5	3.1	4.8	3.1	1	2.3	3.7	1.1	2.8
	SD	3.6	3.5	3.6	2.8	1.8	2.7	3.2	2.1	3.1
household size	Mean	6.4	7.4	6.5	6.7	7.6	7.1	6.6	7.6	6.9
	SD	2.3	2.7	2.3	2.2	2.8	2.5	2.2	2.8	2.5
dependency ratio	Mean	0.4	0.5	0.4	0.4	0.5	0.4	0.4	0.5	0.4
	SD	0.2	0.2	0.2	0.2	0.2	0.2	0.2	0.2	0.2
% population with:										
remittances from Laos	Mean	5.6	2.8	5.4	3.8	2.0	3.1	4.3	2.1	3.6
	SD	0.2	0.2	0.2	0.2	0.1	0.2	0.2	0.1	0.2
remittances from abroad	Mean	4.0	5.3	4.1	3.2	2.5	2.9	3.4	2.7	3.2
	SD	0.2	0.2	0.2	0.2	0.2	0.2	0.2	0.2	0.2
pension and life insurance	Mean	1.9	1.9	1.9	0.2	0.7	0.4	0.7	0.8	0.7
	SD	0.1	0.1	0.1	0.0	0.1	0.1	0.1	0.1	0.1
% population living in village with:										
road	Mean	99.7	98.8	99.6	81.1	66.6	75.2	86.8	68.8	80.8
	SD	0.1	0.1	0.1	0.4	0.5	0.4	0.3	0.5	0.4

(continued)

Appendix Table 1 (*continued*)

		Urban			Rural			Total		
		LaoTai	Non-Lao-Tai	Total	La-Tai	Non-Lao-Tai	Total	La-Tai	Non-Lao-Tai	Total
electricity	Mean	97.5	93.3	97.1	44.3	16.1	32.9	60.7	21.5	47.6
	SD	0.2	0.2	0.2	0.5	0.4	0.5	0.5	0.4	0.5
primary school	Mean	83.6	70.2	82.2	87.6	80.0	84.5	86.4	79.3	84.0
	SD	0.4	0.5	0.4	0.3	0.4	0.4	0.3	0.4	0.4
lower-secondary school	Mean	29.2	22.7	28.6	16.6	3.9	11.5	20.5	5.2	15.4
	SD	0.5	0.4	0.5	0.4	0.2	0.3	0.4	0.2	0.4
upper-secondary school	Mean	11.3	14.1	11.6	4.9	1.0	3.3	6.8	1.9	5.2
	SD	0.3	0.3	0.3	0.2	0.1	0.2	0.3	0.1	0.2
technical school	Mean	8.0	2.1	7.4	0.4	0.4	0.4	2.8	0.5	2.0
	SD	0.3	0.1	0.3	0.1	0.1	0.1	0.2	0.1	0.1
hospital	Mean	9.0	15.2	9.6	1.3	1.1	1.2	3.7	2.1	3.1
	SD	0.3	0.4	0.3	0.1	0.1	0.1	0.2	0.1	0.2
dispensary/health post	Mean	23.2	24.3	23.3	14.6	5.7	11.0	17.3	7.0	13.8
	SD	0.4	0.4	0.4	0.4	0.2	0.3	0.4	0.3	0.3
Number of observations		7,897	1,358	9,255	21,002	19,532	40,534	28,899	20,890	49,789
Nonpoor										
Household characteristics										
school years of head of household	Mean	7.1	5.7	7	5.1	2.9	4.4	5.8	3.1	5.1
	SD	4.2	4.1	4.2	3.4	2.9	3.4	3.8	3.1	3.8
school years of household's spouse	Mean	5.2	3.4	5.1	3.4	1.1	2.7	4	1.3	3.4
	SD	3.7	3.6	3.7	2.9	2	2.9	3.3	2.2	3.3

household size									
Mean	6.2	6.8	6.2	6.2	6.9	6.4	6.2	6.9	6.4
SD	2.2	2.7	2.2	2	2.6	2.2	2.1	2.6	2.2
dependency ratio									
Mean	0.4	0.4	0.4	0.4	0.4	0.4	0.4	0.4	0.4
SD	0.2	0.2	0.2	0.2	0.2	0.2	0.2	0.2	0.2
% population with:									
remittances from Laos									
Mean	6.4	5.0	6.3	3.8	1.9	3.2	4.7	2.2	4.0
SD	0.2	0.2	0.2	0.2	0.1	0.2	0.2	0.1	0.2
remittances from abroad									
Mean	4.2	6.7	4.4	3.5	4.4	3.8	3.8	4.5	3.9
SD	0.2	0.3	0.2	0.2	0.2	0.2	0.2	0.2	0.2
pension and life insurance									
Mean	1.7	1.8	1.7	0.2	0.5	0.3	0.7	0.6	0.7
SD	0.1	0.1	0.1	0.0	0.1	0.1	0.1	0.1	0.1
% population living in village with:									
road									
Mean	99.8	99.6	99.8	83.9	72.8	80.4	89.3	74.9	85.7
SD	0.0	0.1	0.4	0.4	0.4	0.4	0.3	0.4	0.3
electricity									
Mean	97.8	92.9	97.4	47.0	19.4	38.2	64.4	25.2	54.6
SD	0.1	0.3	0.2	0.5	0.4	0.5	0.5	0.4	0.5
primary school									
Mean	82.4	80.5	82.3	88.1	79.1	85.2	86.1	79.2	84.4
SD	0.4	0.4	0.4	0.3	0.4	0.4	0.3	0.4	0.4
lower-secondary school									
Mean	30.6	26.6	30.3	18.4	4.7	14.0	22.6	6.4	18.5
SD	0.5	0.4	0.5	0.4	0.2	0.3	0.4	0.2	0.4
upper-secondary school									
Mean	11.8	18.2	12.3	6.4	2.0	5.0	8.3	3.2	7.0
SD	0.3	0.4	0.3	0.2	0.1	0.2	0.3	0.2	0.3
technical school									
Mean	8.5	3.0	8.1	0.6	0.8	0.6	3.3	1.0	2.7
SD	0.3	0.2	0.3	0.1	0.1	0.1	0.2	0.1	0.2
hospital									
Mean	9.3	8.8	9.3	1.7	1.3	1.6	4.3	1.9	3.7
SD	0.3	0.3	0.3	0.1	0.1	0.1	0.2	0.1	0.2

(continued)

Appendix Table 1 (*continued*)

		Urban			Rural			Total		
		Lao-Tai	Non-Lao-Tai	Total	La-Tai	Non-Lao-Tai	Total	La-Tai	Non-Lao-Tai	Total
dispensary/health post	Mean	24.1	32.7	24.7	15.0	6.1	12.2	18.1	8.2	15.7
	SD	0.4	0.5	0.4	0.4	0.2	0.3	0.4	0.3	0.4
Number of observations		6,562	762	7,324	14,726	9,362	24,088	21,288	10,124	31,412
Poor										
Household characteristics										
school years of head of household	Mean	5.8	4.9	5.6	3.9	2.5	3.1	4.3	2.7	3.5
	SD	3.9	2.9	3.7	2.9	2.7	2.9	3.2	2.7	3.1
school years of head of household's spouse	Mean	3.9	2.6	3.6	2.3	0.8	1.5	2.6	0.9	1.8
	SD	2.9	3.3	3.1	2.4	1.7	2.2	2.6	1.9	2.4
household size	Mean	7.7	8.2	7.8	7.9	8.3	8.1	7.8	8.3	8.1
	SD	2.3	2.5	2.3	2.3	2.8	2.5	2.3	2.7	2.5
dependency ratio	Mean	0.5	0.5	0.5	0.5	0.5	0.5	0.5	0.5	0.5
	SD	0.2	0.2	0.2	0.2	0.2	0.2	0.2	0.2	0.2
% population with:										
remittances from Laos	Mean	2.1	0.0	1.6	3.7	2.1	2.8	3.4	2.0	2.7
	SD	0.1	0.0	0.1	0.2	0.1	0.2	0.2	0.1	0.2
remittances from abroad	Mean	2.7	3.4	2.9	2.4	0.7	1.5	2.5	0.9	1.7
	SD	0.2	0.2	0.2	0.2	0.1	0.1	0.2	0.1	0.1
pension and life insurance	Mean	3.1	2.0	2.8	0.2	0.8	0.5	0.8	0.9	0.9
	SD	0.2	0.1	0.2	0.0	0.1	0.1	0.1	0.1	0.1
% population living in village with:										

road	Mean	99.2	97.8	98.9	74.1	60.7	66.8	79.3	63.0	71.0
	SD	0.1	0.1	0.1	0.4	0.5	0.5	0.4	0.5	0.5
electricity	Mean	96.1	93.8	95.6	37.5	13.0	24.1	49.7	17.8	33.6
	SD	0.2	0.2	0.2	0.5	0.3	0.4	0.5	0.4	0.5
primary school	Mean	89.6	57.0	82.2	86.6	80.8	83.4	87.2	79.3	83.2
	SD	0.3	0.5	0.4	0.3	0.4	0.4	0.3	0.4	0.4
lower-secondary school	Mean	22.5	17.6	21.4	12.1	3.3	7.2	14.3	4.1	9.1
	SD	0.4	0.4	0.4	0.3	0.2	0.3	0.3	0.2	0.3
upper-secondary school	Mean	8.7	8.7	8.7	1.0	0.2	0.5	2.6	0.7	1.6
	SD	0.3	0.3	0.3	0.1	0.0	0.1	0.2	0.1	0.1
technical school	Mean	5.8	1.1	4.7	0.0	0.0	0.0	1.2	0.1	0.6
	SD	0.2	0.1	0.2	0.0	0.0	0.0	0.1	0.0	0.1
hospital	Mean	7.5	23.3	11.1	0.3	0.9	0.7	1.8	2.3	2.0
	SD	0.3	0.4	0.3	0.1	0.1	0.1	0.1	0.1	0.1
dispensary/health post	Mean	18.8	13.5	17.6	13.6	5.4	9.1	14.7	5.9	10.2
	SD	0.4	0.3	0.4	0.3	0.2	0.3	0.4	0.2	0.3
Number of observations		1,335	596	1,931	6,276	10,170	16,446	7,611	10,766	18,377

Notes: Dependency ratio is defined as 1-ratio of number of workers to household size. For categorical variables, standard deviations (SD) are of proportions rather than percentages. Means and SD are estimated for the individual population.

Source: LECS 2002–2003.

Appendix Table 2. *Descriptive statistics of variables included in the regressions*

		Urban			Rural			Total		
		Lao-Tai	Non-Lao-Tai	Total	Lao-Tai	Non-Lao-Tai	Total	Lao-Tai	Non-Lao-Tai	Total
Real per capita expenditure (log)	Mean	12.144	11.775	12.094	11.89	11.606	11.76	11.962	11.617	11.826
	SD	0.594	0.551	0.601	0.535	0.467	0.524	0.564	0.475	0.557
Real per capita expenditure (1000 kips)	Mean	230.0	152.8	219.7	171.4	124.3	149.8	188.0	126.2	163.6
	SD	200.8	100.9	192.3	129.5	83.9	113.4	155.4	85.4	135.7
Household size	Mean	5.688	6.308	5.771	5.984	6.558	6.248	5.9	6.541	6.153
	SD	2.083	2.445	2.144	2.148	2.649	2.408	2.134	2.636	2.365
Lao-Tai household	Mean	1	0	0.867	1	0	0.541	1	0	0.606
	SD	0	0	0.34	0	0	0.498	0	0	0.489
Share of elderly	Mean	0.084	0.075	0.083	0.08	0.069	0.075	0.081	0.069	0.077
	SD	0.15	0.132	0.148	0.145	0.128	0.138	0.147	0.129	0.14
Share of male adults, 17 to 55	Mean	0.262	0.22	0.257	0.23	0.214	0.223	0.239	0.215	0.229
	SD	0.142	0.123	0.14	0.119	0.118	0.119	0.127	0.118	0.124
Share of female adults, 17 to 55	Mean	0.276	0.244	0.272	0.246	0.228	0.238	0.255	0.229	0.245
	SD	0.137	0.136	0.137	0.118	0.115	0.117	0.125	0.117	0.122
Share of males, 6 to 16	Mean	0.145	0.168	0.148	0.162	0.144	0.154	0.157	0.145	0.153
	SD	0.157	0.157	0.157	0.154	0.144	0.15	0.155	0.145	0.151
Share of females, 6 to 16	Mean	0.141	0.143	0.141	0.154	0.147	0.146	0.15	0.146	0.149
	SD	0.151	0.139	0.15	0.15	0.141	0.146	0.15	0.141	0.147
Share of boys, 0 to 5	Mean	0.049	0.078	0.053	0.064	0.101	0.081	0.06	0.099	0.076
	SD	0.099	0.116	0.101	0.107	0.124	0.116	0.105	0.123	0.114
Share of girls, 0 to 5	Mean	0.042	0.071	0.046	0.063	0.098	0.079	0.057	0.096	0.072
	SD	0.091	0.11	0.094	0.105	0.119	0.113	0.102	0.119	0.11
Male head of household	Mean	0.904	0.953	0.91	0.959	0.971	0.965	0.943	0.97	0.954
	SD	0.295	0.212	0.286	0.198	0.167	0.184	0.231	0.17	0.209
Age of head of household	Mean	47.052	43.075	46.521	44.177	41.348	42.878	44.992	41.463	43.6
	SD	11.332	10.804	11.34	11.737	12.498	12.174	11.694	12.398	12.1

Highest education of
most-educated member:

Preprimary	Mean	0.005	0.033	0.009	0.027	0.164	0.09	0.02	0.155	0.074
	SD	0.071	0.179	0.093	0.161	0.37	0.286	0.142	0.362	0.261
Some primary	Mean	0.052	0.136	0.063	0.164	0.38	0.263	0.132	0.364	0.224
	SD	0.222	0.344	0.244	0.37	0.486	0.44	0.339	0.481	0.417
Completed primary	Mean	0.077	0.108	0.081	0.218	0.223	0.22	0.178	0.216	0.193
	SD	0.266	0.311	0.273	0.413	0.417	0.415	0.382	0.411	0.395
Some lower-secondary	Mean	0.091	0.141	0.098	0.171	0.108	0.142	0.149	0.11	0.133
	SD	0.288	0.349	0.297	0.377	0.31	0.349	0.356	0.313	0.34
Completed lower-secondary	Mean	0.167	0.221	0.174	0.188	0.075	0.136	0.182	0.085	0.144
	SD	0.373	0.416	0.379	0.39	0.264	0.343	0.386	0.279	0.351
Some upper-secondary	Mean	0.081	0.089	0.082	0.068	0.014	0.043	0.072	0.019	0.051
	SD	0.273	0.286	0.275	0.252	0.117	0.204	0.258	0.136	0.22
Completed upper-secondary	Mean	0.209	0.122	0.197	0.081	0.019	0.053	0.117	0.026	0.081
	SD	0.407	0.328	0.398	0.273	0.137	0.223	0.322	0.159	0.273
Vocational training	Mean	0.189	0.099	0.177	0.071	0.013	0.045	0.105	0.019	0.071
	SD	0.392	0.299	0.382	0.258	0.115	0.207	0.306	0.137	0.257
University	Mean	0.129	0.052	0.118	0.012	0.003	0.008	0.045	0.006	0.03
	SD	0.335	0.222	0.323	0.11	0.055	0.089	0.208	0.079	0.17
Received remittances from abroad	Mean	0.04	0.042	0.041	0.029	0.017	0.024	0.032	0.019	0.027
	SD	0.197	0.201	0.197	0.169	0.13	0.152	0.177	0.136	0.162
Highlands	Mean	0.041	0.154	0.056	0.155	0.623	0.37	0.123	0.591	0.308
	SD	0.198	0.362	0.23	0.362	0.485	0.483	0.328	0.492	0.462
Lowlands	Mean	0.846	0.528	0.804	0.623	0.218	0.437	0.686	0.238	0.509
	SD	0.361	0.5	0.397	0.485	0.413	0.496	0.464	0.426	0.5

Notes: A household is defined as Lao-Tai if there are equal or more Lao-Tai than non-Lao-Tai members.
Source: LECS, 2002–2003.

References

Alderman, Harold and Jere R. Behrman. 2006. "Reducing the Incidence of Low Birth Weight in Low-Income Countries Has Substantial Economic Benefits," *World Bank Research Observer* 21(1): 25–448.

Arnold, Fred, Minja Kim Choe, and T. K. Roy. 1998. "Son Preference, the Family-Building Process and Child Mortality in India." *Population Studies* 52(3): 301–315.

Baird, Ian G. and Bruce Shoemaker. 2007. "Unsettling Experiences: Internal Resettlement and International Aid Agencies in Laos," *Development and Change* 38(5): 865–888.

Behrman, Jere and James Knowles. 1999. "Household Income and Child Schooling in Vietnam," *World Bank Economic Review* 13(2): 211–256.

Bhalotra, Sonia and Christopher Heady. 2003. "Child Farm Labor: The Wealth Paradox," *World Bank Economic Review* (17): 197–227.

Butler, J. S., Richard V. Burkhauser, Jean M. Mitchell, and Theodore P. Pincus. 1987. "Measurement Error in Self-Reported Health Variables." *The Review of Economics and Statistics* 69(4): 644–650.

Cohen, Paul. 2000. "Resettlement, Opium and Labour Dependence: Akha-Tai Relations in Northern Laos." *Development and Change* 31: 179–200.

Edmonds, Eric. 2008. "Child Labor," *Handbook of Development Economics*, Volume 4, T. P. Schultz and J. Strauss (eds.). Amsterdam: Elsevier B. V. Press.

Evrard, Olivier and Yves Goudineau. 2004. "Planned Resettlement, Unexpected Migrations and Cultural Trauma in Laos." *Development and Change* 35(5): 937–962.

Finch, Caleb and Eileen Crimmins. 2004. "Inflammatory Exposure and Historical Changes in Human Life-Spans," *Science* 305: 1736–1739.

Ireson, Carol and Randall Ireson. 1991. "Ethnicity and Development in Laos," *Asian Survey* 31(10): 920–937.

Jalan, Jyotsna and Martin Ravallion. 2002. "Geographic Poverty Traps? A Micro Model of Consumption Growth in China," *Journal of Applied Econometrics* 17(4): 329–346.

Mishra, Vinod, T. K. Roy, and Robert Retherford. 2004. "Sex Differentials in Childhood Feeding, Health Care, and Nutritional Status in India," *Population and Development Review* 30(2): 269–295.

Orazem, Peter and Elizabeth M. King. 2008. "Schooling in Developing Countries: The Roles of Supply, Demand and Government Policy," Chapter 55, *Handbook of Development Economics*, Volume 4, T. P. Schultz and J. Strauss (eds.). Amsterdam: Elsevier B. V. Press.

Phimmasone, Kotsaythoune, Inpanh Douangpoutha, Vincent Fauveau, and Phonethep Pholsena. 1996. "Nutritional Status of Children in the Lao PDR," *Journal of Tropical Pediatrics* 42: 5–11.

Pholsena, Vatthana. 2006. *Post-War Laos: The Politics of Culture, History, and Identity.* Ithaca: Cornell University Press.

Planning Committee and National Statistical Center. 1999. *The Households of Lao PDR: Socio and Economic Indicators 1997/98.* Vientiane.

Ravallion, Martin and Quentin Wodon. 1999. "Poor Areas or Only Poor People?" *Journal of Regional Science* 39: 689–712.

Richter, Kaspar, Roy van der Weide, and Phonesaly Souksavath. 2005. *Lao PDR Poverty Trends 1992/3 – 2002/3.* Washington, DC: World Bank.

Rigg, J. D. 2006. "Forests, Marketization, Livelihoods and the Poor in the Lao PDR," *Land Degradation and Development* 17: 123–133.

van de Walle, Dominique and Dileni Gunewardena. 2001. "Sources of Ethnic Inequality in Vietnam," *Journal of Development Economics* 65: 177–207.

World Bank. 2006a. *Lao PDR: Rural and Agriculture Sector Issues Paper.* Working Paper No. 37566, East Asia and Pacific Region, World Bank, Washington, DC.

2006b. *Lao PDR: Poverty Assessment Report. From Valleys to Hilltops: 15 Years of Poverty Reduction.* Report No. 38083, East Asia and Pacific Region, World Bank, Washington, DC.

8

Vietnam

A Widening Poverty Gap for Ethnic Minorities

Hai-Anh Dang

INTRODUCTION

Vietnam is a tropical country with a land area of around 331,000 square kilometers in Southeast Asia, and is bordered by China to the north, Lao PDR to the northwest, and Cambodia to the southwest. The population of Vietnam was approximately 85 million in 2007, ranking it among the countries with the highest population densities in the world. Income per capita was estimated at US$1,052 in 2009; the value-added shares of GDP for agriculture, industry, and services in 2009 were 22 percent, 39 percent, and 39 percent, respectively (World Bank 2010.)

Vietnam has fifty-four ethnic groups. Almost all these ethnic groups' languages belong to the five language families of Southeast Asia and can be considered as sharing "the same historical and cultural horizon of the past which spread from south of the Yangtze River to the Islands of Southeast Asia" (Dang et al. 2000). Some of these groups have been in Vietnam since the earliest times (for example, the Viet and the Tay-Thai groups), while some arrived as recently as around the seventeenth to nineteenth century (for example, the Hanhi, the Lahu, and the Lolo groups) and some came to Vietnam throughout different periods, but mostly in the last millennium (for example, the Hoa, the Nung, and the Vankieu groups) (Dang et al., 2000). The Kinh or Viet (ethnic Vietnamese) is the largest group, accounting for 86 percent of the population. The next largest groups are the Tay, the Thai, the Muong, the Khmer (ethnic Cambodian), the Hoa (ethnic Chinese), and the Hmong, which together represent 10 percent of the population, and the remaining ethnic groups make up 4 percent of the population (GSO 2001a).

Although terms such as *indigenous people* have been used to refer to ethnic groups of smaller size than the majority group in certain countries (see, for example, United Nations Development Group 2008), the preferred terminology in this chapter is *ethnic minority groups*. This term is considered to be the closest translation for the Vietnamese term *dân tộc thiểu số* that is widely used in both official documents and popular speech.[1] This chapter defines the ethnic majority group as consisting of the Kinh and Hoa ethnic groups and ethnic minority groups as the remaining ethnic groups.[2]

Despite government assistance efforts, ethnic minority groups still lag behind in living standards (Swinkels and Turk 2006; World Bank 2009). Worse still, concerns were voiced that ethnic minority groups are subject to stereotypes that portray them negatively as backward, superstitious, and conservative (Jamieson et al. 1998; Asian Development Bank 2002). The World Bank, in its Country Social Analysis report (World Bank 2009), identifies six areas where ethnic minorities have a disadvantage compared with ethnic majorities:

- Ethnic minorities have less access to education, higher dropout rates, and later school enrollment. There is lack of ethnic minority teachers and bilingual education for ethnic minorities. School fees also represent a burden for ethnic minorities.
- Ethnic minorities have less mobility, with Kinh migrant households enjoying better benefits from government programs and their social networks. Kinh migration even has had negative effects on local minorities in certain places.
- Ethnic minorities have less access to formal financial services.
- Ethnic minorities have less productive land and are more dependent on swidden agriculture; they also have less off-farm employment.

---

[1] The term *dân tộc thiểu số* is usually shortened to *dân tộc* in everyday spoken Vietnamese. This practice of categorizing ethnic groups into minority or majority groups rather than indigenous or nonindigenous people can perhaps be traced back to the origin of most major ethnic groups in Vietnam, which were considered to come as branches of the common *Bách Việt* (multiethnic Viet) race from 5000 B.C. to around 700–800 A.D. (Tran 2001). In addition, the Vietnamese terms closest to "indigenous people" are *người bản địa* or *người bản xứ* and these terms in current usage usually refer to people that have already been living in a certain place before anyone else arrives – for example, the natives in America.

[2] By definition, except for the Kinh group, all ethnic groups can be considered ethnic minority groups because of their small size. However, the Hoa ethnic group is not usually considered an ethnic minority in Vietnam because of their high cultural assimilation with the majority ethnic Kinh group, and they are also one of the wealthiest ethnic groups in Vietnam. This approach is also used in earlier studies such as van de Walle and Gunewardena (2001).

- Ethnic minorities have lower market access and poorer returns from markets. Although this varies among ethnic groups, ethnic minorities engage in trading activities less than the Kinh group.
- Ethnic minorities are subject to stereotyping and misconceptions, not just among Kinh households, but even among ethnic minorities themselves, which can considerably hinder participation by ethnic minorities in their own development.

Even though these results are well-illustrated through a mix of research methods including literature reviews, focus group discussions, and household surveys, they may not be nationally representative because the report focuses on three provinces in Vietnam with the highest ethnic minority poverty (World Bank 2009).

This chapter further investigates the welfare of ethnic groups, using several nationally representative surveys. For policies to be efficiently implemented, this chapter aims to identify the areas with the largest disparities between the ethnic groups. This chapter begins by reviewing the demographics of ethnic groups in Vietnam and major government programs for ethnic minority groups. The subsequent sections provide a mostly quantitative analysis of the welfare outcomes between Vietnamese ethnic groups in poverty, education, labor market participation, earnings, child labor, health, nutrition, and social protection.[3] The final section summarizes the main findings and offers policy recommendations.

BACKGROUND ON COUNTRY'S ECONOMIC HISTORY

Since the *doi moi* (renovation) process in 1986, Vietnam's economy has made remarkable progress. Figure 8.1 shows that it took Vietnam just four years after 1986 to catch up with and grow faster than most countries in the world. Between 1986 and 2009, the average per capita growth rate for Vietnam was 5.2 percent, almost double the rate of 2.9 percent for low- and middle-income countries and three times higher than the rate of 1.7 percent for high-income countries.[4] These steady growth rates have considerably increased living standards in Vietnam and have been found to benefit the

---

[3] For a more detailed coverage of these issues (not just for ethnic groups) for Vietnam in the 1990s, see, for example, Glewwe, Agrawal, and Dollar (2004); for the welfare impacts of land reforms, see Ravallion and van de Walle (2008).

[4] Notably, Figure 8.1 shows that even though high-income countries had negative growth rates per capita in 2009 (most likely as a result of the global financial and banking crisis), Vietnam still enjoyed a 4.2 percent growth rate during this year.

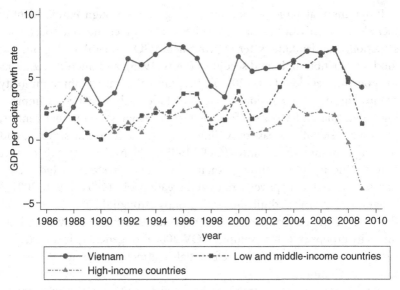

Figure 8.1. GDP per capita growth rate for Vietnam versus other countries, 1986–2007.

poor more in the 1990s (Glewwe and Dang, 2011); still, a question can be raised on whether the benefits are shared equally between ethnic groups.

GOVERNMENT POLICIES AND PROGRAMS FOR ETHNIC MINORITIES

The government of Vietnam (GOV) has paid much attention to the welfare of ethnic minority groups. There is a ministerial-level government body, the Committee for Ethnic Minority and Mountainous Area Affairs (CEMA), which is in charge of management functions for ethnic minorities and mountainous areas. In geographically strategic areas or areas with an ethnic minority population of 5,000 or more, CEMA has its own representative agency down to the district level (GOV 2004a).

Programs that specifically target ethnic minority groups are numerous and cover a wide range of issues including poverty reduction, resettlement and sedentarization, forest land allocation, education, health, and communication. They benefit those minority groups through several channels such as: (1) their ethnic identity, (2) their (usually mountainous or remote) residence areas, (3) their (usually poor) economic status, and (4) general social programs for households with war martyrs, war invalids, or individuals recognized as having contributed to the government.

Programs that target ethnic minority groups through ethnic identity include such activities as cash subsidies on land reclamation, house construction, and drinking water improvement (GOV 2004b), cash grants on food, production tools, and seedlings (GOV 1995), and interest-free loans for poor households (GOV 2007a). Programs that target ethnic minority groups through their residence areas include such activities as improving commune and village infrastructure, developing communal centers, planning residential areas, providing agricultural extension services, and training commune-level cadres (GOV 1998a, 2007b). Programs that target ethnic minority groups through their poor economic status include activities such as reducing poverty rates and creating jobs (GOV 1998b, 2001).[5] Programs that target ethnic minority groups through their contribution to the wars or the government can be provided either especially for ethnic minority groups (see, for example, GOV 2005a) or generally in a variety of legal documents that include preferential-treatment clauses for those with such contribution.

In particular, major programs such as Program 135 (GOV 1998a, 2007b) target all the poor communes in ethnic, mountainous, and remote areas, and laws such as the 2005 Education Law (NA 2005) stipulate the beneficiaries under all four different channels listed earlier. The government of Vietnam also gives preferential treatment such as price and transportation subsidies to businesses that operate in mountainous and ethnic areas (GOV 1998c, 2002). Teachers working in these areas can be entitled to 70 percent supplemental salary increase (GOV 2006a), and government officials assigned to these areas can be promoted one year earlier than generally prescribed (GOV 2006b).

However, concerns have been expressed by both the donor community and the government itself that these numerous programs may be overlapping and may not be very efficiently and adequately supervised in their implementation (Asian Development Bank 2002; GOV 2005b; World Bank 2009). In addition, although these programs clearly contribute to the welfare of ethnic minority groups, to our knowledge, their costs and benefits have not been evaluated.

DATA AND METHODOLOGY

Data for analysis are nationally representative and include two rounds of the Vietnam Living Standards surveys (VLSS) (World Bank 2000, 2001)

---

[5]   A detailed review of these programs is provided by Phuong and Baulch (2007).

and three rounds of the Vietnam Household Living Standards Surveys (VHLSS) (GSO 2001b, 2004, 2006) between 1992 and 2006,[6] as well as the 2002 Vietnam Demographic and Health Survey (VDHS) (CPFC and ORC Macro 2003). However, to keep a reasonable sample size and time span for analysis, the main data are from the 1997–1998 VLSS and 2006 VHLSS. Other sources of data include a smaller but nationally representative survey on test scores[7] and the World Development Indicators Online database (World Bank 2010).

Both descriptive statistics and multivariate regression methods are used. As shown later, ethnic minority groups usually reside in more remote areas. Thus, to reduce the heterogeneity caused by differences in ethnic residence areas, most of the regressions control for this heterogeneity at the commune level[8] either through commune fixed-effects or random-effects models. The choice of fixed-effects or random-effects models is mainly determined by currently available computing software and sample sizes.[9]

For random-effects models, commune-level variables are also controlled for in regressions to further reduce this heterogeneity, and include commune poverty status (i.e., the share of poor households in the commune), commune topography (i.e., whether the commune is in a lowland or midland area versus mountainous area), and the distance from the commune to the nearest town. However, because there are a number of households missing observations for these commune-level variables, the main models for interpretation are the models without these variables and models using these variables mostly serve as robustness checks. For lack of space, the main estimation results using these models are discussed in this chapter, and the full results with regression tables are only provided in the working paper (Dang 2010).

---

[6] In this chapter, sometimes the author's calculations from the 2006 VHLSS are cited in the text and not shown in a table. Such cases are noted by (VHLSS 2006), and full tables are available from the author on request.

[7] This survey collects data on reading and mathematics scores for young students and adults in about 1,350 households across Vietnam, which are a subsample of the 2006 VHLSS. See Dang and Glewwe (2008) for more details on this survey.

[8] In Vietnam, communes are administrative units larger than villages (lowest administrative unit) and smaller than districts. The VLSS and VHLSS collect data from households as well as the communes in which these households reside.

[9] Whereas it is straightforward to compute linear fixed-effects models, it is not always the case with nonlinear fixed-effects models such as probit models with fixed effects (see, for example, StataCorp 2009). Additionally, sample sizes would be reduced in fixed-effects models, because communes with only one ethnic group would be left out.

The following sections offer a quantitative analysis of the welfare for different ethnic groups in Vietnam.

DEMOGRAPHICS

On average, ethnic minority groups have a gender ratio similar to that of ethnic majority groups, but they are younger, likelier to be married, and living in larger households (Table 8.1). Ethnic minority groups live predominantly in rural areas, although more of them were living in urban areas in 2006 compared to 1998. However, in 2006, whereas around 71 percent of ethnic minority groups lived in the mainly mountainous northeast, northwest, and central highlands, approximately 64 percent of the ethnic majority groups lived in the mainly lowland southeast and the Red River and Mekong River deltas. Overall, these mountainous and lowland regions accounted for 21 percent and 58 percent of the total population, respectively (VHLSS 2006).[10]

INCOME AND POVERTY

Income

Ethnic minority groups are overrepresented in the lower tail of the population consumption distribution and underrepresented in the upper tail of the consumption distribution. As much as 72 percent of the population of ethnic minority groups fall into the poorest three consumption deciles, and 88 percent of ethnic minority groups fall in the lower half (50 percent) of the consumption distribution (VHLSS 2006).

Did this situation improve or worsen over time? Figures 8.2 and 8.3 compare the expenditure distributions of ethnic minority groups with those

---

[10] There are currently sixty-four provinces in Vietnam. According to GSO classification (GSO 2007), eight regions house the following cities and provinces: (1) Red River Delta: Ha Noi, Hai Phong, Vinh Phuc, Ha Tay, Bac Ninh, Hai Duong, Hung Yen, Ha Nam, Nam Dinh, Thai Binh, Ninh Binh; (2) North East: Ha Giang, Cao Bang, Lao Cai, Bac Kan, Lang Son, Tuyen Quang, Yen Bai, Thai Nguyen, Phu Tho, Bac Giang, Quang Ninh; (3) North West: Lai Chau, Dien Bien, Son La, Hoa Binh; (4) North Central: Thanh Hoa, Nghe An, Ha Tinh, Quang Binh, Quang Tri, Thua Thien- Hue; (5) South Central Coast: Da Nang, Quang Nam, Quang Ngai, Binh Dinh, Phu Yen, Khanh Hoa; (6) Central Highlands: Kon Tum, Gia Lai, Dak Lak, Dak Nong, Lam Dong; (7) South East: Ho Chi Minh city, Ninh Thuan, Binh Phuoc, Tay Ninh, Binh Duong, Dong Nai, Binh Thuan, Ba Ria- Vung Tau; and (8) Mekong River Delta: Long An, Dong Thap, An Giang, Tien Giang, Vinh Long, Ben Tre, Kien Giang, Can Tho, Hau Giang, Tra Vinh, Soc Trang, Bac Lieu, Ca Mau.

Table 8.1. *Basic demographics, Vietnam 1998–2006 (percent)*

	Ethnic minority		Ethnic majority		Total population	
	1998	2006	1998	2006	1998	2006
Male	49.2	49.7	48.3	48.9	48.5	49.0
Average age	25.2	27.0	28.7	32.1	28.2	31.4
Married (for those aged 15 and over)	63.2	65.0	59.1	60.5	59.7	61.1
Household size	6.1	5.8	5.4	4.7	5.5	4.9
Urban	1.6	7.4	25.9	29.8	22.5	26.7
Households	699	1,384	5,300	7,805	5,999	9,189
N	3,832	7,064	24,791	32,007	28,623	39,071

Sources: VLSS 1998 and VHLSS 2006.

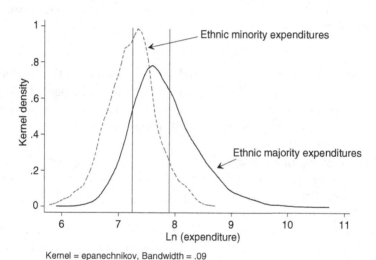

Figure 8.2. Income distribution for ethnic majority and ethnic minority groups, Vietnam, 1998.

of the ethnic majority groups in 1998 and 2006. Over this time span, the consumption distributions for both ethnic minority and majority groups in Vietnam shifted to the right, indicating an overall increase in living standards for all groups. However, a closer visual inspection suggests that the two distributions stand further apart in this same period. Indeed, whereas consumption levels doubled for all ethnic groups from 1998 to 2006, the gap in average consumption levels between the ethnic minority group and the

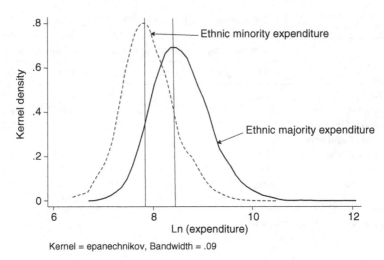

Figure 8.3. Income distribution for ethnic majority and ethnic minority groups, Vietnam, 2006.

ethnic majority group actually widened from D 1,500,000 to D 3,100,000[11] in the same period. Thus, these graphs indicate that although all ethnic groups appear to enjoy similar economic growth rates in Vietnam in recent years, ethnic minority groups are actually falling behind in terms of absolute consumption levels.

In fact, ethnic minority people seem to continue falling behind ethnic majority groups. In the period between 1992 and 1998, Glewwe, Gragnolati, and Zaman (2002) find that ethnic minority people have a lower probability of escaping poverty than ethnic majority people.

The disparities in living standards between ethnic groups are analyzed. This disparity has been decomposed using earlier rounds of the VLSS into differences due to endowments and the returns to these endowments. Van de Walle and Gunewardana (2001) and Baulch et al. (2004, 2007) find that a major share of this gap is due to the returns to endowments for Vietnam in the 1990s. Baulch et al. (2007) also find that ethnic minority groups that assimilated most with the ethnic majority (Kinh) society enjoy improved living standards, whereas the less-assimilated groups have been left behind.[12]

---

[11] The exchange rates in 1998 and 2006 were around US$1 for D 14,000 and D 16,000, respectively (IMF 2006, 2007).

[12] In a similar vein, Nguyen et al. (2007) also find that the gap in living standards between urban and rural areas in Vietnam in 1992–1993 is mostly the result of differences in

Poverty

As a result of the recent economic growth, poverty rates have been steadily decreasing over time in Vietnam. Poverty numbers – both general poverty and extreme (food) poverty – are shown in Table 8.2 for the different ethnic groups and the whole population. (See also Box 1 for an overview of the different poverty lines used in Vietnam.) The general poverty rates have decreased from approximately 58 percent in 1993 to 16 percent in 2006; the corresponding figures in the same period for the extreme poverty rates were 25 percent and 6 percent. Thus, from 1993 to 2006, every year has seen an average reduction rate of 3.2 percent and 1.5 percent, respectively, in general and extreme poverty in Vietnam.

However, not all ethnic groups enjoy the same decreases in poverty rates. Table 8.2 also shows that ethnic minority groups lag behind the ethnic majority groups in their struggle against poverty. Whereas the general poverty rate for the ethnic majority group declined by 71 percent [(54–10)/54 = .71] from 1993 to 2006, the general poverty rate for ethnic minority groups declined by only 42 percent in the same period. Similarly, the extreme poverty rates decreased by 85 percent for the ethnic majority group but decreased by only 48 percent for ethnic minority groups from 1993 to 2006. Consequently, poverty rates for ethnic minority groups over those of ethnic majority groups actually diverged over time, and the ratios of poverty rates for ethnic minority groups over those of the ethnic majority groups are estimated to increase by around three times or more from 1993 to 2006 (Table 8.2, last column).[13]

The determinants of household poverty status are further examined in a multivariate regression framework.[14] Factors that increase the probability that a household is poor include ethnicity, number of young or old household members, and the household's residence area (compared to the

endowments, but the gap in 1997–1998 is mainly caused by differences in the returns to endowments.

[13] During this same period, both the depth and severity of poverty – as measured by the poverty gap index and the Foster-Greer-Thorbecke (FGT) index, respectively – are reduced at a faster rate for the ethnic majority group than those of ethnic minority groups (70 percent versus 40 percent for both indexes). In 2006, ethnic minority groups' poverty gap index and the FGT index were seven to eight times higher than those for the ethnic majority groups (VHLSS 2006).

[14] The estimation model is a commune random-effects probit model. Two regressions are run, one controlling for ethnicity, household demographics, head of household's work sectors, regional, and urban dummy variables, and the other adding commune topography and the distance from the commune to the nearest town.

Table 8.2. *Poverty headcount, 1993–2006 (percent)*

Income group	Ethnic minority			Ethnic majority			Total population			Ratio of poverty rates for all
	Rural	Urban	All	Rural	Urban	All	Rural	Urban	All	
1993										
Not Poor	12.9	51.5	13.6	37.6	75.6	46.2	33.6	75.1	41.9	0.3
Poor	87.7	48.5	86.4	62.4	24.4	53.9	66.4	24.9	58.1	1.6
Extreme Poor	53.3	12.9	52.0	24.5	7.8	20.8	29.1	7.9	24.9	2.5
1998										
Not Poor	23.8	91.8	24.8	61.2	90.8	68.9	54.5	90.8	62.6	0.4
Poor	76.2	8.1*	75.2	38.8	9.2	31.1	45.5	9.2	37.4	2.4
Extreme Poor	42.4	0.0*	41.8	13.4	2.5	10.6	18.6	2.5	15.0	4.0
2002										
Not Poor	27.9	65.9	30.7	70.9	94.5	72.9	64.4	93.3	71.1	0.4
Poor	72.1	34.1	69.3	29.1	5.5	23.1	35.6	6.7	28.9	3.0
Extreme Poor	43.2	21.3	41.6	8.3	1.1	6.5	13.6	1.9	10.9	6.4
2004										
Not Poor	37.3	70.5	39.3	82.1	97.2	86.5	75.0	96.4	80.5	0.5
Poor	62.7	29.5	60.7	17.9	2.8	13.5	25.0	3.6	19.5	4.5
Extreme Poor	35.5	14.3	34.2	4.8	0.4	3.5	9.7	0.8	7.4	9.8
2006										
Not Poor	46.0	68.9	47.7	86.6	97.2	89.7	79.6	96.1	84.0	0.5
Poor	54.0	31.1	52.3	13.5	2.8	10.3	20.4	3.9	16.0	5.1
Extreme Poor	30.0	19.3	29.2	4.3	0.5	3.2	8.7	1.2	6.7	9.2

Notes: * fewer than twenty observations.
Source: VLSSs 1993, 1998 and VHLSSs 2002, 2004, 2006.

Box 1. *Which Poverty Lines Are Used In Vietnam?*

Correct measurement of poverty is an important issue faced by almost all countries in the world and can also be a source of much debate. Although having high-quality household surveys that are nationally representative, Vietnam is no exception.

There can be at least three main approaches to measuring poverty in Vietnam. The first approach is the calorie-intake approach, which considers the poverty line as the cost of a food and nonfood consumption basket allowing a healthy lifestyle, with the food component providing a daily intake of 2,100 calories per person per day (World Bank 2007). Thus individuals are considered poor if their daily per capita expenditure cannot afford this basket, and extremely poor (or food poor) if their daily per capita expenditure is not enough to purchase this amount of calories were they to spend all their expenditure on food. Under this approach, the yearly food poverty lines and poverty lines for Vietnam were approximately D 1, 915,000 and D 2,560,000 in 2006 (Glewwe 2008). This approach usually relies on household surveys with expenditure data and is also the approach to calculate poverty rates used in this chapter.

The second approach, used by the Ministry of Labour, Invalids, and Social Affairs (MOLISA), also sets specific poverty lines, by which individuals were considered poor in 2006 if their annual incomes were below D 3,120,000 for urban areas and D 2,400,000 for rural areas (GOV 2005c). However, in practice, local MOLISA officials determine which households fall under these poverty lines through a mix of methods including village discussion, surveys, and local officials' personal knowledge. Thus these poverty lines can vary across administrative units and involve perhaps the most subjective judgment. For example, local officials can set a higher poverty line if they have resources available to help larger numbers of people in their community (World Bank 2006). Under this approach, assuming that the number of households identified as poor in the VHLSS 2006 was nationally representative, the poverty rate was 15.4 percent for Vietnam as a whole, 32 perecent for ethnic minority groups, and 10.9 percent for ethnic majority groups.

The third approach is to use an international poverty line measured in Purchasing Power Parity (PPP) dollars that can be converted to the local currency through comparable international price surveys. This international poverty line is currently proposed to be $1.25 a day or $456.3 a year in PPP dollars (Ravallion, Chen, and Sangraula 2009), which is equivalent to D 2,700,950 (using the individual consumption expenditure by household PPP/local currency exchange rate of $5,919.89 [World Bank 2008]). Under this approach, it can be calculated from the VHLSS 2006 that the poverty rate was 18.3 percent for Vietnam as a whole, 55.5 percent for ethnic minority groups, and 12.5 percent for ethnic majority groups. Whereas the first approach is found to correctly measure poverty only at the national level because of the usual limited sample sizes in household surveys, the second approach perhaps works best at the commune level because of its subjective judgment component (Nguyen and Rama 2007). The third approach appears to work best for cross-country comparison. MOLISA is currently doing research on how to combine the first and second approaches to better measure poverty in Vietnam.

southeast region – the reference region); factors that decrease the probability that a household is poor include the number of working-age members, the head of household's age and years of schooling completed, and whether the household lives in an urban area. When commune-level characteristics including the commune topography and the distance to the nearest town are controlled for, households living in mountainous and more isolated communes are found likelier to be poor. However, as discussed earlier, we focus on interpreting the results from models without these commune-level variables because there are quite a number of missing observations for these variables.

Specifically, it can be calculated that households belonging to ethnic minority groups are 14 percentage points more likely to be poor than households in ethnic majority groups, controlling for other factors. The usual positive relationship of working-age members on household living standards is clearly seen: Whereas one more member in the age group zero to six (or sixty and older) increases the probability of a household being poor by 6 percentage points (or 2 percentage points), one more member in the age group of twenty-five to fifty-nine reduces this probability by 1 percentage point.

Households living in urban areas are 4 percentage points less likely to be poor than those living in rural areas. Households living in all regions except for the Mekong Delta are more likely to fall into poverty status than households living in the southeast region – where Ho Chi Minh city, the

Table 8.3. *Calculated probabilities of household being poor, 2006 (percent)*

	Ethnic minority	Ethnic majority	Total population
Head of Household's Years of Schooling			
0	76.8	24.4	52.2
6	44.8	9.3	15.7
12	10.3	1.6	2.2
16	1.6*	0.1	0.2
Head of household's work sector			
Agriculture only	52.8	8.8	18.6
Service only	15.1	1.2	1.7

Notes: Computed from Table 8.6.
* fewer than twenty observations.
Source: VLSS 2006.

economic capital of the country, is placed. Compared to the southeast region, households living in the northeast, northwest, and north-central regions are 12 percentage points to 27 percentage points more likely to be poor. Notably, ethnic minority groups are heavily concentrated in these three regions: These regions house 64 percent of the ethnic minority population, but they make up only around 29 percent of the total population (VHLSS 2006).

The role of the head of household is important in poverty reduction. One additional year of schooling for the head would decrease the probability of households being poor by 2 percentage points. Compared to heads of household working in more than one sector, those who work in the agricultural sector are only 2 percentage points less likely to live in a poor household, and those working in the service sector are only 5 percentage points less likely to be poor. However, to the extent that heads of household can choose their occupation, their occupation should be considered as a correlate rather than a determinant of household poverty status. This shows that poverty can be reduced through restructuring the economy perhaps toward service-oriented industries.

The probabilities of the household falling into poverty given the head of household's characteristics are calculated in Table 8.3. A household where the head has zero years of schooling has a 52 percent chance of being poor, but has only a 2 percent chance of being poor if the head of household has twelve years of schooling, and almost 0 percent chance of being poor if the head of household has sixteen years of schooling (equivalent to a university degree). A household where the head works in agriculture has a 19 percent chance of being poor, but has only a 2 percent chance of being poor if the head works in services. However, given the same head of household's years of schooling or work sector, ethnic minority households are much more likely to fall into poverty than ethnic majority households. The probabilities range from 9 percentage points to 52 percentage points higher for heads of household with twelve and zero years of schooling, respectively.

EMPLOYMENT

Together with the strong performance in recent years, Vietnam's economy has undergone a restructuring, as shown in Table 8.4. This includes the downsizing of the agricultural sector and the increase in the wage work sector: The share of employment in agriculture decreased from 44 percent in 1996 to 34 percent in 2006, whereas the share of wage work increased from 12 percent to 23 percent in this same period. Whereas there was a decrease in the combined agriculture and service sector, there was a slight increase in the service sector and the combined wage-work-and-service sector from 1998 to 2006. At the same time, the share of self-employed workers decreased from 81 percent to 67 percent, and the share of the private sector increased almost three times from 7 percent to 20 percent. There can be several reasons for this restructuring of the economy. The first reason is that the fast economic growth rate for Vietnam in this period has helped transform the economy (Figure 8.1). The second reason can be due to trade liberalization. Edmonds and Pavnick (2006) shows that trade liberalization helped reallocate labor between the households and the market in the period between 1992 and 1998. It is possible that the same mechanism was at work in the subsequent period.

Although there was a similar change in the occupation redistribution for ethnic minority groups – in fact, ethnic minority groups have higher growth rates in the wage work sector and private sector – these groups still appear to lag behind ethnic majority groups in all modern sectors. In 2006, whereas agriculture accounted for only 30 percent of ethnic majority employment, it made up 55 percent of ethnic minority employment. The wage work sector for ethnic minority people is around 8 percent, less than one-third of that of ethnic majority people, and the service sector is around 2 percent, less than one-seventh of that of ethnic majority groups. A disproportionate share of ethnic minority people are self-employed (85 percent) and this share is around 20 percent higher than that of ethnic majority people. Similarly, the shares of ethnic minority people working in the private sector or the public sector are less than half of those of ethnic majority people.

Table 8.4. *Employment sector for people age fifteen and over, 1998–2006 (percent)*

	Ethnic minority		Ethnic majority		All	
	1998	2006	1998	2006	1998	2006
Work sector						
Wage work only	3.0	7.6	13.2	25.3	11.8	22.9
Agriculture only	67.3	55.2	40.2	30.2	44.0	33.6
Services only	1.4	2.3	13.8	15.2	12.1	13.4
Wage work and Agriculture	18.4	25.0	15.0	16.6	15.5	17.8
Wage work and Services	0.6	0.3*	1.6	1.7	1.4	1.5
Agriculture and Services	8.3	8.3	14.3	10.0	13.5	9.7
Wage work, Agriculture, and Services	1.1	1.3	1.8	1.0	1.7	1.0
Total	100	100	100	100	100	100
Work type						
Self-employed	92.3	84.7	79.4	63.8	81.2	66.6
Work for other households or in private sector	2.3	10.0	8.2	21.8	7.4	20.2
State-owned or collective sector	2.2	5.0	8.9	12.2	8.0	11.2
Foreign-invested sector	0.3	0.3*	1.3	2.2	1.1	1.9
Other sector	2.9	n.a.	2.0	n.a.	2.1	n.a.
Total	100	100	100	100	100	100
Number of observations	2,063		13,663		15,726	

Note: * fewer than twenty observations.
Sources: VLSS 1998 and VHLSS 2006.

The determinants of earnings are also examined using multivariate regression analysis.[15] Controlling for other factors, the average ethnic minority worker earns 15 percent less than the average ethnic majority worker, whereas the average female worker earns 21 percent less than the average male worker. (One more year of schooling will bring a 4 percent increase in earnings; the corresponding figure for one more year of experience is 3 percent.) Workers employed in the private sector, public sectors, or foreign-invested sector earn from 108 percent to 134 percent more than workers employed in the agricultural sector. Whereas the rate of return to education for ethnic majority workers is around 2 percent higher than ethnic minority

---

[15] The estimation model is a commune fixed-effects linear model. Regressions are run for the population, ethnic minority group, ethnic majority group, and separately for men and women in each ethnic group. All regressions control for years of schooling, work experience, number of hours worked in the past twelve months, work sector, and marital status.

workers, their rate of return to the number of hours worked is around 6 percent less than ethnic minority workers. However, given that ethnic majority people have on average 2.5 more years of schooling than ethnic minority people (as shown later in Table 8.7), the former can suggest either lower quality of education or less access to better employment or more discrimination toward ethnic minority workers in the market or any combination of these factors.[16] Perhaps the latter can be partly explained by the law of diminishing returns, because ethnic minority people work two fewer hours per week than ethnic majority people (VHLSS 2006).

In fact, the earnings differential between the ethnic minority group and majority groups can be decomposed into two parts, one due to the differential in endowments and the other due to the differential in returns to endowments or wage structure. The latter part is also known to be caused by unobserved factors such as ethnic differentials in the quality of schooling, individual ability, culture, or labor market discrimination. These differentials are considered in 2006 and in 1998 as well in Table 8.5 using three methods of decomposition: Oaxaca-Blinder, Cotton, and Oaxaca and Ransom.[17]

According to Table 8.5, differences in endowments explain from 66 percent to 74 percent of the earnings differential between the ethnic groups, whereas differences in the wage structure explain from 26 percent to 34 percent of the earnings differential. The range of the earnings differential due to endowments decreased (or the range of the earnings differentials due to the wage structure increased) from 1998, reflecting a wider gap in the unobserved factors between ethnic groups. One such increasing factor can be increasing rates of return to education for ethnic majority groups as shown in Table 8.6.

---

[16] These results are qualitatively similar in the basic Mincerian earnings function where log of earnings is regressed on only ethnicity, gender, years of schooling, and work experience.

[17] The Oaxaca-Blinder decomposition method (Blinder 1973; Oaxaca 1973) breaks down the ethnic differentials assuming either the ethnic minority or majority wage structure will prevail in the absence of discrimination. Thus, depending on which assumption is used, this method will provide a range of estimates. The Cotton decomposition method (1988) uses the employed population shares of different ethnic groups to weight the estimated coefficients to obtain the nondiscriminatory wage structure. Thus, by construction, the wage structure using the Cotton method will be somewhere between the range of estimates using the Oaxaca-Blinder method (and is closer to the ethnic majority wage structure the larger the employed population share the ethnic majority group have). The Oaxaca and Ransom (1989, 1994) method calculates the nondiscriminatory wage structure by combining the Cotton wage structure with a common wage structure derived by an OLS regression using a pooled sample of both ethnic minority and majority groups.

Table 8.5. *Earnings differentials for people age fifteen and over, Vietnam, 1998–2006*

	Percentage of earnings differential due to differences in			
	Endowments		Wage structure	
	1998	2006	1998	2006
At ethnic minority mean	35.6	66.3	64.4	33.7
At ethnic majority mean	94.6	69.9	5.4	30.1
Cotton	86.2	69.4	13.8	30.6
Oaxaca-Ransom	90.9	73.6	9.1	26.4

Sources: VLSS 1998 and VHLSS 2006.

Table 8.6. *Contribution of independent variables to earnings differential between ethnic minority and ethnic majority for people age fifteen and over, Vietnam, 2006*

	Decomposition		Contribution as	
	Endowments	Pay structure	Endowments	Pay structure
Female	−0.008	−0.030	−0.9	−3.4
Married	−0.001	0.101	−0.1	11.5
Years of schooling	0.125	0.116	14.3	13.2
Experience	−0.049	0.098	−5.6	11.2
Experience-squared	0.038	−0.110	4.3	−12.6
Log (hours worked)	0.096	−0.381	11.0	−43.5
Work for other households or in private sector	0.225	0.030	25.7	3.4
State-owned or collective sector	0.128	−0.032	14.6	−3.7
Foreign-invested sector	0.054	−0.002	6.2	−0.2
Constant		0.478		54.6
Subtotal	0.608	0.268	69.4	30.6
Total	0.876		100	

Sources: VHLSS 2006.

The contribution of each of the explanatory variables in the multivariate regression analysis to the earnings differential between ethnic groups is further considered in Table 8.6, with absolute amounts shown in the first two columns and relative amounts (percentage) shown in the last two columns; a positive coefficient indicates advantages in favor of ethnic majority groups and a negative coefficient indicates advantages in favor of ethnic minority groups.

Table 8.6 shows that the higher share of ethnic majority people working in the private sector can explain up to 26 percent of the ethnic earnings differential. The higher mean years of schooling completed by ethnic majority groups can explain 14 percent of the ethnic earnings differential. Ethnic majority people also have higher returns to education as discussed earlier, and these higher returns alone account for 13 percent of the ethnic earnings differential. However, the returns to the hours worked are higher for ethnic minority people than ethnic majority people, thus helping reduce the ethnic earnings differential by 44 percent. It should also be noted that the constant term (the last column in Table 8.6) explains the most – as much as 55 percent – of the earnings differential due to different returns to endowments. This implies that regardless of all factors considered, such as gender, education, working experience, or work sectors, there are unobserved factors in favor of ethnic majority earnings. As discussed earlier in Table 8.6, such factors can include labor market discrimination against ethnic minority groups or differentials in the quality of schooling.

CHILD LABOR

For children ages six to eighteen, approximately 14 percent of ethnic minority children go to school and work at the same time; the corresponding figure for ethnic majority children is more than three times lower, at 4 percent (VHLSS 2006). The disparity in child labor between ethnic groups is illustrated in Figure 8.4, which plots the incidence of child labor for a wider age range of six to twenty-five. A wedge can be seen between ethnic minority children and ethnic majority children, with the incidence of child labor for the former always higher than that for the latter. This wedge is largest at more than 25 percent around age fifteen – the legal working age in Vietnam.

The probability of child work is further considered using multivariate regression analysis,[18] which shows that, controlling for other factors, ethnic

[18] The estimation model is a sequential random-effects probit model, which considers three stages of child work for children ages six to eighteen: (1) whether a child works; (2) conditional on working, whether a child does not go to school; and (3) conditional on working and not going to school, whether a child receives wages. The regressions control for ethnicity, household demographics, household living standards (as measured by consumption expenditure), regional and urban dummy variables, and commune-level characteristics including the share of poor households in the commune, commune topography, and the distance from the commune to the nearest town.

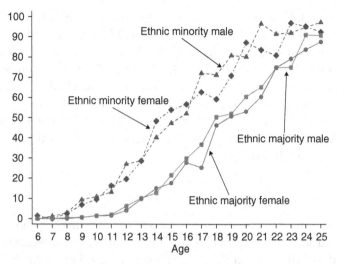

Figure 8.4. Incidence of child labor for age 6–25, Vietnam, 2006.

minority children are 3 percentage points more likely to work than ethnic majority children. Among the working children, ethnic minority children are 16 percentage points more likely to work and go to school at the same time; among the working children that do not go to school, ethnic minority children are 25 percentage points less likely to work for wages. However, the fact that ethnic minority children are more likely to work at home rather than for wages does not necessarily reflect better welfare levels. On the contrary, it can also indicate that the labor market is not well developed and wage work is not readily accessible for ethnic minority children (even if they wanted to work for wages).

Not surprisingly, both the head of household's educational level and household consumption level are negatively correlated with the probability that children work or work for wages. Larger household sizes are correlated with lower probabilities that children can spend all their time attending school.[19] In models that control for commune characteristics, the share of poor households in the commune also are positively correlated with children working; a 10 percent increase in this share is correlated with a 1 percent increase in the probability that children work.

---

[19] Macroeconomic factors such as the economy being more open to international trade can also help reduce child labor. Using data from the VLSS 1992–1993 and 1997–1998, Edmonds and Pavcnik (2005) find that trade liberalization, in particular higher rice prices, are associated with declines in child labor for households that are net rice producers.

324   *Dang*

Clearly, child work should be reduced as much as possible. Child work can have undesirable effects on children's well-being in several ways such as loss of schooling and reduced health. In an earlier study for Vietnam that uses the VLSS 1992–1993 and 1997–1998, O'Donnell, Rosati, and van Doorslaer (2005) find that work undertaken during childhood can have lasting negative consequences on children's health up to five years later. Using the same survey data, Beegle, Dehejia, and Gatti (2009) find that child labor has significant negative impacts on school participation and educational attainment.[20]

EDUCATION

Illiteracy rates have been steadily decreasing in Vietnam, although at a faster rate for ethnic majority groups. From 1993 to 2006, illiteracy rates for individuals ten years and older were reduced from 8.4 percent to 5 percent for ethnic majority groups and from 30 percent to 20 percent for ethnic minority groups (VHLSS 1993 and 2006). It is worrisome that the illiteracy rate for ethnic minority groups in Vietnam in 2006 was much higher than that for ethnic majority groups in 1993. However, the gap in literacy rates between ethnic groups seems to be narrowing over time.

The general educational achievement for different ethnic groups is shown in Table 8.7. Ethnic minority groups can almost catch up with ethnic majority groups in the share of people aged fifteen and older who are still in school. However, these numbers can be misleading for several reasons. First, ethnic minority people can start school later than their ethnic majority peers. Second, ethnic minority groups can repeat or drop out of classes more often. Third, the quality of education may not be the same between the different ethnic groups. These issues will be discussed in more detail later in the chapter.

For people who are out of school, Table 8.7 shows the highest educational achievement that they obtain. In general, educational achievement for ethnic majority groups is similar to that of the total population and appears to follow a roughly bell-shaped distribution. In this distribution, the share of people with a completed primary degree is highest at 26 percent, followed by the share of people with a completed lower-secondary degree (25 percent),

[20] Beegle, Dehejia, and Gatti (2009) also find that child work is associated with an increased likelihood of wage work. However the authors also acknowledged that they could not estimate the impact of child labor on future earnings in the absence of more precise wage and labor productivity data.

Table 8.7. *Educational achievement, people aged fifteen and over,*
Vietnam, 2006 (percent)

	Ethnic minority			Ethnic majority			All Population
	Male	Female	All	Male	Female	All	
Still in school (%)	12.2	10.9	11.5	13.7	11.3	12.5	12.4
If not still in school, highest education achievement							
None	15.3	31.2	23.5	3.0	8.0	5.6	7.8
Incomplete Primary	25.2	22.2	23.7	12.9	20.1	16.6	17.5
Complete Primary	29.1	22.2	25.5	26.3	25.7	26.0	26.0
Complete Lower-Secondary	18.2	15.5	16.8	27.5	24.5	25.9	24.8
Complete Upper-Secondary	8.1	7.2	7.6	17.3	13.9	15.5	14.5
University	1.2	0.6*	0.9	5.9	4.7	5.3	4.7
Vocational Education	2.9	1.1	1.9	7,2	3.2	5.1	4.7

Note: * denotes number of observations fewer than twenty.
Source: VHLSS 2006.

followed by the share of people with incomplete primary education (20 percent), and the share of people with a completed upper-secondary degree (14 percent). The share of people with a tertiary degree is somewhat similar to the share of people with a vocational education, at 5 percent.

However, the distribution of educational achievement for ethnic minority groups is strongly skewed (right-skewed) toward higher school levels. In this distribution, the share of people with a completed primary degree is highest at 26 percent, followed by the share of people with an incomplete primary education (25 percent), the share of people with no education (24 percent), and the share of people with a completed lower-secondary degree (17 percent). Around 8 percent of ethnic minority people have a completed upper-secondary degree, and less than 1 percent of them have a tertiary degree; these numbers are, respectively, approximately one-half and one-fifth of the corresponding ones for the ethnic majority groups.

The pattern of lower educational achievement for ethnic minority groups is confirmed in Figure 8.5, which looks at the mean years of schooling attained for different birth cohorts from 1945 to 1985. (The year 1985 is chosen as the last year to allow for the fact that the majority of people may not finish schooling until twenty years old or so.) There is a consistent gap of around three years of schooling between the ethnic groups across the different birth cohorts. It should be noted that this gap widens around the period between 1966 and 1975, which coincides with the Vietnam War. However, the gap seems to be narrow for recent birth cohorts. In particular, women in

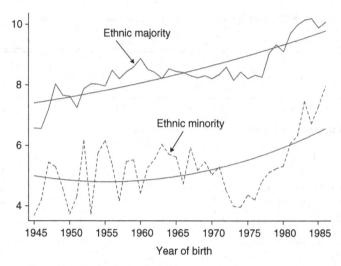

Figure 8.5. Years of schooling, by year of birth, Vietnam, 2006.

birth cohorts further away from the war have higher educational achievement. Further analysis shows that the differences range from half a year to more than one year of schooling for women in different birth cohorts, when controlling for other factors (Dang and Patrinos 2008).

Age-grade distortion, which is defined as the percentage of students who are more than one year behind the age appropriate for their grade, is considered in Table 8.8. For example, the age-grade distortion for grade 3 in Vietnam is 19 percent, indicating that 19 percent of students studying in grade 3 are older than age eight, which is the appropriate age for this grade level. Age-grade distortion is a particularly serious problem for ethnic minority people, with a rate higher than 30 percent at all primary grades except for grade 1. Table 8.8 shows that there is a large disparity in the age-grade distortion rates between ethnic minority groups and ethnic majority groups. This disparity ranges from approximately 3 percent for the first grade to more than 20 percent for the second grades and higher.

While age-grade distortion is a useful indicator of educational achievement, its large scope of definition can include several different problems such as late enrollment, class repetition, and school discontinuation (that is, dropping out of school and then reenrolling). Thus the factors determining school enrolment for young people ages seven to fourteen are considered in more detail using multivariate regression analysis.[21]

[21] The estimation model is a commune random-effects probit model. The regressions control for ethnicity, individual characteristics (i.e., age, gender), household demographics, head

Table 8.8. *Age-grade distortion, Vietnam, 2006*

	Ethnic minority	Ethnic majority	All Population
First grade	4.48	1.22	1.72
Second grade	31.64	8.74	13.09
Third grade	36.30	15.24	19.30
Fourth grade	36.11	12.33	16.42
Fifth grade	34.57	14.30	18.11
Number of observations	1,091	3,500	4,591

Source: VHLSS 2006.

Factors that increase the probability of school enrollment are an individual's age (although age-squared has a negative relation), the head of household's education, the household expenditure level, and residence areas. The positive association with age may be the result of late enrollment for some people, as can be seen in the high percentage of age-grade distortion in Table 8.8. Controlling for other factors, one more year of schooling for the household increases the probability of school enrollment by 0.2 percentage points, and people living in all geographic regions except for the Mekong Delta are 1–2 percentage points more likely to enroll in school than people living in the southeast region. Keeping other factors fixed at the mean, ethnic minority people are 0.6 percentage points less likely to enroll in school than ethnic majority people.

The finding that household expenditure level increases the probability of school enrollment concurs with an earlier study for Vietnam by Glewwe and Jacoby (2004). Using panel data from the VLSS 1992–1993 and 1997–1998, Glewwe and Jacoby (2004) find that child enrollment increased faster in households that gained greater increases in wealth, and grade attainment increased by 0.25 for these households.

The probabilities of being enrolled in school for those aged seven to fourteen are calculated in Table 8.9. Keeping other characteristics fixed at the means, the probability that a child age seven to fourteen is enrolled in school is 88 percent in a household where the head of household has zero

of household's years of schooling, household living standards (as measured by consumption expenditure), regional and urban dummy variables, and commune-level characteristics including the share of poor households in the commune, commune topography, and the distance from the commune to the nearest town. Estimation results are rather similar whether or not commune characteristics are controlled for. In fact, the coefficients on the numbers of household members and commune characteristics are statistically insignificant, suggesting that these variables can be left out.

Table 8.9. *Predicted probability of being enrolled in school,*
seven- to fourteen-year-olds, Vietnam, 2006 (percent)

	Ethnic minority	Ethnic majority	All
Head of Household's Years of Schooling			
0	86.7	89.5	87.9
6	96.6	97.4	97.2
12	99.4	99.6	99.6
16	100*	100	100
Extremely poor	87.7	92.0	89.0
Poor	90.3	94.0	92.0
Not poor	95.9	97.9	97.6

* fewer than twenty observations.
Source: VLSS 2006.

years of schooling. This probability increases to 97 percent or 100 percent
if the head of household has six or twelve years of schooling, respectively.
At the same time, the probability that a child is enrolled in school is 92 percent for a poor household and 98 percent for a nonpoor household. Thus,
the association with a head of household with twelve years of schooling on
school enrollment rates is very similar to (although slightly higher than)
that of a nonpoor household. Depending on the relevant cost-benefit scenarios, this would clearly suggest alternatives for improving school enrollment to policy makers.

Quality of Education

The determinants of reading and mathematics standardized test scores are
also examined using data from a nationally representative survey.[22] Factors
that significantly affect test scores include an individual's years of schooling, age (and age-squared), ethnicity, household consumption, and head of
household's education.

[22] The estimation model is a commune random-effects linear model. The regressions control
for ethnicity, individual characteristics (i.e., age and gender), head of household's years of
schooling, household living standards (as measured by consumption expenditure), and an
urban dummy variable. The control variables are limited because of the small sample sizes.
When commune characteristics are included, the coefficients on the ethnic variables are
still negative but are significant only at the 10% level for reading scores and insignificant
for math scores. However, estimation samples are reduced by around 30% in these models,
and the commune variables are either statistically insignificant or marginally significant
at the 10% level. See Dang and Glewwe (2008) for more details on this survey and the
test scores.

Controlling for other characteristics, whereas one more year of education for the head of household can raise test scores by less than 0.1 standard deviation, one more year of schooling for the individual can raise test scores from 0.1 to 0.3 standard deviations. A 270 percent increase in per capita expenditure can increase test scores by 0.2 to 0.3 standard deviations. Ethnic minority individuals score from 0.2 to 0.5 standard deviations lower than ethnic majority individuals. This suggests that even if ethnic minority individuals have the same years of schooling as their ethnic majority peers, the quality of their education is lower. This concurs with an earlier World Bank study on grade 5 students in Vietnam, which finds that students who always spoke Vietnamese outside of school or belonged to the ethnic majority Kinh group were likely to have higher test scores than students who never speak Vietnamese outside of school or belong to the ethnic minority groups (World Bank 2004).

There can be several reasons for lower education quality for ethnic minority groups. First, as discussed earlier, ethnic minority groups have a lower consumption level than ethnic majority groups, thus ethnic minority students may not have the same learning materials or opportunities (for example, books or computers) as ethnic majority students. Second, ethnic minority students are more likely to drop out of school and have higher age-grade distortion rates (Table 8.8). Third, the general educational achievement levels for ethnic minority groups are lower than those of ethnic majority groups, implying that ethnic minority parents may not be able to help with their children's studies as much as ethnic majority parents do. Fourth, ethnic minority students have to travel longer distances to get to school, which can reduce their time and energy for studies.

An important difference in learning opportunities between ethnic groups is extra classes or private tutoring, which is a popular phenomenon in Vietnam and can have a strong impact on student learning outcomes (Dang 2007, 2008, forthcoming). It can be calculated from the 2006 VHLSS that ethnic majority students are from 33 percent to 43 percent more likely to attend extra classes than ethnic minority students.

HEALTH

There is a large improvement in health for the total population from 1998 to 2006, with the share of the total population who are sick or injured in the four weeks preceding the survey decreasing from 41 percent in 1998 to approximately 23 percent in 2006 (VHLSS 2006). However, Table 8.10 shows that both the infant mortality rate and the under-five mortality

Table 8.10. *Child mortality rates, Vietnam, 2002 (per 1,000 live births)*

	Ethnic minority	Ethnic majority	Urban	Rural	All population
Infant mortality rate	30.4	22.5	13.0	26.2	23.9
	(5.7)	(2.3)	(3.7)	(2.4)	(2.1)
Under-five mortality rate	41.1	27.7	15.6	33.0	30.0
	(6.8)	(2.5)	(4.2)	(2.8)	(2.4)

Note: Standard errors in parentheses.
Source: VDHS 2002.

Table 8.11. *Vaccination rates for children ages 12–23 months, Vietnam 2002 (percent)*

	Ethnic minority	Ethnic majority	Urban	Rural	All population
BCG	82.3	95.8	99.1	92.1	93.4
DPT (three doses)	48.3	77.7	89.7	68.5	72.4
Polio (three doses)	58.3	79.9	94.8	71.8	76.1
Measles	68.1	86.5	94.3	80.7	83.2
All (BCG + DPT + Polio + Measle	38.1	73.4	87.1	62.5	67.1
Number of observations	71	396	99	368	467

Note: Standard errors in parentheses.
Source: VDHS 2002.

rate for ethnic minority groups are higher than those for ethnic majority groups. The infant mortality rate for ethnic minority groups is 30 per 1,000 live births, whereas the corresponding figure for ethnic majority groups is 23 per 1,000 live births (but note the large standard error of the estimate for ethnic minority groups). The under-five mortality rate for ethnic minority groups is much higher, at 41 per 1,000 live births, than the corresponding figure for ethnic majority groups at 28 per 1,000 live births. These differences suggest that ethnic minority groups have yet to enjoy the same health levels that ethnic majority groups have. However, these differences also appear to be strongly correlated with (the remoteness of) the residence area for ethnic minority groups. Table 8.10 also shows that the mortality rates in rural areas are more than twice higher than in urban areas in Vietnam.

The vaccination rates for children aged twelve to twenty-three months are shown in Table 8.11. A child is considered to be fully vaccinated if the child has received a Bacillus Calmette-Guerin (BCG) vaccination against

Table 8.12. *Medical insurance, 1998–2006 (percent)*

	1998			2006		
	Ethnic minority	Ethnic majority	All population	Ethnic minority	Ethnic majority	All population
Have medical insurance	8.18	16.98	15.73	33.45	41.74	40.61
Have free medical insurance				44.36	7.66	12.63
Have no medical insurance	91.82	83.02	84.27	22.19	50.60	46.75
Total	100	100	100	100	100	100
Number of observations	3,817	24,687	28,504	7,064	32,007	39,071

Source: VDHS 2002.

tuberculosis, three doses of diphtheria, pertussis, and tetanus (DPT) vaccine, at least three doses of polio vaccine, and one dose of measles vaccine (WHO 2005.) The age range is limited to children aged twelve to twenty-three months because a child should have received these vaccinations at these ages. Children in Vietnam are most likely to be vaccinated against BCG (93 percent), followed by measles (83 percent), polio (76 percent), and DPT (72 percent). The same trend holds for children belonging to different ethnic groups and living in urban and rural areas (but the vaccination rates for measles and polio are almost equal for urban areas). The overall vaccination rate for Vietnam stands at 67 percent; however, the rate for ethnic minority children is much lower at 38 percent, almost half that of 73 percent for ethnic majority children.

Most of this gap in health care, however, can be attributed to factors other than ethnicity, such as differences in living standards or residence areas. It was estimated that, controlling for other factors, poor ethnic minority children aged eleven to twenty-three months living in rural areas are 15 percent less likely to be fully vaccinated than their ethnic majority peers (Thang et al. 2007).

Table 8.12 shows that health care appears to have improved for ethnic minority groups in recent years. From 1998 to 2006, health care has improved for the whole population, but at a faster rate for ethnic minority groups compared to ethnic majority groups. The share of the total population without any medical insurance decreased by almost half, from 86 percent in 1998 to 46 percent in 2006, but the share of ethnic minority groups fell more than fourfold, from 91 percent to 21 percent, in this same period. In particular, in 2006, the share of ethnic minority groups with free medical insurance was 44 percent, more than five times higher than that of ethnic majority groups. (Unfortunately, there were no disaggregated data on free medical insurance in the 1998 VLSS, thus we cannot examine any difference in this category between ethnic groups that year).

This is perhaps due to a number of preferential government policies during this period, targeted at ethnic minority groups, notably among them Program 139 established in 2002. After two years of implementation, 4.15 million poor people were issued free health care certificates under this program. As discussed in the preceding section, because ethnic minority groups represent a larger share of the poor in Vietnam, they understandably account for a proportionately larger share of people who are granted free health care certificates. However, having a free health care certificate does not necessarily mean better-quality health care for ethnic minority groups. It has been noted that the treatments readily accessible to poor ethnic minority people at the commune health centers are deficient and constrained by expenditure ceilings. Furthermore, as shown later in Table 8.15, ethnic minority groups live in communities with much less access to health facilities than ethnic majority groups.

In absolute terms, ethnic minority groups also have lower health care expenditure. An average ethnic minority outpatient spends only D 493,000, and an average ethnic minority inpatient spends only D 3,038,000, which represent 18 percent and 34 percent of the corresponding expenditures for the average ethnic majority patients (VHLSS 2006).

Is it possible that this lower health care expenditure is a result of a higher proportion of health insurance usage among ethnic minority people? The answer appears to be no. A recent study using earlier rounds of the VLSS shows that health insurance can reduce health expenditure by as much as 35 percent (Sepehri, Sarma, and Simpson 2006), but even if this is taken into account, ethnic minority people still have much lower health expenditure than ethnic majority people.

The number of visits to a hospital is further investigated using multivariate regression analysis.[23] Controlling for age, gender, log of per capita

---

[23] The estimation model is a commune fixed-effects Poisson model. The regressions control for ethnicity, individual characteristics (i.e., age, gender, years of schooling completed, and marital status), and household living standards (as measured by consumption expenditure).

Table 8.13. *Knowledge about AIDS for ever-married women ages 15–49, Vietnam, 2002 (percent)*

	Ethnic minority	Ethnic majority	Urban	Rural	All pop.	No. of observations
Ever heard about AIDS	85.5	97.1	98.8	94.6	95.4	5660
Perception about AIDS	62.5	80.2	84.5	76.2	77.8	5397
Know ways to avoid AIDS	85.7	93.6	93.8	92.2	92.5	5397

Note: Standard errors in parentheses.
Source: VDHS 2002.

expenditure, marital status, and years of schooling, ethnic minority people are 16 percent (100 – 84) less likely to visit a hospital when they are ill, compared to ethnic majority people. However, there is no statistical difference between the incidences of inpatient treatment for the different ethnic groups. Not surprisingly, richer and more educated households are found, all else being equal, to visit hospital more often, both as outpatients and inpatients. This result is consistent with the findings from a recent study on parents' seeking care for their children's illness: Although self-prescribed care is the most common response of ethnic majority and minority parents to childhood illness, ethnic minority parents are less likely to seek professional health care for their sick children compared to ethnic majority parents (Teerawichitchainan and Phillips 2008).

As shown in Table 8.13, knowledge about AIDS is rather good in Vietnam for women who are ever-married and in the age group of fifteen to forty-nine, with 95 percent of these women having heard about AIDS at some point in their lives. However, out of those who ever heard about AIDS, only 78 percent have the correct perception about AIDS (that is, a healthy person can contract AIDS), and 93 percent know of a way to avoid AIDS.

There is a difference in knowledge about AIDS for different ethnic groups. Compared to women belonging to ethnic majority groups, women belonging to ethnic minority groups are 12 percent less likely to have ever heard about AIDS, 18 percent less likely to have the correct perception about AIDS, and 8 percent less likely to know ways to avoid AIDS. This difference is much larger than the urban-rural divide in knowledge about AIDS, which only ranges from 2 percent to 8 percent. This implies that there is still room for improvement in promoting AIDS awareness among ethnic minority women.[24]

HOUSEHOLD/ COMMUNITY SERVICES
AND SOCIAL PROTECTION

Overall, ethnic minority people have higher access to social programs such as preferential credit, free health care, tuition exemption or reduction, and agricultural promotion activities (VHLSS 2006). However, they appear to have lower access to community services.

Utility access and household assets are considered for ethnic groups and urban-rural areas in Table 8.14. For all utilities including potable water, electricity, sanitary conditions, Internet connection, housing, and garbage collection, ethnic minority people have lower access than ethnic majority people. The same situation is true for people living in rural areas compared to people living in urban areas. The gap in utility access can range from 4 percent to as much as 50 percent in favor of ethnic majority groups, and from 5 percent to 39 percent in favor of people in urban areas. For example, only 57 percent of ethnic minority people have potable water, whereas 90 percent of ethnic majority people have potable water. The corresponding numbers for people living in rural and urban areas are 82 percent and 96 percent.

A similar pattern can be seen with household assets including radio, television set, video recorder/stereo system, refrigerator, washing machine, motorbike, bicycle, air conditioner, desk telephone, mobile telephone, and computer, where ethnic minority people have less than ethnic majority people and people living in rural areas have less than people living in urban areas. Again, the gap can range from 4 percent to 30 percent in favor of ethnic majority people and from 5 percent to 46 percent in favor of people living in urban areas. The two exceptions are home ownership and bicycle ownership. Ethnic minority people are 2 percent more likely to own a home and people in rural areas are 3 percent more likely to own a home than people in urban areas. People in rural areas are 9 percent more likely to own a bicycle than people living in urban areas.

---

[24] More generally, ethnic minority women can be particularly at risk with regards to nutrition and health functioning. Using data from the earlier VLSS, Molini, Nube, and van den Boom (2010) find that between 1993 and 1998, the adults' BMI (Body Mass Index) growth for ethnic minority women is lower than that for ethnic minority men, and even lower than that for the ethnic majority groups.

Table 8.14. *Utility access and household assets, Vietnam, 2006 (percent)*

	Ethnic minority	Ethnic majority	All	Rural	Urban
Utility access					
Safe drinking water	57.0	90.3	85.8	82.0	96.3
Electricity	80.6	98.1	95.7	94.5	99.1
Sanitation facility	15.1	64.9	58.2	47.7	86.9
Internet connection*	16.6	20.5	20.5	13.4	23.0
Temporary housing	29.6	13.4	15.6	18.7	6.9
Assets					
Home ownership	98.5	96.0	96.3	97.2	93.8
Radio	12.0	15.8	15.3	14.0	18.6
TV	63.4	89.8	86.2	82.9	95.2
Video recorder/Stereo system	32.8	53.8	50.9	45.0	67.1
Refrigerator	4.7	26.6	23.7	12.2	55.0
Washing machine	0.4	10.8	9.4	2.2	28.9
Motorbike	47.2	67.2	64.5	57.7	83.0
Bicycle	54.6	72.2	69.9	72.2	63.4
Air-conditioner	0.0	3.4	2.9	0.4	9.7
Desk telephone	6.2	36.0	31.9	19.6	65.7
Mobile telephone	2.6	21.6	19.0	10.3	43.0
Computer	0.6	9.7	8.4	3.0	23.3
Number of households	1,384	7,805	9,189	6,882	2,307

Note: Internet connection is for households with computers only.
Source: VHLSS 2006.

However, these exceptions do not necessarily imply that ethnic minority people or people in rural areas are better off in these respects. Table 8.14 also shows that ethnic minority people and people in rural areas are more likely to have housing of lower quality, and are less likely to own a motorbike, which is fast becoming a popular means of transport in Vietnam. Table 8.14 also shows that ethnic minority groups are the most disadvantaged in the country. Except for home ownership, ethnic minority people have lower utility access and less household assets than people in rural areas.[25]

[25] In Table 8.14, Internet connection rates are only calculated for households with computers. Thus, among households with computers, Internet connection rate for ethnic minority groups appears to be close to that for ethnic majority groups; however, for the whole population, Internet connection rate is around twenty times lower for ethnic minority groups.

Table 8.15. *Availability/distance to community facilities, Vietnam, 2006 (km)*

	Ethnic minority	Mixed ethnic groups	Ethnic majority	All
Proportion of communes that have				
Cultural house	29.6	30.5	40.9	35.2
Radio station	30.6	74.9	92.5	80.8
Distance to school				
Primary school	0.8	0.9	0.7	0.8
Lower-secondary school	2.2	1.9	1.2	1.6
Upper-secondary school	14.8	6.6	4.5	5.6
Distance to health facilities				
Commune health center	0.0	0.1	0.0	0.1
Polyclinic	15.5	10.9	7.6	9.6
District hospital	21.6	13.4	9.4	11.9
Provincial hospital	86.0	46.3	29.9	40.6
State pharmacy	17.4	9.3	6.6	8.4
Private pharmacy	22.0	3.6	1.9	3.4
Distance to other community amenities				
Paved road	1.2	1.0	0.2	0.6
Public transportation	8.4	3.1	1.9	2.8
Agricultural extension center	20.1	12.1	8.5	10.9
Daily market	18.1	3.8	1.9	3.5
Periodic market	10.1	6.1	3.0	4.6
Wholesale market	37.0	17.1	9.9	14.3
Commune's people committee	3.1	1.9	1.1	1.6
Post office	8.7	2.6	1.6	2.4
Bank/bank branch	18.4	8.7	5.3	7.6
Town	23.0	12.9	9.0	11.5
Provincial/city capital	88.0	48.1	31.3	42.0
Major cities	385.6	188.1	135.2	170.0

Note: Major cities include Hanoi, Hai Phong, Da Nang, Can Tho, and Ho-Chiminh City.
Source: VHLSS 2006.

Access to community facilities for communes with only ethnic minority groups, mixed ethnic groups, and only ethnic majority are depicted in
Table 8.15. Generally, ethnic minority communes are least served by the
available community facilities, followed by mixed-ethnicity communes
and ethnic majority communes. For example, 31 percent of ethnic minority communes have a radio station, whereas the corresponding figure is 75
percent for mixed-ethnicity communes and 93 percent for ethnic majority communes. Whereas the provincial hospital is 86 kilometers away for
ethnic minority communes, it is much closer at 46 kilometers for mixed-ethnicity communes, and around two-third nearer at 30 kilometers for ethnic

majority communes. The average distance to a paved road is around 1 kilometer for ethnic minority communes and mixed-ethnicity communes – a figure five to six times larger than that for ethnic majority communes. However, there are also some exceptions; for example, the distances to primary schools or commune health centers are almost equal for the different communes.

CONCLUSIONS

Despite much progress in living standards, health, and education in recent years, ethnic minority groups still lag behind ethnic majority groups in Vietnam. In 2006, the general poverty rate for ethnic minority groups was 52 percent, more than five times that of ethnic majority groups; the extreme poverty rates for ethnic minority groups was 29 percent, more than nine times that of ethnic majority groups. Ethnic minority people have lower-quality health care than ethnic majority groups, and they are 16 percent less likely to visit a hospital when they are ill. Ethnic minority infant and under-five mortality rates are higher than those of ethnic majority groups, and ethnic minority women are less like to know or have the correct perception about AIDS. The illiteracy rates (for individuals aged ten years and older) for ethnic minority groups are 20 percent, four times higher than that of ethnic majority people; the mean years of schooling attained is 5.6 for ethnic minority groups, 2.5 years less than that of ethnic majority groups.

Even though there has been a restructuring of the Vietnamese economy in recent years, more than half (55 percent) of ethnic minority groups still work in agriculture; the corresponding number for ethnic majority groups is less than one-third (30 percent). About two-thirds of the earnings differentials between ethnic groups can be attributed to differences in endowments, and one-third due to differences in the returns on endowments. Ethnic minority children are more likely to drop out of school and work than ethnic majority children.

Despite various government assistance programs specially targeted at ethnic minority groups, ethnic minority people still suffer from lower utility access and household assets than ethnic majority people. Ethnic minority groups' utility access and household assets are also lower than those of people living in rural areas, placing them as the most disadvantaged groups in the country.

Policies to level out the disparities between ethnic minority groups can be roughly divided into either a short-term approach or a longer-term approach. Short-term policies arguably would take less effort to implement and can be targeted at urgent issues, whereas long-term policies may take longer and require more resources to come into effect. Clearly, the criteria to categorize policies are highly context-specific and can be subjective, but we believe that this division may help focus ideas and stimulate more discussion.

In that respect, short-term policies can include such measures as:

1. Building more roads for ethnic minority communes. Table 8.15 shows that ethnic minority groups are much farther away from commune facilities than ethnic majority groups. Thus, one way to reduce this distance and to immediately improve the welfare of ethnic minority groups is to provide them with easier access to the economic, political, and cultural centers such as schools, hospitals, markets, post offices, and town centers. One recent study also shows that building roads has significant and robust impacts on primary school completion rates in Vietnam, and poorer communes tend to benefit more (Mu and van de Walle 2007). However, it also argued that building roads is not always the best solution because it can bring negative impacts on the environment as well as ethnic minority communities' lifestyle. Obviously, there is some trade-off that needs to be carefully considered with this policy.

2. Increasing knowledge about AIDS among ethnic minority women and increasing rates of vaccination among ethnic minority children. Perhaps few will disagree that vaccination for children is a rather cost-effective measure against disease. In addition, because the vaccination rate (for all four diseases) for ethnic minority children is so low, their welfare can be significantly improved with more vaccination.

However, improving the well-being for ethnic minority groups would require more and sustained efforts in the long term. Several main policies can be considered, such as:

1. Emphasizing the importance of improving educational outcomes for ethnic minority groups in all development plans or government campaigns. This chapter has shown that educational achievements play an important part in reducing poverty, increasing cognitive skills and earnings, increasing the use of contraceptive methods among married women, and reducing child labor. Furthermore, education also has strong intergenerational impacts on increasing educational

accomplishments for future generations. There seems to be no over-emphasizing the role of education in improving welfare and reducing the disparities between ethnic groups, and this is true not just for Vietnam but for other countries as well (see other chapters in this book, as well as Hall and Patrinos 2006).

2. Diversifying employment opportunities for ethnic minority groups. Even though their occupation is becoming more diversified, ethnic minority groups are still mostly occupied in agriculture. It might not be easy to map out good strategies to change the occupation for these groups, but it is important that the government include the economic development of ethnic minority groups among the top priorities in development plans. For example, tax incentives or preferential loans can be given to enterprises employing more ethnic minority people. Or special job training centers can be established in ethnic minority communes.

3. Applying lessons with social safety net or transfer programs from other countries to Vietnam. For example, welfare-improving programs specially targeted at poor and disadvantaged groups, such as conditional cash transfer programs, have been extensively used in a number of countries (see, for example, Das, Do, and Ozler 2005.) Vietnam can perhaps experiment with such programs to increase school attendance rates and reduce child labor for disadvantaged groups, including – but not limited to – ethnic minority groups.

4. Using more quantitative methods to better evaluate the different government programs for ethnic minority groups. The government can make use of technical assistance from international organizations and/or involve local researchers more in designing these programs.

5. Better monitoring the welfare for ethnic minority groups through implementing, perhaps special, nationally representative surveys that can provide detailed analysis for each ethnic group.

ACKNOWLEDGMENTS

I would like to thank Harry Patrinos, Gillette Hall, Carrie Turk, Van-Can Thai, and participants at a workshop at Georgetown University for insightful comments on earlier drafts. I would like to thank Vietnam's General Statistical Office and the World Bank office in Vietnam for permission to use the data. I would also like to thank Cong-Minh Nguyen for capable research assistance.

References

Asian Development Bank. (2002). *Indigenous Peoples/Ethnic Minorities and Poverty Reduction Vietnam*. Manila: Philippines. Environment and Social Safeguard Division, Regional and Sustainable Development Department.

Baulch, Bob, Truong Thi Kim Chuyen, Dominique Haughton, and Jonathan Haughton (2004). "Ethnic Minority Development in Vietnam: A Socioeconomic Perspective." In Glewwe, Paul, Nisha Agrawal, and David Dollar (Eds.) *Economic Growth, Poverty, and Household Welfare in Vietnam*. Washington, DC: World Bank.

——— (2007). "Ethnic Minority Development in Vietnam". *Journal of Development Studies* 43(7): 1151–1176.

Beegle, Kathleen, Rajeev Dehejia, and Roberta Gatti. (2009). "Why Should We Care about Child Labor? The Education, Labor Market, and Health Consequences of Child Labor." *Journal of Human Resources*, 44(4): 871–889.

Blinder (1973). "Wage Discrimination: Reduced Form and Structural Estimates." *Journal of Human Resources*, 8(4): 436–465.

Committee for Population, Family and Children (Vietnam) and ORC Macro (CPFC and ORC Macro). (2003). "Vietnam Demographic and Health Survey 2002." Calverton, MD: Committee for Population, Family and Children (Vietnam) and ORC Macro.

Cotton, Jeremiah. (1988). "On the Decomposition of Wage Differentials." *Review of Economics and Statistics*, 70(2): 236–243.

Dang, Hai-Anh. (2007). "The Determinants and Impact of Private Tutoring Classes in Vietnam." *Economics of Education Review*, 26(6): 684–699.

——— (2008). *Private Tutoring in Vietnam: An Investigation of Its Causes and Impacts with Policy Implications*. Amsterdam: VDM Verlag Dr. Mueller Publishing House.

——— (2010). "Vietnam: A Widening Poverty Gap for Ethnic Minorities." Working paper version.

——— (forthcoming). "Private Tutoring: A Review of Current and Little Explored Issues in the Context of Vietnam." In Janice Aurini, Julian Dierkes, and Scott Davis (Eds.) *Out of the Shadows: What Is Driving the International Rise of Supplementary Education?* Berlin: Springer Press.

Dang, Hai-Anh and Paul Glewwe. (2008). "An Analysis of Learning Outcomes for Vietnam." Working paper.

Dang, Hai-Anh and Harry Patrinos. (2008). "The Impacts of War on Gender Differences in Educational Achievements and Labor Market Outcomes: The Case of Vietnam." Paper presented at the IZA/ World Bank Conference on Employment and Development, Rabat, Morocco.

Dang, Nghiem Van, Chu Thai Son, and Le Hung (2000). *Ethnic Minorities in Vietnam*. Hanoi: The Gioi Publishers.

Das, Jishnu, Quy-Toan Do, and Berk Ozler. (2005). "Reassessing Conditional Cash Transfer Programs." *World Bank Research Observer*, 20: 57–80.

Edmonds, Eric V. and Nina Pavcnik. (2005). "The Effect of Trade Liberalization on Child Labor." *Journal of International Economics*, 65: 401–419.

——— (2006). "Trade Liberalization and the Allocation of Labor between Households and Markets in a Poor Country." *Journal of International Economics*, 69: 272–295.

Evans, Grant (1992). "Internal Colonialism in the Central Highlands of Vietnam." *Sojourn*, 7(2): 274–304.

General Statistical Office (GSO). (2001a). *Population and Housing Census Vietnam 1999*. Hanoi: Statistical Publishing House.

(2001b). "So Tay Huong Dan Nghiep Vu Dieu Tra Muc Song Ho Gia Dinh 2002" (Interview Guidebook for the Vietnam Household Living Standards Survey 2002). Hanoi: Statistical Publishing House.

(2004). "Khao Sat Muc Song Ho Gia Dinh 2004: So Tay Huong Dan Nghiep Vu" (Interview Guidebook for the Vietnam Household Living Standards Survey 2004). Hanoi: Statistical Publishing House.

(2006). "So Tay Khao Sat Muc Song Ho Gia Dinh 2006" (Interview Guidebook for the Vietnam Household Living Standards Survey 2006). Hanoi: Statistical Publishing House.

(2007). *Statistical Yearbook of Vietnam 2006*. Hanoi: Statistical Publishing House.

Glewwe, Paul. (2008). "Mission Report for Trip to Vietnam October 2007." Report submitted to the World Bank.

Glewwe, Paul, Nisha Agrawal, and David Dollar (Eds.). (2004). *Economic Growth, Poverty, and Household Welfare in Vietnam*. Washington, DC: World Bank.

Glewwe, Paul and Hai-Anh Dang. (2011). "Was Vietnam's Economic Growth in the 1990's Pro-Poor? An Analysis of Panel Data from Vietnam." *Economic Development and Cultural Change*, 59(3): 583–608.

Glewwe, Paul, Michele Gragnolati, and Hassan Zaman. (2002). "Who Gained from Vietnam's Boom in the 1990s?" *Economic Development and Cultural Change*, 50:773–792.

Glewwe, Paul and Hanan Jacoby. (2004). "Economic Growth and the Demand for Education: Is There a Wealth Effect?" *Journal of Development Economics*, 74(1): 33–51.

Government of Vietnam (GOV). (1995). "Quyết định số 862/QĐ-TTg ngày 30/12/1995". (Decision 862/QĐ-TTg on 30/12/1995).

(1998a). "Quyết Định Số 135/1998/QĐ-TTg ngày 31/7/1998". (Decision 135/1998/QĐ-TTg on 31/7/1998).

(1998b). "Quyết Định Số 133/1998/QĐ-TTg ngày 23–7-1998". (Decision 133/1998/QĐ-TTg on 23-7-1998).

(1998c). Nghị Định số 20/1998/NĐ-CP ngày 31/3/1998. (Decree 20/1998/NĐ-CP on 31/3/1998).

(1999). "Quyết Định Số 188/1999 /QĐ-TTg Ngày 17–9-1999". (Decision 188/1999 / QĐ-TTg on 17–09-1999).

(2001). "Quyết Định Số: 143/2001/QĐ-TTg Ngày 27–9-2001". (Decision 143/2001/QĐ-TTg on 27-9-2001).

(2002). Nghị Định số 02/2002/NĐ-CP ngày 3/1/2002. (Decree 02/2002/NĐ-CP on 3/1/2002).

(2004a). Nghị Định số 53/2004/NĐ-CP ngày 18/2/2004. (Decree 53/2004/NĐ-CP on 18/2/2004).

(2004b). Quyết định số 134/2004/ QĐ-TTg ngày 20/7/2004. (Decision 134/2004/CP on 20/7/2004).

(2005a). "Quyết Định Số 92/2005/QĐ-TTg ngày 29/4/2005". (Decision 92/2005/QĐ-TTg on 29/4/2005).

(2005b). "Quyết Định Số 1277/QĐ-TTg ngày 07/12/2005". (Decision 1277/QĐ-TTg on 07/12/2005).

(2005c). "Quyết Định Số 170/2005/QĐ-TTg ngày 8/7/2005". (Decision 170/2005/ QĐ-TTg on 8/7/2005).

(2006a). Nghị Định số 61/2006/NĐ-CP ngày 20/6/2006. (Decree 61/2006/NĐ-CP on 20/6/2006).

(2006b). "Quyết Định Số 56/2006/QĐ-TTg ngày 13/3/2006". (Decision 56/2006/QĐ-TTg on 13/3/2006).

(2007a). "Quyết Định Số 32/2007/QĐ-TTg ngày 05/3/2007". (Decision 32/2007/QĐ-TTg on 05/3/2007).

(2007b). "Quyết Định Số 113/2007/QĐ-TTg ngày 20/7/2007". (Decision 113/2007/ QĐ-TTg on 20/7/2007).

Hall, Gillette and Harry Patrinos (Eds.). (2006). *Indigenous Peoples, Poverty and Human Development in Latin America*. London: Palgrave Macmillan.

International Monetary Fund (IMF). (2006 and 2007). *International Financial Statistics*. Washington, DC: International Monetary Fund.

Jamieson, Neil L., Le Trong Cuc, and Terry A. Rambo (1998). "The Development Crisis in Vietnam's Mountains." *Special report #6*. Honolulu: East-West Center.

Molini, Vasco, Maarten Nube, and Bart van den Boom. (2010). "Adult BMI as a Health and Nutritional Inequality Measure: Applications at Macro and Micro Levels." *World Development*, 38(7): 1012–1023.

Mu, Ren and Dominique van de Walle. (2007). "Rural Roads and Poor Area Development in Vietnam." World Bank Policy Research Working Paper No. 4340.

National Assembly, Government of Vietnam (NA). (2005). "Luat Giao Duc" (Law on Education).

Nguyen, Binh T., James W. Albretch, Susan B. Vroman, and M. Daniel Westbrook. (2007). "A Quantile Regression Decomposition of Urban–Rural Inequality in Vietnam." *Journal of Development Economics*, 83: 466–490.

Nguyen, Nga Nguyet and Martin Rama. (2007). "A Comparison of Quantitative and Qualitative Poverty Targeting Methods in Vietnam." Q-Squared Working Paper No. 32.

Nguyen, Thi Thu Phuong and Bob Baulch. (2007). "A Review of Ethnic Minority Policies and Programs in Vietnam." Working paper.

O'Donnell, Owen, Furio C. Rosati, and Eddy van Doorslaer. (2005). "Health Effects of Child Work: Evidence from Rural Vietnam." *Journal of Population Economics*, 18:437–467.

Oaxaca, Ronald. (1973). "Male-Female Wage Differentials in Urban Labour Markets." *International Economic Review*, 14(1): 693–709.

Oaxaca, Ronald L. and Michael R. Ransom. (1989). "Overpaid Men and Underpaid Women: A Tale of the Gender Specific Wage Effects of Labor Market Discrimination." Paper presented at the International Economic Association World Congress, Athens, August 28–September 1.

(1994). "On Discrimination and the Decomposition of Wage Differentials." *Journal of Econometrics*, 61: 5–21.

Ravallion, Martin, Shaohua Chen, and Prem Sangraula. (2009). "Dollar a Day Revisited." *World Bank Economic Review*, 23(2): 163–184.

Ravallion, Martin and Dominique van de Walle. (2008). *Land in Transition: Reform and Poverty in Vietnam*. New York: Palgrave Macmillan and World Bank.

Sepehri, Ardeshir, Sisira Sarmab, and Wayne Simpson. (2006). "Does Non-Profit Health Insurance Reduce Financial Burden? Evidence from the Vietnam Living Standards Survey Panel." *Health Economics*, 15: 603–616.

StataCorp. (2009). *Stata: Release 11. Statistical Software*. College Station, TX: StataCorp LP.

Swinkels, Rob and Carolyn Turk. (2006). "Explaining Ethnic Minority Poverty in Vietnam: A Summary of Recent Trends and Current Challenges." Draft Background paper for CEM/MPI meeting on Ethnic Minority Poverty, September 28. Hanoi: World Bank.

Teerawichitchainan, Bussarawan and James F. Phillips. (2008). "Ethnic Differentials in Parental Health Seeking for Childhood Illness in Vietnam." *Social Science and Medicine*, 66: 1118–1130.

Thang, Nguyen Minh, Indu Bhushan, Erik Bloom, and Sekhar Bonu. (2007). "Child Immunization in Vietnam: Situation and Barriers to Coverage." *Journal of Biosocial Science*, 39: 41–58.

Tran, Linh T. and Pierre G. Walter. (2010). "National Unity and Ethnic Identity in a Vietnamese University." *Comparative Education Review*, 54(4): 483–511.

Tran, Ngoc Them. (2001). *"Tim ve Ban Sac Van Hoa Viet Nam" (Discovering the Identity of Vietnamese Culture.)* Ho Chi Minh City: Ho Chi Minh City Publishing House.

United Nations Development Group. (2008). "United Nations Development Group Guidelines on Indigenous Peoples' Issues." Accessed November 2009 at http://www2.ohchr.org/english/issues/indigenous/docs/guidelines.pdf

van de Walle, Dominique and Dileni Gunewardena (2001). "Sources of Ethnic Inequality in Vietnam." *Journal of Development Economics*, 65: 177–207.

World Bank. (1999). "Vietnam Development Report 2000: Attacking Poverty." Poverty Reduction and Economic Management Unit, East Asia and Pacific Region, Washington, DC.

    (2000). "Viet Nam Living Standards Survey (VNLSS), 1992–93. Basic Information." Poverty and Human Resources Division, Washington, DC.

    (2001). "Viet Nam Living Standards Survey (VLSS), 1997–98. Basic Information." Poverty and Human Resources Division, Washington, DC.

    (2004). "Vietnam: Reading and Mathematics Assessment Study. Volumes 1, 2 and 3." Human Development Sector Reports.

    (2006). "Vietnam Development Report 2007: Aiming High." Joint Donor Report to the Vietnam Consultative Group Meeting, Hanoi, December 14–15.

    (2007). "Vietnam Development Report 2008: Social Protection." Joint Donor Report to the Vietnam Consultative Group Meeting, Hanoi, December 6–7.

    (2008). "Global Purchasing Power Parities and Real Expenditures: 2005 International Comparison Program." Washington, DC.

    (2009). "Country Social Analysis: Ethnicity and Development in Vietnam. Volumes 1 and 2." Social Development Unit, East Asia and Pacific Region, Washington, DC.

    (2010). World Development Indicators Online.

World Health Organization (WHO). (2005). "Users' Guide on How to Use and Adapt an Excel Workbook for Conducting Immunization Coverage Cluster Survey, Based on a Standard Template." Geneva: Switzerland.

9

Latin America

Gillette H. Hall and Harry Anthony Patrinos

INTRODUCTION

In Latin America – where indigenous peoples comprise some 10 percent of the population – despite decades of attention to the issue, political openings, and constitutional changes, and so on, real progress in economic terms is absent. In 1994, the first regional assessment of living standards among indigenous peoples (Psacharopoulos and Patrinos 1994) found systematic evidence of socioeconomic conditions far worse than those of the population on average. More than ten years later, a follow-up study (Hall and Patrinos 2006) found that even though programs have been launched to improve access to health care and education, indigenous peoples still consistently account for the highest and "stickiest" poverty rates in the region.

INDIGENOUS POPULATIONS IN LATIN AMERICA

The history of Latin America is interwoven with that of the region's indigenous peoples. Indigenous inhabitants – estimated to have numbered at least 40 million prior to the arrival of European colonizers – were members of highly developed civilizations with vast cities and trade networks spanning the region (Mann 2006). Colonization quickly decimated these cultures via the combined processes of disease and economic displacement. Those remaining were engaged in slave-like relationships in the new economy, or escaped to remote mountain habitats. Five hundred years on, the existence of so many different indigenous groups in the region – with well more than 100 living native languages and cultures – is owing at least in part to the "triumph" of self-imposed geographic and economic isolation over the inevitable march of progress. Yet for many indigenous peoples across the continent this is a hollow achievement that has allowed them to survive but not to thrive. Recent evidence for the five countries with the largest indigenous populations – Bolivia, Ecuador, Guatemala, Mexico, and Peru – finds that most live in materially impoverished conditions, with poverty, education, and health outcomes far worse than their nonindigenous counterparts (Hall and Patrinos 2006).

Historically, indigenous peoples in Latin America were most commonly identified according to language spoken; early census data for Mexico and Peru dating to the 1800s uses this metric. Yet, over the past two decades, as a slow progression toward greater recognition of indigenous rights has occurred across the region, so has a shift toward self-identification as the prevalent means of identifying members of indigenous groups (Hall and Patrinos 2006). In some cases, this new form of identification has caused measurable shifts in the estimated number of indigenous peoples. In Peru, for example, when language is used as the key identifier, approximately one-quarter of the population is considered indigenous. However, self-identification yields a number closer to half of the total population (Trivelli 2006). In Guatemala, on the other hand, self-identification produced lower numbers for the estimated indigenous population during the war, but after the Peace Accords in 1996, the number of people willing to self-identify increased (Layton and Patrinos 2006).

Estimates of the region's indigenous population vary depending on method and source, but are in the range of 20 to 30 million. Thus, they represent a relatively small share – less than 10 percent – of the total global indigenous population. Yet, perhaps in part because in many countries the relative size of the population is large (close to half by some measures in Guatemala and Peru, and more than half in Bolivia), they are a relatively powerful force in national politics and a well-recognized population both within and outside the region.

Internationally, Latin America's indigenous peoples burst on the scene in 1994, as news spread across the globe that a small group of armed indigenous rebels had taken control of San Cristobal de las Casas in the heart of deeply impoverished Southern Mexico on New Year's Day. Their purpose – to protest the introduction of the North American Free Trade Agreement – became symbolic of the plight of indigenous and other groups worldwide seen as victims of the march of progress and globalization. Since that time, Latin America's indigenous peoples have gained ever-increasing political power across the region. The Zapatista movement has become a force to be contended with in Mexican politics; indigenous movements toppled presidencies in Ecuador and Bolivia in the late 1990s; and several countries across the region, including Peru and Bolivia, have elected indigenous presidents. Recent analysis of

Table 9.1. *Average annual per capita growth rates in Latin America by decade, 1980–2009*

Years	Bolivia	Chile	Ecuador	Guatemala	Mexico	Peru	Latin America
1980–1989	–2.6	2.7	–0.4	–1.4	0.1	–2.0	–0.2
1990–1999	1.7	4.7	–0.1	1.7	1.7	1.4	1.3
2000–2009	1.7	2.6	3.4	1.0	0.8	3.8	1.9

Source: World Development Indicators, World Bank.

evidence of indigenous poverty outcomes through the mid-2000s suggests, however, that increased political muscle has not translated into significant economic or social gain, at least not yet (Hall and Patrinos 2006).

GROWTH PERFORMANCE AND INCOME
DISTRIBUTION IN LATIN AMERICA

In general, Latin America's growth performance has been weak over the past three decades. The debt crisis triggered by Mexico's default on its international debt in 1982 heralded the end of what had been a golden age of development. Growth rates ground to a halt across the region as the cracks in import-substitution policies became apparent. The heavy public subsidies this strategy required could no longer be financed by international borrowing, and debt service owed skyrocketed with rising international interest rates. The toll paid has been enormous. In most cases, average annual per capita growth rates were negative in the 1980s and have remained below 2 percent since. A singular exception is Chile, which under quickly embraced export-led growth by the mid-1980s and since then has, on average, outperformed every other economy in the region (Table 9.1). In recent years, the region has experienced an economic resurgence, with many economies experiencing steady growth rates since the mid-2000s, although the recent global financial crisis and consequent slump in demand for the region's exports has dampened this recovery. Peru's growth performance has been exceptional during this period. Since 2005, the country has consistently posted annual growth rates of more than 6 percent (peaking at 9.8 percent in 2008); as the fastest-growing economy in the Americas (World Development Indicators), it has yielded an average annual per capita growth rate of 3.8 percent for the decade of the 2000s (Table 9.1).

Income distribution in Latin America is widely held as being the most unequal in the world (Deininger 1996). Contributing factors appear to be the

Table 9.2. *Inequality (Gini coefficient) in Latin America by decade, 1980–2009*

Years	Bolivia	Chile	Ecuador	Guatemala	Mexico	Peru	Latin America
1980–1989	n/a	56	50	59	46	46	50
1990–1999	58	56	54	56	54	46	49
2000–2009	58	53	58	55	49	52	52

Note: Where the World Development Indicators database provides a Gini coefficient for more than one year during a given decade, the table shows the average Gini coefficient for that country during that decade.
Source: Individual country scores from World Development Indicators, World Bank. Latin America median 1980–1989 and 1990–1999 from Morley (2001); 2000–2009 from Lopez and Perry (2008).

highly unequal distribution of education, land, and the growth of the labor force, which together depress earnings for unskilled labor (Morley 2001). The Gini coefficient is the most common measure of inequality, taking a value between 0 (perfect equality) and 1 (perfect inequality). Worldwide, in the 1990s, the median Gini coefficient ranged from less than 30 in Eastern Europe to near 50 in Latin America (Morley 2001). Inequality in the region has been persistently high – dipping just slightly between the 1980s and 1990s but on the rise again in the 2000s (Table 9.2). Among the six countries considered in this chapter, Bolivia – with the largest indigenous population as share of its total – also has consistently the highest inequality, with a Gini coefficient of 58. Chile and Guatemala also have high rates, but inequality has been declining over the past three decades; in Ecuador and Peru, it is on the rise (Table 9.2). Overall, the region's inequality problem is evident in the countries studied here.

PUBLIC POLICY FOR POVERTY REDUCTION AND INDIGENOUS POPULATIONS

The countries with the largest share of indigenous peoples in their populations have experienced significant downturns in their economies, and only some have managed to improve over time. A summary of their achievements over the last couple of decades suggests some interesting developments.

Bolivia

As the political landscape has shifted dramatically in Bolivia, so has the thrust of public policy. The country's Nueva Politica Economica of the

1980s represented one of the most aggressive structural adjustment programs ever implemented, embracing rapid deregulation, trade liberalization, and privatization of public entities (Klasen et al.2004; Spatz 2006). The
results were disappointing, however, and Bolivia registered one of the worst
growth performances in the region, an average of −2.7 per year during
the 1980s (Table 9.1). A second reform wave in the 1990s led by President
Gonzalo Sanchez de Losada largely failed to deliver palpable benefits to the
poor, comprised of the majority indigenous population, who led a coalition
toppling the Losada government in 2003 (Hall and Patrinos 2006). A series
of interim governments culminated in the eventual election of the country's
first indigenous president, Evo Morales, in 2005 and again in 2009.

In parallel, the focus of public policy has shifted to nationalization of
major industries such as oil, mines, and public subsidies for basic items
such as food and gasoline, along with an explicit effort to strengthen indigenous peoples' rights via constitutional change. Following a 2009 national
referendum, a new constitution was signed into law recognizing Bolivia as
a pluri-national state according indigenous peoples the right to representation (reserved seats in congress and on the constitutional court), territory,
language, and freedom of religion and allowing them to practice traditional
forms of community justice (Miller-Llana 2009; Hasan 2010). It is too early
to tell whether any of these reforms will bear fruit. Public subsidies and
price controls will be difficult to sustain; the new constitution has been recognized on the one hand as a landmark achievement for indigenous rights
(Miller-Llana 2009) but criticized on the other hand for weakening property rights, containing vague wording, and curtailing human rights in the
embrace of community justice (Romero 2008; The Economist 2009).

Chile

Chile is widely considered to have the highest-quality public policies in all
of Latin America and among the best in the world (Kharas et al. 2008). An
early reformer, by the late 1970s, Chile had opened its economy to trade
and curtailed inflation by rationalizing public expenditures and securing
the independence of the Central Bank. These and other reforms allowed it
to weather the debt crisis with relative ease. Chile emerged as one of the few
Latin American countries to produce positive growth during the 1980s, and
led the region's growth charts through the 1990s (Table 9.1). Social policy
advances were also considerable, modernizing pension, health, and education systems and extending "universal benefits" throughout the urban-
industrial core of the country. The combined impact of these economic and

social reforms made Chile a virtual island of stability and prosperity in a region otherwise plagued by social turmoil and at best stop-start growth performances.

The 2000s may have revealed some cracks in the model, however. Chile's per capita growth rates fell to an average of 2.6 percent from 2000 to 2010 (Table 9.1) – still strong but no longer the regional leader. Recent evidence also points to a core of extreme poverty and excluded groups (geographically remote households, the elderly, the disabled, etc.) beyond the reach of long-standing social policy interventions (Silva 2004). The government has responded with a bridge program (*Programa Puente*) designed to link these excluded groups to services and benefits. But by some accounts, the Chilean policy model is at capacity, and a more inclusive growth strategy following the East Asian model, including widespread investments in human capital and incentives for innovation, may be required to jump-start a return to the high-growth path (Kharas et al. 2008).

Ecuador

Ecuador's capacity to undertake public policies directed at poverty reduction has been limited by the persistent economic and political instability that has plagued the country in an on-again, off-again cycle since the 1980s, and by the low level of public expenditures devoted to poverty reduction. Economic instability was fed throughout the 1980s and 1990s by stabilization measures that were inconsistently applied and then relaxed, leading to lost credibility and repeated crises. Hyperinflation and another political crisis in 2000 led to drastic measures including the adoption of the U.S. dollar as the national currency. The resulting exchange rate and price stability along with rising oil prices yielded positive growth rates during the 2000s.

Against this backdrop, modest efforts at social policy reform have ensued. The Bono de Desarrollo Humano, originally an unconditional cash transfer with ill-defined eligibility criteria, has been transformed by the use of a proxy-means test to target the poorest Ecuadorians (World Bank 2004a), and has become the backbone of social policy. But a factor limiting the impact and reach of social policy is poor targeting in general; as of 2004, only 10 percent of social spending was directed toward programs explicitly targeted to the poor – the Bono de Desarrollo Humano, school breakfast programs and infant care, for example (World Bank 2004b). Further, social programs are not generally targeted toward indigenous peoples, and evaluations find that when it comes to the general,

poverty-targeted programs such as the Bono de Desarrollo, social insurance, school breakfast, and temporary labor training, indigenous peoples – who are technically eligible – access these programs at rates lower
than the poor within the general population; this may be because of discrimination or poor information flow about program access (Borja-Vega
and Lunde 2007). Indigenous peoples in Ecuador have achieved a measure
of civil rights and political recognition at least in name, owing in large
measure to the national mobilization of indigenous communities via the
Confederation de Nacionalidades Indigenas de Ecuador (CONAIE). A
new constitution (1998) provides for collective rights, territory, and self-
determination (Plant 1998; Uquillas and Van Nieuwkoop 2003), but many
of these rights have yet to be fulfilled in practice.

Guatemala

Guatemala's economic policies broadly follow those of other Latin American
countries, moving from greater state intervention to price and trade liberalization since the 1980s. But the path has been steadier than in most other
countries – relatively sound macroeconomic management has yielded low
but steady growth rates, low inflation, and the country has not experienced
any macroeconomic crises in recent decades. Against this backdrop, the
end of the civil war and signing of the 1996 Peace Accords set out a new
agenda for poverty reduction emphasizing broader citizen engagement in
development, increases in social expenditures, and better coverage of social
services such as education and health (World Bank 2003).

In 2001, the government set forth the *Estrategia de Reduccion de Pobreza*
(Poverty Reduction Strategy) emphasizing rural poverty reduction and
better targeting via a poverty map to address a fragmented system of more
than thirty different social assistance programs that failed to add up to a
coherent safety net. Recent assessments indicate that there has been some
consolidation into four main programs that make up 75 percent of social
assistance expenditures – school feeding (Glass of Milk and Glass of Atoll)
and fertilizer and electricity and housing subsidies – but this mix hardly
comprises a coherent system of social protection, and targeting continues
to be an issue. Some programs yield pro-poor targeting results, such as
school feeding; others, such as the subsidies, provide most of their benefits to the nonpoor (World Bank 2009). With regard to policies explicitly
directed toward indigenous development, the 1995 Accord on the Identity
and Rights of Indigenous Peoples declared Guatemala a multilingual,

multicultural, and multiethnic nation and included proposals for antidis-
crimination legislation, education reforms, and recognition of traditional
forms of land ownership. Later attempts to pass these proposals into law via
constitutional reform failed (Fazio 2007). Guatemala is, however, one of the
only countries in the region to have created an Indigenous Development
Fund (FODIGUA), established in 1994. The country's social assistance programs provide roughly equal coverage to indigenous and nonindigenous
households, although nonindigenous households receive a larger absolute
share of total transfers (World Bank 2003).

Mexico

Mexico is home to what may be the most notable poverty reduction initiative in Latin America – the conditional cash transfer. Coming out of the
1994 "tequila crisis," the program was devised in 1997 as part of a broader
effort by then-Finance Minister Santiago Levy to rationalize Mexico's historically inefficient public expenditures. Replacing costly and poorly targeted public subsidies for basic food items like the tortilla, the program
delivered immediate cash benefits to poor families while encouraging them
to invest in their children's human capital (Levy 2006). Begun under the
name Progresa, the program's primary innovation is to fight both short-
term and long-term poverty in one combined effort. It does so by offering
an immediate and regular cash transfer to poor households conditioned on
certain desirable behaviors, such as keeping their children in school, taking
them for regular health checks, or other human development investments.
Now called Oportunidades, the program has been the subject of rigorous impact evaluations showing gains in school attendance and poverty
reduction. Because of these measurable achievements, the program – in
various formats – is now being implemented across Latin America and
indeed worldwide.

From the perspective of efforts to combat indigenous poverty, what is
interesting is that by efficiently targeting Mexico's poorest families, the conditional cash transfer program has indigenous families as a large proportion
of its beneficiaries, yet it is not specifically designed for or targeted to indigenous groups (Hall and Patrinos 2006). Instead, its design features emphasize poverty-targeting and good design, reporting, and evaluation features
in general. This mirrors the government's broader approach of focusing on
a national poverty reduction strategy as opposed to a parallel, indigenous-
specific approach. Indigenous-specific initiatives do exist – Mexico has

guaranteed the provision of bilingual education to indigenous children at all levels since the 1940s, for example – but they are often underfunded, minor players in the public policy landscape and less than functional in practice. Indigenous schools are poorly funded and monitored, with teachers who do not always speak the local children's indigenous language; as such, those children enrolled in regular national schools perform better than those in the parallel, indigenous school system.

Peru

The Peruvian government's slow embrace of structural reforms after the 1980s debt crisis, combined with an active terrorist network that repeatedly brought the economy and government to its knees, has left a legacy that until recently allowed little scope for meaningful public policy reform in favor of poverty reduction or indigenous peoples. The government of Alberto Fujimori, elected in 1990, implemented a major stabilization effort and quelled the terrorist problem, yielding a slow return to growth and stability during the 1990s and the creation of several antipoverty programs (the social investment fund FONCODES being the largest), none of them being particularly well targeted but together providing 60 percent of the population with some form of assistance (World Bank 1999; Cotlear 2006). The 1990s came to a close, however, with faltering growth, and in 2000, the Fujimori government collapsed under accusations of corruption.

The 2000s ushered in a slow return to macroeconomic stability, and by the second half of the decade, Peru had become the fastest-growing economy in the region. Modest efforts at social policy reform ensued, beginning with the 2001 Guidelines for a Poverty Alleviation Strategy and Economic Opportunities for the Poor, which laid out a national framework for reform focusing on better targeting and consolidation of programs (Hasan 2010). Introduction of the conditional cash transfer Juntos followed in 2005, modeled after the Mexican program Oportunidades. The government's strategy for indigenous peoples within this framework is not clearly articulated. The 1993 constitution recognizes the "ethnic and cultural plurality of the nation" (Article 2, Republic of Peru 1993) but offers few guidelines for doing so. Select government initiatives (FONCODES and the rural agricultural program PRONAMACHCS, for example), do have components that specifically target indigenous development; the country also has an official policy of bilingual "intercultural" education, although there are significant gaps in its implementation (Garcia 2004).

SUMMARY

Across most of Latin America, economic policy has failed to deliver sustained high growth rates since the debt crisis of the early 1980s. Income distribution across the region continues to be among the most unequal in the world; by and large, there has yet to be evidence of a social contract between citizens and government prioritizing equity and shared growth. Targeted interventions for poverty reduction are on the rise, however. In terms of recent public policy initiatives for poverty reduction, Latin America is perhaps most well known for the conditional cash transfer, a Mexican innovation that is now implemented in various forms worldwide. In some countries, public expenditure reviews have revealed the historically skewed nature of public spending toward nonpoor groups. This in turn has highlighted one reason why social spending across the region may be ineffective at achieving poverty reduction outcomes (Hall and Patrinos 2006). In some cases, a parallel effort to reorient (better target) social spending toward poor populations has begun, often linked to the cancelling of some programs with poor targeting and reorienting funds toward conditional cash transfers or other programs that promise better outcomes for poverty reduction. Such was the case in Mexico, for example, where the introduction of Progresa was funded in large measure by phasing out the ill-targeted tortilla subsidy. Several other countries in the region have followed suit, phasing out long-standing programs with ineffective targeting outcomes and implementing national conditional cash transfer programs (Ecuador, Peru). Few cases emerge, however, of attempts to specifically reorient significant public funding toward indigenous poverty reduction, or to enact significant and meaningful indigenous development strategies.

POVERTY OUTCOMES

Against this backdrop, what has been the trend for indigenous poverty rates in Latin America, and how does this trend compare to the evolution of national poverty rates? This section extends the analysis in Hall and Patrinos (2006). Figures 9.1 through 9.6 present the trends in poverty rates by country from the earliest year to the latest year available. In all cases, the same data series is used and the national poverty rates are computed.

As in the previous analysis, the update for Bolivia shows a consistent gap between indigenous and nonindigenous poverty rates, and at the same time very little change overall in poverty rates. In the latest year, however, there is a slight divergence in poverty rates, with nonindigenous poverty declining

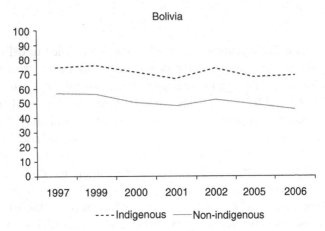

Figure 9.1. Trends in poverty over time, Bolivia.
Source: Hall and Patrinos (2006), with new poverty estimates for 2005 and 2006 using same source data (MECOVI household survey) and methodology.

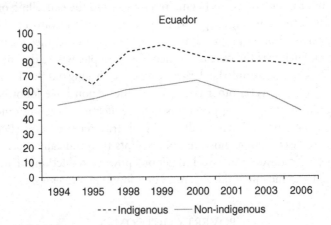

Figure 9.2. Trends in poverty over time, Ecuador.
Source: Hall and Patrinos (2006), with new poverty estimates for 2006 using same source data (ECV) and methodology.

slightly while indigenous poverty remains relatively constant. Ecuador shows a similar pattern. The nonindigenous poverty rate has started to decline while the indigenous poverty rate has remained constant.

In the previous analysis, Guatemala displayed significant poverty declines, up to 2000, although the nonindigenous poverty rate declined quicker. However, the update using 2006 data shows that there have been no further improvements over time and the gap has remained.

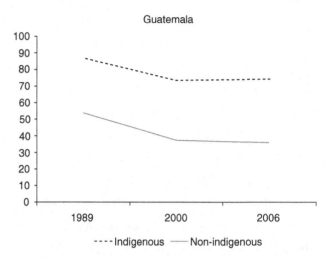

Figure 9.3. Trends in poverty over time, Guatemala.
Source: Hall and Patrinos (2006), with new poverty estimates for 2006 using same source data (ENCOVI household survey) and methodology.

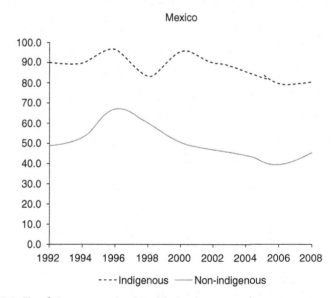

Figure 9.4. Trends in poverty over time, Mexico.
Source: Hall and Patrinos (2006), with new poverty estimates for 2004, 2006, and 2008 using same source data (ENIGH household survey) and methodology.

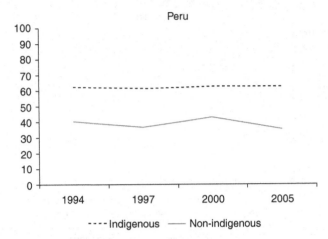

Figure 9.5. Trends in poverty over time, Peru.
Source: Hall and Patrinos (2006), with new poverty estimates for 2005 using same
source data (ENIGH household survey) and methodology.

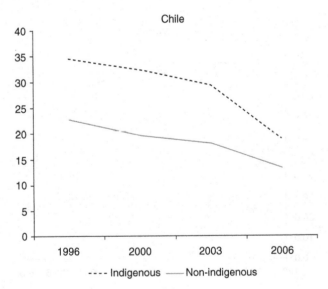

Figure 9.6. Trends in poverty over time, Chile.
Source: CASEN household survey, 1996, 2000, 2003, and 2006.

Previously, Mexico displayed a growing divergence in poverty rates.
The nonindigenous population was improving significantly while indigenous poverty had remained constant. Updating the analysis shows continued declines in poverty up to 2006, but with an increase in poverty for

nonindigenous between 2006 and 2008. In other words, the gap has now decreased, perhaps for the first time in Mexico.

Peru shows no change over time, although the nonindigenous poverty rate is declining. Overall, there is significant growth and poverty reduction in Peru in recent year.

The biggest standout is Chile. There has been considerable poverty reduction in Chile over time. Overall there has been a rapid reduction in poverty in Chile, from more than 45 percent in 1987 to 23 percent in 1996 for the population as a whole (Foxley 2004). Poverty continues to decline for the nonindigenous population to reach a level less than 14 percent by 2006. The indigenous poverty rate declined from a high of 35 percent in 1996 to less than 20 percent in 2006. Thus, the indigenous poverty rate declined by 46 percent and the nonindigenous rate by 39 percent, representing a very different scenario from most Latin American countries.

References

Borja-Vega, C. and T. Lunde, 2007. "Economic Opportunities for Indigenous People in Ecuador." In *Economic Opportunities for Indigenous People in Latin America*. Washington, DC: World Bank.

Cotlear, D. 2006. *A New Social Contract for Peru: An Agenda for Improving Education, Health Care and the Safety Net*. Washington, DC: World Bank.

Deininger, Klaus and Lyn Squire. 1996. "A New Dataset Measuring Income Inequality." *World Bank Economic Review*, 10(3): 565–591.

Fazio, M. V. 2007. "Economic Opportunities for Indigenous People in Guatemala." In *Economic Opportunities for Indigenous People in Latin America*. Washington, DC: World Bank.

Foxley, Alejandro. 2004. "Successes and Failures in Poverty Eradication: Chile." A case study from Reducing Poverty, Sustaining Growth – What Works, What Doesn't, and Why: A Global Exchange or Scaling Up Success: Scaling Up Poverty Reduction: A Global Learning Process and Conference, Shanghai, May 25–27.

Garcia, M. 2004. "Rethinking Bilingual Education in Peru: Intercultural Politics, State Policy and Indigenous Rights." *International Journal of Bilingual Education and Bilingualism*, 7(5): 348–367.

Hall, Gillette and Harry Anthony Patrinos (eds.) 2006. *Indigenous Peoples, Poverty and Human Development*. London: Palgrave-Macmillan.

Hasan, Mahreen. 2010. "Poverty in Bolivia." Background paper.

Klasen, S. et al. 2004. "Operationalizing Pro-Poor Growth – A Country Case Study on Bolivia." University of Gottingen and Kiel Institute for World Economics.

Kharas, Homi, Danny Leipziger, William Maloney, R. Thillainathan, and Heiko Hesse. 2008. "Chilean Growth through East Asian Eyes." Commission on Growth and Development Working Paper 31. Washington, DC.

Layton, H. and H. A. Patrinos. 2006. "Estimating the Number of Indigenous Peoples in Latin America." In G. Hall and H. A. Partrinos, eds., *Indigenous Peoples, Poverty and Human Development in Latin America*. New York: Palgrave Macmillan.

Levy, Santiago. 2006. *Progress Against Poverty: Sustaining Mexico's Progresa-Oportunidades Program*. Washington, DC: Brookings.

Lopez, Humberto and Guillermo Perry. 2008. "Inequality in Latin America: Determinants and Consequences." Policy Research Working Paper 4504. World Bank, New York.

Mann, Charles. 2006. *1491: New Revelations of the Americas before Columbus*. New York: Vintage Books.

Miller-Llana, Sara. 2009. "Bolivia Sets New Global High Mark for Indigenous Rights." *Christian Science Monitor*, January 27.

Morley, Samuel. 2001. *The Income Distribution Problem in Latin America*. Santiago de Chile: CEPAL.

Plant, Roger. 1998. "Issues in Indigenous Poverty and Development." Indigenous Peoples and Community Development Unit. SDS. Inter-American Development Bank. Washington, DC.

Psacharopoulos, G. and H. A. Patrinos. 1994. *Indigenous People and Poverty in Latin America: An Empirical Analysis*. Washington, DC: World Bank.

Republic of Peru. 1993. Political Constitution.

Romero, Simon. 2008. "A Crisis Highlights Divisions in Bolivia." *New York Times*, September 14.

Silva, Veronica. 2004. *The Programa Puente: Bridging the Gap Between the Poorest Families and Their Rights*. Santiago de Chile: FOSIS.

Spatz, Julius. 2006. *Poverty and Inequality in the Era of Structural Reforms*. Berlin: Springer.

The Economist. 2009. "Bolivia's New Constitution: A Passport to Utopia." January 22.

Trivelli, C. 2006. "Peru." In G. Hall and H. A. Patrinos, eds., *Indigenous Peoples, Poverty and Human Development*. New York: Palgrave Macmillan.

Uquillas, J. E. and M. van Nieuwkoop. 2003. "Social Capital as a Factor in Indigenous Peoples Development in Ecuador." World Bank Sustainable Development Working Paper No. 15, Indigenous Peoples Development Series. Washington, DC.

Weisbrot, M. and L. Sandoval. 2008. "The Distribution of Bolivia's Most Important Natural Resources and the Autonomy Conflicts." Issue Brief. Center for Economic and Policy Research. Washington, DC.

World Bank. 1999. *Poverty and Social Developments in Peru, 1994–1997*. Washington, DC: World Bank.

   2003. "Poverty in Guatemala." Report No. 24221-GU. Washington, DC

   2004a. "Ecuador: Creating Fiscal Space for Poverty Reduction: A Fiscal Management and Public Expenditure Review." Report No. 28911-EC. Washington, DC.

   2004b. "Ecuador: Poverty Assessment." Report No. 27061-EC. Washington, DC.

   2005. "Mexico: Determinants of Learning Policy Note." Report No. 31842-MX. Washington, DC.

   2009. "Guatemala Poverty Assessment: Good Performance at Low Levels." Report No. 43920-GT. Washington, DC.

10

Conclusion

Gillette H. Hall and Harry Anthony Patrinos

Indigenous peoples are widely held to be among the worlds' poorest. Yet there is no global source drawing together the available evidence to assess the degree to which this holds across countries and over time. This book provides a cross-country assessment of poverty and socioeconomic indicators for indigenous peoples. It builds on a small but growing body of work that until now has focused on indigenous peoples in rich countries (the United States, Australia, and New Zealand) and more recently in Latin America.

The joining together under a common identity as indigenous peoples is a relatively new phenomenon in the world (Chapter 2), and has accompanied a process among some groups of "reclaiming" identity – as, for example, among the Manchu in China. It is born of common differences, with tremendous variety in individual and group characteristics. It is best seen as a political identity and a social movement. Levi and Maybury-Lewis in this volume argue that groups come together under the banner of indigenous peoples to demand the "Four R's" of the indigenous movement: representation, recognition, resources, and rights.

Being indigenous, or the term "indigenism," can describe "the international movement that aspires to promote and protect the rights of the world's 'first peoples'" (Niezen 2003). Increasingly over the last two decades, disenfranchised peoples from around the world are discovering the liberating potential of the term "indigenous" and claiming this identity as a badge of pride wrested from oppressive conditions, thereby allowing actors from diverse local cultures access to a universal category of collective empowerment predicated on primordial attachments. Put simply, these groups are *becoming indigenous.* Comparing indigenous movements in Africa and the Americas, there are increasing numbers of historically marginalized groups becoming indigenous by joining international networks that promote mobilization and demand recognition of rights (Hodgson 2002). The indigenous movement is a social movement, not a social stasis. It can be described as more of a process than a category (see Box 1). And because issues of indigenous identity also become entwined with demands for political recognition and rights such as those over territory or resources, disagreement over who is and is not indigenous can become heated. This report makes no attempt to resolve these questions, and takes no position on – nor is designed to inform – ongoing or future disagreements over identity.

Box 1. *The usefulness of the concept of identity (Chapter 2)*

"When we are introduced to a man in the village of Mishongnovi on Second Mesa in Arizona, in the southwestern portion of the United States, we are told his name and that he is a member of the Bear Strap Clan. When he goes on business to the nearby town of Window Rock, capital of the Navajo Nation, he specifies that he is a Hopi; at a lecture he delivers in Chicago he claims to be Native American and at the Palais Wilson in Geneva, as he sits between a Dayak woman from Kalimantan, Indonesia and an Ogiek man from Kenya while attending an international human rights conference, he identifies himself, and is identified by others, as indigenous. The same man has claimed four different identities, yet none are inconsistent and all are true."

Following the United Nations and the World Bank (2005), this study does not put forth a rule of what does or does not constitute "indigenous." Such an approach would contribute little and would by definition invite controversy over perceived errors of inclusion or omission. The approach taken is instead a pragmatic one. Chapter 2 provides a minimum set of MDG-like indicators for a definition-conditional assessment of indigenous peoples' development. That is, where data allow, it includes indicators for any people who any government or recognized organization – including self-identified indigenous organizations such as International Working Group for Indigenous Affairs, Indigenous People of Africa Coordinating Committee, Africa Commission on Human and Peoples' Rights, or Asia Indigenous Peoples Pact – has described as indigenous. The country case studies use terminology and population breakdowns typical in that country. Thus, in China, Vietnam, and Laos, the term "ethnic minority" is used and, where possible, groups are broken down into further subcategories; in India, the constitutionally recognized term "Scheduled Tribes" forms the basis of our analysis. In Africa, where the data available are far more limited, the case studies focus on the Pygmy populations for whom data can be disaggregated from household survey data in three countries: DRC, Gabon, and the Republic of Congo.

Chapter 2 presents a set of core socioeconomic indicators for indigenous peoples in low- and middle-income countries. Information is drawn from Demographic and Health Surveys (DHS) in the past twelve years and, where such is not available, the latest Multiple Indicator Cluster Survey (MICS), with some exceptions.[1] DHS and MICS data sets have the advantage of typically providing information on the respondent's self-identified ethnicity or the respondent's language, either spoken at home or spoken by the enumerator with the respondent, in addition to the socioeconomic indicators of interest. The five indicators selected for this analysis most closely measure progress under the Millennium Development Goals (MDGs) while being computable for as many countries and peoples as possible given data limitations. These indicators include:

1. Under-five mortality rate
2. Safe-water deprivation (proportion of individuals with a water source more than fifteen minutes away from where they live, or with access only to surface water or unimproved springs)
3. Nutrition deprivation (proportion of children under three years of age whose height-for-age ratio is less than −3 standard deviations for the international reference population)
4. Male and female literacy rates
5. Male and female country-specific net primary enrolment rates.

These results, presented in a series of World Development Report-style tables, are augmented by tables replicating similar data on indigenous peoples residing in high-income countries, drawn from existing research. Results can be summarized as follows:

With some exceptions, MDG indicators for indigenous groups across Asia are below (worse than) population averages. Under-five mortality rates are only available for Nepal and India; for the Nepalese Janajati, infant mortality rates are distributed across the national level, but as a whole are below (better than) the national level. In India, however, infant mortality among

---

[1] Although data are more limited, for some countries, per capita household consumption relative to the national average is also presented from a variety of budget and expenditure surveys. An appendix contains details and sources of the methodologies used.

the Scheduled Tribes is uniformly higher (worse) than the national average, whereas water deprivation rates both exceed and fall short of their national levels. Among the Hill Tribes in Thailand, the Kammu and Leu samples in Laos, and the Hmong, Muong, and BaNa peoples in Vietnam, these rates are the worst in the region. Male literacy rates are only available for the Scheduled Tribe sample of India and the Nepalese Janajati sample; the Scheduled Tribe sample exhibits the worst among these, whereas the Gurung sample from Nepal exhibits the best. The lowest female literacy rates are found among the Hmong samples in both Vietnam and Laos. Across New Zealand and Australia, all indicators are worse for the Maori and Aborigines than national averages.

Indigenous peoples in Latin America have uniformly worse outcomes across all five MDG indicators, although again, some differences by group stand out. Under-five mortality levels are mostly higher than the national averages, with the worst being speakers of the Mam language in Guatemala and those who identify as Quechua in Bolivia. Water deprivation rates are generally evenly dispersed across the national levels, the worst being sampled speakers of the Q'eqchi, with nearly seven times that of the national level. Child nutrition deprivation rates are generally higher, with Mam-speakers from Guatemala and Quechua in Peru having nearly double the national rates. The lowest female literacy rates are among the Quechua-speaking sample in Peru.

Data coverage is far more limited in Africa, making overarching conclusions difficult. In Africa, survey coverage is spotty. In many cases, available data do not cover core groups widely considered to be indigenous due to their small size (for example, the Ogiek in Kenya) while covering groups for which there is less consistent agreement on status as indigenous (for example, the Maasai in Kenya and the Fulani in West Africa). The data that do exist show that under-five mortality rates tend to be the highest among West African groups, such as the Fulani and Tuareg, and the lowest among the Maasai and Ethiopian group. However, these latter groups also experience the highest rates of water deprivation. Education indicators are uniformly worse; even in countries with higher levels of literacy, such as Namibia, the male literacy rate for San males is less than half that of the national sample and for females less than one-third.

RESULTS: CASE STUDIES

The detailed country case studies in this book include countries from Africa and South and Southeast Asia: Central African Republic (CAR), China,

Table 10.1. *Indigenous population in our case studies*

Country	Year	% Indigenous in Country	Indigenous Population	% of world's indigenous
CAR	2003	1.2	46,380	0.02
China	2005	8.0	106,403,568	35.90
DRC	2005	0.2	132,000	0.04
Gabon	2003	0.1	1,455	0.00
India	2005	8.1	92,987,668	31.37
Laos	2002	42.0	2,361,232	0.80
Vietnam	2006	13.4	11,539,619	3.89
Total			**213,471,923**	**72.02**

Source: Authors' estimates.

the Democratic Republic of the Congo (DRC), Gabon, India, Lao People's Democratic Republic (Laos), and Vietnam. The population of interest in each country ranges from very large to very small. Among the largest representations of indigenous/ethnic minorities, two countries make up more than two-thirds of the world's indigenous population: China and India. Overall, the country cases account for 72 percent of the world's indigenous peoples (Table 10.1). Combined with earlier case studies for five Latin American countries (Hall and Patrinos 2006), the results cover almost 80 percent of the world's indigenous population.

INDIGENOUS PEOPLES AND GLOBAL POVERTY

Estimates suggest that indigenous peoples make up about 4 percent of the world's population (Chapter 1). Given the previously mentioned population numbers, poverty rates in China and India largely determine global poverty estimates for indigenous peoples. Of course, any estimate of the number of the poor depends on the poverty line used. Arriving at a global poverty estimate based on our results is tricky given that what this study contributes is national poverty figures (derived from national poverty lines that are designed to most accurately represent the consumption level it actually takes to be poor in a particular country). Although conceptually comparable across countries in a sense that what we want to discern is precisely the number of people whose consumption levels are below the poverty level, national poverty lines use different dollar values and are thus not strictly comparable across countries. Further, we do not generate poverty estimates beyond our country case studies, leaving out around 20 percent of the global indigenous population.

Table 10.2. *Indigenous poverty as proportion of total*

Country	Indigenous population (millions)	Indigenous poverty rate	Number of indigenous poor
China	106.4	0.048	5.1
South Asia	94.9	0.438	41.6
Former Soviet Union (Russia)	0.4	0.002	0.0
Southeast Asia	29.8	0.515	15.4
South America	16.0	0.800	8.7
Africa	22.0	0.783	17.2
Central America/Mexico	12.7	0.800	9.4
Arabia	15.4	0.050*	0.8
USA/Canada	5.6	0.270	1.5
Japan/Pacific Islands	0.8	na	0.0
Australia/New Zealand	1.1	0.390	0.4
Greenland/Scandinavia	0.1	na	0.0
Total	299.2	–	100.1

Notes: * Not representative.
Source: Computed from country studies, using national poverty lines.

With these caveats, a rough estimate of the number of indigenous people in poverty can be generated as follows. For all countries covered by case studies (representing about 80 percent of the world's indigenous population), poverty rates are multiplied by the indigenous population estimate. Beyond these countries we extrapolate as follows. For South Asia, we apply the poverty rates for India to the whole region. For Southeast Asia, we use the poverty rates for Laos and Vietnam. For the Former Soviet Union, the only poverty estimate available is a national rate for Russia. For Africa, we use the poverty rates generated for CAR, DRC, and Gabon. For South and Central America and Mexico, we use the poverty rates reported in Hall and Patrinos (2006). For Arabia, we use the only available general poverty rates for two countries: Algeria and Morocco. For Greenland/ Scandinavia, Japan, and the Pacific Islands, we do not have disaggregated poverty figures.

Table 10.2 presents a rough estimation of indigenous poverty rates by region. Using the indigenous poverty rate for the country or region, or a reasonable approximation, we estimated the number of poor according to the country's national poverty numbers. We add up the total numbers, which admittedly are not comparable, to arrive at a rough estimate of the number of indigenous poor worldwide. According to this rough estimate, 100 million indigenous peoples worldwide are poor, out of a total indigenous population of almost 300 million. Taking the global number of poor

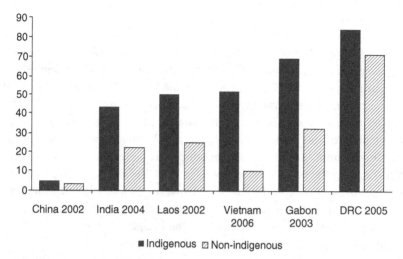

Figure 10.1. Poverty headcount (%).
Source: Authors' compilation.

people in the developing world, which is estimated at 1 billion (but is based on a comparable poverty line that is usually lower than the national poverty lines used later in the chapter), one can crudely estimate the share of the world's poor that are indigenous.

Estimates appear to confirm that worldwide, indigenous peoples are over-represented among the poor. According to our estimates, indigenous peoples make up more than 10 percent of the worlds' poor; yet they account for only 4 percent of the world's total population. Thus, indigenous peoples do in fact make up a disproportionate share of the worlds' poor. This confirms a cocktail-napkin estimate that suggests the same. Given the concentration of indigenous peoples in China and India, and because poverty rates are slightly higher for ethnic minorities in China, and higher still in India and the rest of the world, the share of indigenous in the world's total poor is higher than their population share.

In China, both the national and indigenous poverty rates are strikingly low. Elsewhere, indigenous poverty rates approach or exceed 50 percent. Although the majority of indigenous peoples come from China and India, the proportion of the indigenous poor is more spread out across regions given lower poverty rates in these two countries, particularly China. In other countries, indigenous peoples have disproportionately high poverty rates – meaning that they deviate from the nonindigenous poverty rate by a great margin. Figure 10.1 shows the poverty rates for indigenous and nonindigenous peoples from our case studies.

POVERTY OVER TIME

Evidence of rapidly declining poverty rates – even among indigenous peoples – is emerging in Asia. Research from Latin America, and to some degree also in Australia, Canada, New Zealand, and the United States, shows a sticky persistence of poverty rates for indigenous peoples over time. Yet for the few countries for which, over time, data on indigenous poverty exist in other parts of the world (China, India, and Vietnam), we see significant declines in both overall and indigenous poverty rates. In Vietnam, almost two-thirds of the population was poor in 1993. By 2006, only 16 percent of the population was classified as poor. However, progress in reducing poverty was unequal; the poverty rate fell by more than 80 percent for the non-indigenous, but only by 40 percent for the indigenous. The same pattern appears in India (see Figures 10.2a, 10.2b, and 10.2c).

For the three countries of our study for which we have over-time data, we find significant improvements in standards of living over the last decade. China shows exceptional progress. Poverty decreased even over a short period of time, and poverty reduction was more rapid for the indigenous (see Table 10.3). However, overall poverty rates were very low in China, at only 6 percent in 1998, and although indigenous peoples improved considerably, they are still 1.5 times more likely to be poor than nonindigenous people in China.

This is exceptional progress. In the case of Latin America, poverty rates changed at a lower rate, and even when there was poverty reduction, indigenous poverty reduction was always less and in most cases insignificant (see Figure 10.3). In fact, over the period from the mid-1990s to 2004, few gains were made in income poverty reduction in Latin America, especially among indigenous peoples. In cases where gains in poverty reduction are being made, indigenous people are benefiting less, and when indigenous poverty rates fell, they did so at a slower pace than for nonindigenous people. In the case of Latin America, we concluded that the incomes of indigenous peoples are less affected by macroeconomic trends, whether positive or negative. The situation seems much different in Asia, with overall very large and significant reductions in poverty.

Reform policy efforts in Asia, notably in China and India, promoted high growth for all groups; in other words, the gains from growth were widely distributed. The growth policies in China undid the damages of past policy failures, but built on the relatively low inequality in access to productive inputs such as land and human capital (Ravallion 2010). In other words, China's high-growth-promoting policies and initial relative low inequality

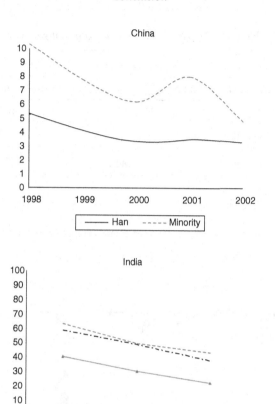

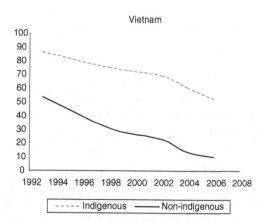

Figure 10.2a, 10.2b, 10.2c. Poverty rates over time.
Source: Authors' compilation.

Table 10.3. *Poverty rates decreased significantly in Asia*

Less so for indigenous, except in the case of China		
Percent change in headcount poverty rate between early and later survey year		
Country	Nonindigenous	Indigenous
China (1998–2002)	37.7	53.4
India (1983–2005)	44.0	31.0
Vietnam (1993–2006)	80.9	39.5

Source: Authors' compilation.

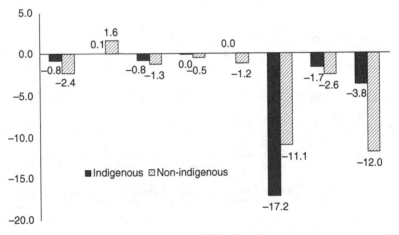

Figure 10.3. Annual rate of change in poverty headcount.
Source: Authors' compilation.

explain the rapid reduction in poverty. This would help explain the relative gains of China's ethnic minorities, who benefited both from the relatively equal access to productive inputs at the outset and the growth-promoting policies after the reforms began. China's growth has been phenomenal, averaging more than 10 percent a year in the early 1990s and more than 7 percent since the mid-1990s.

Initially high income inequality may hinder future growth and poverty reduction. India's pro-growth policies – resulting in growth rates averaging more than 4 percent since 1994 and more than 5 percent since 2000 – in the same period have much in common with the corresponding policies in

China. However, their inequalities in human capital may be a future handicap (Ravallion 2010). High income inequality to begin with is a severe handicap on future growth and poverty reduction, as is the case for Brazil, where despite otherwise good policy intervention in favor of equity, much higher growth rates as a result are needed for significant success against poverty (Ravallion 2010). The same could be said for the Latin American countries with large indigenous populations studied here.

The relative success in equalizing access to human capital in Latin America will not result in rapid poverty reduction, or equitable distribution to indigenous peoples, if the policy reforms do not result in high growth rates. During the 1990s and early 2000s, the Latin American countries studied in this volume experienced growth rates of no more than 1 percent. Lack of growth and development policies that do not include the indigenous populations will not reduce overall poverty rates, let alone benefit indigenous peoples. In this regard, the Asian countries studied here have the necessary conditions for sustained poverty reduction, namely equitable access to productive inputs (especially China and Vietnam) and high growth rates. Moreover, the growth policies favor broad-based development. This suggests that despite the relative success in equalizing access to human capital and other services in the Latin American countries studied here, poverty reduction will not be rapid, or equitably distributed to indigenous peoples, if the policy reforms do not result in high growth rates.

This is not to say that indigenous peoples should not receive policy attention. Rather it is the type of attention that matters. In Latin America, indigenous rights are now well established, indigenous peoples are represented, and many countries have programs that target indigenous peoples. Yet the high inequality as initial conditions, the lack of growth overall, and failure to include the indigenous populations when growth did occur mean that indigenous progress in poverty reduction has failed to materialize. These "rights" approaches and distributive programs may have other benefits, but they have not resulted in promoting poverty reduction among indigenous peoples, except perhaps for the case of Mexico's conditional cash transfer program, Oportunidades. On the other hand, direct redistributive interventions have not been prominent in China's efforts to reduce poverty (Ravallion 2010). India's phenomenal growth record, focused since the 1980s on moving from a state-controlled, inward-looking economy, to a market-led, outward-oriented economy (Bosworth and Collins 2008), has not been dampened by their poorly performing targeted programs (Lanjouw and Ravallion 1999; Ravallion 2010). This suggests that growth is a necessary condition for poverty reduction, as many have argued (see, for example, Dollar and Kraay 2002).

Poverty reduction strategies in the successful Asian countries followed the establishment of sustained high growth and inclusive policies. China's growth strategy and poverty reduction strategy coincided in the years following the introduction of the economic reforms of the late 1970s. That is, the primary strategy for poverty reduction was rural economic growth. After 1985, however, it was recognized that growth is a necessary but insufficient condition for poverty reduction, so government adopted a development-oriented strategy providing assistance through various programs to designated poor regions to help them develop income-generating activities (World Bank 2009). Similarly, Vietnam's remarkable gains in economic growth and poverty reduction were the product of market reforms and loosening of state control (Dollar, Glewwe, and Litvack 1998). It was only after the growth record was established that policy makers turned their attention to poverty reduction strategies and ethnic minority development (Baulch et al. 2007). Therefore, only after growth has spread did the government turn its attention to poverty alleviation programs, and even then they were designed to develop local economic activities. These policies are in contrast to Latin American-style programs that focus primarily on targeting the poor.

It can be hypothesized that Latin America has not been successful in promoting in general the policies necessary to create the conditions for high economic growth and inclusive outcomes.* At least the Latin American countries studied here have been much less successful than, say, some East Asian countries, at promoting growth in general. Even the relatively successful targeted programs have promoted access to essential services for the poor and indigenous, but they are not in general promoting poverty reduction to the extent required, except perhaps for Mexico's Oportunidades. Their growth policies are not as inclusive of all regions and therefore – one might hypothesize – do not include their indigenous populations, thus not resulting in equitable growth distribution or poverty reduction. In any case, the growth record has not been of sufficient magnitude to even create the gains that can be redistributed.

Great gains in economic growth and poverty reduction may lead to subsequent inequalities. China and Vietnam's policies have also resulted in growing inequalities in their countries. This is inevitable in the early stages. This is one area where Asia can stand to learn from Latin America. Mexico, for example, has a successful anti-poverty program that targets efficiently and is regarded as a significant component of the country's anti-poverty efforts, which have benefited indigenous peoples disproportionately. Brazil also has a similar anti-poverty program that has also been recommended for Asia to follow (Ravallion 2010).

Table 10.4. *Poverty gap (FGT1) by minority/indigenous status across countries*

China (rural), 2002	Minority	2.0
	Han	0.9
	All	–
India, 2005	Scheduled Tribes (ST)	10.6
	Scheduled Castes (SC)	7.9
	Non-ST/SC	4.4
	All	5.6
Vietnam, 2006	Ethnic minority	15.4
	Ethnic majority	2.0
	All	3.8
Laos, 2003	Non-Lao-Tai	13.2
	Lao-Tai	5.4
	Total	8.0
DRC, 2005	Indigenous	39.4
	Nonindigenous	32.4
	All	32.3
Gabon, 2003	Indigenous	30.0
	Nonindigenous	10.7
	All	10.7

Source: Authors' compilation.

POVERTY GAP

A sizeable poverty gap remains. The poverty gap, which is the mean shortfall from the poverty line (counting the nonpoor as having zero shortfall), expressed as a percentage of the poverty line. This measure reflects the depth of poverty as well as its incidence. It is expressed as the total amount of money that would be needed to raise the poor from their present incomes to the poverty line, as a proportion of the poverty line, and averaged over the total population. This measures the depth of poverty. In all cases, the poverty gap measure is higher for indigenous/minority groups, in some instances substantially higher, such as the cases of Vietnam, Laos, and Gabon (Table 10.4). In the case of China, the minority group would require about twice as much money as the majority to escape poverty. A similar story emerges for India's Scheduled Tribes. In Gabon, the indigenous would need three times as much income. In Vietnam, the poverty gap index for the ethnic minorities is more than seven times greater than for the majority; this implies that it would take seven times as much income for the minority group to escape poverty.

Table 10.5. *Poverty gap (FGT1) by minority/indigenous status across countries and over time, early to latest estimates*

		Early	Latest
China, 1998–2002	Minority	2.8	2.0
	Han	1.5	0.9
India, 1994–2005	Scheduled Tribes	12.2	10.6
	Scheduled Castes	12.2	7.9
	Others	6.8	4.4
	All	8.4	5.6
Vietnam, 1998–2006	Ethnic minority	24.2	15.4
	Ethnic majority	7.1	2.0
	All	9.5	3.8

Source: Authors' compilation

Further, the indigenous poverty gap in many countries has been widening over time. Data allowing poverty rates to be tracked over time are more limited, but where available, the results show that the poverty gap index has also declined over time (Table 10.5). The index has declined for the minority population in each case, but not by as much as the decrease for the majority population. That is, the gap in the Poverty Gap Index has widened over time. This widening ranges from slight in the case of China to significant in the case of Vietnam. In 1998, the poverty gap index for the minority was three times as large as for the majority in Vietnam; in 2006, the gap was seven times that. In India, the poverty gap index was the same for Scheduled Tribes and Scheduled Castes in 1994; in 2005, while the index declined somewhat for the Tribes, it fell more significantly for the Castes, by 35 percent, which is the same decline that the non-Caste, non-Tribe population experienced. Thus the gap declined between Castes and others but widened between Tribes and others.

EDUCATION GAP

A persistent gap in schooling attainment remains. Minority groups have increased their overall schooling attainment, but so has the majority population. Therefore, despite significant schooling progress overall, the gap between groups remains (see Figure 10.4 for India, Scheduled Tribe [ST] and non-Scheduled Tribe [non-ST] comparison).

There is evidence of greater vulnerability to shocks – in this case, in education. In Vietnam, there is, over time, a significant increase in schooling

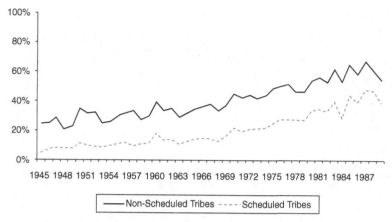

Figure 10.4. India: Post-primary attainment rate by year of birth and ST status.
Source: India National Sample Survey, various years.

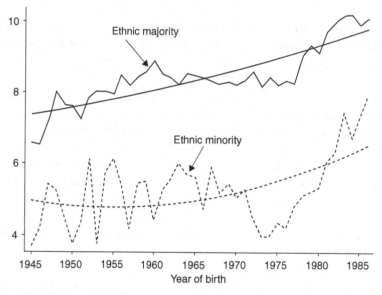

Figure 10.5. Vietnam: Schooling attainment by year of birth and minority status.
Source: Vietnam Living Standards Survey, various years.

attainment overall. This is evident in Figure 10.5, and for both majority and
minority groups. However, there is a large break in the trend beginning in
the 1970s and coinciding with the Vietnam War. What is interesting about
this break is that it affected the ethnic minority groups more than the rest
of the population. That is, the gap in schooling widened during the war

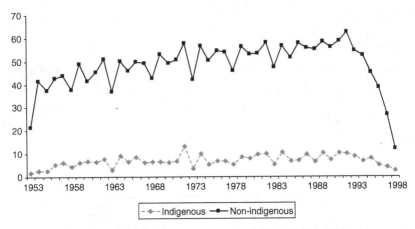

Figure 10.6. Percentage of people who have ever attended school in CAR.
Source: Own calculations.

and remained larger after the war. This finding adds further evidence that crises and interruptions affect the indigenous more and/or differently, as was the case after economic crises in Latin America (Hall and Patrinos 2006).

In Africa, there is evidence of a widening education gap. In Africa, while there is progress in schooling attainment overall, there is evidence of a widening gap in the share of people who report ever having attended school in the Central African Republic (Figure 10.6). Indigenous females are particularly disadvantaged, in CAR as well as in Gabon. Note, however, that from 1993, there is a significant declining levels of school attainment in the case of indigenous; most likely the cohort is still too young to give us good numbers. The double disadvantage of ethnic/indigenous females has been documented elsewhere as well (see, for example, Psacharopoulos and Patrinos 1994; Hall and Patrinos 2006; Lewis and Lockheed 2006). Even in countries with far higher average schooling rates, such as Laos, we find hidden pockets of low schooling in rural areas, as well as for girls. In rural Laos, 34 percent of non-Lao-Tai females have never attended any school, whereas only 17 percent of non-Lao-Tai males never attended and only 6 percent of Lao-Tai females never attended.

EARNINGS

Much of the earnings disadvantage of minority workers is a result of lower levels of human capital endowments. Yet the returns to schooling are not necessarily lower for minority workers. However, given limited sample sizes, as well as the location and type of work concentration for indigenous peoples, it is not always possible to estimate labor supply or earnings functions. In Latin America, there is evidence that indigenous peoples face significant disadvantages in the labor market (Psacharopoulos and Patrinos 1994; Hall and Patrinos 2006; Skoufias, Lunde, and Patrinos 2010). The portion of the difference in earnings between indigenous and nonindigenous peoples that is "unexplained" – perhaps because of discrimination or other unidentified factors – represented one-quarter to more than one-half of the total differential, with the average at about 42 percent. This means that whereas about half of the earnings differential can be influenced by improvements in human capital (education, skills, and abilities that an indigenous person brings to the labor market), another half may result from discriminatory labor market practices or other factors over which the indigenous person has little control. In terms of labor market earnings, indigenous peoples experience significantly lower returns to a year of education, averaging 40 percent lower returns.

There is evidence in some countries of strong returns to education among indigenous populations. In Laos, for example, controlling for other characteristics, there are significant and large returns to education, although the pattern of returns differs across groups. In urban areas, returns to lower levels of education are not significantly different from the returns to no or some primary schooling for the indigenous, whereas the nonindigenous get significant returns from the completion of lower- and upper-secondary schooling. The picture is quite different in rural Laos, where there are pronounced and significant returns to schooling at all levels, although the completion of a schooling level tends to do more for consumption than having only completed part of the level. Still, the returns tend to be larger and more consistently statistically significant for the nonindigenous. For example, the impact on per capita consumption of the most-educated household member having completed primary school is 10 percent of original consumption for the indigenous versus 17 percent for the nonindigenous. Completion of lower-secondary school results in a per capita expenditures increase of 15 percent for the rural indigenous and of 26 percent for the rural nonindigenous. The returns to vocational education are strongest for the urban indigenous and those to university are strongest for the rural nonindigenous. In Vietnam, the rate of returns to education for ethnic majority workers is around 2 percent higher than for ethnic minority workers. Earnings functions show significantly lower labor earnings for indigenous peoples. There is also evidence consistent with labor market discrimination. In Vietnam,

Table 10.6. *Earnings differentials, Vietnam, 1998–2006 (age fifteen and over)*

| | Percentage of earnings differential due to differences in | | | |
| | Endowments | | Wage structure | |
	1998	2006	1998	2006
At ethnic minority mean	35.6	66.3	64.4	33.7
At ethnic majority mean	94.6	69.9	5.4	30.1
Cotton	86.2	69.4	13.8	30.6
Oaxaca-Ransom	90.9	73.6	9.1	26.4

Source: Vietnam Living Standards Survey 1998 and 2006.

unexplained differences in wage structure accounted for 26 percent to 34 percent of the wage differential in 2006 (Table 10.6).

Indigenous workers in Latin America, in almost all cases, receive lower rates of return to a year of schooling (Hall and Patrinos 2006). This is similar to what indigenous workers experience in Australia (Daley and Lui 1995), Canada (Patrinos and Sakellariou 1992), New Zealand (Brosnan 1984; Brosnan and Hill 1984) and the United States. By contrast, in China the minority groups have higher returns to schooling. Overall, in China, the returns are 8.1 percent, broken down into 6.9 percent and 9.1 percent for men and women, respectively. For minority men, they are 9.1 percent and only 6.6 percent for majority men; they are 10.7 percent for minority women compared to 9.1 percent for majority women.

HEALTH

Despite generally improving conditions in many countries, health deficits among indigenous populations are severe. Indigenous groups are more likely to suffer from health issues and they are less likely to seek or receive medical attention, even the most basic preventive care. For example, in both India and Vietnam, where poverty reduction achievements have been sizeable, indigenous peoples (known as Scheduled Tribes and ethnic minorities, respectively) are less likely to be covered by health programs or receive vital vaccinations than members of non-Scheduled Tribes and ethnic majorities, respectively (Table 10.7). There is good coverage against tuberculosis (BCG vaccine), but ethnic/tribal groups in Vietnam and India are less likely to be vaccinated against DPT, polio, and measles. There is a large ethnic gap in vaccination against DPT in Vietnam. Only about one-third of ethnic/tribal groups are vaccinated against all diseases. This is as true in Vietnam, where

Table 10.7. *Vaccination rates for India and Vietnam, latest year (percent)*

	BCG	DPT	Polio	Measles	All

	Percent of children 12–23 months				
	BCG	DPT	Polio	Measles	All
Vietnam (2002)					
Ethnic minority	82	48	58	68	38
Ethnic majority	96	78	80	87	73
All	93	72	76	83	67
India (2005–2006)					
Scheduled Tribes (ST)	72	42	65	47	32
Non-ST	79	57	80	60	45
All	78	55	79	59	44

Notes: BCG=bacille Calmette-Guérin, a vaccine for tuberculosis; DPT= Diphtheria Tetanus whole cell Pertussis vaccine.
Sources: Vietnam Demographic and Health Survey 2002; National Family Health Survey 2005–2006.

overall vaccination rates are high, as it is in India, where overall vaccinations are relatively low.

SOCIAL PROGRAMS

There are significant discrepancies in access to basic infrastructure and services. For example, in the case of Vietnam, only 5 percent of minorities have access to safe drinking water, compared to 25 percent of the ethnic majority population. Whereas electricity and (interestingly enough) Internet connections are fairly evenly available to both groups, ethnic minorities are less likely to have garbage collection services and more likely to live in temporary housing.

However, there is also evidence of higher incidence rates among ethnic minorities as beneficiaries of major social programs in Vietnam (Table 10.8). In India, the Scheduled Tribes are more likely – especially the poorest 20 percent – to be beneficiaries of the Integrated Child Development Services program, and appear well represented as beneficiaries of the National Rural Employment Guarantee scheme. In China, the Han are well represented as beneficiaries of social insurance programs such as unemployment insurance, pensions, and basic medical insurance; yet, not all minority groups are underrepresented, with the Manchu just as likely to be covered by unemployment insurance, and the Hui more likely to be so; the same goes for pensions; and in the case of medical insurance, the Hui are just as covered as the majority Han, but just 50 percent of the rural Uyghur have medical

Table 10.8. *Social program coverage by expenditure quintile, Vietnam, 2006 (percent)*

	Expenditure Quintile				
	1	2	3	4	5
Preferential credit for poor people					
All	36.3	39.9	31.6	36.5	36.0
Ethnic minority	40.4	45.1	45.2	38.7*	100.0*
Ethnic majority	33.0	38.7	30.8	36.5	34.5
Free health care					
All	77.5	70.2	62.2	63.8	74.6
Ethnic minority	83.1	78.9	89.3	71.9*	100.0*
Ethnic majority	73.0	68.2	60.5	63.4	74.0
Tuition exemption and reduction					
All	59.6	46.9	44.3	22.0	11.2
Ethnic minority	73.0	56.9	67.2	54.0*	0.0*
Ethnic majority	49.1	44.7	42.9	20.8	11.5
Agriculture, Forestry, and Aquaculture promotion					
All	27.6	15.1	9.5	4.7	2.5
Ethnic minority	41.1	25.8	27.4	54.0*	0.0*
Ethnic majority	16.9	12.7	8.4	2.7	2.5
Number of households	4,247	1,420	582	361	68

Note: * fewer than twenty observations.
Source: Vietnam Living Standards Survey 2006.

coverage. In Laos, there is a very low incidence of access to pension and life insurance – less than 1 percent – and majority and minority populations are about equally likely to be covered.

UNDERSTANDING INDIGENOUS PEOPLES' POVERTY

Drawing on the theories highlighted in Chapter 1, and the detailed country findings, we summarize the implications of the study. Our findings, while documenting falling poverty rates in some regions, also reveal a persistent gap in basic indicators of well-being (poverty, health, and education outcomes) for indigenous peoples worldwide. This result prompts the question of causality: What causes indigenous peoples on average to be significantly poorer than the rest of the population?

SPATIAL DISADVANTAGE

Despite some urbanization, indigenous peoples worldwide continue to live predominantly in rural areas. For various historical and cultural reasons, they also inhabit remote locations to a far greater degree than the rest of the population. A growing literature suggests a strong role for geography in poverty outcomes, driven both by externalities such as climate and topography as well as limited access to infrastructure and services. Spatial inequality (variations in well-being between regions) is well documented. Cross-country studies find that differences between regions account for up to a third of inequality in a given country (Kanbur and Venables 2007; Shorrocks and Wan 2005).

What explains these regional differences? In China, there is some evidence that geographical characteristics trump household characteristics in accounting for poverty reduction and growth in income or consumption (Jalan and Ravallion 1997, 2002, 2004). Borooah, Gustafsson, and Shi (2006) also find that rural inequality in China is driven to a large extent by location, whereas in India, inequality between rural areas is driven to a greater degree by education levels. In Mexico, Esquivel (2000) finds that two-thirds of differences in state income are driven by natural characteristics (climate, vegetation). Others, however, show that once differences in households' access to private and public (infrastructure and basic services) assets is accounted for, pure geography (altitude, temperature) does not affect household well-being (Torero et al. 2004).

In China and Laos in particular, we find results that are consistent with the notion that poverty among minority groups is driven to a significant degree by geographic location. In China, more urbanized groups, and groups not concentrated in poor regions, have much reduced disparities with the Han population. But China also shows, like India, that some minority groups have lower urbanization rates, and thus live in a "disadvantaged context" in terms of access to infrastructure and opportunity. Overall, minorities in China are twice as likely to live in isolated, remote villages with difficult topography and poor infrastructure. Further, the disparity between Han and ethnic minority groups diminishes when household and individual characteristics are taken into account, but also strikingly diminishes when geographic differences are taken into account – again suggesting that much of what appears as cross-ethnic differences has to do with regional development. Similarly, in Laos, the sizeable discrepancy in returns to education declines significantly once controls for village fixed effects are included.

Evidence drawn from related micro-studies yields mixed results. For instance, Van de Walle and Gunewardena (2001) find that in Vietnam, residing in disadvantaged areas reduces returns to productive characteristics of households (such as education and household structure) for all groups, but the effect was significantly stronger for ethnic minorities. Similarly, in Mexico, Borja-Vega et al. (2006) find that while indigenous peoples concentrate in poorer, more marginalized locations, poverty and human development outcomes are still worse for indigenous families when compared to nonindigenous families in equally marginalized locations. It seems that although geography may be a powerful explanatory variable, it alone does not explain high and persistent poverty rates among indigenous peoples.

HUMAN CAPITAL

Human capital is often used to explain poverty and its persistence over time. Fewer years of schooling and lower academic achievement (test scores) are strong correlates of poverty across rich and poor countries alike (Glewwe 2002). An extensive literature also explores the role of human capital in explaining racial differences in income, particularly in the United States (Browne and Askew 2005). In the development literature, education is also considered one of the main vehicles through which poverty is transmitted across generations (Behrman, Birdsall and Székely 1999).

There is a small but growing body of work exploring the relationship between human capital and poverty outcomes among indigenous groups. Recent evidence finds continued disadvantage among indigenous groups in terms of schooling and health outcomes in Latin America (Hall and Patrinos 2006), Africa (Ohenjo et al. 2006), Asia (Hannum 2002), as well as in developed countries. Several studies from Latin America also find lower income mobility among excluded groups such as indigenous and Afro-descendants (Ferreira and Veloso 2004).

Our results document significant progress over time with regard to education and health status, with indigenous peoples gaining as part of national upward trends. In all cases, however, a gap persists between indigenous peoples' outcomes and national averages, and in Africa, there is some evidence that the gap is widening (see Wodon in this volume). In countries where further disaggregation by group is possible, differences do come to light. Despite massive educational achievements in China, national averages hide major pockets of low education among subgroups such as the Miao, a quarter of whom remained illiterate in 2005. In Laos, the Chine-Tibet population fares significantly worse and is the reason behind the low non-Lao-Tai averages (see King and van de Walle in this volume). Yet across several dimensions of the MDGs, including female literacy and infant mortality, the Aymara in both Peru and Bolivia do significantly better than the Quechua, and are converging with national averages (see Macdonald in this volume). In China, a further degree of nuance emerges, and there appears to be some "bifurcation" of human capital status across urban and rural regions, even among members of the same group: The Hui in urban areas are highly educated but significantly disadvantaged in terms of education outcomes in rural areas (see Hannum and Yang in this volume).

But what does education produce for indigenous peoples in terms of incomes gains, and how important is it as a determinant of poverty? Here the story appears to be more nuanced than it first appeared when based solely on results for Latin America. Much of the earnings gap of minority workers is a result of lower levels of schooling, and yet the returns to schooling are not necessarily lower for all minority workers. In Laos, there are significant and large returns to education, but the pattern of returns differs across groups. In Vietnam, the rate of returns to education for ethnic majority workers is two percentage points higher than for ethnic minority workers.

ASSET THRESHOLDS, POVERTY TRAPS, AND VULNERABILITY

Beyond human capital, there is a vast literature suggesting that the lack of a critical "threshold" level or combination of assets holds families in poverty, constituting a "poverty trap." Dasgupta and Ray (1986) note that something as simple as the minimum level of nutrients needed for productive work may represent a threshold "lump" investment unattainable by the poorest. Assets may also be complementary, with access to one enhancing returns to another; in rural Vietnam, for example, the net marginal benefit of irrigation investments increases with the education of the household (Van de Walle 2003). Related work suggests that low asset endowments hinder the capacity to insure against shocks, heightening vulnerability, prompting "negative coping," and thus locking households in chronic poverty (Murdoch 1994).

To the extent that we document lower combined assets and higher poverty among indigenous households in all countries studied, our results are consistent with theory. On the other hand, the gains that indigenous peoples have made in moving out of poverty in countries such as China and India refute the point; at a minimum, these track records indicate that for some members of the indigenous population in countries where dramatic poverty reduction has been achieved, the poverty-trap theory no longer holds.

Nevertheless, in many countries, indigenous peoples do appear to be on the "front line" of vulnerability. Evidence in this report finds that the

Vietnam War had a differential impact on ethnic minorities, depressing education levels further – and for a longer period of time – than for the rest of the population (see Dang in this volume). The evidence for China underscores a slightly different point, which is that "relative vulnerability" is rising. Despite widespread progress enhancing the asset base and income levels of vast swaths of the population, exclusion from education benefits, for example, is becoming a much more pronounced feature of minority groups in China. In India, tremendous achievements in poverty reduction have translated to poverty gains among scheduled tribes, *but not equally so*, both according to the poverty headcount and the poverty gap. And despite significant education and health gains, scheduled tribes also continue to have lower endowments of these human capital assets (see Das et al. in this volume).

Latin America presents a somewhat different story, in that national achievements in poverty reduction have been more limited. But like India, where poverty has declined, it has not been at commensurate rates among indigenous peoples (Hall and Patrinos 2006). Low asset endowments do help explain low overall returns to all assets among indigenous peoples (Skoufias, Lunde, and Patrinos 2010), and there is also evidence of heightened "vulnerability." In Mexico and Ecuador, during economic downturns, indigenous consumption levels took longer to regain pre-crisis levels (Hall and Patrinos 2006). In Bolivia, shocks (droughts and floods) have large income effects on indigenous households, and there is evidence of negative coping in the form of selling key assets to finance current consumption (Velasquez 2007). Overall, little work exists testing asset-based theories to explore the determinants of indigenous poverty. Given the results now emerging at a global scale, this is likely to be a promising area for further research.

SOCIAL, CULTURAL, AND INSTITUTIONAL DRIVERS OF INDIGENOUS POVERTY

The findings in this report contribute less in terms of empirical evidence that can be drawn on to assess the degree to which social, cultural, and institutional factors drive poverty and disadvantage among indigenous peoples. A related body of work, however, points unambiguously to their importance in drawing a comprehensive picture of the forces behind disadvantage, and offers rich avenues for exploration in further research applied to indigenous peoples.

Social exclusion and discrimination

It is widely held that outright discrimination may also explain a portion of the observed differential in poverty outcomes among minority groups (Becker 1971). There is evidence consistent with labor market discrimination for indigenous peoples in Latin America, Australia, Canada, New Zealand, and the United States (Brosnan 1984; Patrinos and Sakellariou 1992; Daley and Lui 1995; Kimmel 1997; Hall and Patrinos 2006), where indigenous peoples receive lower rates of return to a year of schooling. But more recent work in the United States finds that 90 percent of the Native American wage differential can be explained by characteristics rather than wage structure. Our findings on labor market returns are consistent with discrimination in some countries (Latin America, as well as Laos and Vietnam) but less so in others. In China, minority groups overall have higher returns to schooling (27 percent higher for males and 15 percent for females). Qualitative research points to discrimination restricting access to social services in Africa (Ohenjo et al. 2006), and that exclusion from social networks inhibits access to services and credit in India (Parker and Kozel 2007). But overt tests for discrimination of indigenous peoples, such as those in the United States comparing call-back rates for blacks and whites with otherwise similar profiles (Bertrand and Mallainathan 2004), are distinctly lacking.

Culture and institutional path dependence

Another vast body of work draws attention to culture and history as determinants of gaps between minority groups and the wider society in which they live. Wilson (2009) finds that beyond structural factors (low incomes or education), poverty among African Americans stems from informal "cultural frames" or codes of conduct that are learned behaviors in response to a history of oppression. Neckerman (2007) traces the roots of inner-city school failure to institutional history and education policy in the United States. Peer-effects – where assumptions on cultural identity, when overtly stated, determine outcomes on test scores (Steele and Aronson 1997, 1995; Hoff and Pandey 2006; Fryer 2010) – have also been detected. Echoing Chapter 1, which positions indigenous identity as a demand for rights and recognition, Will Kymlicka, the leading international voice on cultural minorities, links distributional conflict to the worldwide tendency of dominant cultures to reject demands for the "permanent differentiation in rights" (Kymlicka 1996). Pointing to culture and history as determinants of indigenous poverty, Mexican anthropologist Aguirre Beltran (1967) coined the term *"regiones de refugio"* (shelter zones) in reference to areas characterized by physical isolation and hard topography to which indigenous peoples retreated to escape exploitation and adverse integration into non-indigenous society. In Africa, Hitchcock and Vinding (2004) link lack of land and other resources among the San and Khoe of southern Africa to "systematic patterns of social exclusion and discrimination" associated with cultural identity.

Summary

It seems that while geography may be a powerful explanatory variable, it alone does not explain high and persistent poverty rates among indigenous peoples. Education still may be the great equalizer for many groups, but the returns to schooling continue to be lower on average for indigenous peoples, suggesting that either the quality of schooling indigenous children receive is inferior, the relevance of their education is not appropriate, or the labor market does not value their education because of low quality or because there is still significant discrimination. Nonetheless, efforts to improve the quality and relevance of schooling that indigenous children receive should continue, but it does seem that human capital alone does not explain away the disadvantage experienced by indigenous households in most societies. To the extent that we document lower combined assets and higher poverty among indigenous households in all countries studied, our results are consistent with theory. On the other hand, the gains that indigenous peoples have made in moving out of poverty in countries such as China and India refute the point; at a minimum, these track records indicate that for some members of the indigenous population in countries where dramatic poverty reduction has been achieved, the poverty-trap theory no longer holds.

CONCLUSIONS

This study brings together information about indigenous/ethnic/minority groups for a number of counties that have not been studied systematically in a comprehensive manner. The study systematically assesses the socioeconomic situation of groups in Asia and Africa, and adds value by interpreting the empirical results in a manner consistent with previous research in other regions, thus giving – perhaps for the first time – a more global understanding of indigenous peoples' socioeconomic development. Prior to this study, detailed work providing comparative national estimates of poverty and other living-standards indicators on indigenous peoples has focused on Latin America, Australia, Canada, New Zealand, and the United States. Even though the populations in these countries represent a minority of the world's indigenous peoples, results have been taken to suggest that indigenous peoples tend to be among the poorest of the poor, with little progress in poverty reduction and a persistent gap with the nonindigenous population.

Poverty rates have declined substantially among indigenous peoples in Asia. Our analysis adds data for only seven additional countries, yet by population, these represent about 72 percent of the world's indigenous population worldwide, of whom two-thirds reside in Asia. The results presented here, especially for Asia, present an important nuance to the general finding. Indigenous peoples have a higher poverty rate in all countries studied, but the general pattern of failure to progress or catch up does not hold in all countries. In fact, widespread and sustained growth and poverty reduction appears to have brought large numbers of indigenous peoples out of poverty in Asia. This puts previous multi-country evidence in a new light, in particular suggesting that the Asian success at achieving sustained growth and poverty reduction has positively impacted major segments of the indigenous population in those countries in terms of poverty, health, and education outcomes.

Despite this progress, a poverty gap persists between indigenous and nonindigenous populations. This result holds across all countries without exception, but the size of the gap, as well as whether it is growing or shrinking, does vary across cases. Whereas the gap is narrowing in China, it is stable or widening in most other countries. Further, within countries, some specific subgroups among the indigenous population appear to be particularly disadvantaged. Here there appears to be multiple sources of disadvantage at play. Ethnic disadvantage among these groups is driven in part by topography and other characteristics of land inhabited, compounded by limited access to infrastructure and services leading to, among other things, low levels of endowments, but also low combined endowments of several assets at once (low human capital, poor land, poor access to credit). Ethnic and gender disadvantage also compound, and there is evidence consistent with discrimination in labor markets, although little overt evidence to prove or disprove the extent of it.

In some countries, spatial or geographic factors may be the predominant cause of indigenous disadvantage (China, Laos, and, to some extent, India). Most ethnic minorities in China and Scheduled Tribes in India reside in rural areas and face the economic challenges of isolated rural communities – highly overrepresented in relatively poorly paid agricultural occupations. Access to basic infrastructure and services is an apparent driver of indigenous poverty in these cases. Yet, it is not obvious how to address these constraints most effectively. Delivering basic infrastructure to small, dispersed populations in remote areas is not cost-effective, and resettlement strategies, where they have been attempted, are not only contentious, but have largely failed (Laos).

In Latin America, indigenous disadvantage appears to be more complex, driven not only by geography, but also low returns on human capital and other assets, leading to significant differences in earnings and, consequently, poverty status. That these differences have endured despite several decades of progress in reducing human capital gaps may be indicative of the lack of complementary investments and less-than-optimal national growth and poverty reduction strategies. That is, if at the national level one is willing to accept slow growth and inequality, then not much can be expected for indigenous peoples.

Reform policy efforts in Asia, China, India, and Vietnam, promoted high growth for all groups. In other words, the gains from growth were widely distributed. Poverty reduction strategies in these successful economies followed the establishment of sustained high growth and inclusive policies. The relative success in equalizing access to human capital in Latin America did not result in rapid poverty reduction or in equitable distribution to indigenous peoples, nor will it do so in the future if the policy reforms do not result in high growth rates. The Latin American countries studied here have not been successful in promoting the policies necessary to create the conditions for high economic growth and inclusive outcomes. Initially high income inequality may hinder future growth and poverty reduction. At the same time, great gains in economic growth and poverty reduction may lead to subsequent inequalities.

There is no overwhelming evidence that programs targeted specifically at the indigenous population will substantially erase the gap between groups, especially in the absence of broad-based growth and poverty reduction. In Latin America, we only found evidence of poorly performing targeted programs, and even in cases where programs could help – such as bilingual education – they were poorly implemented. On the contrary, the one program that as of 2006 had reached indigenous groups successfully and on a large scale – Oportunidades in Mexico – did so as a poverty-targeted as opposed to indigenous-targeted program. Because of its success, this program is now being replicated across the region, and it will be important to monitor results for indigenous peoples across the region. In Asia, ethnicity-targeted programs such as the resettlement strategies in Laos are generally appraised as failures. China, like India, has implemented some pro-indigenous policies, in this case easing access to political office, looser fertility restrictions, and affirmative action policies for matriculations into colleges and universities along with subsidies, the appraisal of which is mixed. In sum, the evidence that can be pieced together so far suggests that general economic improvement (as in China and, to some extent, India and Vietnam) or generally poverty-targeted programs such as Mexico's Oportunidades have had a greater impact on indigenous poverty.

Well-designed targeted programs are also likely to be important, but their success is probably contingent on countrywide growth and poverty reduction. Widespread growth and poverty reduction may be the necessary but insufficient condition for eliminating the indigenous poverty gap. That is, the first step in improving indigenous peoples' outcomes is likely to be to identify and address the binding national country's constraints on poverty reduction. Evidence suggests that within this context, vast segments of the indigenous population will benefit. Yet, the indigenous movement is made up of varied groups of people, some of whom will be likely to benefit substantially from widespread growth and poverty reduction strategies, and others that will require focused strategies to address multiple sources of disadvantage. Country- and group-specific solutions, however, are likely to be complex; as David Maybury-Lewis in this volume note, the question is not if we are going to have development in the indigenous world, but how. However, it will be very difficult for efforts designed to tackle group-specific disadvantage to succeed unless implemented against a backdrop of successful widespread poverty reduction strategies.

AREAS FOR FURTHER RESEARCH

Causal mechanisms of indigenous poverty

The results presented in this book document a persistent gap in poverty outcomes between indigenous and nonindigenous peoples across the developing world. Against this backdrop, several key research priorities emerge. First, further work should be done examining the correlates of indigenous poverty (in more countries, and continued over time) to test and refine the results presented in the five case studies here. However, given the nature of unobservables, one can never clearly claim causality. Thus, a second and equality important priority is to use impact evaluation tools to rigorously assess what policy tools and programs actually works – and which do not – in improving indigenous peoples' outcomes. For example, ascertaining that a given program actually works to raise indigenous children's test scores in primary school provides a valuable policy model that can be applied in other settings and countries. Third, more precise estimates of indicators and the differences in those indicators between groups are important. Such work is feasible, even with survey data. In the case of Vietnam, using repeat cross-section household surveys and the Vietnam War as an instrument for schooling, the determinants of earnings were calculated (Dang and Patrinos 2008). It was found that the gap increased as a result of the war, and although there has been improvement over time, the gap that opened during this crisis remains.

Determinants of success

A second and related research priority is to gain a better understanding of the policies that underlie the falling indigenous poverty rates in Asia (China, India, and Vietnam). A decomposition of the results assessing the portion of these income gains to indigenous peoples that can be purely attributed to growth versus redistribution, and an assessment of what kinds of policies have worked to achieve these "shared growth" results, would offer important lessons. Furthermore, careful work to unpack the determinants of income, education, and health gains among particular "outlier" groups would be extremely valuable. Our results underscore the fact that there are particular groups or subgroups that deviate positively from average indigenous outcomes – both in countries that are already doing relatively well with regard to growth and poverty reduction (in China, the Hui and Manchu groups) as well as in poorly performing countries (in Peru, the Aymara). Untangling the factors that explain the success of these groups will help provide policy models of use in other settings, and is hence a priority for future research.

Education

Third, given overwhelming evidence on the role of human capital, research specifically focused on improving education outcomes among indigenous peoples is also critical. In particular, a promising area for research concerns the question of language of instruction. This may be relevant not only for improving access, but also for making education more relevant – to the indigenous communities themselves and for improving the quality of that education as measured by standardized test scores. Therefore, evaluating bilingual programs could be a promising area of future research (Patrinos and Velez 2009). Also, among the multiple sources of inequality identified in this study is the precarious position of rural minority girls and women. Besides relevance of schooling, other improvements must be made to ensure that minority girls participate in schooling. Scholarship programs such as Mexico's Oportunidades (conditional cash transfers) have proven very successful in getting poor children into school and was even more successful in reducing the indigenous/nonindigenous gap in schooling (Lopez-Calva and Patrinos 2008); it is now being tried in other countries, but should be in cooperation with indigenous communities and have a quality or supply-side corresponding element.

Country coverage and data collection

Although we cover most of the indigenous population of the world by including both China and India, there are nevertheless many countries where this type of work is not yet done, and should be. This study demonstrates that it is possible to come up with indicators for indigenous populations in a large number of countries using existing survey instruments. Therefore, the call to disaggregate data used for official international programming (MDGs) and country-specific programming is possible and should be done.

In cases where data is lacking, a concerted effort is then needed to introduce items in standard data-gathering instruments to identify different population groups. In surveys, questions on identity can focus on self-identification, language, and geography. The need to develop a list of standardized questions for surveys in different years and countries is apparent. That list could include self-identification, language (mother tongue, commonly used language, language used at home, secondary language), and parents' mother tongues. Ideally, each question would allow respondents to identify a specific group. Statisticians must also recognize that indigenous areas are often undersurveyed due to civil conflict and geographic isolation, thus there may be a need to impute the underrepresentation of groups, particularly if changes in the size of the indigenous population would affect policy.

However, beside the usual self-identification questions, a special survey module for indigenous peoples could be highly useful. Statistics agencies could include a special survey module for indigenous peoples. That module could study traditional medicine practice, religious/community activities, land ownership, bilingual schooling, intermarriage, and other aspects. Some countries have used separate surveys for indigenous peoples. It is unclear whether such separate surveys are more useful for researchers than are national surveys including both indigenous and nonindigenous peoples. More useful, from a research and policy perspective, are supplements to national censuses (such as Canada's Aboriginal Peoples Survey, designed and implemented in partnership with national Aboriginal organizations). It goes without saying that, as indigenous peoples themselves have been requesting, this effort can only be done successfully to the extent that they play a role in the conceptualization and implementation of the data gathering, as well as policy formulation.

References

Aguirre Beltran, G. 1967. *Regiones de Refugio*. Mexico: Instituto Indigenista Interamericano.

Baulch, B., T. Chuyen, D. Haughton, and J. Haughton. 2007. "Ethnic Minority Development in Vietnam." *Journal of Development Studies* 43(7): 1151–1176.

Becker, G. S. 1971. *The Economics of Discrimination*. Chicago: University of Chicago Press.

Behrman, J. R. , N. Birdsall, and M. Székely. 1999. "Intergenerational Mobility In Latin America: Deeper Markets and Better Schools Make a Difference." In N. Birdsall and C. Graham, eds., *New Markets, New Opportunities? Economic and Social Mobility in a Changing World*. Washington DC: Brookings Institution and Carnegie Endowment for International Peace.

Bertrand, M. and S. Mallainathan. 2004. "Are Emily and Greg More Employable than Lakisha and Jamal? A Field Experiment on Labor Market Discrimination." *American Economic Review* 94(4): 991–1013.

Borja-Vega, C., T. Lunde, and V. G. Moreno. 2006. *Economic Opportunities for Indigenous People in Mexico*. Washington, DC: World Bank, Human Development Network.

Borooah, V., B. Gustafsson, and L. Shi. 2006. "China and India: Income Inequality North and South of the Himalayas." *Journal of Asian Economics* 17: 797–817.

Bosworth, B. and S. M. Collins. 2008. "Accounting for Growth: Comparing China and India." *Journal of Economic Perspectives* 22(1): 45–66.

Browne, I. and R. Askew. 2005. "Race, Ethnicity and Wage Inequality among Women: What Happened in the 1990s and Early 21st Century?" *American Behavioral Scientist* 20(10): 1275–1292.

Brosnan, P. 1984. "Age, Education and Maori-Pakeha Income Differences." *New Zealand Economic Papers* 18: 49–61.

Brosnan, P. and C. Hill. 1984. "New Zealand Maori/non-Maori Labour Force Income Differentials." *Journal of Industrial Relations* 25: 327–338.

Daley, A. E. and J. Lui. 1995. "Estimating the private rate of return to education for indigenous Australians." Centre for Aboriginal Economic Policy Research Discussion Paper No. 97.

Dang, H. A. and H. A. Patrinos. 2008. "The Long-Run Educational and Labor Market Costs of the Vietnam War: Gender and Ethnic Minority Impacts." Draft, Human Development Network, World Bank, Washington DC.

Dasgupta, P. and D. Ray. 1986. "Inequality as a Determinant of Malnutrition and Unemployment, 1: Theory." *Economic Journal* 96(4): 1011–1034.

De Meer, K., R. Bergman, J. S. Kusner, and H. W. A. Voorhoever. 2005. "Differences in Physical Growth of Aymara and Quechua Children." *American Journal of Physical Anthropology* 90(1): 59–75.

Dollar, D. and A. Kraay. 2002. "Growth is Good for the Poor." *Journal of Economic Growth* 7(3): 195–225.

Dollar, D. , P. Glewwe , and J. Litvack, eds., 1998. *Household Welfare and Vietnam's Transition.* Washington, DC: World Bank.

Esquivel, G. 2000. "Geography and Economic Development in Mexico." RES Working Papers 3089, Inter-American Development Bank, Research Department.

Fryer, R. 2010. "The Importance of Segregation, Discrimination, Peer Dynamics, and Identity in Explaining Trends in the Racial Achievement Gap," in J. Benhabib, A. Bisin, and M. Jackson, eds., *Handbook of Social Economics* Volume 1. Amsterdam: North-Holland.

Glewwe, P. 2002. "Schools and Skills in Developing Countries: Education Policies and Socioeconomic Outcomes." *Journal of Economic Literature* 40(2): 436–482.

Hall, G. and H. A. Patrinos. 2006. *Indigenous Peoples, Poverty and Human Development in Latin America.* London: Palgrave.

Hannum, E. 2002. "Educational Stratification by Ethnicity in China: Enrollment and Attainment in the Early Reform Years." *Demography* 39(1): 95–117.

Hitchcock, R. and D. Vinding (eds.) 2004. *Indigenous People's Rights in Southern Africa.* Copenhagen: International Work Group for Indigenous Affairs.

Hodgson, D.L. 2002. "Introduction: Comparative Perspectives on the Indigenous Rights Movement in Africa and the Americas." *American Anthropologist* 104(4): 1037–1049.

Hoff, K. and P. Pandey. 2006. "Discrimination, Social Identity, and Durable Inequalities." *American Economic Review* 96(2): 206–211.

Jalan, J. and M. Ravallion. 1997. "Spatial Poverty Traps?" World Bank Policy Research Working Paper No. 1862. Washington, DC.

2002. "Geographic Poverty Traps? A Micro Model of Consumption Growth in Rural China," *Journal of Applied Econometrics* 17(4): 329–346.

2004. "Household Income Dynamics in Rural China," in S. Dercon (ed.), *Insurance against Poverty.* Oxford: Oxford University Press: 108–124.

Kanbur, R. and A. J. Venables. 2007. "Spatial Inequality and Development: Overview of UNU-WIDER Project." In D. Held and A. Kaya, eds., *Global Inequality.* Cambridge: Polity Press.

Kimmel, J. 1997. "Rural Wages and Returns to Education: Differences between Whites, Blacks, and American Indians." *Economics of Education Review* 16(1): 81–96.

Kymlicka, W. 1996. *Multicultural Citizenship.* Oxford University Press.

Lanjouw, P. and M. Ravallion. 1999. "Benefit Incidence and the Timing of Program Capture." *World Bank Economic Review* 13(2): 257–274.

Lewis, M. and M. Lockheed. 2006. *Inexcusable Absence: Why 60 Million Girls Still Aren't In School and What to Do About It.* Washington, DC: Center for Global Development.

Lopez-Calva, L. F. and H. A. Patrinos. 2008. *Child Labor, School Attendance, and Indigenous Households: Evidence from Mexico.* Washington, DC: World Bank, Human Development Network.

Lunde, T. 2008. "Indigenous Peoples and Theories of Poverty." Background paper.

Maybury-Lewis D. 2002. *Indigenous Peoples, Ethnic Groups and the State.* Needham, MA: Allyn & Baker.

Murdoch, J. 1994. "Poverty and Vulnerability." *American Economic Review* 84(2): 221–225.

Neckerman, K. 2007. *Schools Betrayed: Roots of Failure in Inner City Education.* Chicago: University of Chicago Press.

Niezen, R. 2003. *The Origins of Indigenism: Human Rights and the Politics of Identity.* Berkeley: University of California Press.

Ohenjo, N., R. Willis, D. Jackson, C. Nettleton, K. Good, and B. Mugarura. 2006. "Health of Indigenous People in Africa." *The Lancet* 367: 1937–1946.

Parker, B. and V. Kozel. 2007. "Understanding Poverty and Vulnerability in India's Uttar Pradesh and Bihar: A Q-squared Approach." *World Development* 35(2): 296–311.

Patrinos, H. A. and C. N. Sakellariou. 1992. "North American Indians in the Canadian Labour Market: A Decomposition of Wage Differentials." *Economics of Education Review* 2(3): 257–266.

Patrinos, H. A. and E. Velez. 2009. "Costs and Benefits of Bilingual Education in Guatemala: A Partial Analysis." *International Journal of Educational Development* 29(6): 594–598.

Psacharopoulos, G. and H. A. Patrinos. 1994. *Indigenous People and Poverty in Latin America: An Empirical Analysis.* Washington, DC: World Bank.

Ravallion, M. 2010. "A Comparative Perspective on Poverty Reduction in Brazil, China, and India." *World Bank Research Observer* 26(1): 71–104.

Shorrocks, A. and G. Wan. 2005. "Spatial Decomposition of Inequality." *Journal of Economic Geography* 5(1): 59–81.

Skoufias, E., T. Lunde, and H. A. Patrinos. 2010. "Indigenous Peoples in Latin America: Economic Opportunities and Social Networks." *Latin American Research Review* 45(2): 49–67.

Steele, C. M. and J. Aronson. 1995. "Stereotype Threat and the Intellectual Test Performance of African Americans." *Journal of Personality and Social Psychology* 69(5): 797–811.

1997. "A Threat in the Air: How Stereotypes Shape Intellectual Identity and Performance." *American Psychologist* 52(6): 613–629.

Torero, M., J. Saavedra, H. Ñopo and J. Escobal, 2004. "An Invisible Wall? The Economics of Social Exclusion in Peru." In M. Buvinic, J. Mazza, and R. Deutsch, eds., *Social Inclusion and Economic Development in Latin America.* Washington, DC: Inter-American Development Bank

Van de Walle, D. 2003. "Are Returns to Investment Lower for the Poor? Human and Physical Capital Interactions in Rural Vietnam." *Review of Development Economics* 7(4): 636–653.

Van de Walle, D. and D. Gunewardena. 2001. "Sources of Ethnic Inequality in Vietnam." *Journal of Development Economics* 65: 177–207.

Velasquez Castellanos, I. 2007. "Extreme Poverty: Vulnerability and Coping Strategies among Indigenous People in Rural Areas of Bolivia." *Ecology and Development Series* No. 51. ZEF, University of Bonn.

World Bank. 2009. *From Poor Areas to Poor People: China's Evolving Poverty Reduction Agenda.* Report No. 47349. Washington, DC.

Index

Printed in the United States
By Bookmasters